The Khoja Shia Ithna-Asheries of East Africa:
Their Quest for a New Socio-religious Identity (1860 – 1960)

The Khoja Shia Ithna-Asheries of East Africa:
Their Quest for a New Socio-religious Identity (1860 – 1960)

DR SIBTAIN AKBERALI PANJWANI

Introduced and Edited by

DR IMRANALI PANJWANI

The Awakening Project
Mimbar - Madrasah - Family

Published by
Sun Behind the Cloud Publications
PO Box 15889, Birmingham, B16 6NZ

The first edition published in 2023

Copyright © Dr Sibtain Panjwani 2023

The moral rights of the author has been asserted

All rights reserved

A CIP catalogue record of this book is available from the British Library

ISBN: 978-1-908110-86-2

www.sunbehindthecloud.com
info@sunbehindthecloud.com

I dedicate this work for the pleasure of Allah (SWT).

In memory of my beloved parents and grandparents.

I am grateful for the support and sacrifice afforded to me by my dear wife, Nasim, my beloved children: Imranali, Sabikah, Fatema-Zahra and Ali-Reza, and my grandchildren: Maryam and Isa-Jawad.

I am ever thankful for the wonderful times spent with my mentor, Asgharali M M Jaffer or Mullasaheb, as he was fondly known.

It is only right that we also remember all those who sacrificed their lives for the good of the community and whose efforts have allowed a book such as this to come into existence.
May God bless them all. Ameen.

CONTENTS

Acknowledgements — xi
Welcome Note from Africa Federation — xv
Forewords — xvii
Preface — xxi

Introduction: Interpreting History, Human Struggle and the Qur'anic Spirit of Reflection on the Past — 33

Part 1: The Khoja Shia Ithna-Asheries of East Africa
Our Collective Past
   1.1 *Satpanthi* and the Khoja connection — 51
   1.2 Scholars' Consensus on Khoja community — 58
   1.3 Aga Khan I's Arrival — 59
   1.4 Aga Khan I and the Court Cases — 60
   1.5 The Khoja Case of 1866 — 62
   1.6 The definition of Khojas — 64
   1.7 The Emerging Khoja Shia Ithna-Asheries — 65
   1.8 The Haji Bibi Case — 69

Part 2: Migration to A New Land
   2.1 The Earliest Arrival — 76
   2.2 Migratory Influences in the 1830s — 79
   2.2.1 Famine in Kachchh — 80
   2.2.2 The Abolition of Slavery in 1833 — 81
   2.3 Indian Ocean Trading World Opportunities — 83
   2.4 Influences of the Omani Sultanate — 89
   2.5 Khoja Settlement in Zanzibar — 91
   2.6 European Powers and the Fall of the Busa'idi — 93
   2.7 The Khoja of Zanzibar under the British Colonial Project — 98
   2.8 The *Dukawalla* Mindset — 104
   2.9 Internal Migration — 106

Part 3: Arrival of Khoja Shia Ithna-Asheries in Zanzibar and Shifting Patterns of Interaction
   3.1 The Arrival of Khojas in Zanzibar — 115
   3.2 Early Pioneers — 118

3.3	Swahili Environment: Its Impact on the Socio-Religious Stability of the KSI	131
3.4	Separation in Zanzibar	137
3.5	Challenging the Narrative	144
3.5.1	Finding Faith	148
3.5.2	Turbulent Times	151
3.6	*Mehfils* and Female Influencers	160
3.7	Qur'an Reciters	170
3.8	Activism and Media	171
3.9	Commemorations and Celebrations	178

Part 4A: Socio-Economic and Socio-Religious Change: Settlement Patterns in East Africa

4A.1	Overview of Settlement in East Africa	185
4A.2	Distinctive Settlement in East Africa	307

Part 4B: Socio-Economic and Socio-Religious Change: Evolution into a Distinct Community in East Africa

4B.1	A Singular Rule-Based Community	311
4B.2	Philanthropy	316
4B.3	Entrepreneurship and Permanency	320

Part 5: The Structural Institutionalisation of the Khoja Shia Ithna-Asheries In East Africa

5.1	The Idea of Centralising	333
5.2	The First Conference of Khoja Shia Ithna-Asheries of East Africa	342
5.3	Khoja Shia Ithna-Asheries and the Changing Political Backdrop	370

Concluding Remarks	375
Notes	393
Bibliography	433
Interviews & Talks	442
Appendices	445

Acknowledgments

I am eternally grateful to Allah (SWT) that He provided me with the opportunity to write this book and contribute to our understanding of who we are as a community. It has been the labour of many months, and by His grace, I have been able to complete it, *Alhamdulillah*.

I cannot forget my dear father, Alhaj Akberali Panjwani, who encouraged me to be aware of my own family history and thus influenced me greatly in the writing of this book. My dear mother, Laila Panjwani, was always, without fail, a loving mother who provided me and the rest of my siblings with that calming and positive influence required to follow our life pursuits. I must also mention my dear grandparents, Alhaj Gulamali Jivan Panjwani and Sherbanu Panjwani, whose family spirit and legacy of community service continue until today through their offspring. May God bless them all.

Writing this book has not been an easy task. When I began to research the history of the Khoja Shia Ithna-Asheri community of East Africa, the complexity became evident in terms of the many threads that met up as the community evolved. My biggest help was my son, Imranali, who took the time to steer me - with his clarity of thought and precision of expression - to bringing the various strands together in the shape of the narrative for this book. He stood by me to the end of this mammoth task I had undertaken. May Allah (SWT) bless him and give him *tawfiqaat* to carry on His work for His pleasure. Ameen.

This book would also not have been possible without the help, support and encouragement of many people. At the very beginning of my journey, I remember the encouraging words of Roshanbhai Fazal – the past chair of the Archive Section of Africa Federation - regarding this project. He gave me a couple of old books from his library that have been extremely helpful in my research.

I cannot forget the immense help Alhaj Asgerbhai Dhanji provided to me when © The Awakening Project needed support. In his polite and pragmatic way, he got the consent of the Jamaat leadership and opened the door for me to launch 'The Awakening Project for Khoja Shia Ithna-Asheri Jamaats' to the Dar es Salaam community. This led me to share The Awakening Project research with communities in London, Peterborough, Leicester, Birmingham, Toronto, Vancouver, Orlando (Florida), Sydney, Dar es Salaam, Arusha, Bhavnagar, Ahmedabad and many other places.

I fondly remember Alhaj Murtazabhai Jivraj, who was Chair of the Africa Federation Archive section and sadly departed from us in 2021 whilst holding that position. For me, he was a talking encyclopaedia on the history of our community in East Africa. Together with Sister Arifa Somji (Archive Section-Africa Federation), they provided me with valuable historical material and many relevant articles about the community. The Khoja Reading Circle that was established under Mulla Asghar Resource Centre met twice a month to share the historical events in our community as understood by the authors at the time. This allowed me to engage with both the history of that time and the present.

I would like to thank Professor Abdul Sheriff, Professor Iqbal Akhtar and Dr Imranali Panjwani for writing the Forewords and Introduction to this book respectively. In particular, I am grateful to Fatma Jaffer for editing this work. With her invaluable experience, she provided much-needed conciseness to my writing style and always made incisive and constructive comments. I would also like to thank Tehseen Merali, Director of Sun Behind the Cloud Publications, who was always ready to give excellent guidance on how the editing and publishing process works.

The Chairman of Africa Federation, Alhaj Shabir Najafi, along with his colleagues Alhaj Aunali Khalfan, Alhaj Amine Nassor, Alhaj Zainul Chandoo and Alhaj Zuhair Jaffer encouraged me by supporting the publication of this book financially. It is fitting that this book that acknowledges and honours the journey of this institution is coming out as Africa Federation celebrates its 75th anniversary. The money from the sale of this book will, *insha'Allah*, be utilised by Africa Federation for its various beneficial projects.

Finally, I thank all the chairmen and members of the Seniors of Hujjat Jamaat group, Stanmore, who provided their platform at various times to talk about The Awakening Project and the history of our community.

In this journey, there were many people within and outside of the community who encouraged me and I am thankful to every one of them. If I have forgotten to mention anyone, please forgive me as it was not intentional in any way.

Dr Sibtain Panjwani

Founder & Head of © The Awakening Project of KSI Muslim Communities

12th June 2022/11th Dhul Qad 1443

WELCOME NOTE
FROM AFRICA FEDERATION

It is often said that communities that fail to preserve their history become dead communities and are in no time forgotten. *Khoja Shia Ithna-Asheries of East Africa: Their Quest for a New Socio-religious Identity (1860-1960)* authored by Dr Sibtain Panjwani and edited by Dr Imranali Panjwani is a welcome contribution to the valuable record of our community's hard work, struggles and successes. I consider it a privilege to write a welcome note to this great work.

The achievements of the Khoja Shia Ithna-Asheri community of East Africa need to be understood from their own lens. This book provides the narrative that shows their capacity to adapt to a challenging new environment, their style of management coupled with their spirit of cooperation and mutual respect for the indigenous communities. Coming to East Africa nearly one and half centuries ago, they transformed the landscape in the areas where they settled. They had a spirit of togetherness that prompted them to set up *jamaats*, prayer facilities, cemetaries, social, welfare and educational institutions. They set up religious education centers on the socio-religious side and business infrastructure on the economic side, going out to remote rural areas to set up shops and bring essential commodities within reach of the local population.

Whilst this book extensively deals with the period between 1860 to 1960, three major events beyond 1960 impacted the communities in East Africa that I hope will be covered in the second volume of this publication. They were: the revolution in Zanzibar (1964), the expulsion of Asians from Uganda (1972) and the political crises in Somalia (1990s). The communities represented by Africa Federation played an exemplary role in evacuating fellow community members from Zanzibar and Somalia, aided by Alhaj Sajjad Rashid of Mombasa and his team who led the Somali evacuation at the risk of their lives.

The Ugandan crisis led to the expulsion of almost 4000 Shia Ithna-Asheries from Uganda. Their migration to the West exposed them to the principles of democracy and human rights; it also made them realise the importance of higher education that could provide better opportunities for the younger generation.

It is a proven fact that the people of Gujarat - where Khoja Shia Ithna-Asheries hail from - have business "in their blood", yet dedication and sincere devotion to the cause are preconditions for sustainable economic activity.. The business success of Ugandan Asians in Europe, North America and elsewhere generated the interest of Western academia who were keen to find out how individuals who arrived with a mere £50 became a net contributing community to the economy of the countries where they settled within a span of three to four decades.

The generation that came out of East Africa in the wake of the 1972 Uganda Asian expulsion were mainly "*Dukawallas*". They added skill and acumen to experience and became the owners of multimillion dollar businesses. Today, they own multinational companies, formidable business complexes and fast growing international trade houses; their children have gone on to become highly-educated professionals. I am sure that the authors of this book will comprehensively cover Khoja Shia Ithna-Asheri successes and challenges after 1960 to the present in their next work.

I am confident that this current in-depth study of our community will be a source of inspiration to all Khoja Shia Ithna-Asheries in East Africa, from East Africa and beyond. Once again, I congratulate Dr Sibtain Panjwani and Dr Imranali Panjwani for this wonderful study of our early pioneers and its timely publication. May the Almighty give them appropriate rewards and blessings for their great service to the community. Ameen.

Alhaj Shabir Najafi
Chairman
Federation of Khoja Shia Ithna-Asheri Jamaats of Africa
01 June 2022

Foreword

Dr Sibtain Panjwani's book, *Khoja Shia Ithna-Asheries of East Africa: Their Quest for a New Socio-religious Identity (1860-1960)*, is a remarkable contribution to the academic field of Khoja Studies. The book catalogues the history of the Khoja community from inception until 1960, focusing on the East African experience. His next book will bring this history to the present day.

What motivates Dr Panjwani is the sense of loss among the younger generation in the United Kingdom. Most British Khojas are not aware of their heritage and not particularly interested in learning about the history of migration, challenges, and accomplishments from their family's East African experience. And yet, it is ever-present as a difference in the larger construction of the British Muslim identity, which is dominated by Sunni Muslims of Pakistani origin. The educational and economic success of the Khoja community separates them from the majority of British Muslims, yet blends into the idea of a pan-Shia identity advocated by Arab and Iranian origin Shia British Muslims. The question then becomes, what makes the Khoja unique, and why should successive generations retain this ethnic identity, particularly as intermarriage now challenges traditional endogamy?

Dr Panjwani's answer to this question is his decades-long 'Awakening Project,' which advocates awareness of religion and the Khoja identity through the *'madrasah, mimbar,* and family unit.' For years he has researched and spoken about the importance of documenting our community's rich heritage. He has also served as the Secretary-General of the Khoja community's highest organization, the World Federation of Khoja Shia Ithna-Asheri Muslim Communities, headquartered in Stanmore.

This book is a compilation of years of primary and secondary research, as well conversations we have had in the Khoja Heritage Project Reading Circle initiated by Dr Hasnain Walji. It is organized chronologically, drawing mainly on secondary research in the beginning chapters, then incorporating more primary research from the community's Gujarati texts and oral interviews with the community's elders. It is an encyclopedia of the East African Khoja legacy that provides minute details of names, dates, and events that have shaped the community's collective identity in the diaspora. This book includes detailed biographical inserts of Khoja pioneers, such as Alhaj Shermohamed Sajan. In meticulous detail, the journeys are recorded from cities and villages of 19th century British India to colonial East Africa providing the data points required for mapping the unique mix of local Indic cultures and languages that came together in East Africa.

We are indebted to community scholars such as Dr Panjwani for his painstaking efforts over a lifetime in recording and assembling these histories that are contextualized through his lifetime of ethnographic observations of the community. This book is essential for any study of the Khoja of East Africa and will serve as a resource for succeeding generations of Anglophone Khojas in the Western diaspora interested in learning about their unique heritage in our multicultural, globalised world.

The success of the diasporic Khoja community is due to its entrepreneurial spirit, shaped by the successes and losses of its East African experience. Panjwani's book can help British-born Khojas understand the loss and trauma their parents' generation endured due to the British presence in post-colonial East Africa, as well as appreciate the extent and impact of the political upheavals that led to their parents' migration.

Iqbal Akhtar
Florida International University
Miami
25 March 2022

Foreword

Dr Sibtain Panjwani's *Khoja Shia Ithna-Asheri's of East Africa* is a long-awaited sequel to the *Trade Directory of the Federation of East African Khoja Shia Ithna-Asheri Jamaats*. About half the Directory includes some of the most enchanting life histories of the pioneers of our community. It was compiled in the early 1960s by Marhum Rafiq Somji, then Secretary of the East African Federation, into whose shoes Dr Sibtain has stepped. In the same way that Marhum Rafiq was driven by Marhum Ebrahim Sheriff, then President of the East African Federation, Dr Sibtain has been inspired by Marhum Mulla Asgharali Jaffer's commitment to serving the community in the World Federation.

Alongside Dr Sibtain's successful career as a dentist, he accepted an invitation from Mulla Asghar to serve the community and is now devoting his years of retirement to writing its history. Dr Sibtain has dug deep to trace the origin of the Khoja community, going back to its *Satpanth* connections and Pir Sadrudin. He has explored the twists and turns our forefathers had to take before finally emerging with the Khoja Shia Ithna-Asheri identity. Our community spread across the Indian Ocean to East Africa in the 19th century, and has now crossed another boundary to populate Europe and North America.

Dr Sibtain has also been driven by his concern about the extent to which our community has let 'its heritage and language go'. This is a perennial problem faced by communities defined by caste and language, often having to confront the social processes of the history of wider integration, like the Parsi community whose number is comparable in size to ours. This phenomenon had led Marhum Hassan Ali Mohammed Jaffer to bemoan our state as '*The Endangered Species*'.

As a historian, and especially one from Zanzibar - where these processes had gone the farthest before the community began to migrate to the West, I feel compelled to consider why we applaud our religious evolution from *Satpanth* ties and the Pirs of the past under the guidance of Ayatollah Mazindarani and Mulla Qadir Husain, yet fear social evolution as a threat to our survival as a community.

Our earliest religious teachers were Iranians who settled around us and whome we grew up with. As a young boy, I used to go to Mehfile Abbas in Muharram during our school break to listen to Seyyid Abbas. He was a member of the Bahraini Shia Ithna-Asheri community in Zanzibar that was led by Ahmed b. Numan, the first envoy of the Sultan of Zanzibar. Seyyid Abbas preached in Kiswahili, which was neither his mother tongue nor ours, but was a language we could all understand. Were they part of our community?

The question in my mind is what exactly defines our community: our fundamental religious beliefs or our caste social practices? This is the issue that Dr Sibtain begins to grapple with at the end of this book. It will become even more challenging when he discusses the community across the second boundary to the West, to which his second volume will be devoted, and for which many will be waiting with bated breath.

Professor Abdul Sheriff
Zanzibar
21 October 2021

Preface

In the summer of 1996, I was requested to accept the position of Secretary-General of the World Federation of the Khoja Shia Ithna-Asheri Muslim Communities (WF) by then President, Marhum Mulla Asgharali M M Jaffer (affectionately known as "Mullasaheb"). I had no idea of the enormity of the position and the responsibility that went along with it nor did I fully understand what he or the global Khoja community expected from me.

I do remember it being a particularly hot day. I was attending the quarterly Executive Committee meeting of the WF in Birmingham, UK in my capacity as an elected councillor. When the meeting adjourned for a short break, Mullasaheb, in the presence of the Vice President Alhaj Manzoor Kanani, requested me to join them. He asked me to consider the position of Secretary-General of the WF until the end of his term in October 1997 because Alhaj Hasnain Walji, who had held this position, had migrated to the United States of America. I asked for two days to consider this proposal.

On the way back home to Chelmsford - a journey of almost three hours - his proposal remained etched in my mind but I continued to mull over it. Considerations such as the scale of responsibility involved and the time I would have to give from other commitments weighed heavily in my mind. However, the prospect of working alongside a personality and inspirational leader I had adored from a young age also thrilled me.

I knew Mullasaheb from afar as an observer, listening to his religious, historical, and communal lectures. Beyond that, I had only been in his presence when I participated in deliberations at the WF Executive Council meetings in my capacity as President of the Muslim Shia Ithna-Asheri Jamaat of Essex or as his appointed/elected councillor. The thought of accepting his proposal of becoming Secretary-General and getting to work alongside him, to debate and discuss the many challenges facing the community, thrilled me.

Zeal Meets Doubt

Despite my enthusiasm, doubts lingered in my mind. What if I was unable to carry out the duties expected of me by the community? Or if I had a disagreement on a point of principle? Many 'what ifs?' reverberated in my mind but always, the opportunity of working alongside Mullasaheb returned to tempt me. Stuck in a quandary, I concluded that the best way to resolve my concerns was to have a face-to-face discussion with Mullasaheb himself. Our chat was amicable and one of the main things I took away from the discussion was his candid approach to resolving disagreements. It showed his remarkable foresight, patience, sincerity and - above all - his humbleness, which led me to accept the appointment of Secretary-General of the WF.

As the Secretary-General and his colleague, I worked alongside him for nearly four years. I came to know him as well as many of his close colleagues. There were many days when I would sit with him and discuss the community; its history, as well as its future. Many a weekday - and sometimes weekend - was spent listening to his thoughts on various contemporary challenges facing the community and learning about his vision. His ideas about how to put forward an argument or what the message to the community at large should be, all played a part in my steep learning curve.

Those were some of the best days of my life and I am thankful to Allah (SWT) for them. One of his habits that left a lasting impact on me was the manner in which he would correct mistakes by relating anecdotes that had both philosophical depth and wisdom. These stories were gems to treasure.

We Exist to Serve

One afternoon, I remember we were walking together towards the WF office entrance from the men's entrance of Hujjat Imambada, Stanmore - a distance of about thirty steps. During this short walk, he shared with me the importance of the position of the Secretary-General. For him, it was a symbolic representation of our global community. Accordingly, the public see our community reflected through the Secretary-General. When he articulates in public space, they hear the community speak through him. His movements in public are the actions of the community through him. The best etiquette for the Secretary-General, he emphasised - as I recollect - was to be humble and dignified with poor and rich alike when adversity demanded it.

At the time, as we approached the office, I remember asking him about the role and purpose of our community. I believed this subject to be fundamental for anyone wishing to serve the community and was eager to know his thoughts. He waited until we were in the WF office in the Hujjat Annexe and he had sat on the chair behind his desk. Then he motioned to me to take the seat opposite, gazed his eyes towards me and explained that

> In our short history as a community, we have passed through some anxious and trying times to survive...Our community's heightened capacity to withstand these trying times (in order) to preserve our faith and values has provided us our tryst with destiny and that is: we exist to serve Allah (SWT).

To me, these words were inspirational. They expressed candidly the objective of the community. At the same time, I was curious to know more about both the insight of the man who expressed these words and the historical legacy he had referred to. What were the trying times that we had faced as a Khoja Shia Ithna-Asheri community? And how did those events that shaped the community lead him to arrive at this impressive phrase: 'we exist to serve', which was the title of my Secretary-General's report (1994-1997) and subsequently became the motto of the World Federation.

I could not ask these questions then. We were busy attending to community matters so my curiosity had to wait for other opportune times. For almost four years, I took advantage of those special moments whenever they arose so that I could know - as best as one could ever know or be allowed to know - a dear colleague, leader and brother.

As I worked closely with him, I tried to understand his thoughts on many subjects, relating to our community as well as outside of it. What struck me was his capacity to touch people through the warmth of his personality, the candour of his speech (which spurred the community to action on many occasions!), the courage of his faith and the deep, abiding feeling he had for the less fortunate of the society. These qualities made him unique and as a leader, he was highly appreciated by our community and others who also looked up to him as a figurehead.

On various occasions when we travelled together, I took the opportunity to further probe his thoughts so that I could understand what led him to express that 'we exist to serve'. We had many discussions on a variety of topics: his understanding of the history of our community, the role played by previous generations of leaders, his thoughts on future leadership in the community, his vision for its institutions, and our community's constructive role in the affairs of the Muslim and Shia communities.

Everything I heard from him fascinated me. I began to understand foundational historical concepts, his ideological stand and his amazing ability to contextualise decisions within a historical background. He had a unique perspective that, blended with his foresight, benefited the community more than they would ever realise. Having grasped as much as I could, I began to see how appropriately the phrase 'we exist to serve' encapsulated his vision for the Khoja Shia Ithna-Asheries.

My Travels and Learning about Our Heritage

In November 1999, I had the opportunity to accompany Mullasaheb to visit WF projects in Baltistan, a region of Pakistan at the foothills of the Himalaya mountain range. Skardu, its capital, is extremely cold in the evenings and we soon found that spending them around a burning stove provided us much needed warmth. It was the perfect place to engage in a deeper conversation with Mullasaheb. One night, the subject happened to be the history of the Khoja Shia Ithna-Asheries, their language and cultural heritage. Naively, I thought I had a good understanding of how rich we were culturally and tried to defend my stand. However, after hearing from Mullasaheb, I began to appreciate the sad reality of our community i.e. that the extent to which our community had let its heritage and language dissipate was astonishing.

By the 1990s, the majority of the Khoja Shia Ithna-Asheries from East Africa could neither read nor write Gujarati. They had little or no knowledge of their own languages - Gujarati and Kachchhi - and lacked an appreciation for their literature. To this day, our literary heritage is almost non-existent within our communities from East Africa. A point that did not escape me was that had we preserved the rich tradition of our own language and literature, our community would have increased in its knowledge about its existence and as a result formed a well-rooted identity for itself.

This is not merely a question of history, but a question of the basis of one's identity, morals and way of life. A community that does not have an interest in its own language and literature will not have a deep understanding of its history or culture and will ultimately lose sight of its future. As a result, such a community will remain nomadic, hanging onto the language and culture of others. Until we, as a community, don't take a deeper interest in our own culture and dialect (or indeed in any other that we choose to adopt, be it Swahili, Urdu or English) and engage with its literature, we will remain a community without a deep understanding of the language we speak, its poetry and poets.

A community that has the vantage points of language and literature will go on to develop a deeper insight and meaning of its own existence and this will bring about its progress and allow it a place in human history. In order to produce a younger generation that will carry on our heritage and purpose, we need to empower them with a critical appreciation of the factors and people that have shaped their lives and given them opportunities to prosper. This was my sombre but realistic assessment when we retired for the night.

Visit to Skardu in 1999. In the background is the mountainous landscape of Skardu, Baltistan.

Skardu visit - 1999
Marhum Mulla Asgharali M M Jaffer together with Shaykh Mohsin Najefi (Founder of Jamia Ahle Bait, Islamabad) in a meeting with their colleagues. Under the supervision of Jamia Ahle Bait many projects were completed in Baltistan, Punjab and Islamabad.

A Sobering Reflection

Faced with this sobering reflection, it was inevitable that I would want to know why we began our journey to East Africa (the country in which I was born) and set up a community there. How did we survive the challenges of this journey and what type of experiences shaped our present state? It was the quest to find these answers that propelled me to write this book, which is the first of a two-part series.

This first book begins around the 1860s with a brief description of the tensions in the Khoja community in India, followed by the emergence of the Khoja Shia Ithna-Asheri community in East Africa and by 1960, its institutionalisation. It is the result of my efforts to chart out what motivated our ancestors to leave their country of origin - India, and why they settled in East Africa. The second book I am writing (God-Willing) will look at the period from the 1960s onwards beginning with the rise of African nationalism and the withdrawal of British colonial rule which led to the establishment of an independent East African government in the early 1960s.

These events brought about a dramatic change within the Khoja Shia Ithna-Asheri milieu in East Africa, which had hitherto prospered in sheltered enclaves during colonial times. The degree of change that these events brought would demand a total overhaul in the community's social organisation and aspirations. How did Khoja Shia Ithna-Asheries respond to these changes? What were the repercussions of these events on their socio-religious identity? How did these events affect their economic prosperity and viability? These questions will be explored in the next book.

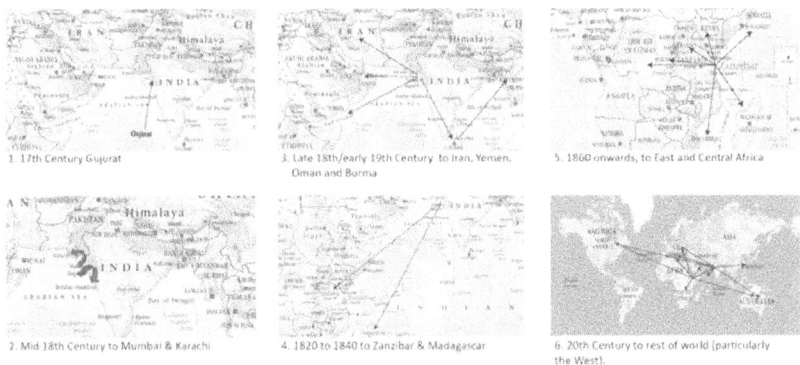

Phases of Migration of the Khoja Community (Courtesy of Fatima Ladak, UK)

A matter of utmost importance that should be borne in the minds of anyone who studies the Khoja Shia Ithna-Asheri Muslim Community is that it is essentially a religious community. It has a history in Islam of over 700 years. In East Africa, the Khoja Shia Ithna-Asheries began first arriving in Zanzibar around 1839. These early settlers laid down the formative socio-religious principles for the later Khoja Shia Ithna-Asheries, giving them their identity in a foreign land.

Around this core background, a highly differentiated structure was constructed founded on a constitution that upheld faith-based values. This structure was then modified as required in response to the impact of external events and internal organisational developments. The continuity of both faith and culture provided an essential base of formation for the community. Specifically, the Khojas' confidence in being Shia Ithna-Asheries frequently acted as a spur for them to evolve; they believed Shi'i principles were influential enough to maintain their communal unity as well as engage in *tabligh* (propagation) towards others. In addition, the Shi'i faith was flexible enough to adapt to societal changes so that they could practice their religion amidst changing political and economic environments.

In this sense, the Khoja Shia Ithna-Asheries of East Africa created a communal system of objectives derived from their Ithna-Asheri faith. When there was disparity between faith-based objectives and the organisational functioning of the community, internal tensions between these two key facets were experienced; this continues to manifest to this day. Such tensions can easily disrupt the smooth running of the community; at worst, they can be the basis for a complete rupture. The only way to alleviate them is to realign the community with the values at its core - 'the Shia Ithna-Asheri faith'. The nature of religious beliefs, therefore, does show a large degree of compatibility with important structural and organisational features of the Khoja Shia Ithna-Asheri community.

Secondly, any research pertaining to the Khoja Shia Ithna-Asheries is in the context of them being Indians. A cursory look at various papers on Indians in East Africa shows a study of their maritime history and migration over the Indian ocean, their cultural expressions, explanations of their business success and an analysis of their demographic position as a minority in a decolonising context. Whilst I am cognisant of this and I do draw upon their research, my focus in this book is to examine how the Khoja Shia Ithna-Asheries in East Africa formed an independent faith from the main Khoja community and then began the quest to establish their own identity in East Africa.

In my research, I have not relied solely on academic sources and official archives, but also on individuals whose narratives are unlikely to be part of a record. Archives, particularly from colonial (German and British) sources, as well as academia, privilege certain authoritative voices. I have chosen to give preference to the ordinary voices from the community in the hope of capturing a very interesting snapshot of the complicated intersecting lives of Khoja Shia Ithna-Asheries of East Africa. In doing so, I am keen not to touch on any collective sense of East African Khoja identify or to discuss the notion of "Wahindi" (a name given in Swahili to East African Indians as a collective).

I have no interest in exploring the community-community dynamic amongst East African Indians of various sects or castes. My focus instead is solely on the Khoja Shia Ithna-Asheries of East Africa and their search for a separate identity. This is the story of Khoja Shia

Ithna-Asheries, a relatively small community mainly from Kachchh and Kathiawad, told within the context of Indian self-interest in East Africa and their competitive as well as cooperative relations with Europeans, Africans and Arabs in Zanzibar.

The discrete categorisation of these groups can provide a sense of neatness and order in any narrative but, at the same time, unduly simplify complex issues relating to racial tensions, social relationships and mutual influence. Rather than take this mode of narrative for granted, I have chosen to explore their identity from within their heritage, beliefs and the way they saw themselves adapting to the prevailing socio-political landscape they found themselves.

In the process, terms such as 'Khoja', 'Community', 'Diaspora', 'Roots', 'Home' and 'Identity' and many others evolved within the Khoja Shia Ithna-Asheries, giving each word a new definition according to their own understanding of its roots and purpose. All this adds a marked voice to the literature dealing with East African Indian experiences.

It is also important to be aware that the aforementioned groups and their systems have also influenced the "distinct" voices of the Khoja Shia Ithna-Asheries themselves. They have been the victim of a large colonial political project and so at times, it may be difficult to distinguish between the voices that are truly authentic (if we can ever achieve such a position) and those that are not. However, I believe we must continue to explore the roots of the Khoja Shia Ithna-Asheries in accordance to their own narrative as much as possible. This will help delineate the more organic formative elements relating to their own language, culture and aspirations to other factors that externally influenced them as they searched for their own identity.

The Structure of this Book

I have divided this journey into four parts. Firstly, it is necessary to go into the historical background of the Khoja community as understood presently. I will briefly survey the available scholarship, as well as take into account some events of decisive importance that could have influenced the nascent Khoja Shia Ithna-Asheries to form a distinct community in Zanzibar.

Secondly, I will look at the major events that took place around 1839 which is the first recorded year of arrival to Zanzibar from Kachchh, as well as the existence of the Indian Ocean trading route. These two factors spurred the migration from the Khoja community (mainly from Kachchh, Kathiawad and Mumbai) to Zanzibar and the coast of East Africa.

Thirdly, I will look at the developments that led to the emergence of the first structurally organised Khoja Shia Ithna-Asheri Community (KSIC) in 1877 in Zanzibar. I will also refer to those settled in the East African coastal towns of Lamu, Mombasa, Bagamoyo, Kilwa, Dar es Salaam and others in the interior.

Fourthly, the early Khoja Shia Ithna-Asheri settlers in East Africa found themselves in a setting strikingly different from the land they had left. mThe new environment presented challenges both internally and externally within this fledgling community that called for important modifications in the socio-religious structure of the community. I will look at the process of socio-economic and religious change the Khoja Shia Ithna-Asheries adopted until 1960.

The pattern of settlement of the Khoja Shia Ithna-Asheries in their endeavour to institutionalise and establish a community in East Africa is worthy of in-depth exploration. In describing these settlements, I have purposely sought to provide names of Khoja Shia Ithna-Asheries who were among the earlier settlers. Whilst the names mentioned are not exhaustive, the intention for doing so, however, is to evoke interest within the community generally and their family members in particular and hopefully motivate them enough to bring out historical material of interest to the community.

I hope that the places and the names mentioned in this book will also jog the memory of those reading it and provide a window to glean and record from. There is a need to collect comprehensive historical data from family archives and from the memory of the elderly members of the community. In time, a detailed contextual research for each place of early settlement needs to be carried out and their history written down for posterity.

A Gujarati book on "Satpanth" written in 1962
(Courtesy: Mulla Asghar Memorial Library & Resource Centre [MARC])

INTRODUCTION:

Interpreting History, Human Struggle and the Qur'anic Spirit of Reflection on the Past

> *'We did not send [any apostles] before you except as men to whom We revealed from among the people of the towns. Have they not travelled over the land so that they may observe how was the fate of those who were before them? And the abode of the Hereafter is surely better for those who are Godwary. Do you not apply reason?'*
>
> *(The Qur'an, 12: 109)*

The fundamental aim of this book is to critically capture and assess two historical norms of the Khoja Shia Ithna-Asheries of East Africa which continue to manifest themselves in the present. These are migration and religious identity. Dr Sibtain Panjwani has painstakingly researched 100 years of history of the Khoja Shia Ithna-Asheri community to present a record to future generations of how their religious and cultural identities formed amidst economic, political, legal, social, cultural, and religious struggles.

It is an honour to write this introduction for my father but more importantly, I would like to comment on his methodological approach to interpreting history and how, within the narrative of the book, he arrived at key norms that have defined (and continue to define) the worldwide Khoja Shia Ithna-Asheri community. It is my hope that this introduction will, for scholars and non-scholars alike, concisely present the themes of this book within the context of how history can be interpreted, how historiography is approached from the perspective of both Western academia and the Qur'an and how historians from minority communities trace their background from a decolonial perspective using a combination of oral, written and community-based archives.

Structure and Themes of the Book

The book is divided into five chapters; the first, entitled 'The Khoja Shia Ithna-Asheries of East Africa - Our Collective Past' investigates the origins of the term "Khoja" and the emergence of the collective Khoja identity (religiously and culturally) in India before and after the arrival of Aga Khan I in Mumbai in 1846. The Khojas were originally part of the trading caste known as Lohanas and Bhatias and upon their joining the *Satpanth* tradition, Pir (missionary) Sadr al-Din gave them the Persian title "Khwaja" (which most likely got corrupted into Khoja). There appears to be a consensus that the pre-colonial Khojas possessed a distinct blend of Hindu and Muslim, as well as Shia and Sunni, customs and beliefs which through a genuine search and struggle for a consistent religious identity gradually transformed into the Shia Ithna-Asheri faith.

Part 2 deals with the causes and opportunities (such as famine and the potential of trade) that led the Khojas in the 1830s (who were either of Ithna-Asheri inclination, Khoja Ismaili, Sunni or a mixture of Muslim and Hindu) to migrate to Zanzibar. Here, the early Khoja migrants had to carve out a life within the British and German colonial systems as well as the Omani Sultanate, and support their families through the *dukawalla* (shopkeeper) enterprise. It is also at this point we see internal migration from Zanzibar to other parts of East Africa as well as the establishment of significant trading enterprises using the natural materials of the land. The gradual economic stability throughout 1860-1900 gave confidence to the emerging Khoja Shia Ithna-Asheries to establish *imambadas* (congregation halls used for religious and social events) and mosques - the first mosque and *jamaat* (community) being Kuwwat Mosque of Zanzibar in 1881.

The third part documents the significant divisions that emerged between Khoja Ismailis and Khoja Shia Ithna-Asheries as well as within the Khoja Shia Ithna-Asheries themselves. For example, when Aga Khan III visited Zanzibar and Mombasa in 1899 and 1905 respectively, he observed the economic stability, formation of religious identity and gradual institutionalisation of the Khoja Shia Ithna-Asheries. Instead of supporting this development, he issued *farmans* (proclamations) that restricted social activities to within the Khoja Ismaili grouping only. Marriages and social interactions between members of the Ismaili and Ithna-Asheri groups were forbidden. Communal worship and gatherings in the Jamaatkhana were now strictly limited to the followers of Aga Khan. Courageous individuals, however, such as Adelji Dhanji Kaba (1863-1923) took it upon themselves to challenge this Aga Khan Ismaili narrative. The *farmans* and subsequent challenges caused violence and divisions within families between the two communities leading to Khoja Shia Ithna-Asheries being ostracised by Aga Khan III.

The ex-communication of the Khoja Shia Ithna-Asheries in the early 20th century came approximately 50 years after the Aga Khan case in 1866 when Sir Joseph Arnould judged that Aga Khan I, Hasan Ali Shah, was the head of the Bombay Khoja community. The case was, in reality, a property dispute between a group of dissident leaders of the Bombay Khojas and the Aga Khan, a Persian nobleman who had arrived in Bombay in 1846 and was regarded by his followers, including most Khojas, as their rightful leader and the 46th Imam of the Nizari Ismaili Muslims. The dissidents rejected Aga Khan's claim of authority by arguing that he was not a Khoja and that the Khojas had always been Sunni Muslims.

The Khoja Shia Ithna-Asheries also had to contend with internal divisions within their own community when a jurisprudential dispute arose between Agha Abdulhussein Mar'ashi (a scholar who had come from Najaf to Zanzibar as a spiritual guide) and Molvi Gulamhussein from Hyderabad (an eloquent scholar who captivated many community members). This dispute coincided with the formation of the religious identity of the community through the adoption of *matam* (expression of lamentation) - notably influenced by Persian and Bahraini Shias, the establishment of the *mehfil* (small gatherings) and the rise of the *zakireen* (reciters) class - men and women who delivered sermons and spiritual recitations from the Qur'an and supplications from the Ahlul Bayt (the People of the Household).

Another important dispute arose in the 1890s involving Ghulam Ali Haji Ismail, known popularly as Haji Naji. He had studied in the seminary of Mulla Qadir Husain in Bombay and then embarked on *ziyarah* (visitation) of the shrines of the Twelver Imams in Iraq and Iran with his family in 1883. There he met Ayatullah Shaykh Muhammad Husayn who encouraged Haji Naji to propagate the Shia Ithna-Asheri faith in India. Haji Naji returned to Gujarat and began publishing classical Islamic texts and faith-based materials widely in Gujarati to increase the religious literacy of the Khoja Shia Ithna-Asheri community. The most important project he embarked on in Amadavad was a translation of the Qur'an (with exegesis) in Gujarati in the 1890s. However, he was met with opposition to the extent that he had to flee from Amadavad. As Iqbal Akhtar concisely explains

> His project broke a five-century prohibition among the Muslims of Gujarat on transliterating the Qur'an into a "non-Islamic" Indic vernacular. As word spread about this translation project entitled 'Illuminating Discourses and Commentary on the Qur'an', Muslims in opposition to his work in the city rose to the point where he was forced to flee to Khambhat, some 80 km to the south. To abate any further opposition upon his return to Amadavad, Haji Naji obtained Islamic legal rulings from two prominent Near Eastern Shia clerics of the time. By the mid-20th century, his Gujarati transliteration scheme for classical Arabic and Persian has become the standard scheme for all Khoja texts until the present day, even employed by the Agakhani Khoja in the transmission of their sacred prayer (*dua*).[1]

The aforementioned internal scholarly disputes within the Khoja Shia Ithna-Asheri community demonstrated two significant developments in their religious literacy and identity. The first was a deeper understanding of Shia Ithna-Asheri tenets and classical Islamic disciplines in order to arrive at a consistent concept of the faith that would provide stable religious values from which the emerging community institutions and programmes could function. The second was greater confidence in how to interpret and propagate Shi'ism within the socio-geographical contexts of India and East Africa. As the jurisprudential dispute between Agha Abdulhussein Mar'ashi and Molvi Gulamhussein demonstrated, but in particular, Haji Naji's innovative project in translating the Qur'an to Gujarati, the Khoja Shia Ithna-Asheries were now in a position to decide not merely what the faith meant to them but how they should interpret and apply it based on their needs and context (an issue which continues in the present day for Khoja Shia Ithna-Asheries who have migrated to the West and other parts of the world).

Part 4 deals with the socio-economic opportunities and challenges that the Khoja Shia Ithna-Asheries faced within the various parts of East Africa they had migrated to. By 1960, the Khoja Shia Ithna-Asheries had a combined estimated population in East Africa (Tanganyika, Zanzibar, Kenya and Uganda) of around 10,050 individual heads. This steady growth in numbers was not without difficulty. Poverty always remained a threat to the extent that the more adventurous Khojas who attempted to explore economic opportunities in the interior parts of East Africa fell prey to thieves, wild animals and death by disease. At the same time, one could see measurable economic success - for every 10 individuals there was one business or roughly one business per two Khoja Shia Ithna-Asheri families. This success came through a period of struggle with the British and German colonial governments who treated Indians as second-class, discriminated against them and simply termed them as 'Asians'.

Part 5 demonstrates the vision and foresight of the Khoja Shia Ithna-Asheries in centralising and institutionalising their religious, communal and social identity. In 1933, Seth Dawood Haji Nasser had the idea of creating the Kachchh Federation which later inspired the creation of the Africa Federation in 1945.[2] As Abdulhussein Sachedina, the editor of the monthly Gujarati magazine *Munadee* (the Herald) expressed in 1932

> progress without reform and organisation is difficult. We need a strong, fortified set of laws, which should bring about order and discipline in all our Jamaats, big and small, and should open up the stifled path of progress and advancement. This has got to be

our goal, and the easiest way to achieve this is to form a Central Council of the Shia Ithna-Asheri Community in East Africa.[3]

By the 1960s, the Khoja Shia Ithna-Asheris of East Africa could, without any doubt, be called a community in the fullest sense of the term with socio-religious institutions (such as *jamaats* and a federation) that cemented their beliefs and communal aspirations with a distinct consciousness of who they were and where they had come from.

The Meaning of History and Historiography

The term 'history' is the study and documentation of the past which somewhat differs from the term, 'historiography', which is the study of the way in which history was written with a view to critically examine its sources and the implications this has on how we derive meaning from it.[4] Simply put, historiography is the discipline of investigating how history has been conceptualised and what it means to us. From here, we can make an important distinction within historiography itself between history as a process and the knowledge of that process. This distinction is central to understanding the methodological approach of Dr Sibtain Panjwani in writing about the history of the Khoja Shia Ithna-Asheries of East Africa.

History as a process means how history is formed in and of itself just as, to give a simple example, how the movements and orbits of planets take place according to their own natural laws. History, though, is somewhat unlike mathematics as mathematics may operate on 'formal, technical procedures to solve problems within a specified range'[5] (though the constant evolution of quantum physics casts doubt on the specified range of mathematics).[6]

I do not profess to be an expert in quantum physics and/or mechanics or mathematics but only want to illustrate that the process of history in itself does not operate on easily identifiable parameters whereby one can quickly point to specific patterns within a set range and yield consistent, logical results as in the case of a defined scientific experiment or mathematical equation. For example, if one were to, prima facie, read about the migration, struggles and initially mixed religious identity of the Khoja Shia Ithna-Asheries in this book, it would not appear likely (according to a scientific calculation of material factors such as economic resources, geographical space, legal documents and family size, for example) that they would have survived as a cohesive community up until the present time. So then it begs the question – how did they survive and according to what consistent patterns? How can this information educate the next generation of Khoja Shia Ithna-Asheries?

The apparent unquantifiable nature of historical trends does not mean that patterns and expected consequences cannot be found in history; indeed they certainly can and this is why many have attempted to conceptualise what these patterns of history are, how they are created by humankind themselves and what they mean to us. For example, Ibn Khaldun (1332-1406) argues that human social organisation is necessary for human beings to withstand the power of predatory animals (and also an unjust human being who exploits his fellow men and women 'for aggressiveness and injustice are in the animal nature of man').[7] Mutual co-operation is therefore crucial for human beings to exist and flourish

> When, however, mutual co-operation exists, man obtains food for his nourishment and weapons for his defence. God's wise plan that man(kind) should subsist and the human species be preserved will be fulfilled. Consequently, social organization is necessary for the human species. Without it, the existence of human beings would be incomplete. God's desire to settle the world with human beings and to leave them as His representatives on earth (Q 2:30) would not materialize. This is the meaning of civilization, the object of the science under discussion.[8]

Another trend we may extract from history is human self-reflection through past actions and overcoming obstacles and limitations through self-realisation. This is arguably Georg Wilhelm Friedrich Hegel's (1770-1831) understanding of the process of history which is based on the idea of a subject–object identity; in history, humankind confronts itself and is constantly writing its own autobiography through struggle and self-consciousness

> Intellectual reflection bounces thought, as it were, off its object and back into the self. A consciousness caught in this interaction is thereby released from fixity and implicated in a process of

mediation and movement. In particular, it is provided with a ladder to higher levels of self-consciousness. For the reflective interaction with its object is at the same time a distancing from the self, a bringing of it under scrutiny from a new vantage point and, thereby, a means of transcending the self-conception with which the process started.[9]

As will be observed from this book, the Khoja Shia Ithna-Asheries were propelled to organise themselves into a cohesive community in East Africa because of the myriad of forces of power, from Aga Khan to British and from the Germans to the Omani sultanate, that attempted to either change their belief system into an Ismaili one, rule over their economic assets, subjugate their rights or make their socio-religious identity uniform like other 'Asians.' Yet the fact that the Khoja Shia Ithna-Asheries have survived until the present was not a guaranteed outcome when one analyses their history. They could easily have disintegrated due to these vying forces of power. Therefore, there was an unquantifiable, non-material factor that led to the survival of this community; it was a deep desire within some of the courageous pioneers of this community to struggle, reflect and forge a new identity that accurately reflected their beliefs and aspirations – arguably the very trends commented upon by Ibn Khaldun, Hegel and other philosophical historians. This struggle and the threat of disintegration, however, will always continue for this and all human communities since history represents a process of human triumph, failure and self-reflection.

Using his methodology of topical exegesis (*al-tafsir al-mawdui*),[10] Shahid Muhammad Baqir al-Sadr (1935-1980) argues that history is fundamentally connected to the Qur'an. Although the Qur'an is not a history book but a book of guidance, it links to the process of change that occurs in human beings due to fixed Divine laws which constitutes the Divine-human relationship. He states

> Here the Qur'an talks about the second aspect of the process of change and tells man his weak and strong points. It speaks of man's rectitude and deviation; and of the conditions conducive to his activity and inertness. This shows that the discussion of laws of history is a subject that concerns the Qur'an as a Book

of Guidance and as a book that leads man from the darkness of perdition to the light of rectitude, for the practical or the human aspect of this process is influenced by the norms of history.[11]

Al-Sadr believes that we can abstract universal trends for human beings from history but positions the Qur'an as the fundamental basis for this abstraction precisely because its aim is to guide human beings and take them out of "darkness into light".[12] God intends for us to discover norms of human history so that we can avoid the errors of civilizations before us. From this basis, al-Sadr extracts Divine norms that will affect all human beings, but which human beings have the capacity to respond to since God has given them free-will. For example, norms such as nations (not just individuals) will also have an appointed time of death; there is a natural indiscriminatory consequence of injustice to the perpetrators, victims and bystanders (i.e. all groups suffer) and no soul shall bear another soul's burden of accountability in the hereafter.

An interesting example that al-Sadr gives pertains to the immense suffering experienced by Prophet Musa and Imam al-Husayn ibn Ali, the grandson of Prophet Muhammad (pbut):

> When as a result of their misconduct Israelites were doomed to roaming about in the desert, this punishment did not remain confined to the wicked. It equally affected Prophet Musa, who was the most pure and active person of his time and who most courageously had faced the tyrant and his tyranny. Prophet Musa being a member of the community had to share the chastisement inflicted on the community as a whole for its wickedness. Consequently, he also had to wander about in the desert for 40 years along with other Israelites.

> Whereas when as a result of their deviation from the right path the Muslims were afflicted with a calamity and Yazid ibn Mu'awiyah was imposed on them to ride roughshod over their lives, property, honour and creed, it was not the wrongdoers among the Muslims society alone who suffered. Even the infallible Imam Husayn (pbuh) who was the most virtuous and the most upright person on the face of the earth, was killed along with his companions and the members of his family. All

this is in consonance with the logic of the norms of history. When a punishment in this world comes to a society it does not remain confined to the unjust of that society. That is why the Qur'an says: *'Guard yourselves against a chastisement which cannot fall exclusively on those of you who are wrongdoers, and know that Allah is severe in punishment.' (Surah al-Anfal, 8:25)*[13]

Our purpose, therefore, is to deeply reflect on the Qur'an so that we can forge a better destiny for ourselves towards God. The Khoja Shia Ithna-Asheri community is no different to any other human community. We will also fall foul to any injustice committed by others or indeed ourselves if we are not just in our actions. In the 1850s-60s, the internal strife within the emerging Khoja Shias in India due to wealth, caste and language allowed Aga Khan I to assert his authority and dominance on these Khojas thereby gaining control of the wider Khoja community. Had this internal strife not occurred, we may not have suffered or may have been in a stronger socio-political position today. These are, of course, lessons from history - lessons which the Qur'an pointedly tells us to reflect on. It states:

> *'We did not send [any apostles] before you except as men to whom We revealed from among the people of the towns. Have they not travelled over the land so that they may observe how was the fate of those who were before them? And the abode of the Hereafter is surely better for those who are Godwary. Do you not apply reason?'* [14]

Allamah Tabrisi (1073-1153) in his major *tafsir* work, *Majma' al-Bayan*, expounds this verse to mean

> Why haven't these polytheists who deny your Prophethood, Oh Muhammad, travelled in the earth so that they can reflect on what the fate was of those before them from amongst the nations which denied their prophets and how God destroyed them with a punishment of excision. Therefore, they should take a lesson from them and be warned about the like of what befell them.[15]

Allamah Tabatabai (1904-1981) in *Tafsir al-Mizan* states the verse is a warning to the nation of Prophet Muhammad (pbuh) to take a lesson from previous nations.[16] And Allamah Fayd al-Kashani (1598-

1860) cites a narration from Shaykh al-Saduq's (923 – 991) hadith (narration) compilation, *Uyun Akhbar al-Rida* in which the importance of reflecting upon the fate of those who previously denied their own prophets is emphasised.[17]

What is clear from the aforementioned Shia exegeses is that reflection and consideration of past events are crucial to prevent present and future mistakes in a society – in this context following God's commands through the propagation of His Prophets. Secondly, reflection on past events is an activity which should be undertaken not just by those who may deny a prophet's prophethood but also by those who are currently following Prophet Muhammad (pbuh). Hence this present book offers a significant opportunity for the present Khoja Shia Ithna-Asheri community to reflect not only on the struggle of their ancestors in arriving at the Shia Ithna-Asheri faith and how they organised themselves into a community but also on any mistakes they made in the way they formed this community and understood their socio-religious identity. The goal, according to the Qur'an, is to reflect on how best we can journey towards God, and the way past civilisations lived gives us the strongest opportunity to do so.

The Interpretation and Knowledge of History

The importance of attempting to understand history as a process is equally coupled with knowledge of that process. Knowledge of the historical process refers to the type of theories of historical knowledge we use to understand history and why. It constitutes the epistemology of history and focuses on how we may arrive at reliable historical knowledge. There are numerous theories on this but a few suffice as examples.

In order to arrive at reliable knowledge of the past, historical sources must be checked against each other so that we can assess not only the reliability of the information conveyed in them but also see if there were any competing interests involved in the production of those sources. One source, therefore, is not sufficient to defeat doubts about a particular historical event.[18]

It is at this point that we find a distinction between primary and secondary sources emerging. From a Western academic perspective, primary sources consist of written material produced more or less at the same time as the object of research which, ideally, would be observed and recorded by eyewitnesses. An appropriate example would be parliamentary debates in which the participants are party to the proceedings and record in verbatim what was said. What is significant about primary sources is that the distance in time between the event and the record of the event is small and so doubts about the unreliability of information are minimised.

Secondary sources, however, constitute those written sources that are produced a considerable length of time after the historical event and are not recorded by eyewitnesses. For example, a compilation of narrations from Prophet Muhammad (pbuh) and his family such as *Uyun Akhbar al-Ridha* by Shaykh al-Saduq who lived during 923-991 but compiled the sayings, actions and events of the 8th Shi'i Imam, 'Ali bin Musa al-Rida (pbuh) who lived during the period 766-818. At least 167 years passed before Shaykh al-Saduq compiled narrations pertaining to 'Ali bin Musa al-Rida (pbuh)'s life. From a Western academic perspective, this *hadith* compilation would be regarded as a secondary source but from the Islamic perspective – specifically within *'ilm al-hadith* (the science of narration) and *'ilm al-tarikh* (the science of history), oral sources have a primary position over written sources since oral narration was the fundamental mode of transmission in Prophet Muhammad (pbuh)'s lifetime and immediately thereafter. Notwithstanding scholars' genuine attempts to capture events of the past and keeping in mind that definitions of primary and secondary sources may differ amongst different disciplines, one factor remains important and that is a source's reliability and authenticity. Hence, more investigative work needs to be done when using any secondary source.[19]

For other historians checking sources against each other is not enough; what is equally important is 'the way the results of historical research are synthesized into a textual whole (Darstellung) and presented to an audience'.[20] However, the approach of synthesis presumes that it is possible to obtain knowledge of other minds i.e. 'the mental states of others, such as thoughts and intentions, separated from the knowing subject in both time and space - the typical problem of the historian...'[21] Is it possible for us to accurately or at least, reasonably, capture what other people in the past thought and how and why they acted in a particular manner? Are we, today, the same subjects as those of the past? We may often say to each other in heart-warming jest, 'how our times were so different to the times of youths today!' There is actually much truth to this statement because how human beings in the past behaved and perceived events could be very different to the way we perceive them today and so the synthesis of history is extremely difficult.

Those that argue against this sceptical position state that we can understand and interpret people's past behaviours because by the basic unity of humankind, there is a fundamental unity of subject and object of knowledge in the human sciences. We are human beings today just as there were human beings in the past and this, in itself, means we can understand the lives, values and aspirations of those before us. This is what is known as the ontological argument for the possibility of historical interpretation to produce knowledge because 'history is fundamentally the process in which mankind expresses and develops itself in the form of diverse cultures; and because mankind has made history, it is capable of knowing history in a direct way, according to this argument, just as the writer of an autobiography knows the history in case in a direct way'.[22] Once this presumption is accepted, one may abstract universals from the particulars of objects of knowledge.

For example, a simple particular of events in the past (and present) is the constancy of death which we can put into a deductive syllogism by stating, 'All human beings die. I am a human being. Therefore, I will die.' However, a more complex particular which requires inductive (or abductive) reasoning is: 'All the Khoja Shia Ithna-Asheries I have met are businessmen. Therefore, all Khoja Shia Ithna-Asheries are businessmen.' We know, of course, that this conclusion is wrong because Khoja Shia Ithna-Asheries are also doctors, lawyers, opticians, pharmacists and more. However, we can make the conclusion stronger by making it more probable: 'All the Khoja Shia Ithna-Asheries I have met are businessmen. Therefore, most probably Khoja Shia Ithna-Asheries are businessmen.' Again we can challenge this conclusion but there is an element of greater truth here which is exactly what historians attempt to discover by examining a particular trait in history and making a generalised conclusion about it.[23]

The *dukawalla* (shopkeeper) enterprise in East Africa from the early 20th century was instrumental in giving prosperity to family units and the emerging Khoja Shia Ithna-Asheri community as a whole; trading the natural materials of the land was also an essential ingredient of the early Khoja migrants. We may therefore form a probable conclusion about why the Khoja Shia Ithna-Asheri community was able to survive the colonial period whilst being new to a foreign land – entrepreneurship. There was an entrepreneurial spirit within the early community in East Africa which by and large has continued today wherever the Khojas have migrated. We also know, however, that this essential ingredient of the community is constantly being transformed to the extent that the young generation of Khoja Shia Ithna-Asheries have chosen diverse professions that were not available to their forefathers. Does this mean that we no longer have an entrepreneurial spirit or conversely, that this spirit has evolved? How do we account for this changing trend? Do human communities lose their formative characteristics (for example, and arguably a sad one at that - our mother tongue, Gujarati) or rather, adapt to changing geographical and economic circumstances? These are even harder questions to answer for the historian.

The final issue with the reliability of historical knowledge concerns our own bias and perception of others. Even after checking other sources to arrive at the veracity of a historical event with the presumption that we can understand and synthesise our past into a consistent narrative (which is what Dr Sibtain Panjwani is attempting to do), there always remains a concern about how objective historians can be. Bias is part and parcel of our human makeup because we all come from different cultural, linguistic and genetic backgrounds. Therefore the subjective way in which we look at the world is natural.

Indeed, God states in the Qur'an:

> Among His signs is the creation of the heavens and the earth, and the difference of your languages and colours. There are indeed signs in that for those who know.[24]

Yet our backgrounds should not be a cause for pride and arrogance that we look down upon the 'other' as if those apparently different to us should be accorded a lesser intellectual and moral status. This was the reason for the revelation (*sabab al-nuzul*) of the following verse:

> O mankind! Indeed We created you from a male and a female, and made you nations and tribes that you may identify yourselves with one another. Indeed the noblest of you in the sight of Allah is the most Godwary among you. Indeed Allah is all-knowing, all-Aware.[25]

Allamah Tabrisi states that the aforementioned verse was revealed to show that males and females '[originate] from Prophet Adam and Lady Hawwa and the meaning is that all of you are equal to each other in lineage because all of you return in lineage to Adam and Hawwa; Allah, Glory be to Him, prevents you from pride over lineage'.[26] The verse was also revealed in the historical context of Arabia in which some Arabs were haughty over the tribes (*qabaail*) they belonged to in contrast to the nations (*shu'uban*) who were deemed foreigners to the Arab society and accorded a lesser status in society.[27] These 'foreigners' were often exploited and treated as slaves like Bilal ibn Rabah who, although born in Makkah, descended from Habasha (Ethiopia). As is well-known from history, Prophet Muhammad (pbuh) freed him from slavery and gave him the honoured status of being the first *mu'adhin* (one who calls to prayer) in Islamic history.[28]

Despite these important verses of the Qur'an, Muslims and non-Muslims alike have subjugated each other using religion, skin colour, tribal descent, language, money and societal status. In the field of history and indeed other intellectual sciences, the subjugation occurs by demeaning or ignoring a so-called 'primitive' or 'lower cultures' own history, language and values because they are not superior to others. This can be termed as an orientalist, colonial and/or Eurocentric way of looking at the world which deems cultures different to the West as lower and therefore insignificant and in need of being educated or colonised.[29] This dangerous model of historical knowledge which is intellectually violent and destroys or manipulates other communities' histories is now readily acknowledged within Western academia:

> According to the same nineteenth-century conception, nonscriptural or 'low' cultures were primitive by definition and simply had no history comparable with 'high cultures.' In this way the scriptural, source-based conception of historical method

defined – and limited – the object of academic history to the history of 'high cultures,' especially the history of the West. It would last until the second half of the twentieth century before these biases in the very conception of historical method would be seriously criticized, especially by 'history from below' and by postcolonial theory. It dawned on an increasing number of historians that entangled with the history of 'the West' there was and is a history of 'the rest.' As a consequence, global and world history have been on the rise since the 1990s, using comparative and transnational approaches (Haupt and Kocka, 2010).[30]

Methodology and Concluding Reflections

This book is a sincere attempt to present the history and voice of the Khoja Shia Ithna-Asheri community to its future generations and also to others as an intellectual history from its own archives and sources. Based on the analysis of historiography I have presented above, Dr Sibtain Panjwani's methodology is three-fold. The first is that his conception of history is both cyclical and evolutionary. Cyclical because as per the Qur'an, there are natural causes for the triumph and failure of civilisations; greater injustice than justice leads to the ostracisation and subjugation of others. This is exactly what happened to the early Khoja Shia Ithna-Asheries who were ostracised by the mainstream Khoja Ismailis but with determination and struggle, were able to survive and form their own Shia Ithna-Asheri identity. As the early Khoja Shias migrated to East Africa (and now other parts of the world such as the West), they evolved from *dukawallas* to traders and entrepreneurs. This evolution continues today where Khoja Shia Ithna-Asheries have arguably maintained their entrepreneurial spirit but diversified into an array of professions.

The second dimension of his methodological approach is to combine primary and secondary sources to determine what exactly transpired in the Khoja Shia Ithna-Asheri community during the period spanning 1860 to 1960. These primary sources include the participants or eyewitnesses who recorded business information or gave their views about how their ancestors migrated and struggled.[31] This approach attempts to present more of a people's history rather than a historian's history of the Khoja Shia Ithna-Asheri community.[32]

The final dimension of his methodology of history is to synthesise sources to produce a coherent narrative of the past that continues till the present day of which he is a contemporary participant. This may be termed as an experiential, participatory epistemology of history that focuses on historical consciousness. As one will read towards the end of this book, apart from the observable characteristics of language and religious beliefs, the Khoja Shia Ithna-Asheries who began to settle in various parts of East Africa were able to identify with each other through a mutual awareness of the following factors: their families' journeys from India to East Africa, a common longing to construct a new home but one that was not completely disconnected to their origin and roots i.e an Indian home within East Africa or a 'home away from home', their yearning for economic stability, the happiness of being part of a community and ultimately, a deep-rooted search for a faith that would give them solace in this life and the next. In sum, the aforementioned dimensions of mutual awareness can be called a type of consciousness that permeated amongst virtually all Khoja Shia Ithna-Asheries that migrated to East Africa from India.[33]

The task of the next generation of Khoja Shia Ithna-Asheries, including myself, is to deeply reflect on the nature of this consciousness and how it informs our present life, values and visions for ourselves. This reflection, which is an injunction in the Qur'an, is necessary in order to learn from the courage of our respected ancestors who risked everything for not just a better life but a deeper identity; not to repeat their mistakes and forge an even better destiny for ourselves that is rooted in God-consciousness, God Willing.

Dr Imranali Panjwani

Senior Lecturer in Law, Anglia Ruskin University and Head & Founder of Diverse Legal Consulting, UK

PART 1

The Khoja Shia Ithna-Asheries of East Africa:
Our Collective Past

1.1 *Satpanthi* and the Khoja connection.[1]

Given the scarcity of available material about Khojas in the pre-colonial era[2], the work of scholars such as Nanji become an essential study; he is a rare historian who has studied the *Satpanth* tradition and provides a detailed narrative of it.[3] According to this tradition, the Khojas were originally part of the trading castes known as Lohanas[4] and Bhatias[5] and upon their joining the *Satpanth* tradition, Pir (missionary) Sadr al-Din gave them the Persian title "Khwaja" which most likely got corrupted into Khoja.[6]

Pir Sadr al-Din is widely accepted to be a *Satpanthi Dai* (preacher), credited with founding the first *jamaatkhana* (Khoja communal space).[7] The *ginan*[8] *'Dasa Avatara'* - historically a key aspect of Khoja beliefs and practices - is also attributed to him.

Due to the lack of academic work on the pre-colonial Khoja community, the capacity for scholars to raise alternative narratives on how the belief system evolved is limited. When examining this scholarship there is a tendency to view the spread of the *Satpanth* tradition within the Khoja milieu solely through the lens of the broader history of Ismailis.[9]

As Parpia explains, the *ginan* tradition[10] had 'tactfully' constructed a 'bridge between Ismailism and Hinduism which permitted the new ideas to enter into the entirely different world of Hindu mentality'.[11] Daftary[12] suggests that the Pirs 'expounded, within a Hindu framework, the doctrine of the Imamate'[13] while Madelung[14] remarks that 'they [*ginans*] include hymns, religious and moral exhortation, and legendary history of the Pirs and their miracles, but contain no creed or theology'. Differing from this approach, however, are scholars like Nanji[15], Khan[16], Purohit[17], Shushan[18], Masselos [19] and Asani[20] who view the tradition through a broadly Indic lens and locate the *Satpanth* from within the South Asia setting[21].

In his interesting paper, Ranjan[22] further discusses Purohit's contention that it was not just a colonial lens but an Arab-centric one also. It appears that, for the British judiciary, the personal laws of *Shari'ah* fitted well with their jurisprudence; it was a classic case of using the one-size-fits-all approach. Moreover, these scholars depict that British colonisation was also a time of transformation for Khojas from being an amalgamation of ideas and beliefs to becoming a community seeking a definitive identity.[23] There is a consensus that the pre-colonial Khojas possessed 'a unique blend of Hindu and Muslim, as well as Shia and Sunni, customs and beliefs'.[24] It is therefore plausible to argue that at that point in time, the Khojas were not part of any clearly defined religious group.

Before 1809, the Khojas were identified as a 'loosely organized "caste"' and appeared in the records of the British as Hindus.[25] In fact, the newspapers repeatedly referred to them as a caste, a definition that seems to have also been ingrained within the psyche of Khojas themselves. This term persisted in documents such as the various "Rules and Regulations" that governed the administrative structures overseeing Khoja bureaucracy in the early 20th century. It also found expression in translations of words like *jamaatkhana* which is rendered in those texts as the "caste house". This is evident, for example, in the revised edition of the "Rules of the Shia Imami Ismailia Councils of the Continent of Africa".[26] In addition, from the account of the 1866 Khoja Case[27], in the early 19th century the Khojas were thought to be a Hindu or a syncretised group.[28] However, there is no firm evidence to confirm this opinion.

What we can say - and this may well be an assumption - is that Khojas were not yet noted as a separate sub-caste under the broader category of Mahomedan as they would be in later censuses and government documents. This is corroborated by the accounts of Captain McMurdo, a British political resident in Kachchh. He read a paper before the Asiatic Society of Bombay in 1818 and stated that the Khojas were 'Mahomedans and considered themselves to be of Persian origin; and that they went on pilgrimage near Ispahan to worship their living Saint, to whom they pay an annual tribute'.[29]

In Pirana village, outside Ahmadabad, Gujarat, the residents follow a Sufi-inspired faith of Imam Shah Bawa's teachings of love and harmony. The sect is an offshoot of Ismaili teachings and it attracted devotees from religions other than Hinduism and Islam too. All 18 communities living in Pirana village, belonging to different castes and religions, are devotees of Imam Shah Bawa.
(Dionne Bunsha, 'The Chains of Pirana', FrontLine, September 10, 2004)

In 1821, an unattributed article entitled *Heterodox Mahomedan* described the Khojas, without naming them, as a people that 'have many singular customs, and adhere more to the notions of the Sheeahs than to those of the Sunies' but that 'most of the other tribes hold them in abhorrence in a very great degree; they even abuse them on every occasion and say that abuse or indignity offered to this race has as much efficacy as a pilgrimage to Mecca'.[30]

However, by 1847, a case tried in Bombay's highest court to determine the personal law of the Khoja community noted that their religious rites and markers of self-definition aligned them with an identity most closely commensurate with being Muslim.[31] There is some evidence of this as exemplified in Habib Ebrahim's testimony in an inheritance case of 1847. Ebrahim, elaborating on his religious identity, said that: 'some say we (the Khojas) are Soonees (Sunnis), some Sheas (Shii). Our religion is a separate religion; Aga Khan is esteemed as a great man amongst us'.[32]

Parpia's seminal paper suggests that prior to arrival of Aga Khan I, Khojas conducted their affairs from different belief sources. For example, they grounded the doctrine of Imamah (religious leadership stemming from Prophet Muhammad's progeny) within the notion of *'Dasa Avatara'*. They did not follow the Muslim laws of inheritance and in most cases did not require their women to observe wearing of *pardah* (veils). On the other hand, their burials and marriages were performed by Sunni *mullahs* (clerics) and they venerated their living Imam[33] in Iran, sent him tithes and, if possible, tried to make a pilgrimage in order to obtain his blessings. Parpia also suggests that they had a strong Ithna-Asheri flavour in their rites, as evidenced by their mourning of the death of Imam Husain (pbuh), and that the Khojas with these leanings began to organise a separate identity from around that time.[34]

Given that the Ithna-Asheries later separated from the Khoja community, the question of whether other practices such as mourning of Imams beyond Ja'far al-Sadiq (pbuh)[35], daily *salaat* (prayers) or payments of *khums* (religious tax) existed before the coming of Aga Khan I needs to be explored.

From the Khoja Shia Ithna-Asheri community archives, there is some indication of a deeper influence than those found in the academic journals. For example, in 1865, in the Gujarati translation of Aga Khan I's autobiography, he expressed his desire to propagate and spread the religion of the last prophet according to the Ithna-Asheri tenets.[36] He claimed that it was not Shah Ismail Safavi,[37] but rather his own ancestors who had spread the Ithna-Asheri faith. Interestingly, at the same time, his advocates were arguing in the 1866 case that he was the Imam of the Ismailis.

In a second book[38] - this one published in the Sindhi language - Aga Khan I provided instructions to his followers on how to perform *aamaal al-Qur'an* (deed of Qur'an) during the holy month of Ramadan. This is one of the prayers performed by the Ithna-Asheries in which the names of their twelve Imams are mentioned. His son, Aga Jangi Shah, confirms this and says that Aga Khan I used to lead this *aamaal*.[39] The Sindhi book also provides detailed directions on how to recite the *ziyarats*[40] of the eighth and twelfth Imams[41] after every prayer.

This information is gleaned from materials such as *Ibratul Afza*, Aga Jahangir Shah's *Risala*, *Kanzul Masaib*, *Kilwa na Sawal Jawab*, *Khoja Panth Durpan*, *Hidayat Prakash* and others resources that exist in communal archives.[42] Particularly because there is such a scarcity of available texts to work with about Khojas in pre-colonial times, these resources should not be dismissed as merely polemical works of no substantial value and should be evaluated in the light of known facts.

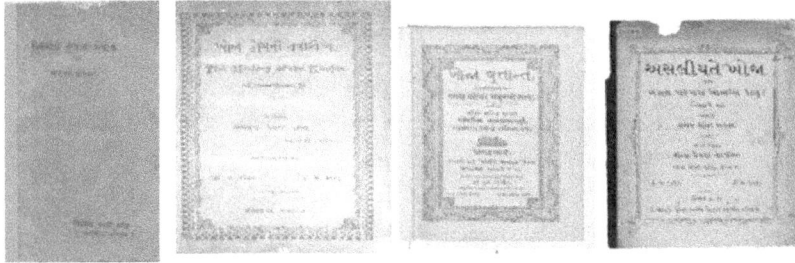

Some of the resource materials available (from left):
'Kilwa na Sawal Jawab', 'Khoja Kaum ni Taarikh', 'Khoja Vrutant' and 'Asliyaate Khoja'.
(Courtesy Mulla Asghar Memorial Library & Resource Centre [MARC])

Here, I would like to make two points. Firstly, the communal archives I have referred to above are based on the personal experiences and opinions of Khoja Shia Ithna-Asheries. They are invaluable in providing us with authentic records that allow us to challenge archival historical data and their interpretation. Oral testimonies of community members - either from personal life experiences or recounted from family members - open a new line of enquiry for scholars. These stories may legitimately produce an alternative history of the Khoja Shia Ithna-Asheri community.

Secondly, from an interpretive angle, one may further argue that such oral and communal works[43] reveal the genuine intentions, motives and feelings of Khoja Shia Ithna-Asheries. Through their study, we are in a better position to understand the cultural dynamics of the Khoja community in Kachchh and Kathiawad prior to the arrival of Aga Khan I in India. This would then allow us to answer questions about why certain religious, social and personal choices were made in the development of their identity. [44]

There is a consensus among scholars that before the arrival of Aga Khan I, the Khojas were a functionally organised community with a strong sense of coherence. The glue that held their collective together was their language, institutions, dress, customs and religious observances. In fact, the Khojas appeared regularly in the Bombay dailies, establishing themselves as part of the fabric of urban life. The arrival of Muhammad Hussein Husseini, more commonly known as either Aga Khan Mahalati, Aga Hasanali Shah or simply Aga Khan I, disturbed this status quo within the Khoja community. He arrived in Bombay in 1845 while charged conflicts were brewing amongst the Khojas. These had initially flared around complex questions of inheritance and upholding custom and had escalated to seeking recourse with the law.[45] Aga Khan I compounded these tensions with his claim of being the *murshid* (guide or teacher) of the Khojas.[46]

In his capacity as the *murshid* of the Khoja community[47], Aga Khan I argued he was entitled to a communal monetary tribute and had sole jurisdiction in the management of the community's affairs, including issuing excommunications from the caste. A small but powerful group, known to ordinary Khojas as *Shethias* (an influential faction), challenged the Aga Khan's obligations. They preferred to continue their own customary form of decision-making and conflict resolution.[48] This group was composed of the mercantile elite of the Khoja community; they were an affluent, socially mobile group and had relationships with influential groups of other communities.[49] Their network gave them visibility and prominence in the eyes of the British colonial establishment.

For the ordinary Khojas, these *Shethias* embodied the prestige and responsibility that was required to look after their affairs; for some of them, the Aga Khan I encroached upon this autonomous balance within the community. The *Shethias* claimed that they had no substantial relationship to Aga Khan I who was a Shia Muslim, whilst according to them, the Khojas were practising the Sunni interpretation of Islam; they therefore distanced themselves from him. An opposing party felt that there was an allegiance owed to the Aga Khan I based on a customary relationship the Khojas had with his ancestors.[50] In their understanding, the Aga Khan's claim to authority over them was legitimate suggesting that by virtue of this relationship they too were Shia Muslims.

Based on the published papers available to us, we can establish that the arrival of Aga Khan I in Mumbai in 1846 made a definitive impact on the Khoja community. He employed tactics to appease some whilst asserting his leadership over others; as a result, his authoritative influence could not be ignored.

During general conversations with community elders, I was also able to obtain several accounts suggesting that the manner in which Aga Khan I imposed his authority resulted in various internal conflicts. There were certain established elements who considered his pretensions blasphemous and resented his demand for the payment of *dasondh*.[51] These people resented his overbearing attitude towards the community and his insistence on controlling the lives of his followers and the communal properties.[52]

Conflict amongst the Khojas escalated and cases were brought to the colonial courts for adjudication (the internal and external powers influencing the Khoja community are an interesting subject that is outside the scope of this book). The courts went on to discuss intricate questions regarding the rights and responsibilities of caste leadership, particularly around a line of hereditary claimants. What ensued, however, was not peaceful negotiation but serious disputes that ultimately deteriorated into futile acts of violence.

Until this point, the Khojas had marked their religious beliefs with relative ambiguity. While there were certain beliefs held and religious practices observed by the Khojas, they had neither been able to insert their faith into the demarcated categories of being a Hindu or a Muslim as demanded by the colonial state,[53] nor were they able to affiliate themselves with the historical divisions of Shia and Sunni as put forth by the Aga Khan. From the available literature, one can reasonably argue that what the Khojas *did* know was that they followed a religious system known as *Satpanth* founded by Pir Sadr al-Din.

The series of prolonged court cases brought to light the glaring lack of clarity around questions such as: how did *Satpanth* - an ideology that emerged and developed in Sindh and Kachchh - merge with Hindu, Muslim, Shia and Sunni beliefs? Was Pir Sadr al-Din acting alone in founding an independent religious tradition or was he representing Aga Khan I's ancestors? Did Pir Sadr al-Din's identify himself as Muslim? And finally, how did he understand the *Satpanthi* ethos?

These questions notwithstanding, what is relevant for this study is the determinative outcome of the famous Khoja Case of 1866 in which Justice Arnould defined the religious identity of Khojas.[54] This ruling led to the splintering of groups from the community, first of the Sunnis and then the Shia Ithna-Asheries; the latter split reaching completion after the Haji Bibi case.[55] Justice Arnould's decision established Aga Khan I's authority over the Khoja community and because he was not immediately challenged, he had the opportunity to start shaping the Khoja community's Ismaili identity.

It was from this time that the Ismaili-*Satpanthi*-Khoja nexus began to be articulated; any Ithna-Asheri influence that may have existed then has not been officially recorded. However, there is a corpus of unexplored written material within the community archives that may hold the answers as to whether Ithna-Asheri beliefs/rituals existed within the Khoja community of the time and to what extent.

1.2 Scholars' Consensus on Khoja community

As described in the previous section, there exist differences in the way various scholars looked at the connection of the Ismaili-*Satpanthi*-Khoja entity. Nevertheless, there is an agreement on various aspects of the community or caste practices as summarised below.[56]

- Various Khoja communities existing prior to Aga Khan I's arrival in India were autonomously functioning. They collectively owned their own places of congregation.[57] They appointed/elected their own *Mukhi* and *Kamadia* who served in an honorary capacity.[58]
- Khojas held meetings to arbitrate and decide on various civil

disputes, such as cases relating to marriage and divorce. However, there was no strict or distinct framework used to judge on an issue.

- The community collected contributions from their members to take care of communal and capital expenses, such as the purchase of cooking utensils (valued at Rs. 20,000 in 1851) and a Khoja burial ground in Bombay.[59]
- Pre-colonial Khoja religious identity was diverse in nature and therefore it is difficult to clearly classify their religious affiliations into any of our modern-day constructs of Hinduism, Islam, Shias, and Sunnis. Masselos argues that the Khojas possessed 'a unique blend of Hindu and Muslim, as well as Shia and Sunni, customs and beliefs'[60] while Bernard Lewis classifies them as 'Hindus under a light Muslim veneer'.[61] In fact, some did not even believe that they were part of any clearly defined religious group as per the earlier mentioned testimony by Habib Ebrahim in 1847.

1.3 Aga Khan I's Arrival

Prior to the arrival of Aga Khan I, the Khoja community lived within their organisation, beliefs and practices. As explained above, most scholars agree that the pre-colonial Khoja religious identity was eclectic and it is difficult to clearly classify their religious affiliations.[62] Indeed, the Khoja Jamaat - or at least a section of it - did not believe that they were part of any defined religious group. Some scholars do suggest that in the mid-19th century, the Khojas distributed into multiple Indic religious traditions, including *Satpanth*, *Brahma Samaj* and *Prarthana Samaj*.[63]

By the time Aga Khan I arrived in India around 1844, there were a considerable number of Khojas - mostly prominent traders - in Mumbai (Bombay). He started an active campaign to impose his authority and began to attend the Bombay Jamaatkhana on special religious occasions. He would give audience to his *jamaat* every Saturday and on each of these occasions, a large number of his followers would turn up to receive his blessings.[64] He also tried to assert his authority over communal property and to make sure that communal dues were paid by all members of the community. This came at a time when the Khoja elite, on the back of their new-found wealth as merchants, had begun to take control of the community's affairs.[65]

This further complicated the evolving power dynamics of the community and several lawsuits, based on the customs of the community, followed as a result of his activities; Aga Khan I lost them all. Unfazed by this outcome, he continued to exert his influence on a more individual level. By 1866, twenty years after his arrival in India, he had gained sufficient control over the Khojas to feel confident asking them to pledge loyalty to him again. This time the majority agreed; only a small group known as the *Barbhai* (Twelve Brothers) felt that what Aga Khan I was doing was unacceptable and they led the dissenting faction.[66]

The *Barbhai* took it upon themselves to rescue the Khoja tradition from the hands of Aga Khan I. They charged him with interference and effectively removing the agency of decision-making from the well-established practices of the *jamaat* (community). In doing so, they claimed, Aga Khan I was imposing an identity upon the Khojas which was contrary to their understanding of their faith. Aga Khan I defended his position by claiming that *Satpanth* was a manifestation of Shia Ismailism that had been collectively forgotten by the Khojas and that he was merely reminding them of it. Thus, the scene was set for a volatile confrontation.

Whatever the merit of these differing positions, there is a minimum consensus amongst scholars such as Asani,[67] Masselos,[68] Purohit,[69] and Shodhan[70] that the arrival of Aga Khan I in Bombay and his assertion of authority triggered opposition within the Khoja community. After a number of public disputes between the *Barbhai* and the supporters of the Aga Khan I, things came to a head in 1866 and the matter unfolded in the courts as well as the media.[71] Eventually, in the same year, a lawsuit followed that would go down in historical records.

1.4 Aga Khan I and the Court Cases

The answer as to why Aga Khan I interfered in the way he did depends on how one views his status. Purohit argues that he used different tactics to persuade the Khoja community that they had a connection to Shia history.[72] Asani views Aga Khan I's authority as an extension of the doctrine of Imamate[73] that had already existed within the Khoja belief system.[74] Many others feel that Aga Khan I's conduct with the community is riddled with ambiguity.

For example, in 1861, he issued a circular declaring the Khojas as Shia.[75] In 1865, in the Gujarati translation of his autobiography he expressed a desire to share Islam according to the rulings of the Ithna-Asheri Imams claiming that it was his ancestors and not Shah Ismail Safavi who had spread the Ithna-Asheri faith.[76] At the same time, his lawyers were arguing in the court of Justice Arnould that he was the Imam of the Ismailis. One wonders whether these contradictions were simply tactics to keep the Ithna-Asheri group within his fold whilst he was confronting the Sunni challenge in court.

Whichever arguments one accepts, the fact is that the internal strife in the Khoja community[77] caused by Aga Khan I's interference resulted in the creation of two main groups: the Khoja elites i.e. the *Barbhai*[78] and the Aga Khan's followers, comprising his immediate family and supporters within the Khoja Jamaat.[79] The resulting tension in the community grew to such an extent that it eventually needed to be resolved by the court.[80]

Prior to 1857, the courts in India were operating on the principle that the ancient usages and rulings of the people took precedence over any other form of law, in effect recognising the inherent customary diversity within both the Muslims and Hindus. Two major court cases that took place before 1857 support this position. These cases were a prime example of a community that did not neatly fit into the legal 'box' set out in the British formulation of Muslim Law.

The first case, tried by Justice Perry was the 1847 Khoja Female Inheritance case.[81] In this case Aga Khan championed the rights of a daughter to inherit property in accordance with the *Sharia* law while the *Barbhai* supported the claim that the wife should be allowed to inherit property from her deceased husband in accordance with Khoja customs. The judgement made by Perry was later credited with being the key ruling responsible for the acceptance of 'custom' as a means to mitigate or ignore the rigid rules found in Muslim and Hindu personal laws in the Bombay 'residency'.[82] The second dispute in 1851 was between Aga Khan and several Khojas over the Jamaatkhana property.[83] In both cases, the judge ruled against the position taken by Aga Khan I.

In 1857, the British decided to apply a uniform set of policies, including legal practices, across their entire territory. They adopted a model that required the terms 'Hindu' and 'Muslim' to be clearly defined and compelled the community to place itself within one of these two categories.[84] The implementation of this model had a significant effect on all Khoja disputes that came to court after 1862.[85] It was this model that the court applied in the Khoja case of 1866 thus helping Aga Khan I become the official Imam of the Ismailis'.[86]

1.5 The Khoja Case of 1866

In 1866, a dispute over the Jamaat's property came up to the British courts in India. This time the courts applied the post-1957 uniform model and classified the Khojas as a Muslim group.[87] The disputed property was termed as a trust held by a religious community for charitable purposes. The court, tasked with ascertaining what kind of Muslims the Khojas were, began an equity suit around the ownership and management of Khoja properties in Bombay.

It quickly transformed into dealing mainly with the community's definition as if the Khoja identity was on trial rather than the community's governance and assets. The court wanted to determine what the foundational beliefs of Khojas were and to that end, it needed to first understand the past of the community so that it could then plot its future.

Each of the parties involved needed to provide a narrative that would link it to the present practices. This meant that each party i.e. the Aga Khan I and his Khoja supporters as well as the *Barbhai* and their supporters drew upon different understandings of the same past. Each group sought to find a link of continuity with the present so that their narrative would undermine their opponent's and gain legitimacy in the eyes of the British colonial establishment.

The plaintiffs' (the Reform Party comprising the *Barbhai*/the Khoja elite) case centred on the contention that Aga Khan I had unjustly asserted his authority over the Khojas and the Ismaili Islam was inherently heretical.[88] These arguments relied on the assumption that the Khojas were and always had been Sunni. Conversely, the Aga

Khan's party argued that the Khojas were Shia and any Sunni elements were a result of *taqiyya* (concealment), which was not needed any more since the British guaranteed them greater religious freedom.[89] Furthermore, they also argued in favour of his authority over the property and contributions of the community.

It is worth noting that the judicial reforms instituted as a result of the British Raj had already started to affect the Khoja identity. The community had significantly moved away from the position that the Khojas had a separate religion and were neither Sunni nor Shia. During the court case, both parties were forced to define themselves with reference to the Qur'an and the categories of Shia and Sunni as defined in the wider "imperial context" and it was up to the courts to decide their true religious identity.[90]

In order to arrive at a decision, the court analysed a variety of evidence and called upon expert witnesses. The list of authorities included various European texts on Islam and Ismaili history such as Sale's *Preliminary Discourse to the Koran*, De Sacy's *Expose de la Religion des Druzes* and Von Hammer's *History of the Assassins*. Besides consulting these Orientalist[91] works, the court also called upon various members of the community to give statements. However, they did not admit the testimonies of these witnesses as evidence; instead, the court looked for clear markers of the individual's religious identity - Shia or Sunni - for example, in their dressing and rituals.[92]

Ginan literature was initially ignored but as the case developed the court had to consider the role it played, if any, and to what extent it influenced the Khoja belief system; it soon became the key piece of evidence in the case. The main argument submitted by Aga Khan I's party was that the *ginan 'Dasa Avatara'* and other such *ginans* were tools used by the pirs to convert Hindus into Shia Muslims and this premise was accepted by the court.[93]

What emerges clearly from these legal encounters are the overlapping notions of Khoja traditions. The records show their rich traditions, practices, sites of devotion, and continuities as well as ruptures. In this fog of contrasting narratives, the defendants, the plaintiffs, and the lawyers and judges wrestled to determine the fate and identity of a community.[94] Ultimately, the court exercised its legal rights to decide what constituted the Khoja tradition.

1.6 The definition of Khojas

Justice Arnould finally decided in favour of the Aga Khan I. To do so, he had to first define who the Khojas were and he said that they were 'a sect of people whose ancestors were Hindus in origin, which was converted to and has throughout abided in the faith of the Shia Imami Ismailis, and which has always been and still is bound by ties of spiritual allegiance to the hereditary Imams of the Ismailis'.[95]

From this point on, there existed a legal definition of what it meant to be a "Khoja"; this ruling changed the way the Khoja identity was understood both by others and by themselves. It is saddening to note, however, that throughout the court disputes, what remained largely ignored was the voice of the ordinary Khojas of that time, which could have provided a more elaborate picture of the community in 19th century India. In the end, Aga Khan I won and this raises an obviously interesting question as to how the Khoja community would have evolved had he not interfered in its workings.

One of the far-reaching consequences of this case and its verdict is the way in which Khoja community history was recorded. Many of the modern chapters of Ismaili and Khoja history take the leadership of Aga Khan I as their starting point and conduct their research within that paradigm. This is not problematic for those who accept the close link between Khoja and Ismaili history as the ruling of 1866 simply confirms their view. One researcher, however, challenges this way of writing history.

Teena Purohit contends that the conclusion in 1866 was the result of a flawed interpretation of the *ginans*. According to the court, *Dasa Avatar* was of Ismaili origin, but she demonstrates that this was wrong. In Purohit's opinion, the Aga Khan Case is not a valid argument to defend the leadership of Aga Khan I over the Khoja community or for writing them into Ismaili history.[96] Her research opens up the exploration of alternative origins of the Khoja community.

The 1866 case implies that Khoja origins and associations have been basic. Through his judgement, Justice Arnould implied that the identity of the community was simplistic, dismissing the richness of its origins and past associations. He condensed a complex past and formalised a diverse Khoja identity into one of a mainly Ismaili origin. The immediate and most pressing result of this was that it established the authority of Aga Khan I over the Khoja community. For some members this ruling was simply not acceptable.

In practice, however, it was difficult to break the ties of mutual dependence that had been built over many years. For many choosing another faith meant making the difficult decision to leave the community and part ways with family, friends, and relations. In time, however, first those of Sunni inclination and then the Shia Ithna-Asheri did eventually secede and form their independent Khoja communities.

1.7 The Emerging Khoja Shia Ithna-Asheries

Whilst the 1866 ruling established Aga Khan I's authority, it did not resolve the internal disputes within the Khoja community. In 1872, a group of Khojas of Shia Ithna-Asheri persuasion went to Karbala for *ziyarat*.[97] When they found out that their understanding and practices were not wholly in accordance with Shia Ithna-Asheri tenets, they requested Sheikh Zain-al-'Abidin Mazindarani (a recognised *mujtahid*[98] of the time) to send *mubaleegheen*[99] to teach them the proper Shia Ithna-Asheri Islam. Sheikh Mazindarani assigned this task to Mulla Qadir Husain of Madras.[100]

Mulla Qadir reached Bombay in 1873 and remained there until 1899. When he first began to challenge the established practices in the Jamaatkhana, there was a fierce campaign against him and his students. These protests came from those loyal to Aga Khan I[101] and generated ill-feeling between families, neighbours and relations to such an extent that those who visited Mulla Qadir or attended his class were no longer welcomed in the Jamaatkhana. By 1877, the opposition to those of Khoja Shia Ithna-Asheri persuasion became so intense that Haji Dewji Jamal[102] and his colleagues were expelled from the Bombay Jamaatkhana.[103] Eventually, Mulla Qadir's life was also threatened.

In his book, Hassan Jaffer describes an interesting conversation between Noormohammed and Mulla Qadir Husain when Mulla was told that 'Khojas believed that Ali is God'. After this conversation, Mulla Qadir took Noormohammed to Shaykh Zainul Abedin Mazindarani. After his subsequent meeting with Mukhi Hashambhai Dossa and finally the insightful conversation with Haji Dewji Jamaal and the intervention of Bakhshi Shujaat, Ayatullah Zainul Abedin Mazindarani requested Mulla Qadir Husain to return to India to serve the nascent Khoja Shia Ithna-Asheri Community.

Left - A rare Photo of Ayatullah Shaykh Zainul Abedin Mazindarani (Courtesy of Ayatullah Sayyid Abbas Kashani, Shaykh Nadir Jaffer, Syed Ridha Syed Mehdi and Marhum Hassan Jaffer, 'The Endangered Species')

Despite all this, a growing number of people began to appreciate the tenets of the faith as presented by Mulla Qadir and his teachings allowed a better understanding of Ithna-Asheri beliefs to develop within the community. The nascent community of the Khoja Shia Ithna-Asheries was finally taking shape.

By the late 1880s, they needed an *alim*[104] to provide socio-religious guidance and direction on a daily basis. At the request of Haji Dewji Jamal, two *alims* came to Bombay between 1889-90: Shaykh Abul Qassim Najafi who stayed in Bombay and Sayyid Abdul Hussein Mar'ashi who went on to serve the community in Zanzibar.

With the arrival of Sheikh Najafi, the small number of Khoja Shia Ithna-Asheries gained moral strength. Friday prayers were established and in 1898, the community – now around 50 members strong - established their own rule-based *jamaat* (community). By 1899, they were able to acquire a burial ground and through the newly-formed Khoja Shia Ithna-Asheri Jame Masjid, Madrasah and Imambara Trust, a *masjid* (mosque) was built by 1900.[105]

The developments achieved by this small, actively emerging Khoja Shia Ithna-Asheri community were all note-worthy and set a precedence for the future successes of its members, but perhaps their greatest achievement was that they were no longer under the authority of Aga Khan I.

Marhum Sayeid Abdulhusain Jawad Mar'ashi Musawi - The first resident Alim of Kuwwatul Islam Jamaat in Zanzibar. He passed away in Mecca in 1905.

'History of Mumbai Jamaat and its Martyrs' (1995) relates the birth of Marhum Ayatullah Shaykh Abul Qassim Najafi, his arrival to Mumbai and his contributions in the formative period of Khoja Shia community in Mumbai. (Courtesy: MARC)

However, the path to independence was not an easy one. Records show that in the quest to establish their own community, four prominent personalities were attacked in 1901 simply for being Shia Ithna-Asheries.[106] Hirjibhai Allarakhia and Laljibhoy Sajan died, while Abdulbhai Lalji and Kassambhai Nanji Miyani survived the attack. The two attackers, Kurji Rajan and Noor Mohammed Ali were both sentenced to death.[107]

*Artist Renditions from photos:
Marhum Sheth Hirjibhai Alarakhiya (left) and Marhum Sheth Laljibhai Sajan assassinated on 9th March 1901 for being Khoja Shia Ithna-Asheries.
(Courtesy: MARC)*

From 1873 until his departure to Karbala, Mulla Qadir Husain prepared a number of his pupils who became well-versed in the tenets of Shia Ithna-Asheri faith. Prominent amongst them were Haji Gulamali

Haji Esmail (Haji Naji), Habib Abji Jetha, Nur Mohammed Meghji, Aladin Ghulamhussein, Hafiz Ali Jiwa, and Abdalla Saleh Sachedina. These personalities were to play an exceptional role in teaching and spreading the faith among the Khoja community of Kathiawad and Kachchh. After Bombay, the first Shia Ithna-Asheri madrasah was established in Mahuva followed by a mosque and *madrasah* (religious school) in Bhavnagar. Another mosque and *madrasah* was established in Dholera followed by *madrasahs* in Talaja, Vertej, Mundra, Ahmadabad, Chamardi and Nagalpur.

Haji Ghulam Ali Haji Esmail
(Haji Naji)

A scholar of immense depth and founder of 'Raahenjat', he published more than 50 thoughtful books in the Gujarati language.

He was the lamp of guidance for the Khoja Shia Ithna-Asheri community in its formative period and after.

(Photo Courtesy of
Haji Naji Memorial Trust - Bhavnagar)

Between 1866 and 1899, the small Khoja Shia Ithna-Asheri community continued to evolve, but no clear break occurred between those who accepted Aga Khan as their Imam and those who believed in the Twelve Imams (Ithna-Asheries). After 1899, the differences became noticeable and it was soon clear that the two groups were heading towards a complete rift. Two processes led to the eventual split.

The first had begun with the arrival of Mulla Qadir Husain and his inspirational teachings that had drawn more and more members of the Khoja community. This process was subsequently accelerated by the arrival of Sheikh Abul Qasim Najafi who became the resident scholar for the emerging Khoja Shia Ithna-Asheri community in Bombay. The second process was the use of *farmans*[108] by Sultan Muhammad Shah i.e. Aga Khan III[109] to establish a distinct Ismaili identity according to his desire. At this time, there also arose a dispute within his own family regarding their entitlement to the monetary contributions received from the community. This dispute ended up in court and became famously known as the Haji Bibi Case.¹¹⁰

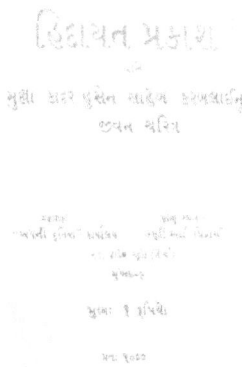

In his Autobiography titled 'Hidayat Prakash' (Light of Guidance), Mulla Qadir Husain Karbalai recalls his experiences and tribulations from his time with the Khoja community.

This autobiography was written in Urdu around 1900 and then translated in Gujarati in 1909 and published in Zanzibar.

It was finally translated and published in English by PET in 1992.

1.8 The Haji Bibi Case

The Haji Bibi case of 1908 arose because the Aga Khan's authority was once again challenged, this time from within his own family. He had to seek legal recourse to maintain his authority over the Khoja community and thus, the Haji Bibi Case took place. Sultan Mohammed Shah, the third Aga Khan, was put on trial by his cousin regarding his handling of money and tributes that came to him in his position as Aga Khan. Whilst the 1866 case had determined that Khoja property and financial tributes belonged to the Aga Khan, the 1908 case asked whether those funds were partly owned by his family, who believed they were equally entitled to those tributes.

Parpia explains the core allegation as being 'that the Khojas were in reality a Shia Ithna-Asheri community and that the voluntary offerings by the Khojas were made to Aga Khan III, not in the capacity of the Imam, but in the capacity of a Sayyid (descendent of Prophet Muhammed (pbuh), a distinction they (his family) shared with the Aga Khan III'.¹¹¹

The fact that the dissenters had declared themselves, and the Khoja community at large, to be Shia rather than Sunnis ensured that they had a stronger footing than the plaintiffs had in the 1866 case. As previously mentioned, the Khojas had a strong Ithna-Asheri flavour in their rites. Furthermore, Aga Khan II and subsequently his wife were both buried at Karbala, giving further credence to the allegations that the Aga Khan III had in fact invented a new religion.[112] However, Justice Russell came out with a detailed judgment in favour of the Aga Khan III, exonerating him of all the charges and reasserting his authority over the community's contributions.[113] This set a precedent for future generations of the community and also formalised another Khoja group.

The 1866 case produced the Khoja Sunnis and the 1908 case cemented the identity of the Khoja Shia Ithna-Asheries. Those that remained loyal to the Aga Khan III after this period became known as Shia Ismailis and became the majority constituents of the now divided Khoja community.

These two pivotal cases - the Khoja Case and the Haji Bibi Case - revealed the changing socio-religious environment of the Khoja community in India as the Sunni and Shia Ithna-Asheri factions sought to forge their own independent identities within the Khoja community. Following the legal battles and tumultuous state of the community ethos, Aga Khan III realised that he needed to secure his position, which he did by introducing changes aimed at clearly defining their religious identity according to his views.[114] In order 'to execute their ambitious programme of reforms, the "Aga Khans" used two important instruments: constitutions and *farmans* (directives).'[115]

The first formal constitutions - introduced by Aga Khan III in the year 1905[116] - and all subsequent constitutions included the Khojas and other indigenous *Satpanthi* groups within the broader category of Ismailis. It clearly stated that Aga Khan III was the leader of this religious community. Aga Khan III also issued various *farmans* that played a key role in shaping the Khoja identity to his preference.[117] Owing to the increasing emphasis on the transcendental stature of the Ismaili Imams, the *farmans* soon became the most important source of guidance for the loyal Khojas since they represented direct instructions of a mystical nature from the Imam of the time.

Aga Khan III's extensive use of the *farmans* began to strengthen his initiative towards centralising authority on him, to the exclusion of any others.[118] These spiritual directives not only became the tool to consolidate power but went further and reframed the beliefs, rituals, and practices of the Ismaili Khojas.

For example, Justice Arnould in the 1866 case explained the difference between the Sunni and Shia *salaat* (prayer) omitting to mention any *dua* (lamentations) or *bandagi* (the rites of prayer Ismailis use in their Jamaatkhana). However, Justice Russell in 1908[119] did not mention *salaat* but provided a full translation of *bandagi* to support the claim of the leadership of Aga Khan III. Furthermore, Justice Arnould mentioned Imam Hassan as 'the second Imam' whereas Justice Russell used the words: 'the Khoja regard the second one, namely Hassan, merely as Pir'.[120] A question arises as to why the two Justices referred to the prayers in such different ways. This seemingly subtle disparity is just one indication that shows how practices and rituals were changing dramatically within the Khoja community.

Another significant event that could have influenced Aga Khan III to issue *farmans* are his visits to Zanzibar, first in 1899[121] and subsequently in 1905[122], both before the Haji Bibi Case. In Zanzibar, he saw an established community of Khoja Shia Ithna-Asheries with their own *masjid* and *imambada* that had been built in 1880.[123] He was well aware of Khojas of Shia Ithna-Asheri persuasion who attended the Jamaatkhana but were not practicing its tenets yet.[124]

He was also aware that in Bombay and elsewhere in East Africa, Khoja Shia Ithna-Asheries had functioning community structures with their own communal and religious facilities.[125] Clearly, this state of affair would not serve his purpose of consolidating his authority as a leader over the entire community.

The Aga Khan began issuing various *farmans* that played a key role in the shaping of the distinct Khoja identity.[126] The *farmans* required those amongst the Khojas who did not show complete loyalty, in the exact way prescribed by Aga Khan III, to be excluded from the community. *Farmans* now represented the direct authority of Aga Khan III and began to emphasis his own transcendental stature.[127] They became the most important source of guidance for the Ismaili Khoja community.

From Zanzibar, he dictated *farmans* to his *wazir* (representative), Vares Kassam, an Ismaili of Junaghad,[128] along the following lines:

- *Majalis* (religious lectures) should be held only during the ten days of Muharram and not on other days.[129]

- After the *majlis* (sing.), only one *ziyarat* (oral salutation to Holy Imams from afar), that of Imam Hussein, should be recited whilst facing *qibla* (Mecca). The other two *ziyarat* (of the 8th and 12th Imams) should be discontinued.

- In the official documents of the Jamaatkhana, the phrase 'Twelve Imams' and 'Fourteen *Masumin*'[130] should be discontinued.

For Aga Khan III, it was imperative to have unanimous and complete loyal servitude from the community. He was not going to tolerate a loose group which looked towards Najaf and Karbala for their religious guidance as a growing number of Khoja's of Shia Ithna-Asheri persuasion were already doing. The idea was to use the vehicle of *farmans* to wean his supporters away from the Ithna-Asheri Khojas and cement his hold over the remaining Khoja community.[131] Following his visit to Zanzibar, the *farmans* that came out were increasingly identifying the Khoja community as Ismaili. Those who held on to the Shia Ithna-Asheri faith could no longer remain within this larger community.

Over the late 19th and early 20th centuries, the journey of the Khoja community played out in a series of momentous events. The judgements of Justices Arnould and Russell and the establishment of the *farman* system completed the split between the Khoja Sunnis, Khoja Ismailis and Khoja Ithna-Asheries. However, even in the years between these milestone events, the community was not at peace.

The toxic religious and social tensions had continued to fester before the final severing of ties. During this period, several well-known personalities and their families suffered a communal boycott. In the Trade Directory, Karimbhai Alarakhiya explains that:

> In Mumbai, due to religious tensions within the Khoja community, Bhai Dewji Jamaal, Alarakhiya Walli, Suleiman Khalfan and Kalyan Gangji were banned from the Khoja

community. Bhai Dewji Jamaal and Alarakhiya Walli together with their respective families migrated to Zanzibar. Suleiman Khalfan settled in Muscat and Kalyan Gangji went to Baghdad. These two families are still residing in Muscat and Baghdad.

Here in Jangbar (Zanzibar), some of the Khoja brothers began to accept the tenets of Ithna-Asheri faith and in 1880, Dewji Jamaal and Alarakhiya Walli brought in a donation of approximately 8000 Indian Rupees and, in Jangbar (Zanzibar), Mohammed Walji Rawji and Walli Nazarali and other brothers assisted in the fund-raising and, in 1880, Kuwwatul Islam Masjid and Imambada was completed....[132]

HAJI DEWJI JAMAAL (1820-1905)

Born in Bhavnagar, India, he was an active member of the Khoja community, he prayed, kept fasts and observed Majlises of Imam Hussein (pbuh). At the same time, like other Khojas, he believed in the Satpanthi ideas of reincarnation and that Imam Ali (pbuh) was the first Imam and tenth incarnation of God.

Around 1873, Dewji Jamal travelled from Zanzibar to Iraq for pilgrimage and in Karbala, met Mulla Qadir Husain and Ayatullah Zainul Abedin Mazindarani who explained to him that the Satpanthi/Ismaili belief of Ali's incarnation was wrong.

Dewji Jamal originally operated his business in Bhavnagar. He moved to Bombay in 1850 and in 1860, opened his first East African branch - Dewji Jamal & Co - in Zanzibar. In 1870, he opened a second branch in Lamu, Kenya, and in 1890, he established a branch in Mombasa.

Dewji Jamal and his sons were Importers and Exporters. Their fleet of dhows transported timber, textile, all kinds of foodstuff, including rice and sugar from India and exported cloves, copra, ivory, seashells and wooden poles (Boriti) etc. from East Africa. They contributed to building mosques, community halls, rest houses, madrasahs, cemeteries and properties for rental income for charitable purposes, both in India and East Africa.

The beautiful mosque on the seashore of Lamu next to the Post Office, the Hyderi Mosque and Imambada, the cemetery at Mombasa, Zanzibar and Lamu, the huge rest house, mosque and madrasah at Bombay and at Kurla (Bombay Suburb) - all are their charities which today hold immense value and provide services to the community. Haji Dewji Jamal died at the age of 85 and is buried in Karbala, Iraq.

(Courtesy: Africa Federation Archives)

These early settlers laid the foundational socio-religious principles that formed a basis on which the Khoja Shia Ithna-Asheries developed their East African identity. In the next part, we will explore the reasons that spurred the migration from Kachchh, Kathiawad, and Mumbai to Zanzibar and the coast of East Africa.

Early Khoja settlers (mainly Khoja Ismailis) of East Africa establishing a foothold in Zanzibar (From Nimira's Blog by Nimira Dewji)

PART 2
Migration to A New Land

According to the Khoja Shia Ithna-Asheri community archival records, the Khojas that came to the East African coast were of three faith persuasions: Shia Ithna-Asheries, of Shia Ithna-Asheri inclination, and Khoja Ismaili.[1] The communal records mention 1839[2] as the earliest year of arrival of the first individuals who would go on to form the Khoja Shia Ithna-Asheri community. While not exclusively Ithna-Asheri, there was an established Khoja community in the region from the 1820s at least. According to the testimony of Tharia Topan (then head of the Khoja community) provided in *Jesa v Hurbayee* in 1837, there were 205 Khoja households in Zanzibar and only 20 Khoja women.[3] Many Khoja men had partners who were *masuria* (concubines).

From 1840, Khoja migration to Zanzibar began to increase and by the 1870s, the Khoja community (of all belief persuasions) in Zanzibar numbered 718 males, 642 women and 540 children.[4] There were Khoja families in other parts of East Africa as well; in Kilwa, there were 59 Khojas and in Bagamoyo, there were 18. The individual narratives found in the Trade Directory bring to light each immigrant's personal circumstances and reasons for migration.[5] From these testimonies, the most favoured first stop was Zanzibar. People then either stayed or travelled onwards to other coastal towns of East Africa, and then to the interior. There are, however, testimonies, particularly from those who arrived from the 1880s onwards that indicate people were starting to land in other coastal towns of East Africa and not just Zanzibar.[6]

2.1 The Earliest Arrival

The earliest recorded arrival to Zanzibar is that of Sachedina Pirani Mawji, popularly known as Haji Sachoo Pira who came in 1839 AD.[7] Oral narrative within the Dar es Salaam community, supported by the Africa Federation archives, say that he was born in Mandvi, most likely in the year 1836.

HAJI SACHOO PIRA (1836 - 1906)

(Courtesy: Africa Federation Archives)

He was only three years old when he came from Mandvi (Kachchh). Whilst travelling towards Kilwa with his parents the dhow carrying them sank and his parents drowned in the tragedy. The orphaned Sachoo Pira was brought to Zanzibar and placed in the care of his uncle. His family history does not reveal any details about his parents or explain how or when his uncle arrived in Zanzibar.

What we do know is that at some point in time, he moved from Zanzibar to Mji Mwema,[8] an area within the Mzizima region,[9] and a convenient commercial fishing village that later developed into the city of Dar es Salaam.[10] According to oral sources there were only two Indian families residing in Mzizima in the 1850s; one of them was the family of Sachoo Pira.[11] From this account at least, we can infer that he was one of the first Khojas to settle there. By 1866, besides

Sachoo Pira, there were around 43 more Khoja residents.[12] There are no records of who they were, their demographics or social interactions.

What is known is that three main groups traded from Mzizima: the Khoja merchants who had been trading along the East African coast for many years, the local Shomvi[13] people, and an inland Bantu tribe known as the WaZaramo.[14] The local economy consisted of farming, coconut harvesting, fishing, hunting and craft-making such as embroidery, woodcarving, metal and leatherwork. Khoja *dukawalla* (shopkeepers) traded in these goods for *merikan*[15] and *khanga*[16] cloths, natural beads from Gujarat, and building materials from Bagamoyo and Zanzibar.[17]

Mzizima, as recalled by the elders of the community, was not conducive to settlement, unlike Bagamoyo with its wealth built on slavery and the trade from the interior caravans.[18] **Nevertheless, the Khojas who had fled the economic miseries and famine of Kachchh wanted a better life for themselves and were keen to make a prosperous living there.**[19]

By 1866, Sultan Majid[20] began building the port at Mzizima into a bustling hub and renamed it Dar es Salaam. However, in 1873, the area's business activities began to decline because of a trade boycott by the WaZaramo traders.[21] This was followed by an outbreak of smallpox in 1882, which killed around three-quarters of the town's inhabitants. The final blow came in the form of drought and famine in 1884. Many Khojas settlers suffered irrecoverable commercial loss due to this series of adversities and had to move to Bagamoyo or Zanzibar to begin afresh.[22]

Things were looking bleak for the region, but its fortunes were soon to change for the better. From 1885, German colonial occupation[23] began and they set up a trading station in Dar es Salaam. Business started to improve and by 1891, the city had become the new capital of German East Africa. Government money flowed in for development projects.

By 1905, Dar es Salaam was the eastern terminus of the Central Railway Line running to the interior; it had two grand German churches: a Bavarian Alpine-style Lutheran church and a Gothic-style Catholic Church, an imposing Government State House, and an equally imposing hospital facing the Indian Ocean and government's main office buildings. With improved living and commercial facilities in Dar es Salaam, the Khojas returned to take advantage of significant infrastructure and opportunity for corporate investment. Their resettlement increased significantly, but it was at the expense of Bagamoyo, which by then had started to steadily decline.[24]

The increased Indian presence in German East Africa posed direct commercial competition for the German settlers who viewed them as unwelcome intruders in their prospective fortune in the region. Harry Johnston reflects this animosity towards Indians in East Africa when he says that 'it is no secret that much of the recent troubles and difficulties of the German Company in East Africa arose from the unwisdom of its employees in endeavouring to rudely and suddenly oust the Indians from their commercial supremacy and thereby making Indian sentiment opposed to the extension of German rule'.[25]

On the other hand, the German administrators viewed the Indian settlers - including the Khoja community - as essential labour. They needed them to make a success of their colonial project but treated them as inferior to German settlers when it came to handing out state benefits.

Sachoo Pira stayed in Mzizima through its evolution from a humble fishing village to the booming business hub that Dar es Salaam became. He witnessed adversity and prosperity, first under the Sultan of Zanzibar and then under the German colonial government. By all the accounts available, he was a successful well-liked businessman. His contributions were directed to all without discrimination and appreciated to such a degree that the government recognised him and allowed him to fly a German flag on his house.[26]

He was an active benefactor especially for the Khoja Shia Ithna-Asheri community to which he donated land for their *masjid* (mosque), *imambada* (religious hall) and *kabrastan* (graveyard). By 1900, the small Khoja Shia Ithna-Asheri community had an *imambada* constructed from corrugated iron sheets standing on the donated land (currently occupied by the Pirbhai Jiwa Bharwani building on Mosque Street).

There are no records in communal sources of how the place was run, who was in charge or even whether the Khoja Shia Ithna-Asheries of Dar es Salaam had an existing *jamaat* prior to the construction of the Mosque Street Imambada. What the older generation considers common knowledge though is that the German authorities requested the community to move their place of congregation from Mosque Street to a different place (at Kaluta Street).

According to Africa Federation archives,[27] the German Governor knew that the Khoja Shia Ithna-Asheri community needed a place of worship. In 1904, he gave the plot of land to Sachoo Pira who donated it to the community; this is where our current *masjid-imambada* complex on Indira Ghandi Street stands. That same year, Sachoo Pira laid the foundation stone for the new *masjid* and personally supervised its construction. He passed away one year later in 1906 and others, including his family members, saw the project to its completion.[28]

Transformation of New Land – Mosque, Imambada and Kabrastan built on the land donated by Haji Sachoo Pira (Courtesy: Africa Federation Archives.)

2.2 Migratory Influences in the 1830s

Sachoo Pira's migration to Zanzibar in 1839 and his subsequent brief life history is the earliest record available in communal sources. They reveal the extent of his role in transforming the landscape of Dar es Salaam where he settled. His example is one among many that show the determination of immigrants to succeed against all odds in a foreign land. But what motivated people like Sachoo Pira to leave their homeland, especially when the risks involved in the journey and the arrival into a new land were perilous? Why did not they internally relocate within Gujarat or India itself? Was the dire economic situation in India sufficient motivation to leave behind everything they knew for a new country?

We do not have much information on what led Sachoo Pira's parents to leave Mandvi for Zanzibar. Nevertheless, we need to find out why they and others would have wanted to leave Kachchh and Kathiawad and cross the ocean to Zanzibar and the East-African coast. In the absence of concrete evidence or records on these early pioneers, we must turn to general historical records of the time period.

With the lack of extensive public, community and family documents, it is difficult to isolate any concrete factor that made these earlier Khoja pioneers leave India and go to East Africa. A study of influential events in Kachchh and Kathiawad during the years in question may provide a small window of understanding as to the cause of the Khoja migration. We begin with Mandvi, as it is the place of birth of Sachoo Pira.

2.2.1 Famine in Kachchh

In the early 1800s, Mandvi was the most populous town in Kachchh. At the time, it engaged in brisk trade with Muscat, Malabar and Bombay. In 1819, a severe earthquake rocked Kachchh and it was followed by a serious cholera outbreak. Subsequent crop failures of 1823 plunged major parts into drought and famine. The calamities did not stop there. The next decades saw natural disasters continuing to descend on the area.[29] The failure of the summer monsoons over west and central India and successive monsoon failures preceded by droughts, affected an area of 476,000 square miles and a population of almost 59 million.

This situation, combined with large planted-crop failures in the rest of India, unsettled inter-regional trades and led to the hoarding of grains. The fear of scarcity further destabilised the supply and prices of the food grains. This famine was amongst the worst in history and known as *Chappanyo Dukal*. It resulted in a mortality rate of 37.9 deaths per 1000 persons - this is a low-end estimate as there was no organized system of counting or reporting.³⁰ It was at this time that the members of the Gujarati-speaking Kachchhi and Kathiawadi communities began migrating in earnest and amongst them were the Khojas.

As rains kept failing and conditions became worse, some people moved internally to places like Mumbai for better opportunities whist others moved out from the ports in Western Gujarat and Bombay to East Africa. The intensity of migration increased with each famine cycle and the local reality of the 1830s could well have pushed young people, possibly the parents of Sachoo Pira amongst them, out of Kachchh in search for better prospects.

From the family archives of community members, we know that drought, famine and subsequent calamities were the core pressure for Khojas migrating to East Africa in search of better opportunities.³¹ Oral accounts state that many were subsistence farmers or farm labourers, some were also engaged in construction work or transportation, and a few had their own businesses.

Daftary refers to the migration of Khojas in 'large numbers' to Zanzibar between 1840 and 1870. He lends credence to the sparse conditions precipitating their decision and observes that 'severe droughts and famine in Gujarat induced many Khoja farmers there to join the caravans of the Khoja traders' immigration to East Africa.'³²

Meagre conditions aside, another factor that could definitely have encouraged enterprising Khojas to migrate was the breadth of the British occupied territories that allowed them - as British subjects - to move around freely with British Overseas Passports. Some chose East Africa as their destination.

2.2.2 The Abolition of Slavery in 1833

Another factor that cannot be ignored is the abolition of slavery in 1833.³³ While slavery was coming to an 'official' end, human labour was still needed to work in the plantations across all occupied territories, including East Africa. Colonial authorities in India arranged with plantation owners to send workers from India to fill this labour gap and in 1834, they constructed the Indian Indentured Labour System.[34] Under this system, contracted Indian labourers were sent in large numbers to plantation colonies producing high value crops such as sugar and sugar-fermented alcohol in Africa and the Caribbean. Many Indians agreed in order to escape the widespread poverty and desperate circumstances prevailing in India from 1800-1900 AD. Some travelled alone while others brought their families with them.

These Indians were mostly young, active, able-bodied people looking for any menial work to sustain their families but they were often ignorant of the places they were being taken to and did not understand the challenges they would face thousands of miles away from the home. Most of them also held British Overseas Passports and the ships that took them out of India recorded their births, marriages and deaths. Interestingly, whenever an indentured Indian labourer gave birth to a child on board a ship, the records give the child's name but the parent is listed simply as 'coolie'.[35]

When this system ended in the 1920s, the documented figures show that nearly a million Indians had left India to work overseas.[36] In the late 19th century, the British government imported large numbers of labourers from India to build the railway line from Mombasa on the coast of Kenya to Kampala, Uganda; in total 32,000 of them came to East Africa.

This large-scale migration from Gujarat to East Africa gave Indian traders a built-in market for their wares of food and sundries. The Khoja Shia Ithna-Asheri communal records show that from 1839, the majority, if not all of the Khojas who arrived in Zanzibar and East Africa were not under the indentured scheme, but independently looking for new, better opportunities.[37]

In Zanzibar, they found a society that was welcoming and accommodated different cultures because of the trade and migration it had seen for centuries. The common language was Swahili[38] and the majority of the residents were Muslims. For Khojas arriving in the 1870s onwards, a majority-Muslim island may have resonated more with their collective psyche, especially as by this time the British colonial authorities had classified them as Muslim.

2.3 Indian Ocean Trading World Opportunities

While we do not specifically know why people like the parents of Sachoo Pira were travelling to Kilwa instead of Zanzibar, the temptation of trade is a very likely factor for their move. Kilwa was a major trading centre from the 8th century and became one of the most powerful settlements along the coast. By the 18th century, the Gujarati merchants among the Indian residents in Kilwa were financiers and moneylenders just as they were at other coastal ports such as Mogadishu, Zanzibar and Madagascar.[39]

Dhows, the sailing ships characteristic of East Africa, would set out from Kilwa and Sofala laden with gold, grain, wood, and ivory. Driven by the monsoon winds across the Indian Ocean, they took their wares to India and China as well as to Arabia and Persia. Europe's growing dependency on hard currency also drove a demand for Swahili gold. In return, Kilwa imported cotton, ceramics, Chinese porcelain, and silk. As it grew richer, the city started to mint its own coins. In short, Kilwa developed a rich commercial history.

It attracted many Indian entrepreneurs including Khojas and the economic opportunities could have been a legitimate reason for the family of Sachoo Pira and others to choose this new land over other more common options. We do not know how many Khojas settled in Kilwa around the 1840s, but we can presume that there were some as it was a trading port for ivory and there is evidence that ivory trading existed amongst Khoja Shia Ithna-Asheries

The Indian Ocean trade influenced Zanzibar and coastal ports of East Africa deeply. These ports were an integral part of the Indian Ocean Trading World from the end of the first century and dominated the trade routes until the 20th century. For millennia the Gujaratis, like the Arabs, plied the Indian Ocean in small sailing ships.[40] Through the Persian Gulf, they traded with ancient Babylon and through the Red Sea with Egypt, Greece, Rome, Axum and Kush.

The earliest account of the East African trade is in the *Periplus of the Erythraen Sea*. Written in the first century by a Greek-speaking Egyptian, this is a trader's handbook on the commerce of the Indian

Ocean. The *Periplus* records that the 'Ausanitic (East African) coast' was by ancient right subject to the sovereignty of whichever state had become the leader in Southern Arabia. We also know that the principal actors in the East African trade were Arab merchants from Yemen and their Indian counterparts from Gujarat.[41]

John Middleton holds that 'Indians (had) settled in and traded with the Swahili towns for many centuries' with 'some Muslim Indian groups...being an integral part of the larger towns'.[42]

Chhaya Goswami also agrees that

> Indian involvement in trade resulted in the formation of settlement in and around Zanzibar. These merchants in their process of settlement influenced the set-up of bazaars and houses of the nineteenth century Zanzibar town. During their stay in Zanzibar whether periodical or permanent, Kutchis retained a particular sense of cultural identity. The Hindus were guided by the codes of conduct of their respective communities and their strict adherence to their religion restricted their assimilation.
>
> Representations of the establishment of communities and the conduct of trade and nature of their settlement are important elements in understanding the culture and custom. Some of the Indians even adopted Swahili as their first language. This shows the impact of local culture on the migrants. In short as in Muscat, the Indians in Zanzibar were an essential part of the East African economy and society.[43]

Based on all this, we can safely conclude that the Indians including Khojas had considerable influence in East Africa's trading activities.

The monsoons were a critical factor for the Indian Ocean communities.[44] They provided Gujarati traders with calm seas and enabled small craft to navigate the ocean. Trading relied upon the winds, which blew dhows in a south-westerly direction from the East African coast to Arabia, India and Persia between April and August. The north-eastern winds reversed the direction bringing the dhows back to East African between December and March. This predictability allowed sailing vessels to time their journeys to and fro with relative precision.

However, waiting for the change in the winds forced the traders to spend a fixed time in port cities leading over time to many long-term social consequences. The Indian Ocean evidenced elements of cohesion in its economic exchanges, climate and movement of people, shared religion and means of travel.[45]

Perhaps most importantly, in his research of the region, K. Chaudhuri emphasized that despite the social diversity, the relationships created across the Indian Ocean basin were highly meaningful for those at its shores. Studying the coastal towns of East Africa within the larger Indian Ocean Region would thus require an approach from the sea rather than from the land. Elaborating on this point, Michael Pearson[46] has argued that port cities such as Mandvi, Muscat and Mombasa shared more features with each other than they did with their own hinterlands. It appears that a far better understanding of Zanzibar and the East African coast can be achieved if the analysis of its people is approached from the perspective of it being part of the Indian Ocean region and not just confined to the interior regions of East Africa.

As evidenced in the substantial works of Professor Abdul Sheriff, the monsoons created shifting patterns of interaction.[47] For example, 300 dhows on average would descend to a port in Zanzibar from Somalia, Yemen, Persian Gulf, and India, bringing up to 6000 sailors who would completely transform the town between the two monsoons. As sailors of different nationalities made homes for a substantial period at either coast, they also created families of mixed race.

The Indian Ocean[48] thus facilitated a unique interaction of trade, religion and culture that created new societies and intercourse between states. These interactions played a major role in the migration of people from one coast to another and beyond. It allowed 'traders, scholars, jurists, officials, and military officers to move between several jurisdictions to seek employment and fortunes'.[49] This mutual interdependence on trade, intermarriage of Africans with minority Muslims, and the subsequent infusion of native religions with Islam gave rise to a distinct culture, predominantly African but with strong Arabic-Persian influences, called Swahili after the Arabic phrase meaning 'of the coast'.

This approach towards the Indian Ocean region provides the opportunity to appreciate the complexity of a dynamic, cosmopolitan, globalised and diverse socio-religious-political culture that scholars refer to as 'Swahili Civilisation'.⁵⁰ Various relationships within it evolved, not by exploitation but by fluid negotiation of ethnicity and social positioning within an integrative space.

Coffee seller serving kahawa (black coffee) on the streets of Zanzibar.

Most Arabs who settled on the coastline gradually adopted Swahili culture and speech, as did numerous other communities including the Khoja Shia Ithna-Asheri.

The social hierarchy of 19th century Swahili society was essentially defined by how close one was to the indigenous culture. For example, established residents, recently-settled immigrants and new arrivals were ranked in terms of how indigenous (*wenyeji*) or how foreign (*wageni*) they were perceived as. As Deckard puts it, it was

> 'Arabs' (*Waarabu*) versus 'Africans' (*Waafrika*), people of the coast (*watu wa pwani*) versus people from inland regions (*watu wa bara*), freeborn (*waungwana*) versus those affiliated with slave or servile ancestry (*watumwa/ washenzi*).
>
> The fluidity of these ethnic categories, whose boundaries were continually in the process of negotiation sharply contrasted the rigidity of the racial hierarchies constructed by European colonial policies of 'divide and rule'.⁵¹

The Indian Ocean with its unique interaction of trade, culture and religion became an integrated part of the East African coastal places like Zanzibar, Lamu, and Mombasa, Bagamoyo, Tanga, Kilwa and others; this is at least true for the period 1750 to 1960.⁵² During these centuries, the peoples of the Indian Ocean shared a history and its inhabitants were involved in a common social, economic and cultural project. This does not diminish the crucial role played by the indigenous people who inhabited the interior of the East African shore; rather, the sea gave unity and coherence to the region and provided these coastal towns references beyond their immediate lifestyle.[53]

This structural flexibility was necessary to accommodate migratory influences and the Khoja community was just one of many that benefitted immensely from it.[54] Understanding the true depth of the connectivity of the Indian Ocean requires us to factor in multiple voices - be they merchants, slaves, indentured labourers, entrepreneurs or explorers - from all cultures and creeds. In this book, we will be focusing on the Khoja Shia Ithna-Asheries.

The mercantile Indian communities, amongst them the Kachchhi and Kathiawadi Khojas, were prominent traders on the Indian Ocean.[55] Having endured Portuguese interference in the triangular trade network between Kachchh, Muscat and Zanzibar, Kachchhi traders regained their position in the early 19th century.

The Kachchhi of Mandvi, well known for their trading prowess, had upward of 800 boats of differing sizes exporting cotton cloth, silk, alum, and ghee, among other things. They conducted inland trade with Malwar, Sind, Gujarat, and Jaisalmar. They also took part in external trade by sea with the ports of Western India as well as the Red Sea, Persian Gulf, East Africa, Mozambique, and beyond.[56] The most economically important port cities were Cambay, Diu and Surat that supplied the East African coastal towns and Swahili people with the largest share of cloth which was the chief category of imported goods.

Economic activities between cities in Western India and East African coastal towns became a critical factor in the formation of enduring socio-political relationships.[57] In the 19th century, trade between Kachchh and Muscat grew rapidly with the latter becoming the major transhipment port between the Persian Gulf, Aden, and India.

Around 1820, when the Indians began to make Muscat their base for the Red Sea and Persian Gulf trading areas, it also became home to many Khojas, Memons, and Bhatias.[58] Gwadar, an Omani outpost, is on the Balouch coast. By the 1830s, Kachchhi Khojas were constantly moving between Gwadar and Muscat where a community of Sindhi Bhatias existed from the 1750s. Kachchhi Khojas, having already gained a foothold in Muscat sought a return to Zanzibar to expand their trading. At the same time, Hyderabadi Khojas (called Luti or Luwatiyas) also came to settle in Muscat and, together with the Kachchhi Bhatias, were one of its most influential Indian merchant communities.

Fortified gate at Mandvi built by Jadeja rulers (mid 16th century)

In the late 18th and early 19th centuries, Mandvi was the greatest, busiest port in India. It was the key point in the triangular trade route between Oman, Mandvi and the Sindh-Punjab hinterland.

As Oman expanded its trade to the Zanzibar coast, the Indian (and Khoja) traders[59] also moved with them. With the Khojas actively involved in the framework, the vessels that left Mandvi were laden with Khoja-owned goods being sent to Zanzibar and other East African ports using either the Buradur[60] route that traded with Somalia, or the Suwalle[61] route that traded with Lamu, Mombasa and Zanzibar.

The evidence of the Kachchhi settlement (including Khojas) in Zanzibar is available through the report of a British officer, Captain Smee.[62] According to his view, the best part of the trade that existed was controlled mainly by the Arabs from Muscat and Indians from Kachchh and Sindh.

Goswami writes that the 'Kachchhi merchants' business connections with East Africa in the late eighteenth and early nineteenth century proved to be instrumental in expanding the trading networks between Muscat and Zanzibar'.[63]

Those Khojas originating from the provinces of Kachchh, Kathiawad and Sindh (present day Pakistan) boarded dhows[64] from the ports of Mandvi, Porbander and Diu located in Western India and came mostly to Zanzibar. Some disembarked in Mombasa, Tanga and southern regions, settling there; others then moved in to the interior.

Khoja trading activities began to expand in East Africa in this way. Because of this expansion, trading opportunities flourished and enterprising Khojas took advantage of them, which resulted in further migration of Khojas from Kachchh and Kathiawad. Thus, the network between Kachchh, Muscat and Zanzibar was firmly established, with Zanzibar becoming a prominent trading base for Khoja traders.

2.4 Influences of the Omani Sultanate

One of the other important factors that influenced the migration of Khojas was the re-establishment of the Omani Sultanate's influence over the island of Zanzibar. Apart from taking advantage of trading opportunities, the Omanis also had an impact on the religious-cultural norms along the East African coast.

The Swahili coast offered Omanis the opportunity to introduce Islam to the indigenous peoples. In the process of integrating, they created harbours at Mogadishu, Malindi, Mombasa, Dar es Salaam, Zanzibar, and Kilwa where wealthy merchants built grand houses with walled courtyards that are still standing in these ports to this day.

Muslims, it appears, incorporated into social structures more easily than the Portuguese they had expelled. Furthermore, establishing Islamic religious and cultural norms was easier for Omani sultanate because over time, Muslim merchants who had frequented the coast had already established religious institutions that governed their transactions and daily lives. The Omani sultanate merely extended this structure.

The long history of Islamic influence along the East African coast are from two major sources: archaeological excavations and the writings of Muslim geographers and historians who visited parts of the region in the 10th century.[65] According to these sources, there existed Muslim Indian traders, Arab traders as well as entrepreneurs and adventurers in the coastal cities of East Africa all the way up to Madagascar.

Around 1150, al-Idrisi writes of an Indian settlement at the mouth of the Zambezi River.[66] Ibn Battuta, the famous Muslim scholar and explorer, visited East Africa in 1331 and was exposed to an Afro-Islamic culture. He does not seem to have any knowledge or mention any evidence of the existence of an Indian population, but describes a couple of Indian linguistic and cultural elements among the coastal peoples of East Africa i.e. the use of *tambuu* (betel leaves) and *popoo* (areca nuts).[67]

By the time Vasco da Gama arrived in East Africa in 1498, there was already a notable presence of Indians there.[68] Cynthia Salvadori relates this story in her book[69] as told by the Kana brothers, Yakub Abbas Kana and Issak Abbas Kana, of Mombasa:

> …you want to know the first member of our family to be in Africa and when? Well, his name was Mohamed, and he was known as 'Kana Maalim'. That name means "Master of the Tiller' because in the language of Gujarati '*bhadala*', which is where we Bhadalas are from, the word for tiller or rudder, is '*sukhan*'. He was the one who showed Vasco De Gama the way from Malindi to India.

And so it was that a Muslim Indian pilot, Kana (Kanji) Maalim, from the sea-faring Bhadala[70] clan took Vasco De Gama's expedition from Malindi, Kenya to the western Indian port of Kalikat.[71]

By all accounts, the conduit for Khojas migrating to East Africa was the Indian Ocean Trading World with the Omani sultanate playing a major role in encouraging increased migration in the middle of the 19th century. The Khoja traders, being familiar with some Islamic terminology and etiquette, should have found adapting to mainly Muslim coastal societies of East Africa easier than other places.

2.5 Khoja Settlement in Zanzibar

In early- to mid-19th century, Khojas took advantage of the Indian Ocean Trading Route to travel for trade as well as to escape poor economic conditions in their birth places. By 1811, there were a few adventurous Kachchhi and Sindhis settled in Zanzibar. They began to set up the socio-economic foundations that would eventually provide opportunities for many of their families and friends to join them as either employees in their enterprises or to help in setting up the much-needed distribution routes for interior regional trading networks.[72] By 1819, there were 214 Indian merchant houses in Zanzibar town alone. The majority of these were Kachchhi.[73]

What further attracted Khojas and other traders to Zanzibar was the economic shift that Bus'aidi rulers wanted in Zanzibar.[74] In the late 18th century, the Busa'idi rulers in Oman assumed the title of Sultan instead of Imam thus abandoning claims to religious authority. This change in title marked a shift in power that focused on establishing a commercial empire independent of religion. In 1837, Sultan Seyyid Said extended the Oman-Zanzibari sultanate across most of the Swahili region, forming an alliance with Lamu's aristocracy and taking control of Mombasa.[75]

The Sultan also marginalised hereditary rulers of East African coastal towns such as Zanzibar's *Mwinyi Mkuu*[76] and instead installed Busa'idi governors (*liwali*) in each principal town or city. As they consolidated their control, the Sultans banned many foreign merchants from direct trade and at the same time made Zanzibar a free port. This attracted a rush of trade and investment and Indian financial houses took advantage of the opportune environment this created. They began offering generous lines of credit, which brought more cash into circulation, fuelled coastal trading ventures to the interior and stimulated agricultural production for export.

Their enterprise was successful, but not without difficulties. They underwent extortion by the ruling class and higher classes of Arabs often cheated them out of their property. Prior to 1833, the Sultan of Zanzibar had levied duty according to Arab custom, but it was unfairly attributed with Arabs paying only five per cent whereas the Indians sometimes paid as high as 20 per cent. They were also expected to pay a high proportion of irregular levies and accommodate the Sultan whenever he needed finance for his projects.[77]

In 1840, Zanzibar exported its first significant cargoes of cloves.[78] The Sultan sent his flagship on a trade mission to New York City laden with Zanzibari cloves, East African ivory, Yemeni coffee, Omani dates and Persian carpets. The trade mission was probably a result of a treaty signed between Muscat and America in 1833. Consequent treaties that were signed with Britain in 1839 and with France in 1844 strengthened Zanzibar's commercial position.[79] As commercial activities became more important to the Sultan, he eventually moved his court from Muscat to Zanzibar.

For the Indian community in Zanzibar, the entry of Americans and Europeans into the trading activities meant competition and the need for extra effort to keep control of their own position in the game. Although they could not influence the arrival of the foreigners, the Indians were able to retain the management of a greater part of import-export trade even after the treaties mentioned. They did this by adapting to the changing circumstances. They began to take on a variety of roles as required: brokers, investors, agents, retailers, intermediaries, wholesalers, shopkeepers, and customs collectors.

The trading activities of Indians in Zanzibar ranged from providing loans against mortgages to handling the export business; Arab property owners employed some as bookkeepers and financial controllers and yet others were simply traders. Goswami writes that

> …gradually except for a few, the Arabs lost their economic power and became dependent upon the financial and commercial expertise of the Indians. Eventually the Arabs found themselves only owners of lands and with the monopoly of political power.
>
> This was so because certain Arabs were reckless borrowers and were not concerned about the repayment of the loans. Consequently, money-lending was risky, and, as a result, money-lenders charged high rates of interest. This suggests the effectiveness of Indian capital and its use in the expansion of commerce.[80]

The move from Muscat to Zanzibar in the 1840s suggests that the primary objective of the Sultan was to establish a mercantile economy over religious adherence and transform the region into a commercial one. With this shift to Zanzibar, they adopted a policy of encouraging Indian traders to settle there. Entrepreneur Khojas from Kachchh, Kathiawad, Bombay and elsewhere flocked to the coast. This lure was aptly conveyed by a well-known saying that is still uttered: *Zanzibar bandari liari kila sheri tayari* that loosely translates to 'Everything is found in Zanzibar, the best of all, near and far'.

The Indian population continued to rise and by the 1840s, they owned clove plantations and tracts of land.[81] This increased influence of the Indian community was evidenced by the appointment of Jairam Siwji, a Hindu Bhatia, as a chief custom collector in Zanzibar. Jairam Siwji served almost 70 years in this position and recruited many Bhatias from India to work under him. He assisted many to set up money-lending businesses in Zanzibar or to start up trade ventures in other parts of the East African coast.[82]

By 1844, there were 800 Indians living in Zanzibar.[83] Records reveal that in almost every trading place along the coast, there was a Gujarati (one can plausibly assume that a Khoja was amongst them).[84]

2.6 European Powers and the Fall of the Busaʻidi

There were also other developments of a political nature unfolding. In the 17th century, European powers fought internally over trade and land domination due to economic challenges there. These powers were forced to seek new markets.[85] What initially attracted the Europeans to Zanzibar was the plantation economy created by Seyyid Said,[86] as well as the existence of trade links to the interior of East Africa. They were keen to establish trade agreements that would serve their own interests and allow them to gain control of the coast and its ready-made rich commercial set-up.

Apart from this, the Europeans also felt that it was their duty to 'educate', as they saw it, the 'uncivilised' people of Africa. They set out to do this through a combination of government direction, missionary instruction and settlers' enterprise. Whilst focused on this task, they tended to ignore the roles of other communities, including the large Khoja presence, in Zanzibar. The European colonial powers directed their attention to 'saving' the native Africans. Indians and Arabs, who were an integral part of the ethos of East African coastal culture,[87] were of peripheral concern to them. The political excuse for their interest in Zanzibar and East Africa was the 19th century movement to abolish slave trade. At the time, Zanzibar was the centre of the Arab slave trade and the British used their campaign to end slavery as a pretext to justify their plot to control Zanzibar.

Slave trade began earlier in East Africa and lasted longer than in the rest of the world. It essentially fulfilled Arab, Portuguese, Dutch, French, and British demands for forced labour to serve their various economies. East Africa and the Indian Ocean slave trade consisted of three phases: the caravan from the interior, the seaborne passage to Zanzibar, Comoros, or Madagascar and the longer oceanic transportation to the ports of Arabia, the Gulf, and the Cape.[88]

Deckard writes that

> on the gruelling caravan marches led by Arab and Swahili merchants, five out of every ten slaves died from starvation or exhaustion, and yet more died in the bellies of dhow ships, stacked together on bamboo decks so closely they could not move. Survivors faced a lifetime of chattel slavery and hard labour, although Islamic slave-owners often treated their slaves more humanely than their Atlantic or Portuguese counterparts and were more liable to free them due to the Koran's guarantee of paradise to any master who educated, freed or married his slaves.[89]

In 1822, the British counsel in Muscat put pressure on Sultan Said to end the slave trade operating out of the East African coast. The first of a series of anti-slavery treaties signed by Said with Britain prohibited slave transport south and east of the Moresby Line from Cape Delgado in Africa to Diu of India. The British prevailed on Said by offering to make up the loss of revenue from the slave trade as well as providing military protection against the Portuguese.

Karim Alarakhiya says[90] that

> In those days[91] Arab dhows use to arrive in Zanzibar during

the season and remain there for [a] few months. From here they use[d] to sail to Bagamoyo, Pangani and other ports of Tanganyika to capture male and female African slaves and bring them to 'Meena Bazaar' (slave marketplace) to be sold to the highest bidder. At this time, slave trading was so entrenched that it continued until the 1880s, even after the British authorities banned it in Zanzibar.

The British Authorities had to take stern measures against anyone involved with slave trade. British navy use to petrol [sic] the Indian Ocean. Any dhows involved with slave trading [were] escorted to a special place in Zanzibar, their goods seized and burnt, and the owner heavily fined. Those businesses that had owned slaves were requested by the British authorities to free them.' (see photo below.)

Under this pretext, the British imperial power used its self-imposed role to gain control over Zanzibar and the East African coast. They extended their power in various ways, the initial step being to set up a British consulate in 1841. This was the first formal presence of a British official in Zanzibar. The consulate acted as an agent of the East India Company with consular authority from the British Crown.[92]

Once they had a foothold, the British Government increasingly used their rule over India to gain control over the Busa'idi rulers and by extension over the economically powerful Indian and Khoja community. After the death of Seyyid Said in 1856, a succession dispute arose between his two sons, Majid and Thuwayn. Initially the

British government remained neutral as long as her interests along the Indian trade routes were not disturbed.

However, when Thuwayn sent an expedition force against Sultan Majid, this was perceived by the British as threatening their interest in Zanzibar and they sent a warship to intercept Thuwayn's expedition, forcing him to submit to arbitration.[93]

The British government appointed Lord Canning (Governor-General of India) to settle the dispute who took this opportunity to advance British interests and divided the Omani Empire into two: Zanzibar and its African dominions were allocated to Majid, while Muscat was given to Thuwayn. All this was endorsed by the Anglo-French Declaration of 1862 that acknowledged mutual respect for the independence of the two Sultans.[94]

The process of disintegration of the Omani Sultanate began in 1861 and the subsequent signing of the 1862 Declaration paved the way for British intervention in Zanzibar's internal affairs and marked the beginning of the decline of Zanzibar's Sultanate sovereignty.

From the mid-19th century the economy of the East African coast grew due to the demand for slaves in the French Islands of the Indian Ocean and an increasing European market for spices and ivory.[95] European competition, particularly between Britain and Germany, to control the region further contributed towards the disintegration of the Busa'idi Sultanate. This coupled with the military inability of the Sultans to protect their dominions, meant they would inevitably fall prey to European plans. In particular, Britain felt that they had the best opportunity to increase their control over the Busa'idi Sultanate given their power over India and how well it was trading with Zanzibar.[96]

As the Busa'idi Sultanate power declined, it sought protection from Britain enabling her to consolidate her power along the coast and lay a foundation for further extension of the Empire into the hinterland of East Africa and beyond. The primary objective for Britain was to prevent annexation of the Sultanate by other European powers, particularly Germany, which had shown an interest in controlling Zanzibar as well as Tanganyika during the partitioning of East Africa.[97]

By extending her influence over Zanzibar, Britain would be able to keep her European rivals from gaining control over the region while retaining a free hand in exercising internal control of the Sultanate.[98] The economic and political instability of the region towards the end of the 19th century paved the way for a complete British takeover.

In 1890, Britain and Germany signed the Heligoland Treaty[99] in which Britain surrendered her sovereignty over Heligoland to Germany in exchange for recognition of British protection over Zanzibar. After the Heligoland Treaty, Britain was able to have her own way and moved to quickly establish a Protectorate over Zanzibar and the Kenya coastal strip from the River Umba to the River Tana; Germany took control of the coastal strip from the River Rovuma (Zambezi) to the River Umba through the German East African Company. Zanzibar and Pemba were declared British protectorates in return for which Great Britain waived all claims to Madagascar in favour of France and ceded Heligoland to Germany.

Supremacy of British interests over the islands was now complete and recognised by both their rivals, France and Germany. The declaration of the British Protectorate marked the last stage in the progressive shrinkage of the Sultan's sovereign powers and of his influence over his dominions. Britain had taken a huge step in achieving its imperialistic vision of conquering the African continent.[100]

By this time, the Khojas were also the dominant economic community in the area.[101] A financial and social pattern had already been established in which the Khojas constituted the vital entrepreneurs in Zanzibar. When the British authorities began taking increasing control of the main resources of Zanzibar, the Khoja community became subject to the vagaries of the British and other European powers' as they struggled for control of the coast. The ever resilient Khoja community had the foresight to begin adapting in order to create a successful outcome for themselves. A mutually beneficial relationship was set to emerge out of these motivations.

At this point in history, Khojas did not have as much control as before over how their economic lives were shaped. In some respects, their destiny depended on how the colonial power perceived them and whether or not it believed the Khojas could serve its interests. There are those in the British establishment that supported Indians in East Africa, but there were others against them. One of the officials who endorsed the settlement and contribution of Indians was Harry Hamilton Johnston, a colonial administrator, who foresaw an active role for Indians in the development of East Africa. He was a special commissioner in Uganda from 1899 until 1901 and felt that 'East Africa is, and should be, from every point of view, the America of the Hindu.'[102] He believed that Indians should be the settlers in East Africa because they were in a better position than the Europeans to strengthen the region.

On the other hand, Lord Delamere was of an entirely different opinion. He came from South Africa to the Kenyan highlands to develop coffee and tea plantations. He would go on to become one of the most influential British settlers in Kenya. He wanted to stop the Indian migration to the colony, his reasoning being that '…physically the Indian is not a wholesome influence because of an incurable repugnance to sanitation and hygiene. In this respect, the African is more civilized than the Indian, being naturally clean in his ways but he [is] prone to follow the examples of those around him'.[103]

Lord Delamere claimed he was the guardian of the so-called innocent and gullible Africans, only to later claim the most fertile lands in Kenya (the so-called 'white lands') from where both Indians and Africans were eventually pushed out.[104]

In fact, in talking to many elders of the community, they confirmed that they had always known that British colonials would eventually promote the rights of their own kind above those of others. The Indians in East Africa now had to learn to defend and maintain their own interests against British colonisers.[105]

2.7 The Khoja of Zanzibar under the British Colonial Project

After establishing Zanzibar as a Protectorate, the British colonial administration embarked on changing the structure and function of the Sultanate. Amongst the reforms was the creation of a Legislative

Council with limited law-making authority; all decrees enacted by the Council were subject to the approval of the British Appointed Resident. British officials occupied the majority of the seats in the Council and they elected the remaining members to represent the different racial communities including Indians. Britain established these councils to portray her colonial project not only as an economic venture but also as a modernizing project aimed at bringing so-called 'civilization' to the colonised people they viewed as inferior.[106]

In this way, the colonial power was able to promote British interests in Zanzibar. Depending on the circumstances, they used a soft hand, a strong one or a combination of both to achieve their aims. If diplomacy didn't work, legal enforcement was the next step and as a last resort, they did not shy away from imposing military rule to dominate the country. The ultimate goal of British colonial system was subjugation and control rather than any sincere desire to enrich or justly govern the people.

For Khojas, this complete shift of power from the Sultanate to the Imperial powers meant that they too had become subjects of the British colonial government. Deliberately and decisively, the British began to attempt to take full control of the Khoja community in Zanzibar. Two incidents stand out as examples of their subtle use of power to achieve this aim.

The first example is the deliberate use of the judgement from The Khoja Case of 1866 to impose British interests in a local Khoja dispute in Zanzibar. This was despite the fact that for a sizable number within the Khoja community, the 1866 ruling was not acceptable.[107] As we have already seen, this ruling was based on flawed logic, manipulated to enforce the leadership of the Aga Khan over the Khoja community.

The judgement relied on an Orientalist interpretation of the *Dasa Avatar* chapter of the *ginans*, to state that it was of Ismaili origin.[108] The British colonial government of Zanzibar took advantage of this 1866 judgment and applied it to the Mnazi Moja burial ground[109] dispute to promote its own interest and that of Aga Khan in Zanzibar.

For the British, the Aga Khan and his followers were 'a useful asset'.[110] In their view, both the Khoja community and Aga Khan III need to 'be managed' so that they could continue to add value to the British government. On the one hand, the British establishment esteemed the Aga Khan III by addressing him as 'His Highness' in their correspondences and on the other, they regarded Aga Khan III and his followers as a 'utility' for the British interest.[111] Aga Khan III was of high value because of his position as the spiritual head of the Shia Ismaili sect; a position that had intentionally been given official credence by the British establishment in the Khoja case of 1866.

Through Aga Khan III, the British hoped to exert strategic influence over the Khojas (particularly the Ismailis) who were a powerful, integral part of the local community. In order to sustain his support, Aga Khan III was, at certain times, permitted to shape some colonial rules. In return for this small concession, the British had at their disposal, an instrument of sustained control over the Khoja community. In his thesis, Pelgrim describes the benefit of this strategy in resolving the claim by the Khojas for access at the Mnazi Moja burial ground. [112]

Mnazi Moja was a piece of land that had been procured by Mohamed Meru, a Sunni Khoja from Surat, Gujarat. There was no actual record of purchase and any title deed that might have existed was lost. The claims of the Khojas mainly rested on the purchase of the property some sixty or seventy years ago by Meru and his dying wish that the property be used as a burial ground for all members of the Khoja community.[113]

Of course, in the years since the death of Meru, the Khoja community had changed substantially. By the early 20th century, the community in Zanzibar had already split into the Ismailis, Sunnis and the Shia Ithna-Asheries. The Sunnis were a small minority within the community, but the tension between the Isma'ilis and Shia Ithna-Asheries was notable.[114]

For the Ismailis, the Ithna-Asheries were seceders and no longer considered to be Khoja according to the farmans issued by Aga Khan III.[115] Since they were not Khojas, they were not entitled to the use of the burial ground. The Ithna-Asheries, however, claimed that no one party could claim the burial ground as it was communal and should be accessible to all Khoja Muslims on the island.

Here, it is interesting to note that in the evolution of the Khoja Shia Ithna-Asheri Muslim Community, the acquisition of their own burial ground became a priority for almost all communities who settled in new places in East Africa[116]. This was because of historical precedents of the right of burial being denied to them in the ancestral Khoja cemetery in Mumbai, when they separated from the Khoja community there. Until then, the Khoja community in Mumbai had functioned as a united community with their mainly tripartite set of beliefs overlapping and regardless of their individual leanings, all members were buried in the common Khoja cemetery.

When the Khoja Sunnis separated in 1862, followed by the Khoja Shia Ithna-Asheries decades later, both these groups were barred from burying their dead in the ancestral common burial ground. In fact, one of the fears that Mulla Qadir Husain had expressed was that those Khojas who had converted to the Shia Ithna-Asheri faith would succumb to pressure and revert to their previous beliefs when the right of burial was denied to them.[117]

At that time, some assurances were available to the recently-converted, practicing Khoja Shia Ithna-Asheries. Khalfan Rattansi and Dewji Jamal had pledged to undertake transporting the bodies of any deceased to Karbala (in Iraq) for permanent burial if the larger Khoja community refused to grant them burial in the local cemetery. For this purpose, Dewji Jamal acquired a piece of land in Karbala and Khalfan Rattansi pledged Rs. 10,000/- (£2500) for expenses.

Following the death of a child in the family, Dewji Jamal - having witnessed the difficulties of the emerging Khoja Shia Ithna-Asheries in Mumbai - bought a private garden in the centre of the Zanzibar and registered it as a family burial ground. Today, this land still exists and is known as *Bustani*. In Mombasa, three sons of Dewji Jamal: Nazerali Dewji, Sheriff Dewji and Jaffer Dewji followed their father's example and also donated a piece of land in 1897 on which the present *kabrastan* stands.

With this background in mind, it will be easy to understand why members of the Khoja community have always given so much importance to possessing a burial ground of their own. At the time of Mnazi Moja dispute (around 1912), the Khoja Shia Ithna-Asheries had their own mosque and *imambada* as well as a cemetery. Nevertheless, some members had drawn up their wills with instructions to be buried at Mnazi Moja. This was unacceptable to the Ismaili Khojas and the ensuing clashes between the Khoja groups set up the perfect scenario for the British to step in and impose their colonial grip over the community in Zanzibar.[118]

The British officials in Zanzibar dealing with the Mnazi Moja dispute immediately recognised its similarities, in foundational principles, to the Khoja Case. They knew that the colonial authority in India considered Khojas to be Ismailis and Aga Khan as their leader. They also knew that the court had decided in favour of the Aga Khan's claim over community property. The British government in Zanzibar took this position as a fact, however, their challenge was how to proceed with the case in Zanzibar, where the Khoja community had split into three groups: the Khoja Ismailies, the Khoja Shia Ithna-Asheries, and the smaller Sunni Khojas.

When the burial ground case ultimately came up for discussion, neither the Khoja Shia Ithna-Asheries nor Khoja Sunnis were at the negotiating table. The reason for their exclusion is not mentioned, but from the way events unfolded, what is clear is that both these groups were given a lower status relative to the followers of the Aga Khan. In fact, it seems that the colonial authority influenced them to give up their right to access the cemetery as expressed in the following telegram from Zanzibar to the Foreign Office in London:

> I obtained letters at the same time from the recognised heads of the Shia Ithna-Asheries and of the Sunni Khoja sects, resigning any claims that they might have to the land which has been given up under this settlement, and I trust therefore that a question which has for many years given rise to a great deal of trouble and unpleasantness has now been finally and satisfactorily adjusted.[119]

How and why the leaders of the other Khoja groups agreed to

renounce their right to burial in Mnazi Moja is a question that is open to speculation. By 1912, Khoja Shia Ithna-Asheries had organised themselves sufficiently not to accept such a defeat. It is, therefore, surprising that the community did not challenge the decision.

Perhaps, given that the British government had placed the Mnazi Moja conflict within the larger context of The Aga Khan Case and that its judgement was upheld in the Haji Bibi case, the Khoja Shia Ithna-Asheries may have thought that based on precedent, fighting for this particular cause was not worth their time and resources. Furthermore, it was known that the Ismaili community had influence within the British establishment and would use it to their advantage.

The matter was ultimately resolved using the legal ruling of the Aga Khan case as a primary condition for determining that Khoja Ismailis had sole entitlement to the Mnazi Moja burial ground. As expected, the British colonial government ignored the justice of the claim and used its authority to pacify the parties involved in order to advance their own interests. Interestingly, this resulted in the Khoja Shia Ithna-Asheries becoming more resilient and independent within Zanzibar.

From the Mnazi Moja Agreement, the British government got part use of the burial site for its own purposes; they also expected Aga Khan III to make sure that his followers now toed the line, as had been agreed during the negotiations. For Aga Khan III, winning this dispute over a small piece of land allowed him to strengthen his position outside the borders of India while staying safely within the legal borders of the British Empire. Furthermore, by removing all other dissenting Khoja groups from the picture, he was now able to establish a loyal Ismaili community that could be molded according to his worldview.

Having succeeded in using their legal prowess to show the Khojas who was in charge, the British turned to another area - the commercial arena - to further drive home the point. In 1859, the colonial British government of Zanzibar prohibited Indians to own clove farms.[120] This limitation, in addition to British anti-slavery policies, restricted Indian subjects of her Majesty and confined them to trading and finance whilst white British expatriates had freedom to own land and trade with financial and legal support from the government.

2.8 The *Dukawalla* Mindset

Under the restrictive colonial government, the entrepreneurial Khojas and other Indians had to be innovative and create their own niche for trade in order to survive. They had come seeking better economic opportunities and were determined not to leave until they had established themselves in this new land. Under the new and discriminatory state restrictions, many Khojas decided that the easiest way forward for them was to set up *dukas* (small shops). The British expatriates did not have the acumen for such enterprise and even if they did, they lacked any interest in such low-level trade. They left this part of trading activities to non-Europeans, which worked out perfectly for the Khojas.

The Khojas began setting up their *dukas* strategically along *bazaar* (market) streets where local producers would pass on their way to sell their produce in the great market (*soko kuu*) of Zanzibar. On their way back, the local producers had cash in their pockets, which they could spend on the wares the *dukawallas* (shop-owners) had to offer. Slowly, these shops began to thrive, expand and soon dominate the small shop trading arena. Thus the *dukawalla* enterprise was born.

In these early years, the lifestyle of the typical Khoja *dukawalla* in Zanzibar was austere. When savings permitted, they sent for their wives whom they had left behind or returned to India to marry and brought their spouses back with them. For most Khojas, a small room covered with an iron roof, hastily constructed behind the shop, became their new home.

It was in such conditions that the pioneer Khoja trader raised his family. He was often aided for a time by his wife or extended family who would work together to build the business. Essentially, the husband-and-wife team ran both the economic and socio-religious household. At times, the husband ran the wholesale side and the wife looked after the retail front end of the shop.

This historical fact gives us an interesting insight into how Khojas viewed the intellectual and business abilities of their women. Rather than restricting them to domestic activities, they considered them economic partners in building the household. This is in fact closely related to the marital model of Prophet Muhammad (pbuh) [121] and his wife, Lady Khadijah (pbuh). It is well known that before she married Prophet Muhammad (pbuh), Khadijah (pbuh) was a highly successful businesswoman and employed him to travel with her caravans and trade on her behalf.[122] It was his honesty and integrity that encouraged her to propose to him. [123] History shows that they did not view their marital positions as one of superiority over each other and the Khojas seemed to reflect this attitude.

This aspect of Khoja Shia Ithna-Asheri history warrants further research into how early settlers and pioneers interpreted Islamic teachings with specific reference to the position of men and women in the household and work. The *dukawalla* partnership model of husband and wife went against certain Arab and even European norms at a time when women were not commonly regarded as equal financial contributors in a household - an issue that continues to be debated within the Islamic world today.[124]

Typical 'Dukawalla' early 19th century. Most dukawallas lived simple lives, working hard to maintain the status quo of success in turbulent, ever-changing times.

An Indian knife sharpener in Zanzibar doing his mobile business house-to-house.

It was under the austere conditions described above that the Khojas had to motivate themselves to succeed. It is proof of their inherent resilience that despite all odds, they created their own economic space, were able to establish a stable communal and family environment and even to prosper. As their economic confidence grew, Khoja families ventured out to set up shop elsewhere. As the British and German colonial powers began to extend their reach into the interiors, the Khojas gained access to other areas in East Africa and began to explore opportunities outside of Zanzibar.

2.9 Internal Migration

In trying to piece together a timeline of the migration and settlement pattern of the Khojas in East Africa we find that the majority of the community members arrived in Zanzibar from around 1885-1890.[125] Records show that the early generation of the Khoja Shia Ithna-Asheri community migrated to Zanzibar and other places along the East African coast initially and later to the interior of East Africa.

They began their journeys mainly from Mandvi, Bhuj, Mundra, Nagalpur in Kachchh and Hariyana, Jamnagar, Lalpur, Bhavnagar, and Mahuva as well as other towns and villages from Kathiawad, Mumbai, and Karachi. Whilst many hardships awaited them in their new life, the voyage to East Africa was an extremely challenging experience.

Before 1914, almost all the Khojas who came did so by dhow. These were small ships 40 to 60 feet long with wooden hulls and lateen sails, weighing 80 to 350 tons. The passengers slept on deck and representatives of different religious communities cooked their own food. There was no privacy to speak of and barely any competent medical service. They had to endure violent storms on the temperamental Indian ocean and seasickness was common.

From personal narrations, it seems that to pass the time - and occasionally allay fears - passengers and crew would recite religious verses to each other or share tales from folk literature. Under the most favourable conditions, the voyage of 2,400 miles to Zanzibar could be made in 26 days, but a storm or lack of favourable winds could extend this by several weeks or even months.

Despite these difficulties, the migrants were pulled towards the East African coast. They were engaged in the dhow trade with Oman and Hadhramaut along the Persian Gulf and the Benadir and Azanian coasts along the Red Sea and were well aware of the cultural diversity and economic opportunities present in Zanzibar.

Initially, almost all Khojas who arrived retained ties to their origins. As they settled in Zanzibar and elsewhere, they wrote to relatives and friends with tales of their journey, their stay and how promising the opportunities were. In this way, they were able to excite the interest of the young and able-bodied from their extended families. Such news would do the rounds in the *jamaatkhanas* and *imambadas* of towns and villages where Khoja communities resided. Brothers attracted brothers; one went then another and soon the entire male line of a family were out in the coastal towns of East Africa.

The first to come were the young men, followed by their wives and children. Though extensive, the actual movement of people took place gradually and on an individual basis, with kinship ties playing a large part in bringing new members of the Khoja community to East Africa.

This pattern is clearly observed amongst Khoja Shia Ithna-Asheries as noted by Alhaj Pirbhai Visram, fondly remembered in the community as 'Pirbhai Kaka'.[126] In 1953, he submitted a settlement history of the community to the Secretariat of Africa Federation at their request. His report[127] covers the four areas where he personally lived: Lamu (1897-1910), Tabora (1905-09), Bukoba (1914-45), and Kampala (1945-53). It provides valuable insight into the families that had settled there, but more importantly showcases how individual families stayed together and helped each other overcome challenges as they struggled to settle in East Africa. These earlier Khoja Shia Ithna-Asheries made proficient use of their family resources to achieve economic stability and success as described in the report.

PIRBHAI 'KAKA' VISRAM

Pirbhai Visram came to Africa in 1897 at the age of 17 and his observations provide a glimpse on the pattern of family settlement and how the Khoja Shia Ithna-Asheri relied on strong family ties as a human resource.

When he first arrived in Lamu, where he lived for five years, he noted that there were around 300 Khoja Shia Ithna-Asheries. The following is a sketch of the family demographics he noted that show how the extended family worked together towards communal prosperity.

Kanji Hasani was from Jam Khambhadia; he had arrived in Lamu around 1885 with his sons Dewji Kanji, Daya Kanji, Panju Kanji, Shamji Kanji and Ramji Kanji who had their own business. Their family numbered 70 individuals.

The family of Hemraj Ladhani from Bagamoyo (originally from Kachchh) consisted of four brothers, Rawji Hemraj, Abdulla Hemraj, Bandali Hemraj and Hasham Hemraj, who each had their own business. Their family numbered 40 individuals and they came to Lamu between 1880 and 1890.

The family of Jessa Bhimani, who had arrived from Jamnagar, also between 1880 and 1890, consisted of Nasser Jessa, Mohamed Jessa and Moti Jessa. They were in involved in the foodstuff business.

The family of Bhimji Kanji of Dabasang, again arriving between 1880 and 1890 from Jamnagar. Pirbhai Kaka writes that two enterprising and brave individuals in this family were Hassan Walji and Hirji Walji. Their business was based in a village called Pokomoni on Tana River inhabited by people with primitive customs and surrounded by wild animals. Despite the imminent dangers, these two individuals crossed the river on regular basis to trade.

The extended family of Dhanji Samji who arrived around 1885 consisted of 20 individuals. They conducted their business by transporting goods on foot or by mules, and on small canoes.

Around the same time, the three brothers Molu Ramji, Walji Ramji and Damji Ramji had arrived in Lamu. There were 20 individuals in this family - mainly dealing in *khangas* and textiles. They employed enough workers to be able to deliver their textile and clothing wares to their customers' shops and homes in the countryside.

Hirji Bhanji, Alibhai Bhanji, Merali Bhanji and Nanji Bhanji of Jodia arrived in 1890. The arrival of these four brothers was a blessing to Khoja Shia Ithna-Asheri community as they had some knowledge of the English language and could communicate with the colonial authority. They traded mainly with Somalis.

The family of Jamal Jessa arrived in Lamu around 1885. There were 15 members in this family. Jiwan Rajan and his uncle Mawji Daya, together with about 20 farmers from the Sindhi and Ahir community - both Hindu and Muslim - arrived in one dhow. They brought Indian farm equipment with them. Pirbhai writes that 'the District Commissioner of Lamu at that time, Mr. Rogers, was a kind man and provided them with a 50-acre plot for farming on a temporary basis'.[128]

The devotion to farming by the pair and the hard work of farmers, accompanied by adequate rainfall, led them to an excellent harvest. However, just as the harvest was due, a fierce disagreement arose amongst the farmers and in the looting that ensued, all the harvest was destroyed. The farmers were immediately deported to India by the authorities. Whilst they failed in their venture, they were the first to attempt agriculture from within the community.

There was also Issa Thawer who was an agent for ships and dhows. He had no family members with him.

Pirbhai Kaka says that there were three Bhatia families involved in bringing cargo from Mandvi. A large number of the Bohra community members were also present. They mainly worked with iron and wood products, and had established themselves as solders and welders. Bohras, along with Khojas, were amongst the early visitors to the East African coast.[129] The first Bohras came to Zanzibar, the first business family being a Surti family from Surat who settled in Mkunazini.

Many others found Mombasa more agreeable and yet others set up trading branches in Lamu and between Lamu and Pate. Though initial settlers were from Surat and Cambay, later arrivals were almost entirely from Kachchh. The Bohras who resided in Lamu had their own mosque and burial grounds and formed a special community since their families usually accompanied them when they emigrated from Kachchh and Surat. Although they devoted their energies to commercial enterprise, many of them were artisans.

Most of the Khoja Shia Ithna-Asheries who first came to East Africa were poor with hardly any skills or education. Passion and motivation to succeed made up for what they lacked. They had the determination to carve out a space for themselves in this new land; this was their primary motivation. A few were businessmen, some were farmers and a large number of them young children between the ages of 12 and 15 years. For example, in 1910, Rashid M Fazal landed in Mombasa, a 15-year-old with no friends or relatives. He was helped by the Khoja Shia Ithna-Asheri community and given a job.

The pattern of settlement as described by communal resources, including oral traditions, shows that most Khoja Shia Ithna-Asheri migrants from Kachchh and Kathiawad initially came to Zanzibar.[130] Some stayed for a short while - usually two years or less - before journeying to other coastal towns like Lamu, Mombasa, Dar es Salaam or Bagamoyo and joining those who came directly to those places. From these coastal towns, others ventured further into the interior of East Africa. By the mid-19th century, trade routes extended from Zanzibar to Lake Tanganyika through Tabora and from Kilwa to Lake Nyasa.[131] There were three major routes linking the coast to the interior.

The first route connected the Busa'idi Sultanate and the Buganda Kingdom through the coastal towns of Bagamoyo and Dar es Salaam and the interior towns of Tabora and Ujiji. Tabora served as the main link between Zanzibar and the Buganda Kingdom.[132] The second route was along the southern coast connecting Kilwa with Lake Malawi passing through the town of Lindi. The third route was from the northern coast, linking Mombasa and Tanga with Lake Victoria.[133]

Khoja Shia Ithna-Asheries used these trade routes to venture out beyond Zanzibar and the coast to trade and settle inland. From the Trade Directory resource and conversations with the elders of the Khoja Shia Ithna-Asheri community of East Africa, Western Europe, United States and Canada, three critical observations can be made about early Khoja Shia Ithna-Asheri pioneers to East Africa.

Firstly, there appears to be a set pattern to their movements. When any enthusiastic Khoja Shia Ithna-Asheri went to a new place, others followed him so that they could benefit from his experience and acquaint themselves with the local people. It appears that there was a sense of comradeship amongst them. Well-established Khoja Shia Ithna-Asheries helped the inexperienced to stand on their feet. We can also assume that new arrivals from India usually came to Zanzibar and after acquiring relevant information and assistance, ventured out to other places. This pattern was followed even by those who disembarked at Lamu, Mombasa, Bagamoyo or Dar es Salaam and went to the interior from there.[134] For example, in 1898, Gulamhussein Rajpar Ladak who was 12 years old arrived in Bagamoyo alone.[135] After a few days, with help from a complete stranger from the community, he began a 400-mile journey to Tukuyu[136] where he found work as an escort to trade caravans.

The pioneers of all the major routes were African traders. Nyamwezi caravans from central Tanzania, reaching the coast about 1800, developed the most important route from their homeland to Bagamoyo on the mainland directly opposite Zanzibar. Kamba ivory traders from central Kenya opened a route that ended at Mombasa. Eventually, this route crossed Kamba and Maasai country, branching east towards Uganda and north to Lake Turkana.

Photo Courtesy: Niti Bhan, 'Trade in East Africa'.

Secondly, the undeveloped Eastern Africa was foreign to the Khoja Shia Ithna-Asheries. They did not know the language, neither did they have any previous cultural contact with the indigenous African.

Before them lay vast, unexplored but inaccessible tracts of lands into which they had to venture. The new environment and prevailing influences called for a quick adaptation to culture and language. They appear to have done this successfully because of the fact that so many of them owned shops in various places along the coast and inland. This is evidence of their determination to make East Africa their home.

Thirdly, the Khoja Shia Ithna-Asheries quest to seek economic stability and further their religious identity resulted in the formation of a community settlement in Zanzibar. They also could have had an influence in the setting up of bazaars and houses of the 19th century Zanzibar town. During their stay, whether periodical or permanent, they began to develop their own particular religious-cultural identity guided by Shia Ithna-Asheri tenets and their strict adherence to its code. Some of them even adopted Swahili as their first language. This shows the impact the local culture had on the evolving Khoja Shia Ithna-Asheri community. In short, together with other Indian communities, Khoja Shia Ithna-Asheries became an essential part of the East African economy and society.

From above observations, most - if not all - of the Khoja Shia Ithna-Asheries came to Zanzibar and acquired whatever experiences and information they needed about the new land and its people before venturing deeper into East Africa. They were novices in the complete sense of the word as far as the culture and language of the people were concerned, yet brave enough to explore these places with a firm belief in their ability to adapt and benefit themselves and those around them.

The new environment presented challenges both internally and externally and demanded important changes in their outlook. They had to learn to accept and respect the ways of the new land, its people, its language and culture if they wanted to create an economically viable environment for themselves. It was also equally important to create their own socio-religious structures to underpin their young and fragile community in order to remain united to preserve their new faith.

The above priorities and the fact that they - unlike the colonial invaders - came with genuine intentions to live and prosper harmoniously amongst the people allowed them to integrate with the communities without becoming assimilated.

1904, Mombasa. Visiting dignitaries from Zanzibar at the opening ceremony of the Kuwwatul Islam Mosque on Old Kilindini Rd. (from Akbarali A. Khatau)

Sitting on the ground: *Bandali Kanji (fourth from l), Abdul Hussein (A.H.), Nurmohamed (fifth from l), Mohammed Sadak Jivraj Meghji (first from r).*

Sitting first row: *Dharamsi Khatu (first from l), Alimohamed Jagani is standing behind Dharamsi Khatau, Pira Valli (center with hooked staff, first president of Kuwwatul Islam Jamat of Zanzibar in 1882), Sayyid Abdulhusein Mar'ashi (first resident alim of Zanzibar Kuwaatul Islam Jamat), Mulla Abdalla Saleh Sachedina is standing behind Sayyid Mar'ashi's left shoulder, a bespectacled Ali Sachedina is behind Mulla Abdallah Saleh.*
Standing back row: *Ismail Kalyan (fifth from l), Jivraj Khatau (sixth from l), Kassamali Jivraj Meghji (seventh from l), Mohamed Valli Dharsi (third from r).*

PART 3
Arrival of Khoja Shia Ithna-Asheries in Zanzibar and Shifting Patterns of Interaction.

3.1 The Arrival of Khojas in Zanzibar

In 1820, there was a small but growing community of Indians in Zanzibar. In 1840, Sultan Sayyid Said bin Sultan Al Busaidi (ruled 1807-1856) of Oman and Zanzibar made Zanzibar his capital. Establishing his seat of power there signalled a symbolic shift of Omani power that began to influence the economic and political ethos of the East African coast.[1] By now, Zanzibar was attracting migrants from Comoros, Somalia, Arabia, Persia, Kachchh and other parts of Gujarat. Indian entrepreneurs and businesses from Vaniya, Khoja, Bohora and Parsi communities were the key support of Zanzibar's economy under Sultan Al Busaidi.[2] These merchants offered lines of credit to local landowners, ship-owners and caravan leaders.

This infusion of socio-economic activity under the Sultan fuelled trading in the interior of East Africa and stimulated agricultural exports, notably cloves produced by slave labour.[3] Sultan Barghash (1837 - 1888) went on to expand commercial activities and enhanced Zanzibar's position as a regional hub using state funds to promote direct trade with Bombay. With direct and reliable services to Zanzibar being available, Bombay trading houses increased their export of Indian and British products to East Africa. This activity sparked an interest for more trade in the interior region of East Africa. Indians (amongst them Khojas), British and American traders took advantage of caravan trading routes to reach the interior markets. These routes began from Bagamoyo, Kilwa and Mombasa.

Apart from attracting trading opportunities, Zanzibar was also a metropolis where many languages, faiths and cultures interacted. Traders, entrepreneurs, and others found this ethos attractive. For new settlers, the diversity created a comfortable atmosphere of understanding while the Swahili language and its cultural nuances acted as a glue to bind them as uniquely Zanzibarian.[4]

Additionally, Zanzibar Sultans allowed significant religious freedoms that provided a positive space for people to practice their respective faiths. An immediate consequence of this was that Zanzibar Town became a centre of both Sunni and Ibadi scholarship and multiple reformist movements took root there.[5] Due to this favourable environment, Khojas - mainly from Kachchh - came in increasing numbers to trade. The Sultan of Zanzibar appreciated their economic competence to the extent that by 1840, he personally approved a commercial treaty with Britain that guaranteed British subjects of Indian origin the freedom to enter Zanzibar.[6]

As British subjects, the Indians enjoyed protection from the British government whilst resident in Zanzibar.[7] For Khojas, this was highly encouraging and soon they were the largest group amongst the Indian migrants. The 1870s census reveals that the Khoja Muslim population consisted of 642 women, 718 men and 540 children.[8]. By contrast, Hindus had a population of 400 to 500;[9] interestingly, they did not have a single woman among them as caste restrictions prevented their wives from crossing the sea.

According to the communal records, the first Hindu woman - the wife of Ibji Siwji - arrived in 1879. A lot of fanfare greeted her arrival and the Sultan of Zanzibar, Seyyid Bargash, sent his private vessel to welcome her to the island, giving her a gift of 250 shillings. In this way, he hoped to encourage more of the Hindu community of Zanzibar to bring their wives with them. He even offered to equip the old fort with water pipes fitted with silver taps to ensure that Hindu women felt comfortable. After 1879, the flow of Hindu women into Zanzibar began to increase. For some, it was a painful process, requiring them to alter some of their religious notions of purity in order to adapt to their new environment.[10] Due to their specific food habits and marriage patterns, Hindus settled with their families later than the Muslims. In time, however, they were able to gain stability and their community began to become more noticeable.[11]

By contrast, the Khoja Muslims had a strong family life early on in their settlement. The majority of Khoja Shia Ithna-Asheri families came from Kachchh, followed by Jamnagar in Kathiawad. Those who came from Jamnagar were referred to as "Nangarias" (Merchants). They were followed by Khojas from Bhavnagar, Mumbai and Muscat. Many of them arrived with little or no money and no skill set, but what they lacked in finances, they more than made up for with their determination to succeed.

These Nangarias worked mainly for other Khojas who were already established entrepreneurs and after a brief apprenticeship, they would start up their own small shops with goods advanced by other fellow entrepreneurs. After accumulating a small saving, they generally returned home to marry and came back to East Africa to repeat at a larger scale the trade for which they had by then acquired both the skills and experience. Only this time, they would have the support of a wife and/or extended family to rely upon.

British archive records also show that Khojas prospered economically.[12] By the 1840s, they had acquired properties and owned clove plantations. This continued until 1859 when the British government prohibited ownership to Indians. Despite such discriminatory practices, Gujarati traders were able to remain prominent and their economic dominance was visible to those who visited Zanzibar in 1872.

James Christie, the Sultan's British Physician, writes that 'the Banyans[13] are the capitalist...in many respects they are the real ruling powers... they have agents at all the ports of the Zanzibar territories where duties are levied...Directly and indirectly they hold almost unlimited sway over the commerce of the place.'[14]

3.2 Early Pioneers

Jairam Siwji, a Hindu Bhatia (and brother to Ibji Siwji), is a striking example of Indian commercial dominance at the time. In 1835, five years before his move to Zanzibar, Said bin Sultan[15] honoured Siwji with three offices: Collector of Customs, Chief Officer of the Port of Zanzibar, and State Banker. While organising the collection of duties associated with the dhow trade, Siwji put other Zanzibari Indian traders as his agents in charge of customs from Kilwa to Mogadishu.

Built in 1892, the elaborate entrance and wooden balcony are typical of Zanzibar architecture.

The engraving above the wooden doors reads:

CHARITABLE CARAVANSERA
*Established and endowed by
Khoja Esmal Ramjee of Cutch Sama Goga*

*For use of only the Khoja Caste travellers in the Reign of H. The Sultan Sayid Ally bin Sayeed of Zanzibar.
December 29, 1892.*

The appellation "Khoja" was a common prefix to indicate the community to which one belonged e.g. "Banyan" was the appellation for Hindus.

(Photo Courtesy: Ismailimail, Zahir K. Dhalla.)

Tharia Topan is another good example of the kind of hard work and resourcefulness thate Khojas brought with them. He was born in 1823 in Lakhpat, not far from Mandvi. He came to Zanzibar in 1835, aged 12, as a stowaway. Once there, he worked as a garden boy. By all accounts, Topan was a quick learner and had an aptitude for how foreign currency exchange worked. He rose rapidly as an entrepreneur and became an influential figure with the Sultan, who appointed him to Jairam Siwji's position.[16]

Topan also had a respected status in the Khoja community and held the powerful position of *Mukhi* within it.[17] According to Khoja Shia Ithna-Asheri oral sources, he was a strict *Mukhi* who upheld Ismaili traditions and did not tolerate dissidents. Many Khoja Shia Ithna-Asheries felt that his intolerant attitude led to the restrictive measures placed on those who followed the Ithna-Asheri rituals. Such measures were part of the reason that eventually led to the breakup of the Khoja Community in Zanzibar in 1880s.[18]

Sultan Bargash (ruled 1870-1888) seen with his advisors. Tharia Topan, Khoja Indian Merchant and custom master, stands behind him.
(Courtesy: Abdul Sheriff)

Sewa Haji Paroo was another successful Kachchhi Khoja from Bhuj. He was one of four sons of Haji Paroo Pradhan who arrived with his brother Jaffer Paroo Pradhan in 1850. By 1860, Haji Paroo had established a small general store in Zanzibar and opened a branch in Bagamoyo. Sewa was born in Zanzibar and worked in the family store until 1869 when he took complete charge of the family company - 'Haji Kanji & Co'. He traded in cloth, beads, copper wire and brass pots in Bagamoyo and from there to the interior. He was a successful businessperson and a philanthropist.

In 1891, when Dar es Salaam became the capital of German East Africa, he helped establish both the 'Sewa Haji Hospital' as well as a Bagamoyo hospital. He also opened a multiracial school for Indian and African children. In his will, he bequeathed the income from all his properties to be used to provide food to lepers in the area and to help run the Bagamoyo hospital. When Tanganyika became a British Protectorate, the Dar es Salaam hospital was named 'Princess Margaret Hospital' and in 1956 it was renamed again to 'Muhimbili Hospital' which exists to this day.[19]

Allidina Visram was born in Kera in Kachchh. He came to Zanzibar aged 12 in 1863 without any money. He found work with Sewa Haji Paroo but after finding his feet, set out independently to organise caravans into the interior. He achieved significant commercial success soon after when he came up with the idea of providing packaged food to hunters and explorers on expedition. During the construction of the Uganda railway, he opened many stores along the track and became the sole supplier of food to the workers along the railway line. In 1904, he branched into agriculture and within a few years bought seven large plantations.

By 1909, he had up to 17 agents operating in the Belgian Congo and had diversified his business into soda factories and furniture shops in Kampala and Entebbe, oil mills in Kisumu and the coast, a soap-making factory in Mombasa, two cotton ginneries (one each in Mombasa and Entebbe), and sawmills near Nyeri. In addition, he was engaged in the transportation business, operating carts overland and boats plus a steamer on Lake Victoria. He also took interest in politics and helped to create the Mombasa Indian Association.

In 1914, he became the founding member of the East African Indian National Congress. His success was an inspiration for many members of the Khoja community in East Africa. For his extensive successful entrepreneurship, his peers and the community at large gave him the title of the 'Uncrowned King of Uganda'. [20]

Murrabi[21] Shariff Jiwa Surti arrived in Zanzibar in 1865. He was 18 years old and found employment with Alhaj Nasser Nurmuhamad in Nosibe, Madagascar. His hard work, loyalty, sincerity and generosity led him to become a respected member of the Khoja Shia Ithna-Asheri community. In 1885, he went to Bhavnagar to get married and upon his return with his spouse, started his own business in Diegoswarez (official name: Antsiranana). At that time, there were only two other Khoja Shia Ithna-Asheri families in the city: the Bachchu Hasham family and the Molu Kanji family.

Murrabi Shariff Jiwa took a keen interest in learning Islam. He communicated with Islamic scholars regularly to increase his religious understanding and donated land in Diegoswarez to build the present moment and *imambada*. In 1908, when there was a protracted dispute within the Khoja Shia Ithna-Asheries in Zanzibar, it was Murrabi Shariff's intervention that succeeded in resolving the misunderstanding.[22] He was a kind, generous man who assisted those in need within the community and for these good qualities, he became known as 'Bapa Shariff' (Grandfather Shariff) among Khoja Shia Ithna-Asheries.

Virjeebhai Muraj Haji, aged 50, came with his wife Kaj-bai from Kachchh to Zanzibar in 1870 and upon arrival, established a small trading shop. According to his family archives, he came from generations of the Bhatia cast that originated from Rajputana, moved to Sindh and from there settled in Kachchh for about 300 years.[23] They were Hindus and then converted to *Satpanth* Ismaili. They used to observe *Namaz* (prayers), *Roza* (fasts), *Kissa* (traditional Khoja recitations) and lamentation recitals of Imam Hussein (pbuh). The ancestors of Virjeebhai Muraj Haji's family were landowners who grew cotton among other crops.

The effects of famines and earthquakes in Gujarat during 1830 devastated many farms and brought hardship for impoverished peasants, some of whom died of starvation. This pushed many Kachchhi Khojas to migrate to various parts of India where they had connections, like Karachi, Mumbai and Gwadar. Some, including Virjeebhai, came to East Africa. It is also likely that Allidina Visram, who had gone to Kachchh to marry Son-bai, Virjeebhai's sister, convinced him to come to Zanzibar.

Virjeebhai had a five-year-old son, Nasser (b.1865 in Kachchh), whom he left with his grandmother in Ratadhya, Kachchh. She looked after the boy for nine years and by all accounts, he grew up to be a courageous, strong young lad. In 1879, aged 14, he travelled from Kachchh to Zanzibar and when he re-joined his parents, he found two new additions to the family, a younger brother, Kassam and a sister, Shireen. For the next four years, Nasser Virjee worked with his father. During this time, the Khoja community in Zanzibar was becoming more aware of Ithna-Asheri tenets. This deeply influenced both Nasser and his brother. They began to follow the teachings of the Qur'an according to Ithna-Asheri principles.[24]

In 1882, Nasser's business acumen led him to set up a business on his own in Mikindani, a thriving port in south Tanzania; he was only 18 years of age. After his father passed away in 1884, he took his wife, mother, grandmother and brother to Karbala, Iraq for pilgrimage. When they returned to Zanzibar, Sultan Saeed had relinquished the coastal strip of Tanganyika to the Germans. Because of this handover of power, considerable unrest ensued, especially in Mikindani and the Virjee's trading store was burnt, and their stock looted. As a result, Nasser and his family returned to Zanzibar.

In 1888, Nasser Virjee and his brother decided to go into a trading partnership with their uncle, Allidina Visram, who was in Bagamoyo. They bought part of Haji Paroo's business and took advantage of the trading opportunities that arose in Bagamoyo once it became the capital of German East Africa. The partnership lasted for four years. When Haji Paroo died, Allidina Visram took over his business and moved to Uganda. Meanwhile, Nasser Virjee expanded his own family business to Tabora, Shinyanga, Mwanza and Bukoba. He owned many properties in Kigoma and Ujiji including the spot where Stanley and Livingstone met - this land was later donated to the government. The Virjee business boomed all over East Africa and beyond.[25]

By all accounts, Nasser Virjee was compassionate and trustworthy. Family and friends remember his insistence on treating all his employees with respect. In turn, the community accorded him high respect. To this day, there are people in Bagamoyo who remember the generosity and honesty of Nasser Virjee. There is an account of one occasion when he had ordered some shirts from India. On arrival, he paid the relevant tax and released the goods. When he opened the parcel, he saw the shirts were of a large size instead of the medium he had ordered. He immediately returned to the port office to pay the extra tax for the larger size. Acknowledged as a trustworthy member of the Bagamoyo society, the German colonial authorities would turn to him to resolve disagreements between various communities.[26]

Nasser Virjee's company often employed new Khoja migrants. As a result, more Khoja Shia Ithna-Asheries began to choose to settle in Bagamoyo. Alhaj Saleh Jacksi, a resident of Zanzibar, used to bring about 20 Khoja Shia Ithna-Asheries from Zanzibar to Bagamoyo during the month Muharram to commemorate the martyrdom of Imam Hussein (pbuh). In this way, many became aware of the opportunities in Bagamoyo and as the community grew in number, they decided to build a mosque. Nasser Virjee & Company contributed toward the fund and under the supervision of Alhaj Saleh Jacksi, the local community was able to construct a mosque and *imambada* structure which were completed in 1889. The visit of Aga Khan III in the same year, followed by official proclamations instructing his followers to break off all social and economic ties with the Ithna-Asheries led to a splintering of the Khoja community in Bagamoyo and generally within East Africa.

In 1900, Nasser Virjee & Co. opened a branch in Mombasa that subsequently became its head office in 1909.[27] At the time, the Nasser Virjee group owned 72 different companies in German East Africa from the East African Coast to Uzumbura (Bujumbura) in Burundi. The German Colonial Handbook mentions the firm of 'Nassor Wirji & Sons' as being merchants in Bagamoyo and Tabora, an import/export firm in Songea, as well as ivory and rubber traders in Ujiji. Such notable entries in the German Colonial Handbook show their economic prowess. Nasser Virjee's family made a significant commercial impact at the time and stood out as an example to others.

Nasser Virjee became financially self-sufficient and was able to perform obligatory Hajj[28] in 1902. There were no passports at that time, but his position in the colonial German government of East Africa was so influential that they issued a special note for him to travel to Mecca.

Certificate issued to Nasser Virjee by the German Colonial Government
(Courtesy Kurban Virji, the grandson of Nasser Virji)

Sadly, Nasser Virjee lost his two-year-old daughter, Khadijah, on this trip. A few years later in 1911, he had to bear the loss of a second child, his eldest son - Mohammed Ali - who died in Bhuj at the age of 21. According to family records, the young man had memorised the entire Qur'an at an early age and was competently running the family business in Mombasa. He had recently married and travelled to Kachchh on business where he contracted dysentery and died. [29]

By 1913, the importance of Bagamoyo was fading and the Virjee family moved to Mombasa to carry on with the business already established there by the late Mohammed Ali. During World War I, there was no demand for the type of products they were trading in. As the war took its toll on the businesses in East Africa, Nasser Virjee had to lend a large amount of money to the government. The government defaulted on the loan and Nasser Virjee had to declare bankruptcy. The only business assets that survived were in Mwanza as these were in his son's name so the family moved again in 1923. In Mwanza, Nasser purchased a 450-acre freehold parcel of land and started the Mwanza Cotton Trading Company Limited. The company had two cotton ginneries and an oil mill. They also cultivated coffee and cashew nuts.

Throughout his journey to success, loss and financial stability once again, Nasser Virjee remained a deeply religious man. He was thankful that he was on the 'Right Path' as attested to in his will, in which he left a message stating: 'I, Nasser Virjee, am following Islam-Ithenaashery religion which is the True Path. To follow this path in which is the pleasure of Allah and of mine too'.[30]

 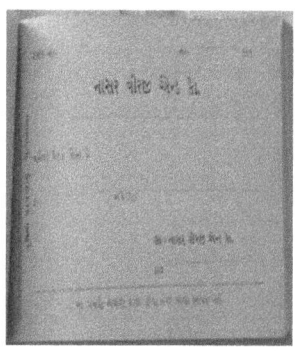 

Alhaj Nasser Virjee kept diaries (from 1923). He had a habit of making notes of transactions on the back of the cash sale receipt book
(Courtesy: Saberabai Jaffer, Grandaughter of Alhaj Nasser Virjee)

*Seated from L to R: Gulamabbas, Abdulrasul, Nasserbhai Virjee, Hassanali, Abdulhussein.
Standing from L to R: Hussein, Mohamed Jaffer, Ebrahim, Shaukat.
(Courtesy: Kurban Virjee, the grandson of Nasser Virjee)*

In 1942, Alhaj Nasser Virjee died and was buried in Mwanza. He had 14 children. One of his sons, Alhaj Abdulrasul Nasser Virjee, served as Chairman of The Africa Federation of Khoja Shia Ithna-Asheri Jamaats in the 1950's. He wrote a book about the solar system in English that was appreciated as a venture in scientific thinking within the community. He was also the recipient of an MBE[31] for outstanding achievement and service to the community at large in East Africa. Another son, Hassanali Nasser Virjee, was the Mayor of Mwanza from 1957-58.[32] A third son, Mohammed Jaffer, had political competence that was recognised by the local political party TANU. When Tanganyika got independence, the party nominated him to become a Member of Parliament. Due to family commitments, he could not take up the position, but he served as a nominated member of Mwanza Town Council and the Vice-Chairman of Mwanza Chamber of Commerce.[33]

Dewji Jamal was one of the few rich Khoja Shia Ithna-Asheri merchants of Bombay.[34] He was born around 1820 in Bhavnagar, India to a mercantile family and originally operated his business in Bhavnagar before moving to Bombay in 1850. The first references of his business activities in Zanzibar appear in consular registers from 1864. Dewji Jamal & Co owned a fleet of dhows transporting timber, textile and all kinds of foodstuff - including rice and sugar - from

India. They exported cloves, copra, ivory, seashells and wooden beams (*boriti*) from East Africa. With the profits they made, they invested in real estate in Zanzibar, Mombasa and Nairobi. Dewji Jamal had 11 dhows which he registered with the British consulate to avoid British naval harassment.[35] According to Professor Abdul Sheriff, his great grandson,[36] many of his captains were Arabs. One dhow, *Salamaty*, bought in 1868, had a Kachchhi captain named Dungersi. Another had a crew of twelve Kachchhi and eight 'Free Swahili'.[37]

Some of his dhows sailed to Bombay and Madagascar under the red flag of the Sultan of Zanzibar, an acknowledgement that the Sultan considered Indian merchants as local traders of the Indian Ocean. Because of this, they could sail to the Mrima[38] coast, which was an exclusive zone for local traders.[39] Other foreign traders were confined to Zanzibar by the Commercial Treaties signed between the Sultan of Zanzibar and the United States and various European powers from the 1830s onwards.[40]

As an entrepreneur, Dewji Jamal traded extensively in East Africa and built a home in Zanzibar in 1866.[41] He also played an influential role in the formation of the early Khoja Shia Ithna-Asheri community there by encouraging the Khojas in Bombay and East Africa to declare their allegiance to the Ithna-Asheri beliefs; many did so upon arrival to East Africa. Abdul Sheriff writes that whilst Dewji Jamal was culturally a Khoja Gujarati, the house he built resembled an Omani mansion in line with local architecture. It was not a Gujarati *haveli* (building) like Jairam Siwji had built or a Gujarati shop-front house of the kind that had begun to sprout along the busy bazaar streets.[42] This was a clear indication of his willingness to adapt to his new homeland.

In 1870, he opened a second branch in Lamu, which by then was a principal port of Kenya. His two sons, Jaffer and Nasser, managed the business in Lamu. In 1887, a third son, Nazerali, moved to Mombasa to establish a new branch of Dewji Jamal & Co. Following this move, Haji Dewji Jamal shifted to Mombasa to take advantage of the opportunities available there, as it was growing into the trading hub of East Africa.[43] Here too, he was active in the socio-religious development of Khoja Shia Ithna-Asheries and donated a plot to build the first mosque and *imambada*.[44]

HAJI JAFFER DEWJI (1860-1934)
A founder of the Mombasa Chamber of Commerce, Indian Association, Indian Congress and The Mombasa Public Library (Seif Bin Salim Library). He was a connoisseur of old china, coins, stamps, carpets, old battle arms, and objects of art. Many notable international personalities came to see his collections.

HAJI NAZARALI DEWJI JAMAL (1842-1930)
Founder of Nazar Ali Imambada, Kurla, and Mumbai (in memory of his father). With his brother-in-law, Noor Mohammed Hemraj, he built and formed the 'KSI Imambargah and Kabrastan Trust' in 1921 for the general benefit of Khoja Shia Ithna-Asheries.

(Photos Courtesy: Archives Section of Africa Federation, 19 June 2020)

The list of Dewji Jamal charitable institutions include mosques, community halls, rest houses, *madrasahs* (religious schools), cemeteries and rental properties whose income went to charities in both India and East Africa. The mosque in Lamu, the Hyderi Mosque and Imambada, the cemeteries in Mombasa, Zanzibar and Lamu, the rest house, mosque and *madrasah* in Bombay and Kurla (a Bombay suburb) all owe their existence to the contributions of Dewji Jamal. He passed away in 1905, aged 85 and is buried in Karbala, Iraq. He left behind six sons: Sheriff, Janmohamed, Peerbhai, Nazerali, Jaffer and Nasser.

Another one of the early Indian migrants to Zanzibar was Natha Gangjee. A Khoja Ismaili and devout follower of the Aga Khan, Natha Gangjee left Jamnagar in 1860.[45] According to the registration records of the British Consulate in Zanzibar, Natha came with three dependents: his wife, one sister and a child. Rashid, his second child was born in Zanzibar in 1875. Upon returning from a trip to Mumbai, a young Rashid - aged 13 - declared to his family that he had adopted the Shia Ithna-Asheri faith. His father disowned him and he had to leave the family house. Determined to remain faithful to his newly adopted faith, Rashid somehow managed to survive without food and shelter. What factors led to Rashid becoming Shia Ithna-

Asheri at such a young age remain unknown. Abdulhussein Akber, Rashid's grandson, believes that it was Mulla Qadir Husain's talks that were persuasive. In Mumbai, the *Darkhana* (the central Ismaili Jamaatkhana), the Khoja Sunni Mosque and the Khoja Shia Ithna-Asheri Mosque are all located in the same area at short distances from each other. Mulla Qadir Husain Saheb ran his *madrasah* near these centres every night.

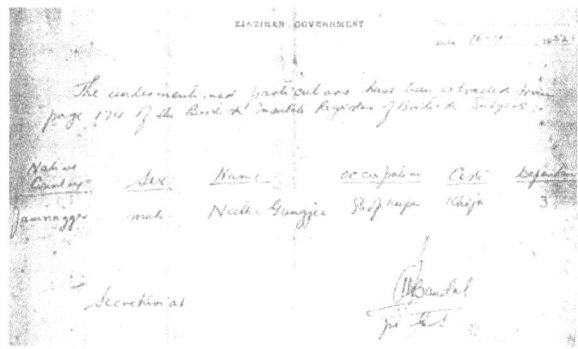

Natha Gangjee's registration at British Consulate in Zanzibar
(Courtesy of Abdulhusein Akber and Archives Section of Africa Federation)

RASHID NATHANI (1875 – 1936)

Rashid Nathani set up a tailoring shop, M. R. Nathani & Co., selling sewing machines and accessories as well as patented medicine.

His first wife was Sherbanu Walli Jamal and he had three children with her: Mohamedali, Fatma and Kulsum. Fatma was married to Mohamedjaffer Sheriff Dewji.

He also adopted two children of Mulla Jaffer of Pangani: Mulla Mohamed Jaffer (father of Marhum Mulla Asgher) and Sherbanu (mother of Marhum Abbas Alidina of Karachi).

After the death of his first wife, Rashid married Zainab Remtulla Nasser. They had seven sons: Abdulhusein, Husein, Mohamed Raza, (Maalim Raza), Mohamedjaffer (Malim Miya), Yusuf (Mulla Yusuf), Sultan and Akber, and one daughter, Sakina who married Abdulrasul Alarakhia Dewji.

When his second wife passed away, he married Fatmabai Kanji, sister of Husein Nazerali (Tabora). In the late 20s or early 30s, Rashid Natha sent his grandson, Hassanali, with Mulla Mohamed Jaffer to study in Lucknow. On their return Mulla Mohamed Jaffer stopped in Mombasa where he married the daughter of Mohamedjaffer Sheriff Dewji. These were the parents of Mulla Asgher M M Jaffer and his siblings.

After the Jamaatkhana's daily *bandagi* (evening prayers), some Khojas would attend Mulla Qadi's traditional *majlis* (lecture with lamentations of Imam Hussein (pbuh)). Mulla often turned these lecture sessions into discussion forums that doubled up as adult classes teaching the basic rudiments of the Islamic faith. It is highly possible that Rashid Natha Gangjee, driven by curiosity, could have attended and been influenced by these sessions along with his local friends.

Dharamsi Khatau came to Zanzibar in 1890. Three years later, he and his brother Jivraj Khatau set up an import business. From this small beginning, they went on to establish 40 branches throughout East Africa including in Mombasa, Lamu, Malindi, Mazeras, Takaungu, Kisumu, Bukoba, Nairobi and Meru. Many of the Khoja Shia Ithna-Asheries arriving into East Africa in the late 1890s and early 20th century worked in these branches before establishing their own businesses.[46]

Dharamsi Gangji (b.1882) from Nagalpur, Kachchh, India was the eldest of six sons of Gangji Sivji, a Khoja subsistence farmer who practiced the Shia Ismaili belief. Following the severe drought of 1899 and subsequent famine, he sent his eldest son Dharamsi to Zanzibar. The 17-year-old arrived with only a determination to succeed and despite not knowing anyone, managed to secure work at a salary of $20 per year. For two years he lived in a clove storehouse and survived on one meal a day. During this time, he gained a good understanding of the local economy and learnt Kiswahili.

At the end of the two years, he had saved $40 and decided to move to Pemba. There he bought a donkey and began transporting farm produce to the town of Chake Chake and bringing tea, rice, kerosene and other necessities to the farmers. In 1903, he opened his own trading shop in Chake Chake.

By 1906, he had saved enough to return to Kachchh and convince his younger brothers - Hashim, Datoo and Peera - of the opportunities in East Africa. They all eventually migrated as well. In 1907, Dharamsi married Sikinabai and returned to Pemba. With the support of his wife, he felt confident enough to invest in a piece of land to grow clove seedlings, fruit trees and vegetables. As the sale of cloves began bringing in profits, he purchased more land at Kipapo, Gagadu, Ndibo, Limani, Mtondoni, Ghombani and Cheche. He was an astute businessperson, investing in property in Pemba and Zanzibar. He was also regarded by the authorities as having enough influence to arbitrate in boundary disputes and farm demarcation.

Dharamsi Gangji
(1882-1956)

Dharamsi started to practice Shia Ithna-Asheri Islam by 1907 and raised his family on the same. He also served as President, Treasurer and Trustee of the Khoja Shia Ithna-Asheri Community of Chake Chake.

In 1926, he supervised and contributed towards the mosque at Chake Chake. Renowned for his charitable work, he set up a trust and the income received from his Ghombani plantation was utilised for the upkeep of the mosque expenses at Chake Chake. He also set up a Medical Clinic at Kipapo for all who needed it.

Dharamsi and Sikinabai Gangji had four children. The eldest was a son, Hussein, followed by another son who unfortunately died in infancy, followed by a girl, Zainab and finally a second girl, Kulsum.

In 1930, Dharamsi's son, Hussein, married Zainab, daughter of Mulyani Kulsumbai (Nanima) Khimji. They were blessed first with a daughter, Rubab, five sons (Mohamedali, Abbas, Muhsin, Jaffer and Ali Akber) and then four more daughters (Fatma, Banu, Raziya and Sikinabai). In 1945, Dharamsi moved his family to Zanzibar.

(Courtesy: Africa Federation Archives.)

The above-mentioned individuals from the Khoja Ismaili and Khoja Shia Ithna-Asheri communities found in Zanzibar - and to some extent Pemba - their first opportunities to learn trade. These towns were where they acquired necessary skills before venturing out to other coastal towns and into the interior of East Africa. Zanzibar gave them stability and a decent environment in which to recoup their strength after the gruelling journey from Kachchh and Kathiawad.

While some migrants failed to adapt to their new environment, Khojas such as Tharia Topan, Sewa Haji Paroo, Allidina Visram, Shariff Jiwa Surti, Virjeebhai Muraj Haji and Dewji Jamaal, Rashid Nathani, Dharamsi Khatau, Dharamsi Gangji and many others appear to have had a strong will to settle and prosper economically in East Africa. In this sense, they were not 'strangers'.[47]

The DHARAMSI GANGJI
Shia Ithna-Asheri School

Constructed by Hussein Dharamsi on Kiponda Road, the school opened in February 1959 to provide much needed extra classes for secondary education.

In the afternoon, the school would run spoken English and vocational classes for girls and by 1960, School Faize evening religious classes had moved here.

3.3 Swahili Environment: Its Impact on the Socio-Religious Stability of the KSI

Beyond economic stability, Khoja Shia Ithna-Asheries were also seeking socio-religious stability in their lives. They were looking to shape their identity and establish a legacy in East Africa. The archival records and recorded conversations show that most of the Khoja Shia Ithna-Asheries who came to Zanzibar were able to uplift themselves economically with assistance from their comrades .

They set down their roots in Zanzibar or the interior and achieved a level of prosperity from which their siblings and children benefitted. Conversations with community elders reveal that many Khojas had adopted the Arabic dress, Arabic names and the Swahili language. Regarding how Khojas lived, Christie[48] wrote as early as 1876 on Khojas that 'they may now be regarded as permanent settlers on the island, most of them having been born there...The outside business is conducted by the husband...and the retail... is attended to by his wife and the junior members of the family.'[49]

By all accounts, Zanzibar was a prosperous place in the 1870s and 1880s; its Stone Town was a beehive of activity. Abdul Sheriff describes it as

> a cosmopolitan metropolis. Its harbour teemed with square-rigged ships from the West and oriental dhows with their lateen sails from many countries in the East, carrying all the colours of the rainbow. Here Yankee merchants from New England drove a hard bargain with Hindu traders in their large crimson

turbans or Khojas in their long coats, exchanging ivory for American cloth; the Marseilles haggled with the Somali for hides and sesame seeds from Benadir; Hamburg entrepreneurs shipped tons of cowry shells to West Africa, where they served as currency; and Arab caravans rubbed shoulders with their African counterparts from the Mountains of the Moon.[50]

Upon their arrival to Zanzibar in the 19th century, the Khoja Shia Ithna-Asheries found themselves in strikingly different surroundings from those they had left. They saw people from many backgrounds, from all sides of the Indian Ocean, all seeking to experience a life interspersed with ordinary and extraordinary experiences. Zanzibar, a centre of commerce along the East African coast, was accepting of many outlooks and brimming with cultural diversity.[51]

The emerging Swahili culture must have resonated with the Khojas as so many of them adapted it into their own ethos. The core of Swahili culture originates from Bantu inhabitants of the coast of Kenya, Tanzania, and Mozambique. The Kiswahili language was a unifying factor. It connected those who came from beyond the coast, including the Khojas, giving the Swahili culture its cosmopolitan outlook. Nowhere was this more obvious than at the Jubilee Gardens Sea Front (famously known as 'Forodhani') in Stone Town Zanzibar.

The picturesque Forodhani overlooked the Indian Ocean. It had an authentic charm with large trees providing natural shade to visitors and various flower patches filling the air with a pleasant aroma. An evening visit to Forodhani would witness different communities gathered in familiar spots. It was a place of relaxation, business and networking over the partaking of food in open air.

Habib Peera,[52] popularly known as Habib *Hathiyar*, had a juice kiosk there where he served ice cream, fruit salads and hot cocoa. He had a jolly nature and almost everyone warmed up to him. He was also a close friend of the then Sultan of Zanzibar, Sayyid Sir Khalifa bin Haroub,[53] and a regular visitor to the palace on Fridays when the Sultan would hold his court. Habib passed away in 1963 leaving five sons. The eldest son, Jaffer, continued to operate the kiosk and one of his other sons, Bashir, became active in community work.

HABIB PEERA KATAW (1888 – 1963)

The picturesque Forodhani Park overlooking the Indian Ocean (Courtesy: Africa Federation Archives)

BASHIR HABIB PEERA (1937-2006)

An affable character who held a very good rapport with other Muslim communities, Bashir Habib Peera was an active community member since his youth.

He was Honorary Secretary of Zanzibar Education Society that established the first Khoja Nursery school in Saateni, Zanzibar. He also taught part-time at Dharamsi Gangji School in Kiponda, Zanzibar. In 1964, he joined the Africa Federation under Marhum Hajji Ebrahim Hussein Sheriff Dewji and held the post of Secretary until 1977.

For 15 years, he was the Secretary of Maulid Celebration Committee in Mombasa.

This was Zanzibar at its best and Swahili was the glue that made it possible for different cultures to cohere as Zanzibaris or "Jangbaris". The Khoja Shia Ithna-Asheries seemed to have more readily adopted the Swahili dialect of Zanzibar, *Kiunguja*, than the other Indian communities. Clothing was another aspect of the culture that was integrated into Khoja Shia Ithna-Asheri community. The men adopted the *kanzu* (long white men's shirtdress) as their daily wear whilst among the women, the *ukaya* (head covering) became a norm.

One important challenge, however, was that Indians were used to the *Jati*[54] system. In Kachchh and Kathiawad, communal membership was based on *Jati* concepts[55] that many Indians understood and practiced. In this system, status was derived from marriage and it was a mechanism to improve one's social status. The patrilineal orientation of many of these communities made marriage outside of their own *Jat* rare, and in instances where such marriages did take place it was only with other Indian communities.[56]

This pattern was less visible among the Khoja community generally and within the Khoja Shia Ithna-Asheries specifically. This was particularly evident after 1880, when they established their own Kuwwat Masjid and Imambada and developed a strong sense of communal identity and interaction. Some of them married spouses from the local community grounding themselves as being more Zanzibari than Indian.

Alhaj Mohammedbhai Khalfan put it succinctly:

> A fair part of success gained by the communities of all faith and culture in settling in East Africa and sharing in developing the countries economically through geographical expansion in trade must be attributed to the congenial disposition and nature of the indigenous peoples of those countries. They were an exception as comparable to those of host countries in other parts of the world.
>
> The indigenous peoples of the East African countries were typically by nature hospitable, readily trusted and also respected the immigrants as they kept arriving in groups over a period of more than a century. When faced by the collective hardship in life they showed the strength of resilience backed by patience, tolerance and spiritual faith. Laughing off their individual hardships come about easily for them. And then others join in the ravishing momentary joy.
>
> These noble characteristics having remained ingrained in nature continued to show even after the countries gained their respective independence and assumed their right to self-rule. The minorities have always been protected as common and equal citizens – when sadly minorities in other certain countries of the same race and themselves indigenous by descent are discriminated against in legislation, governance and policies. Patriotism must never be bruised by misrule.

The Islamic ethos that the Khoja Shia Ithna-Asheries found in Zanzibar and the coast of East Africa suited them. They found it comfortable to live among other Muslim communities. Their inner affiliations were to Islam and to Shia practices such as *Azadari*[57] which allowed them to interact with other Shia communities.

Elders of the community relate that by the beginning of 20th century, the Khoja Shia Ithna-Asheries had already accepted East Africa as their permanent home. They were, perhaps, convinced that history was on their side and confident that they would be able to contribute to the prosperity of this new land that had given many of them opportunities they did not have in Kachchh and Kathiawad.

With this determination, the Khoja Shia Ithna-Asheri began to focus on equal civic and economic rights, including the right to settle on lands reserved for White Europeans. They joined hands with the rest of the Indian community to address the discriminatory practices carried out by German and British colonial authorities towards their non-European subjects. In this regard, the Bagamoyo Indians made formal complaints in 1906 to German officials and a few years later, in 1914 the Tanga Indians submitted a long memorandum on the subject to British administrators.[58]

The discriminatory policies of both colonial powers did not go unnoticed in India as well. In 1913, the Bombay Chronicle wrote a fierce criticism of the discriminatory policies in the British East African Protectorate. It stressed that 'now the Indian cannot acquire property in the uplands, cannot carry weapons, cannot enter the Market House in Nairobi, cannot travel in comfort on the steamers and railways, cannot have a trial by jury, in short, cannot be anything else than an undesirable alien.'[59]

Unable to compete with the Europeans on an equal basis, to defend their properties or protect their families, the Committee of Indians (formed in 1914) reorganized and became the Indian National Association of Zanzibar. In 1923, Yusufali Esmailjee Jivanjee, president of the association, presented a memorandum on the Report of the Commission on Agriculture in which he strongly criticized the government's position that Indians were responsible for the indebtedness of agriculturalists (meaning Arabs and Swahili) in Zanzibar. In addition, he passed judgment on the method of collecting clove duties, which was disadvantageous to Asian clove producers.[60]

He spoke on behalf of the Indian business community (Hindus and Muslims) in Zanzibar. His position to the British was clear in that the Indians living in East Africa were not against any legislation in favour of Arabs and Africans, rather they were against the policy that divided one section of the Zanzibari community at the cost of another.

When the British argued that they had reduced import duties for fresh butter and milk, ghee, and cigarettes, Jivanjee commented incisively that it was the Europeans who used milk to feed their children and not the Africans. The reduction of tax on ghee benefited only the middle and upper classes of the Indian population, not the poorer sections of the community. In the case of cigarettes, Jivanjee demonstrated that Europeans smoked the most and bought them in their thousands adding 'If His Excellency wishes to really benefit the poor natives; we want the duty on rice and *kangas* to be reduced! These are their real necessities. Then alone can we say that the Government is doing something for the natives' concluding 'the policy of the Government underlying this movement is to rob Indian Peter to pay British Paul.'[61]

Yusufali Jivanjee together with others organized protests that eventually led to the establishment of the East African Indian Congress (EAINC), which was modelled on the famous Indian National Congress. The EAINC membership believed that by bringing Indian leaders in East Africa together and presenting their collective case in an organised manner at both colonial and national levels, they would be able to serve Indian interests effectively.

Nevertheless, in the German and British colonial era, Indians, including Khoja Shia Ithna-Asheries, still enjoyed a few privileges: they practised their religions unhindered, some tax rates remained low and their property rights were respected. This came, however, at a cost. The British allowed Indians to indulge in their self-interest as long as it served the colonial interest. This aspect of the Indian activity was viewed by colonial officials with both positivity and negativity. Some colonial officials were very satisfied with the entrepreneurial role Indian communities played within the region. Others characterized

Indians as untrustworthy exploiters of the local economy and tried to alienate them, advocating for them to be denied civic rights and the right to own fertile lands.

This ambivalent relationship between the British colonialists and the Indian communities survived as long as both the British and the Indians got something out of it. In the long run, however, it gave neither a level of political nor economic confidence that the Indians desired; the self-interest of the British colonialist trumped everything else. The German and the British authorities made use of Indian entrepreneurship and their skills for their own colonial project and the Indian communities generally accepted this power imbalance because they knew that they were a strong link essential for the success of the British colonial project in East Africa. Despite understanding these constraints, many in the Indian communities planned their lives for permanent settlement and were not looking to go back.

Once they had made East Africa their home, the Khoja Shia Ithna-Asheries focused their efforts on a most urgent task: to educate their children. This desire ran deep, proven by the fact that as soon as a group of Khoja Shia Ithna-Asheries established a community, they would build or provide facilities for a school as a major priority.[62] Those who could afford to, sent their children abroad for further education because adequate facilities in Zanzibar were lacking. They expected their sons and daughters to return to after completing their further studies and plan their retirement there.

From research and conversations with elders, it is obvious that the mindset of the Khoja migrants was one of permanency.[63] The prevalent ethos of Islam encouraged many to consider building their future in East Africa. Once they landed, they regarded themselves as part of the region and integrated into it almost seamlessly. This is borne out by the fact that many Khoja Shia Ithna-Asheries adopted Arabic dress and spoke the Swahili language as well as the local Zanzibaris.

3.4 Separation in Zanzibar

Considering the positive and communal environment that welcomed the Indians and tempted them to stay on, one might wonder what factors and influences led to the formation of a separate Khoja Shia Ithna-Asheri community in Zanzibar and subsequently the rest of East Africa. Before the 1870s, the cultural life of the Khoja community revolved around the *jamaatkhana*.

Karim Alarakhiya says that 'at that time, there were no sectarian tendencies within the community.[64] Khoja Muslims use to attend the *jamaatkhana* where the Qibla was marked. Those who wanted to pray salaat were free to do so and those who wanted to do *bandagi* could perform it.' In Zanzibar, the *jamaatkhana* - built in 1838[65] - accommodated both types of prayers as well. People gathered there to pray, network and learn the latest news of their families and communities in India. It was a community space that transcended its physical boundaries.

The first Khoja Jamatkhana, Forodhani (Above) was established in the 1830s, with the appointments of Mukhis and Kamadias, during the time of Hasan Ali Shah Aga Khan I. Sultan Muhammad Shah Aga Khan III opened the Darkhana Jamatkhana on 16 August 1905 and established the first Aga Khan School in 1905.

Alarakhiya reminisced that the Zanzibar Jamaatkhana brought together Khojas of diverse beliefs.[66] The community held Ismaili beliefs whilst also including all the normal Islamic rituals such as *salaat*, Muharram commemorations, Ramadhan rituals, etc. They were aware to a certain extent of the stresses present in Mumbai and elsewhere in Kachchh and Kathiawad but more than anything, there was a feeling of belonging and connection amongst the members.

After 1866 case, when Aga Khan I ordered his followers to observe marriage and death ceremonies in accordance with Shia rites, a majority of the Khoja families in Zanzibar accepted this as a unifying move. Outwardly, the murmurings of a possible division halted but not for long as rumours of a split within the Khoja community in Mumbai filtered to Zanzibar. The differences in beliefs began to create tension within the local Khoja community.[67] In 1870, news arrived that members in Mumbai, Kachchh and Kathiawad who had expressed their belief in the Shia Ithna-Asheri faith had been ostracised, among them Dewji Jamal, Alarakhiya Walli, Suleiman Khalfan and Kalyan Gangji.[68] This further widened the rift in the Zanzibar community.[69]

When Dewji Jamaal and Alarakhiya Walli arrived in Zanzibar, people in the community began to take a deeper interest in their faith and the Shia Ithna-Asheri tenets. In the 1870s, they used to meet in the old Faize school building[70] on Kiponda Road, away from the *Jamaatkhana*, to discuss communal and religious issues. Dewji Jamal, Alarakhiya Walli, Mohammed Walji and Walli Nazarali led these discussions and invited Persian and Bahraini Shia Ithna-Asheri scholars who had settled in Zanzibar to guide them.[71]

Despite their eagerness, these fledgling communities had no established centre for their religious gatherings. Alhaj Ahmad bin Na'aman Al Kaabi and Major Mohamed Ahmed Khan[72] were the individuals responsible for obtaining a place - *Matam Baharani* - from Sultan Bargash for them to mark the major events on the Shia calendar.[73]

ALHAJ AHMAD BIN NA'AMAN AL KAABI *(pictured Left)*
and Major Mohamed Ahmed Khan, well respected personalities in Zanzibar and known in the court of Sultan Bargash, approached him with a request to provide a suitable place to hold gatherings on important days in the Shia religious calendar.

Their request was granted and they were allocated a space allocated just behind the Palace and the graveyard on a road leading to Hurumzi Street.

This was the first Matam Baharani (around 1880), the name given by Major Mohamed Ahmed Khan. After a decade, Matam Baharani moved to Kiponda Street (around 1900) where it is currently situated.

Before the construction of the Kuwwat Imambada, many Khoja Shia Ithna-Asheries attended Bahraini gatherings at the *Matam Baharani* and emulated their way of doing *saf matam*.[74] This was probably the source of the fervent '*saf matam*' in Zanzibar that was taken up by other Khoja Shia Ithna-Asheri communities in East Africa.

Matam Baharani, as it is called till today, was named by Major Mohamed Ahmed Khan who was a Bahraini.

It moved to the present site during the reign of the late Seyyid Khalifa bin Haroub (ruled. 1911 -1960). It is said that Sultan Seyyid Khalifa had made 'nazar' (pledge) that if he was blessed with a boy he would fit Persian carpets in the entire Matam Baharani. When his wish was fulfilled, he carpeted the entire Matam and held dinner for the congregation every year. His son, Abdullah, became the Sultan of Zanzibar in the 1960s.

The Arabic inscription reads:

'Al Matam' was established in 1278 A.H. This endowment was made by the honourable leader - the late Captain Alhaj Ahmad bin No'aman Al-Ka'abi Al-Bahrani - may Allah shower his happy place of abode with the endowment's blessings. He was born in the city of al-Basra (Zobair) in 1204, and died in Zanjabar in 1244. Bin Ali al-Shaybani al-Bahrani wrote and carved this memorial for me. The carpentry was completed in 1244. This is the 14th year of the death of the Sultan, our master Khalifa. Thus we became neighbours in Allah's Kingdom.

Inspired by the Persian and Bahraini Shia scholars' interpretation of the faith, the Faize group adopted Ithna-Asheri religious fundamentals, forming their own active, functioning forum. For them, Ithna-Asheri doctrines became a reference point for communal direction. These critical discussions helped them to strengthen their beliefs.

The Khoja Shia Ithna-Asheries in Zanzibar had their Kuwwat mosque in Kiponda area in Stone Town by 1881. They used this for prayers, but the *imambada* had not been built yet.[75] So it was at the old school Faize that they often gathered to pray, listen to lectures and serve *nyaz* (sacred food offering served after a religious lecture).

Many Khoja Shia Ithna-Asheries received their religious grounding by attending the Faize Night School in Zanzibar. Some went on to serve the community as volunteers,[76] religious teachers, preachers, Qur'an and lamentations reciters, community leaders and advisers.

School Fez teachers and students - 1952
Sitting L-R: *Jaffer Boga, Yusuf Alidina, Abdulhussein Nathani, Gulamabbas Kara, Gulamhussein Peera, Abbas Tejani, Mohamedhussein Tejani, Mohamed Jivraj, Raza Nathani, Sayed Jabir Hassan, Agha Mehdi Shustary, Maalim Miya, Mohamedhussein Lalji, Najafali Tejani, Akbar Thaver.*
Standing L-R: *Baker Nathani, Ahmed Bhalloo, Jaffer Tejani, Mohamed Juma, Gulamhussein Saleh, Ahmed Issa, Mohamed Khalfan, Mohamedhussein Kermali, Baker Tejani, Yusuf Sheriff Dewji.*

The first batch qualified in the 1930s. Amongst them was Maalim Najafali Tejani, an amiable and inspirational figure who profoundly influenced the community in Zanzibar and Dar es Salaam. These 'graduates' became a source of inspiration for the next generation.

Maalim Najafali Tejani (1919-2001)

He gave lectures, taught religious education and assisted in preparing madrasah syllabi. Many owe their religious grounding to him. Modest and effable, he would not want to make his presence felt to those around him. Sayed Aqa Haider Saheb, an eminent scholar who served the East African Khoja Shia Ithna-Asheries in the 1970s, recommended him highly to the community.

His pious nature led people to trust him with charity funds for distribution to the poor and needy. He was a source of inspiration to the community.

(Courtesy: Africa Federation Archives)

The wider Khoja community saw the Faize group as a dissident movement and did not tolerate this separation well; the split within the Khoja community of Zanzibar became inevitable. The first signs of schism appeared in the late 1870s and came to a head following the construction of the mosque in 1881.[77]

Leading among the dissidents were the two Walji Rawji brothers, MohamedJaffer and Janmohamed. Heedless of any threats, after receiving moral support from the British Resident in 1880, MohamedJaffer built the mosque adjoining the old Faize School Building while the other brother, Janmohamed, procured the Kabrastan plot at Rahaleo.[78] Dewji Jamaal and Alarakhiya Walli collected around 8000 rupees from donors in Mumbai whilst Mohammed Walji, Walli Nazerali and others added to this amount from Zanzibari donors.

With this fund, the community built the Kuwwatul Masjid and Imambada which were both ready for use in 1881.[79] The registration document at the Zanzibar Archives reads 1294 Hijri[80] as the year of the Jamaat registration. Abdulrazak Sheriff Fazal explains that 'the Hijri date stated in the document at Zanzibar Archives may not be accurate. There is a four-year difference in the Hijra date if the AD conversion is applied i.e making it 1877. It could be that the (Kuwwat) committee was formed four years earlier (1877) and the mosque was made *Waqf*[81] in 1881 after it was built.'[82]

This fact, according to Abdulrazak, makes Kuwwat Jamaat and Kuwwat Mosque the first built by Khoja Shia Ithna-Asheri community. Dewji Jamaal, Wali Nazerali, Nanji Gulamhussein, Daya Punja, Jaffer Kassamali, Peera Walli, Saleh Sachedina, Versi Advani, Remtulla Nurmohammed, Janmohammed Rawji, Saleh Mohamed Hassan and Harji Jamal signed the official document that established the separate identity of Khoja Shia Ithna-Asheries in Zanzibar in 1877.

Despite its Ibaazi[83] sultanate, the Khoja Shia Ithna-Asheries were able to build their own mosque in Zanzibar[84] because of the assistance of Major Mohammed Ahmedkhan[85] of Baluch who obtained the appropriate construction permission for them.[86] Politically, this was possible because at the time the Busa'idi Sultanate was in the process of transformation as it came increasingly under the protection and influence of the British Government. The British were concerned with the emergence of religious movements in the Muslim world, which propagated anti-colonial campaigns as well as the revival of Islamic doctrines in Muslim countries. Their main concern was to prevent the influence of these religious movements on *Qadhis*[87] and Muslim scholars in the Busa'idi Sultanate.

The British colonial authorities had also adopted a policy of categorising colonised people according to their ethnic identities. Khoja Shia Ithna-Asheries did not fall under an ethnic category and therefore, neither the Sultanate nor British colonial authorities had any objections to them building a mosque. The implications of this policy by the British colonial authorities is worth noting, as it had ramifications in later years.[88]

It was 1881 and the Khoja Shia Ithna-Asheries finally came into their own as a *Jamaat*. They had a mosque with an *imambada* built by its side and Pira Walli as their first president.[89] The plot for the *imambada* was secured through the recommendation of Kalbe Aly Khan, one of the wazirs[90] of Sultan of Zanzibar at the time. He also initiated the inclusion of '*Ashahaduanna Aliyun Waliyullah*'[91] in the *adhaan*[92], which was first recited from the new Shia mosque by a Persian teacher, Maalim Maulidi.[93] The *imambada* was partly financed by Remtulla Tejani and carpeted by Mohamed Walli Dharsi.

PIRA WALLI
First President of Kuwwatul Islam Jamaat

Kuwwat Jamaat, Zanzibar.
Built 1881.

Ali Nathoo succeeded Pira Walli and served the community for 23 years.[94] He was a generous contributor and fully financed the new Kuwwat Imambada, that was built upon the old one.[95]

ALI NATHOO
Second President, serving a record 23 years.

Fazal Alarakhiya Siwji recalls that in 1917, when the community in Tanga was ravaged by war, Ali Nathoo generously sent a ship loaded with food and clothes to assist them. Such was his generosity and kindness that he was recognised not only within the community but outside it as well. The British Government offered him a knighthood for his services, which he politely declined. Instead, he requested the colonial government to grant public holidays in Zanzibar for 10th Muharram[96] and 21st Ramadhan.[97] His requests were accepted, and these two days remained public holidays for almost 45 years from 1920 to 1964.[98]

Some of the other Presidents who served the Kuwwat Jamaat in this period of four and a half decades include Husain Sheriff Dewji, Fazel Nasser Mawji, M. D. Kermali, M. A. Saleh, Husain Nazarali, Abdulrasul Khakoo, Sherali Ahmed Ladha and Husain Allarakhia Rahim,[99] who was notably the Public Prosecutor with the Zanzibar Government; he went on to become judge.

3.5 Challenging the Narrative

In 1881, harmony prevailed amongst the Khojas in Zanzibar. There were 250 Shia Ithna-Asheri individuals in the community and the relationship between Jamaatkhana and Kuwwatul Mosque remained cordial with food being shared during big occasions. In addition, members of both factions met up and maintained close social relationships. This stable environment should ideally have pleased

Aga Khan III when he visited Zanzibar and Mombasa in 1899 and 1905 respectively. Instead, the institutionalisation of the Shia Ithna-Asheries was a source of frustration for him. It was a visible reality that a growing number of Khojas were formally rejecting his authority.

After his visit to Zanzibar, Aga Khan III began to issue fiery directives from Bombay. He predicted the demise of the Ithna-Asheri faith worldwide within 100 years and instructed his followers to keep well clear of them, including an order to avoid food and water touched by them.[100] He also introduced constitutions within the Khoja community in Zanzibar that restricted membership only to those loyal to him. It was was one of his priorities to unify the *jamaats* loyal to him and eliminate any dissent. *Farmans* restricted social activities to within the Khoja Ismaili grouping only. They forbade marriages and social interaction between members of the Ismaili and Ithna-Asheri groups. Communal worship and gatherings in the Jamaatkhana were now strictly limited to the followers of Aga Khan.[101] By issuing these *farmans* and consolidating his loyalty within the Khoja Ismaili community, Aga Khan III was able to promote his own socio-religious narrative for the Khoja community.

It was Adelji Dhanji Kaba (1863-1923) of the Khoja community who took it upon himself to challenge this Aga Khan Ismaili narrative. He wrote *Khoja Komna Pustako* (Books of the Khoja Community), a set of 11 books that were available to all the Khoja communities in Mumbai, Gujarat and East Africa. According to his autobiography, he also stayed in Zanzibar for a while and was aware of the socio-religious dynamics within the Khoja communities there.[102] It is possible that his works could have been an influence on the Khoja Shia Ithna-Asheries of Zanzibar in their quest to set up a separate identity. In his various publications, he shared how he came to realise his duty to his community. He explained that (according to him) the Khoja community was surrounded by ignorance and undermined the true nature of Islam. He believed that many non-Islamic beliefs had invaded and corrupted the true teachings of Pirs.

Adelji Dhanji is an interesting figure. His work, classified as polemic, does not have the necessary vigour to be of even marginal interest for those carrying out academic research. Nevertheless, his publications influenced the minds of many ordinary Khojas of his time who were his primary target audience. It is quite feasible to assume that many Khojas at the time were not still fully aware of what it meant to be Ismaili or Ithna-Asheri. Readers would have found the flow of arguments in his work persuasive. One thing appears to be clear from his vastly available writings and that is that given the socio-religious dynamism in the Khoja community, not doing anything was not an option for him. He responded to the situation in the only way he felt would persuade the Khoja community towards his leanings.

In his work, Dhanji makes deliberate assumptions in order to make a point. Why did he do this? To answer this and understand the manner in which he chose to present his narrative, we have to explore the events affecting the Khoja community during his lifetime. These would have shaped Adelji Dhanji's thinking and the way he produced his arguments. During his childhood and years of youth, he would have heard of and witnessed the effects of milestone events in the community such as the Khoja Case, the Sunni split, the emerging Shia Ithna-Asheries group post-1866, the Haji Bibi case as well as Aga Khan III's firm shaping of the Khoja Ismaili identity. Keeping this in mind, Adelji Dhanji's daring conclusions seem less surprising. However, one also wonders if this may have been a deliberate move by him to elicit a reaction from Khoja Ismailis. If so, what was his reasoning and intention?

At that time, Aga Khan III's ideology, coupled with general ignorance on Islamic tenets and wisdom of Pirs as expressed in the ginans, was dominating the Khoja community. This was the '*Rakhshas*' (Darkness of Ignorance), according to Dhanji. It may not have been the only factor, but the content of his writing suggests that it was the main one and he wanted to fight it with everything he had. This idea is what shaped his thinking. The arguments and rhetoric he used in his work was his way of creating enough disturbance to shake an otherwise docile Khoja community out of its slumber, and elicit a reaction to what he was saying.

At the same time, it appears from his work that he wanted to strengthen the Shia Ithna-Asheries position from the perspectives of

both the *ginans* and the Qur'an. He wanted to make following points conclusive:
1. Pirs were Muslims.
2. What is expressed in the *ginans* by the Pirs is supported by what the Qur'an says.
3. The community that properly follows the Pirs and the *ginans* are the Khoja Ithna-Asheries and not Khoja Ismailis.

The raison d'être of his work was that the Khoja Shia Ithna-Asheri were the true followers of Pirs.

In the tense atmosphere of the early 20th century, particularly during the time of Aga Khan III when there was already an impending split amongst the Khojas, his writing was just what the growing Khoja Shia Ithna-Asheri community needed. Dhanji's works were read and widely available and reached even the Zanzibari Khojas. Based on the debates his work generated, there is a definite need to engage his writings more in order to determine the extent of their influence on the Khoja Shia Ithna-Asheries of Zanzibar.

ADELJI KABA *(d. 1923)*
His legacy was to get the community to critically think and evaluate their beliefs.

Excerpts from 'Chaudmi Sadi' magazine, Pustak biju, Jamadil awwal and Rajab edition, 1342 A.H.

According to Dhanji, the Khoja community held beliefs that were at once complementary and contradictory. He argued that the mixing of Hindu and Islamic tenets showed the ignorance prevalent within the Khoja community. He also stated argued that since the Khoja community called itself Muslim, then its beliefs should be Islamic as defined by the Qur'an and followed by the majority of Muslims.[103] He took Ismaili leaders and missionaries to task for cultivating this mixture of beliefs and not setting the correct standard.

In his writings, Dhanji confidently asserts that Khoja Shia Ithna-Asheries are the true followers of Pirs who, according to him, are themselves also Ithna-Asheries. This view, about the Pirs - who originally came from Iran and Afghanistan - was also held by some within the community. Whether the opinion originated from Adelji Dhanji Kaba's work or elsewhere, needs further exploration. There is no doubt however that his writings, and possibly his presence in the early part of the 20th century in Zanzibar, left an impact on the thinking of the Khoja Shia Ithna-Asheries there.

3.5.1 Finding Faith

As the larger Khoja community began to implement the proclamations from Aga Khan III, especially after the Haji Bibi case of 1908, there was a lot of confusion and anxiety within the Khoja community in Zanzibar, followed by conflict. There were instances where the predominant dynamics of the conflict were social and two groups were set against each other, each considering the other as the "out-group". Theological points in this debate, whilst fundamental, were of secondary importance as emotions were roused and discussions within families got divisive.

Once the restrictions began to take effect, instances of fist-fights, stone-hurling and stick-fighting occurred in both communities. Mingling between Khoja Ithna-Asheries and Khoja followers of Aga Khan became difficult. Within families, some remained Khoja Ismailis and others became Ithna-Asheries. Close social and cultural bonds were severed overnight. It was from this time, that the terms Ismaili (or AgaKhani) and Ithna-Asheri became prevalent.

By the second decade of the 20th century, the split was complete both theologically and socially in Zanzibar.[104] The last decade of the 19th century and the first decade of 20th century were a time of great upheaval for the Khoja community. It became the custom to announce the names of the ostracised person or family publicly in the streets of Stone Town in Zanzibar, urging members to boycott the individuals. It was a chaotic scene with claims and counter-claims over the communal properties that needed to be resolved. Families were challenged emotionally and there were those who wanted to convert but feared ostracism if they did.[105] Some of them began to meet privately.[106]

As the Khoja community was dealing with the turmoil amongst its members, the practice of commemorating the martyrdom of Imam Hussein (pbuh) was discontinued in the Zanzibar Jamaatkhana. However, the love for the Imam was such that many Ismailis continued to privately organise these *majlises*. One such place they met at was Mehefile Muhibbane Hussein, otherwise known as "Mehfile Private" (initially known as Mehfil of Abdulrasool Peera Dewji) in Zanzibar. There is also a version of this account that suggests that the Ismailis ran Mehfile Private at Mtendeni[107] where some Ithna-Asheries also joined them. These gatherings began in 1920, shifted to Bustani in 1927, then to a rented house of M D Kermalli until 1930 and from there to Mtendeni until 1932.

MEHFIL-E-MUHIBBANE HUSSEIN (AS) (MEHFILE-E-PRIVATE)

Until 1905, Majalises of Imam Hussein (pbuh) were held in the Zanzibar Jamaatkhana. Varas Kassam Damani, Jetha Valliani, Bhagat Virji and Gulamhussein Teja would read Mukhtar Nama. After Agakhan III's visit in 1899, an order was issued to close Mehfile Private. Majlises continued at the houses of Gangji Dawood, Bhalloo Valli and Mohamed Mussa Rajan.

From 1905, the Muharram majalises at the Jamaatkhana in Zanzibar stopped. In 1907, Janmohamed Master filed a court case against the Jamaatkhana. The proceedings of the case were published in Noore Hidayat.

In 1920, Ithna-Asheri youths rented a place in the Empire Club building and majlises continued jointly with Ismaili youths up to 1927. After the building was sold, majlises shifted to Haji Sheriff Dewji's Bustani and later at M. D. Kermali's house until 1930. Many Ismailis like Abdulrasul Peera Dewji and others joined the Ithna-Asheries.

(Africa Federation Archives)

After 1932, an Ismaili brother, Gulamali Murji Kanji, donated a house for the Mehfil and the religious lectures continued in that building until 1937. Those who attended these *mehfils* discussed their respective religious tenets and conversion was gradual. Given the close family connections between both communities, the conversion process took place over a long period before people were comfortable declaring that they were Ithna-Asheri.[108]

One example of such a conversion was that of Esmail Sabjali Thaver. He was born in Zanzibar in 1902. His parents came from Jaamkhambadia in Gujarat. He was a member of the Ismaili Jamaatkhana, but secretly practised the tenets of the Ithna-Asheri faith. An astute entrepreneur, he owned a variety of businesses, eventually opening his own 'Bhajia Star Bakery' in 1938. Ismail Thaver was a lover of Imam Hussein (pbuh) and although outwardly he acted as an Ismaili, he was punctual in "prayers" as well as "fasts." In 1947, he went for Hajj and the following year he wrote to the Aga Khan Ismaili Provincial Council declaring his faith as Shia Ithna-Asheri and informing them that he had transferred some of his properties to the Khoja Shia Ithna-Asheri Kuwwat Jamaat to be used for religious purposes.[109]

ESMAILBHAI SUBJALI THAWER

Letter to Ismailia Provincial Council Honorary Secretary, H. H. The Agakhan Esmailia Provincial Council, Zanzibar.

Acknowledging your letter no. 1148 of 4-12-48. We had contributed as 'waqf' the income of House No 2518 to the President and Secretary of Khoja Shia Ithnasheri Kuwwatul Islam Jamat to be spent towards a feast in the name of "Panjatane paak" {five infallibles} in 1947, in order to register, the council of chambers has called me to answer on this issue on Wednesday, 8th December 1948 at 7.15.

In reply to this, I regret to inform you that your reporter has presented only about one property {house} By the grace of Almighty Lord and with the intercedence of the five infallibles, in fact I have contributed several properties {houses} income to be utilized for feasts in the name of the five infallibles as this is my religious belief. Your faith is against such deeds thus by this letter, I now detach myself from your jamat and embrace the pure faith of Shiasm.

Signed: Haji Esmail Subjali Thawer.
Translated by; F. Ali, Trade Directory 1960

Another example of conversion was that of Hassanali Salehmohamed. By his own account, he lived in Kaberamaido, Uganda from 1929. Until 1953, the Khoja Shia Ithna-Asheri families and Ismailies there held religious gatherings together. He was an Ismaili at the time and held the position of *Mukhi*. In 1954, a proclamation came from Aga Khan that all his followers had to sign a form declaring that he was god. Hassanali promptly resigned from the *Mukhi* position and with his brothers, Rajabali and Yusuf, converted to the Shia Ithna-Asheri faith. Hassanali and his uncle, Gulamhussein Ladha, went on to build an *imambada* and *musafarkhana* (Travellers Lodge) in Kaberamaido, which was completed in 1958. They also contributed towards the construction of a primary school there.

During conversations with community elders, many such examples of conversion from Ismaili to Ithna-Asheri faith came up. These oral narratives need to be documented in the communal archive or risk being lost forever.

3.5.2 Turbulent Times

Once they had achieved a level of stability, the nascent Khoja Shia Ithna-Asheries in Zanzibar urgently needed to understand their chosen faith better.[110] By 1890, there were two main religious scholars serving the community. One of them was Agha Abdulhussein Mar'ashi who had come to Zanzibar in 1881 form Najaf via Bombay and the other was Molvi Gulamhusein from Hyderabad.

Seyid AbdulHussein Mar'ashi (centre) who was sent to Zanizbar in 1301 A.H. with his son Syed Mehdi (L) and Syed Jawad (R).

When Agha Mar'ashi arrived in Zanzibar with his wife, a daughter and two sons, there were only a few Khoja Shia Ithna-Asheri families in Zanzibar. Once he had surveyed the situation, Agha wrote a letter to Sheikh Mazindarani (an eminent scholar) of Najaf with the names of four people that he requested to be accepted as trustees of the mosque. In reply, Sheikh Mazindarani wrote saying to him: 'my trustworthy wakil, Sayyid Abdulhussein, has written to me to appoint these people as trustees - and I accept and hereby appoint them as (such).'[111]

According to an interview with Agha Sayyid Mehdi Shushtary, as Agha Mar'ashi began to provide religious knowledge and instruction, more families joined the growing Khoja Shia Ithna-Asheri community. The Ismaili's targeted him as the source of what they perceived to be disloyalty and abandonment from their own. He had to endure a lot of hostile behaviour, listen to abusive language and was often attacked. On many occasions, he had dirt thrown on him such that he was forced to return home to change his clothes before going back to the mosque.

SAYYID HUSSAIN SHUSTARY (D. 1945)

Sayyid Mar'ashi wrote a letter to Ayatollah Mazindarani to find a suitable husband for his daughter. Sayyid Hussain Habibullah Shushtary was suggested and the wedding took place at the Musafarkhana of Haji Remtullah Tejani.

After the passing away of Sayyid Mar'ashi, Agha Sayyid Hussain Shushtary arrived in Zanzibar with his wife and children to serve the Khoja Shia Ithna-Asheri community there. He was highly respected by the community and passed away in 1945.

(Courtesy: Africa Federation)

On the other hand, the Sultan and scholars from different sects held Agha Mar'ashi in very high esteem, so much that when there was famine in Zanzibar, Sultan Syed Bargash requested him to pray for rain and when he did, the dry spell came to an end.[112] Agha passed away in 1905 whilst performing Hajj. He is buried in Mecca.

Haji Remtullah Tejani was, a humble generous man who had built a free *musafarkhana* (guesthouse) in Zanzibar. He was well respected not only in his own community but also by the Indian community of Zanzibar for his generosity. His virtuous contributions was recognised officially by Kuwwat Jamaat in 1901. During his visitation to holy place of Najaf, he met up with the Marja of the time and requested the services of Agha Sayyid Hussain Shustary (Agha Mar'ashi's son-in-law) for the community in Zanzibar.[113]

The other scholar - Molvi Gulamhusein - captivated many Khoja Shia Ithna-Asheries with his eloquent sermons.[114] Differences of opinion on some *fiqhi* (jurisprudence) issues arose between Agha Mar'ashi and Molvi Gulamhusein leading to an acrimonious debate that took a divisive turn for the community in Zanzibar. The group that supported Molvi Gulamhusein decided to form another Jamaat and named it Khoja Shia Ithna-Asheri Hujjatul Islam Jamaat (*Nai Misid*). Its initial membership was around 100 members and amongst its prominent pioneers were the families of Lakha Kanji, Ali Mohamed Khalfan, Abdulrasool Datoo, Mohamed Sheriff Dewani, Ali Dungersi, Karim Allarakhia and Dewji Dhanji, all mainly from Jamnagar.

Khoja Shia Ithna-Asheri Hujjatul Islam Jamaat Mosque (Nai Misid)
(Courtesy: Dewani family)

Following the formation of the Hujjatul Islam Jamaat[115], a plot was obtained at the corner of Sokomohogo/Mkunazini for the Hujjat (*Nai*) mosque[116] and two *imambadas* - for women and gents respectively. These were built in 1890 and Mulla Gulamhusein laid the foundation stone himself. The mosque had an attractively styled minaret funded by Mohamed Remtulla Merali. This minaret became Zanzibar's highest structure, commanding a spectacular view. The *muezzin* (one who calls to prayer) would climb up to its top twice daily, at noon and at dusk, to deliver the *adhaan* (call for prayers). On the eve of the end of Ramadhan (month of fasting), the minaret would become the centre of attraction with many faithful climbing it to sight the new moon for the next day's celebrations. Hyderabadi/ Lucknawi influences were also obvious in the architecture of the *imambada*.

It had a long flight of wooden steps ascending to the corridor gallery that opened into an immense oblong *imambada* lined with rows of windows. Rich, colourful Persian and Kashmiri carpets interspersed with straw mats to cover the floor and provide comfortable seating for those attending. From the ceiling hung rows of fans and intricate lights. One of its trademark features were the elegant chandeliers with free-flowing glass pendants that glittered and sparkles when lit up on celebratory occasions. At the front, in a place of honour, stood a replica of the Karbala mausoleum.[117]

Inside the Nai Masjid
(Courtesy: Abdulrazak Sheriff Fazal)

Presidents of Hujjatul Islam Jamaat included well-known personalities such as Abdulrasool Hassan Virjee, Abdulrasool Khalfan, Abdulla Khalfan, Ahmed Lakha, Ahmed Datoo, Ramzan Khamis Damji, Anwer Hassan Virjee, Hussain Hassam Nasser, Yusuf Hassam Nasser, Mussa Ghulamhussein Lakha, Yusuf Salehmohamed, M. A. Rasool, Hussain Remtulla, Pyarali Giga, Akbar Nasser Thawer, Yusuf Karim Allarakhia, Jaffer Karim Jetha and Abbas Mohamed Sheriff.

Some of the members of the community occupied official positions in the Zanzibari society such as Ahmed Lakha and Anwer Hassan Virjee who both became members of the Zanzibar Legislative

Council. Ahmed Datoo was the Commissioner of Customs and Abdulrasool Dewji Dhanji held the position of the Secretary at the main government Secretariat based in Zanzibar.

MULLA AHMED A. M. LAKHA

Born in Zanzibar in 1900, Mulla Ahmed was largely self-taught. He acquired a high level of education as well as spoke many languages including Arabic and Farsi. He served the community as Zakire-e-Hussein for almost 65 years and taught at Sir Euvan Smith Madressa Primary School.

His recognitions include a decoration by the Sultan of Zanzibar in 1936 of a Silver Jubilee medal, nominating him as an Honourable Member of Zanzibar Legislative Council and the decoration of M.B.E. in 1952 by the British Government.

He served as the President of Hujjatul Islam Jamaat of Zanzibar representing them in Federation Meetings. He has also served as the Vice Chairman of the Supreme Council and was awarded the "Hussein Medal" in appreciation of his dedicated services.

Datoo Hemani and Nasser Noormohamed Kasmani were prominent philanthropists who had entrusted their communal properties to the Hujjat Jamaat. The 'Datoo Hemani Kanyashara' provided education for the girls of the community and the 'Khoja Nasser Noormohamed Dispensary'[118] provided medical facilities.

The dispensary building was originally built to commemorate Queen Victoria's Jubilee.[119] In 1901, Kasmani bought the building and decided to convert the upper floors into apartments whose rental income supported the dispensary on the ground floor. The dispensary is now a 'Cultural Centre' and a main tourist attraction in Zanzibar. With its open roof terrace and flamboyant balconies, it stands majestically alongside other architectural structures like the Sultan's Palace (now People's Palace) and Beit Al Ajaib along Forodhani on the seafront.

Kasmani donated the 'Khoja Nasser Noormohamed Dispensary' in memory of his son who passed away at a young age, and this facility benefitted all Khojas, Ithna-Asheries and Ismaili. Practitioners from many faiths served there and the medical practice in those days was based mainly on a doctor's ability to diagnose from examination and a history of symptoms.

THE OLD KHOJA ITHNA-ASHERI DISPENSARY

Located on the seafront on Mizingani Road, this building served as a dispensary in the first half of the 20th century. It is a finely decorated symbol of the multi-cultural architecture and heritage of Zanzibar.

Tharia Topan commissioned the building in 1887 and completed it in 1894. In 1900 the building was bought by Hajji Nasser Noormohamed Kasmani who converted the ground floor into a dispensary and the upper floors into apartments.
(Africa Federation Archives)

Prescriptions until the middle of the 20th century consisted of *puri* (powder) and white or coloured medicines. The "compounders" Husain (Madawa) and Fida Mammu Molu would grind the tablets into *puri*, prepare the mixtures into the prescribed medicine and label the doses on the bottle. They even provided a pack of *malam* (ointment) if prescribed. Hassani, the highly competent male nurse, would apply yellow or red medicine on cuts and boils and then bandage them efficiently.[120] It was common practice for doctors to prescribe homeopathic and local medicines to their patients.

SALEH ALARAKHIYA HIRJI (SALEH MADAWA)

He had a shop selling herbal medicine. Those who visited him would see shelves behind him full of old biscuit tins containing hundreds of medicines. He was an expert on traditional Indian medicine and had a memory so sharp that without looking at labels, he could pull out the right tin with the corrrect herbs.

Saleh Madawa had a number of local assistants from Makunduchi who may have picked up a lot of the knowledge on Indian traditional medicines. After the Saleh family moved to Dar es Salaam, the local assistants inherited the shop and went on to add their own local Zanzibari traditional medicines.

The knowledge he passed on survived his lifetime and the descendants of his assisstants run their own "Duka ya Saleh Madawa" i.e Shop of Saleh's Medicine.

(Courtesy of Abdulrazak Fazal)

Another notable personality from the *Nai Misid* was Haji Rhemtulla Tejani. He opened the Haji Rhemtulla Tejani Dharamsara (guesthouse) in 1900 for community members visiting Zanzibar and the British Resident Governor inaugurated it. The *Bewakhana* (house for widows) was built by Mohamed Alarakhiya Shivji (Mamu Chiku) in 1932. Today, this Bewakhana has been converted into a guesthouse for travellers visiting the community members.

Haji Remtulla Tejani (left) donated Haji Remtulla Tejani 'Musafarkhana' built in 1901 (right).

Haji Mohamed Allarakhia Shivji (left) donated 'Bewakhana' (living space for widows).

Whilst the community was putting social, educational and health infrastructure in place, there were cracks appearing in its religious and spiritual grounding. It is interesting to note that within a period of less than ten years after establishing a separate identity from the main Khoja Community, the Shia Ithna-Asheries were undergoing a further split from within. The reasons for this are not entirely clear.[121]

Was it due to the differences of opinion on religious issues? Was it the charismatic personality of Mulla Gulamhusein that persuaded some community members to break away? Was it a caste/culture related issue in that those who came from Jamnagar felt insecure as they were outnumbered by Kachchhi Khojas who dominated Kuwwat Jamaat (*Juni Misid*) committees under Agha Mar'ashi?

All of these reasons together could have been the cause of the turmoil that resulted in the formation of Hujjatul Islam Jamaat. It may be that after the arrival of Molvi Gulamhusein from Hyderabad and the emergence of differences between the two scholars, Kathiawad Khoja Shia Ithna-Asheries felt more comfortable with him, but there is no evidence of this in communal records. Sadly, for the community, conflicting opinions was not where it ended. Oral traditions show that this division became so intense and passionate, that Khoja Shia Ithna-Asheries of Zanzibar not only boycotted each other's mosque but also avoided wedlock.

While one can speculate on the need for such a decisive split, the true reason needs further exploration. Why the Zanzibari Khoja Shia Ithna-Asheries would choose to split at a time when they were just establishing their new identity and needed to unite against the challenges from the larger Khoja community still remains an intriguing question. From conversations with the elder generation, there is a perception that the core of Hujjat Jamaat (*Nai Misid*)'s members were cultural traditionalists[122] who had stuck to their roots and languages (Gujarati and Kutchi). They were influential and had connections with the Sultans of the time. Being prominent, some even maintained a good relationship with Khoja Ismailis after the split from them to the extent that the Aga Khan would pay a visit to their *pedhi* (shop).

After two splits - one from the main community and a second internal one - over a period of two decades, archival records show that the Khoja Shia Ithna-Asheries of Zanzibar gradually adapted to their differences, accepted both Jamaats as theirs and moved on. Another twenty years down the line, Khoja Shia Ithna-Asheries plunged themselves in to another contentious and challenging *al-musawaat* debate between Allama Haji Naji[123] and Mulla Mohamed Jaffer Sheriff Dewji.[124] This time with drastically different processes and results.

The core issue upon which there was a difference of opinion was the matter of Prophet Muhammed (pbuh) and Imam Ali (pbuh) being *musawaat* (equal). The debate raged on via a number of publications

– the details of each side and expert opinions of qualified scholars on this issue is available to this day. However, the main point of reflection here is in how the Khoja Shia Ithna-Asheries of the 1920s dealt with this new conflict of opinions. They were well aware that a debate of this import could divide the still fledgling community further and weaken the unity they had worked so hard to create after the first split. For them to keep the community together, two fundamental questions needed to be resolved: firstly: what was the etiquette of intellectual engagement in the community? and secondly: what role should the community religious scholars and leaders of the community play?

It is an indication of the underlying wisdom of the community leaders that they they did not choose to simply ignore the issue. Had they chosen the attitude of sweeping problems under the carpet, they perhaps would not have grown intellectually or spiritually as a community in the way that they did. The community chose to deal with this challenge in a reflective way that showed their maturity.

The *al-musawaat* debate between Allama Haji Naji and Mulla Mohamed Jaffer Sheriff Dewji was handled with humility, patience, cordiality and intellectual engagement attesting to the scholarly and pious nature of both individuals.

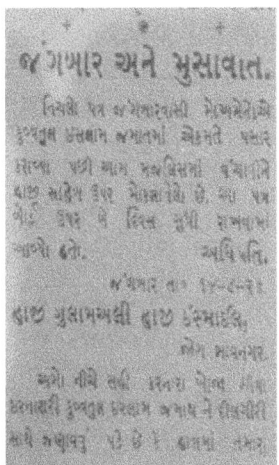
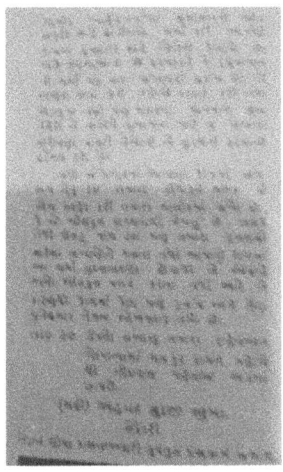

Unanimous resolution, passed by Kuwwatul Islam Jamaat, expressing the feelings and concerns of the community on the issue of 'musawaat'. The letter, written and signed by the secretary of jamaat Ahmed Haji Juma, on 14/8/1923.
(Courtesy: 'Chaudmi Sadi, Pustak biju, Muharram 1342, Ank pahelo)

Neither tried to have the other banned or boycotted and they debated the issues by way of publications in the community forums. In doing so, they emerged as two of the most eminent learned leaders in the Khoja Community. In the 1920s, the Khoja Shia Ithna-Asheries in East Africa had little exposure to scholars from Najaf or Qum. It was home-grown, self-taught personalities like Haji Naji, Haji Mohamed Jaffer Sheriff Dewji and others, who guided the community. They helped build the corpus of religious understanding, accepting diversity whilst keeping the community united on core belief objectives that identified the community.

The way the community handled the issue of *al-musawaat* shows the significant growth that the Khoja Shia Ithna-Asheries in East Africa had achieved by the 1920s. They were not averse to nurturing the minds of ordinary members of the community in order to enhance understanding and propagation of their faith. To achieve this, they relied mainly on a collaborative get-together of scholars, philanthropists, and volunteers. The *al-musawaat* episode clearly showed that such a process assisted the leaders to understand the pulse of their community and manage disagreements in a pragmatic manner without resorting to banning either of the scholars. This process allowed them to maturely resolve not just religious, but also social, economic and political differences within the community.

3.6 Mehfils and Female Influencers.

The cultural and religious importance of *mehfils*[125] cannot be overstated. After the mosque and the *imambada*, *mehfils* were one of the most important aspects of religious life and rituals for the Khoja Shia Ithna-Asheri community. Whilst the two religious scholars, Agha Mar'ashi and Molvi Ghulamhussein concentrated on educating the community on the correct Shia Ithna-Asheri tenets, local speakers gave *majalises* - often at *mehfils* - in Gujarati, Kachchhi and Urdu languages. These were heart-rendering and passionately delivered to the congregation who, in turn engaged with equal emotion, particularly when the rendition of the massacre of the family of Imam Hussein (pbuh) was recounted.

Amongst those who recited lamentations and lectures were Mulla Ahmed Lakha and Mulla Mohammed Walji.[126] Such was the talent of these reciters that they attracted listeners from many communities in Zanzibar and from mainland East Africa as well.

When Agha Mar'ashi and Agha Shustary arrived, they did so with their extended families and as they grew in number . Despite being from non-Khoja backgrounds, their knowledge and cordial nature attracted the Khoja community who frequented their Mehfile Bibi Fatema located at Malindi Lane. Ladies from the Shia Ithna-Asheri community - Khoja and otherwise - would often meet in the evenings and nights for religious lectures. After *majalis* there was time for social interaction as well. With the common Kiswahili language making communication easier, they all bonded over a *paan* (edible leaves with betel) and cigarettes (a common habit in Zanzibar) to the extent that Aghas' families were considered part of the Khoja Shia Community.

The Mar'ashis (L) & Shustarys of Zanzibar (R)
(Courtesy : Abdulrazak Sheriff Fazal)

Mehfils in Zanzibar became an integral part of the religious infrastructure and a model for socio-religious interaction for the community, particularly for women. Over the years, this model of *mehfils* found itself replicated in many Khoja Shia Ithna-Asheri communities across East Africa. These smaller informal institutions provided social and educational support for the community beyond the main *masjid* and *imambada*. Professor Iqbal Akhtar has written a valuable paper on the evolution of *mehfils* in Dar es Salaam that provides a unique insight into the social, cultural and religious utility of these institutions.[127]

The story of Karbala is essential to understanding the context of mehfils and their importance. Commemorating the martyrdom of

Imam Hussein (pbuh) and his family and companions is the oldest, continuously existing tradition within Islamic history. While the lamentations (*azadari*) had a moral aspect in that they promoted understanding and learning, they were also a source of unity for the Khoja Shia Ithna-Asheri community of Zanzibar. Their identity was intertwined with the preservation of this tradition and their passion towards it was evident from the number of renowned reciters the community produced.

Wherever they moved to settle, the Zanzibari Shia Ithna-Asheries replicated their way of *azadari* and promoted the passionate remembrance of events in Karbala in their host community. This unique evolution of *azadari* rituals probably originated from the many *mehfils* that existed in late 19th and early 20th century in Zanzibar, including Mehfile Bibi Fatema and Matam Baharani.[128]

When the Kuwwat mosque was completed in 1881, there was no place yet for holding religious events. Commemorations and celebrations were held at the old School Faize building, but this was not adequate for the growing community. Another location was found at Sokomohogo known as 'Kiwanjani' (*kiwanja* means an open piece of land in Kiswahili) and it became the gathering place for such occasions. The community built separate shelters on this land so that both women and men could take part in the religious ceremonies. The programmes were organised under the leadership of Mulla Abdullah Saleh Sachedina.

Iranian and Bahraini Shia also participated in these programmes, particularly in Muharram. The Zanzibari Khojas - with their classic versatility - soon incorporated the Iranian/Bahraini way of doing *matam*, and slowly spread it to the other Khoja Shia communities in East Africa. In 1926, Mehfile 'Kiwanjani' moved to its present place in Kiponda.

Later Mehfile Shahe Khorasan (named after the Eighth Imam of the Shia Ithna-Asheries) was amalgamated into it and it retains its original name to the present day. Mehfile Bibi Zainab was another popular location where women of the community met in the evenings. The *mehfil* began at Ibrahim Kassam's residence where his mother, Bai

Safia, ran it. It then moved to Malindi and was taken over by her daughter, Bai Nuru (Mrs. Nurubai Mohamed Jaffer Sheriff Dewji).[129]

Mehfile Shahe Khorasan (Kiwanjani)

Left: Gents Entrance   Right: Ladies Entrance

In 1960, there was a grand opening ceremony of 'zareeh' (A symbolic replica of a structure that encloses a grave) of Imam Reza (pbuh) at Kiwanjani. It was brought from India and inaugurated in the presence of community members. It stood on the left side of the pulpit and on the right side was another 'zareeh' of Imam Hussein (pbuh).

In the month of Ramadhan, 'darsa' (recitation of Qur'an) would be held at Kiwanjani and 'istekhan' (black tea) served. 'Iftaar' (breaking of the fast) was also held throughout the month. 'Eid e Zahra' (birthday of Lady Fatema Zahra, daughter of the Prophet of Islam (peace be upon them) celebrations were also a main event. To this day, 'Kiwanjani' still abides by these traditions.

(Courtesy: Abdulrazak Sheriff Fazal and Africa Federation Archives)

At that time, the community did not have *mulyanis* (female religious scholars) or *zakiras* (female reciters) from India or Pakistan to cater for the spiritual needs of the women. Many of the local female members came forward to try and fill this gap. These women dedicated themselves to reading and studying books written in Gujarati and Urdu and then conveying them in Kachchhi and Gujarati, using simple, relevant concepts. They performed these religious duties on a voluntary basis and as they grew older, trained younger women to take over the cause. Over generations, their selfless service inspired an army of committed female scholars, volunteers and philanthropists who continue the tradition of serving the numerous *mehfils* that exist in Khoja Shia communities in Zanzibar and worldwide.

Imambadas and *mehfils* in Zanzibar and other places in East Africa became sacred buildings in which the remembrances of the family of the Prophet Muhammad (pbut) took place. The centrality of the *mehfil's* function was to encourage the women of the community to integrate the lessons from the lives of the Holy family into their own. The lectures given expressed ideal behaviour, doctrines of Islam, Shia theology and laws that were meant to inform local social habits. The mourning assemblies were meant to create an emotive experience that would then motivate the listeners to aspire to higher ideals.

In the formative period of the community in Zanzibar, Khoja Shia Ithna-Asheries excluded women from any intellectual or decision-making gatherings. *Mehfils* provided these women with a sacred, central space in which they could discuss their challenges and chart out their own role within the community. They attended in large numbers, usually bringing their children with them and through recalling and lamenting over the Tragedy of Karbala they accessed the social, ethical and spiritual aspects of the personalities involved to use as exemplars. In this way, the women tried to shape not only their own spiritual and everyday practices, but also of the generation that they were nurturing.

The archive office of the Africa Federation has compiled a list of dedicated female scholars of the East African community from 1881 to date. The list is incomplete and a work in progress, but it does show the dedication of women in meeting the needs of their own. By 2018, there were 74 women from Dar es Salaam, Zanzibar and Pemba, 23 from Arusha, 11 from Bukoba, 1 from Kilwa, 12 from Moshi, 10 from Tanga, 2 from Tabora, 2 from Mikindani, 6 from Kigoma, 3 from Dodoma, 13 from Songea, 7 from Singida, 10 from Lindi, 7 from Mwanza, 6 from Morogoro, 3 from Pangani, 15 from Mombasa and 6 from Nairobi.[130]

Among these female scholars, some were undoubtedly visionary; one of them was Fatimabai Mohamed Shariff. According to some elders, she was a *mulyani* - a female religious scholar - who came from Mumbai, India to Zanzibar and then made her way to Dar es Salaam. She travelled along the coast as well as into the interior of East Africa residing among Khoja Shia Ithna-Asheri communities and observing the womenfolk. She found a general lack of knowledge and neglect regarding the basic understanding of cleanliness, prayers and even male circumcision - which was an obligatory ritual in the Islamic faith.

Appalled by this level of religious ignorance amongst the Ithna-Asheri women, she made it her mission to educate those in Dar es Salaam, mostly through female religious education. She needed a vehicle to disseminate this knowledge effectively to the women and thus, she established a *mehfil* dedicated to Abbas, the brother of Imam Hussein (pbuh). Here, they observed the events on the religious calendar and held classes on religious rituals as well.

While Fatimabai was busy running the daily front of the mehfil activities, she was also embroiled in a dispute in the background that played out over her entire lifetime. There are two versions of what happened. The official document[131] published by Dar es Salaam Jamaat in the 1960s records that Fatmabai originally purchased the land on which Mehfile Abbas stands and the building with funds she collected from the community. The title deed of the land and building were transferred to the Khoja Shia Ithna-Asheri Jamaat of Dar es Salaam on 23 January 1937 and registered on 23 February 1941. In this way, she relinquished ownership to Dar es Salaam Jamaat. The aforementioned publication also provides the minutes for the discussion about Mehfile Abbas, as well as an exchange of letters between the officials of Dar es Jamaat and Fatmabai from 1937 to 1962.

The minutes and the contents of the letters from the publication provide the timeline of the transfer of land. It offers an insight into how elders of the community at the time had their own individual insight in solving an issue. It also reveals, in quite a lot of detail, the subsequent core challenge regarding who should have control of the running of Mehfile Abbas and under whom the control should be vested, the extent of autonomy in decision-making, and ultimately the final decision-making authority over Mehfile Abbas and how any conflict should be resolved.

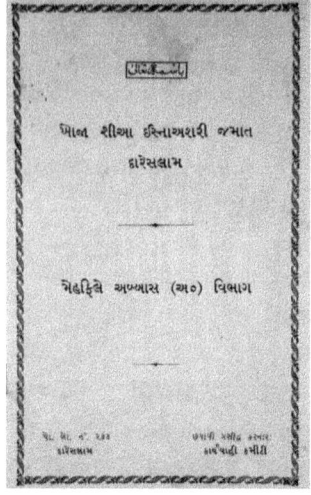

The Front Cover and Page that show the land transfer of Mehfile Abbas

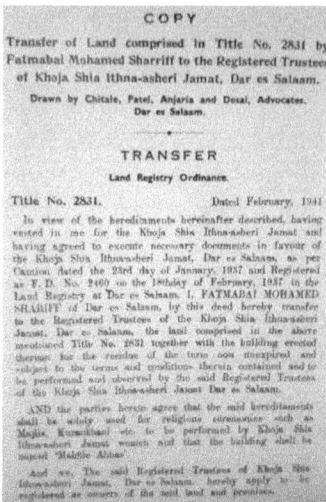

Letter from Fatmabai Mohammed (Fatu Mumbai) written to the President of Dar es Salaam Jamaat in 1962

This is the official version that also states that the possession of Mehfile Abbas happened during the tenure of Alhaj Mohammedbhai Khalfan. He was the Hon. Secretary of the Dar es Salaam Jamaat. He sometimes chaired the meetings of the Management Committee as the President, Alhaj Nurmohamed Nasser, was not keeping well and the Jamaat had no one in the position of Vice-President.

MEHFILE ABBAS 1937 (L) AND MEHFILE ABBAS 2020 (R)
(Courtesy: Africa Federation Archives)

The second version - narrated from observers of the period - recounts that Fatmabai was very successful in her efforts with the women. Under her direct supervision, Mehfile Abbas became a major religious and cultural centre. She became the voice through which the needs of the women were articulated. She touched the lives of many positively and was fondly known by all - men, women and children - as "Fatu Mumbai".[132] According to some members of the community, this success of Fatmabai ultimately threatened the leadership of the Jamaat. They out-manoeuvred her by going to court and applying to have the property re-zoned from a private dwelling to a religious structure thus effectively transferring ownership to the Jamaat.

There were heated debates in the editorial section of 'The Standard' newspaper. Eventually, because of the pressure from the leaders of the community, she gave up the Mehfil to Jamaat control. This was a tremendous setback for her and she felt betrayed by the very people who were supposed to help her promote religion; the shift in control meant a minimization of her role in the programming decision of the Mehfil. This crushed her spirit and eventually she stopped attending altogether. She died broken-hearted a few years later.

Between the official public version available for anyone to read and verbal account of those who were present about the effect this handover had on Fatmabai is an unaccounted state of affairs that was no doubt greatly sensitive. One can only guess how divisive this issue had been for the community for it to take nearly forty years of patient discussion between Fatmabai and the Jamaat to resolve it and for her to eventually relinquish her control of Mehfile Abbas.

Regardless of how the events actually played out, the undeniable fact remains that to date Mehfile Abbas symbolises Fatmabai's reformist action and her courage to initiate a religious awakening for the women of the community of Dar es Salaam. She had the character and personality required to establish Mehfil Abbas with such sincere intention that it not only survived the decades, but has now evolved into a multipurpose centre for the entire community in Dar es Salaam. The Mehfil holds educational and religious events, seminars and conferences and where today, both genders contribute in making decisions on behalf of the community of Dar es Salaam and the broader regions. In the Mehfile Abbas of today, the vision of Fatu Mumbai has come to fruition.

Another remarkable woman in the Dar es Salaam community was Kulsumbai Abdalla Khimji. The contents of her lectures were enthralling and delivered in her distinctive, easy-going style. She encouraged the local women to study spiritual matters and her presentation of religious precepts increased the thirst for more knowledge within the female population of the community. The community bestowed on her the "Fatemi Medal" for her services to the community. She was the first recipient of this medal from the Africa Federation.

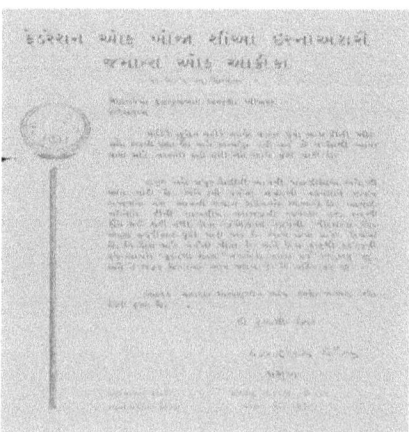

'Fatemi Medal' citation for Kulsumbai Abadalla Khimji from the Federation of Khoja Shia Ithna-Asheri Jamaats of Africa presented by Late Mohamedali Meghji, Chairman.
(27/11/1964)

Kanizbai Chandoo appears in the records as yet another woman who spent her life dedicated to the service of the community. She was born in Zanzibar in November 1927 to Fazal Meghji and Fatmabai Alibhai and the eldest of their five children. At 18 years of age, Kanizbai married Gulamhussein F. K. Chandoo and settled in Tanga. She started teaching Qur'an recitation and religious studies to children of the community from her home. As her class grew in size, it shifted to the community mosque where she continued teaching Qur'an for many years.

Kanizbai or Baiji as she was known was brought up by her grandfather, Marhum Alibhai Dhanji. Her services to the Tanga Jamaat include attending to social and family matters, running the madrasah, volunteering in ghusl/kafan, hosting visiting zakiras and running the Ladies Qur'an Darsa in Ramadhan.

Her family also followed her legacy in serving the community. At her retirement, Kanizbai was honored as the Mother of the Jamaat for her selfless dedication.

(Source: Africa Federation Archives)

KANIZ BAI CHANDOO

Fatmabai Dhirani was born in Bukoba on 20 September 1932 to Fazalbhai and Mariambai Dhirani. After moving to Dar es Salaam, she married Jafferbhai Alidina at the age of 15. She began reciting religious lectures at 18 years and touched many in the community with her words. She was active in community work and taught sewing, reading and writing. She inspired many others to become active members of the community.

"I worked with Fatmabai for many years and she built my confidence and encouraged me to be a Zakira." - Raziabai Janmohammed

"I worked under Fatmabai's guidance and found her a dedicated, sincere and capable leader. She upheld the truth regardless of repercussions. She had good leadership qualities and would consult her team in decision-making. She was a diligent worker and situations did not make her lose courage. She is always in my duas for Allah (SWT) to keep her with her loved ones and all those who served in the community who are no longer with us."
-Fatmabai Rajwani

FATMA BAI DHIRANI

(Source: Africa Federation Archives)

Women formed the unseen backbone of the new Khoja Shia Ithna-Asheri Jamaats in Zanzibar and those springing in many other places in East Africa. As soon as the *jamaats* were established, women emerged within each of them to share their religious knowledge and give their time voluntarily towards uplifting their sisters. There was sufficient awareness among womenfolk about the important role they played within the community that in 1954, when the Husainy Trust of Madras (Chennai) appealed for funds to build an orphanage in Husainabad, Madras (Chennai) it was the women of the community who came forward in large numbers to donate towards the noble project. Many became members of the Trust as yearly contributors.[133]

Sadly, despite the gallant efforts of many women over the years, community leadership hardly recognised their contributions in the early years. However, by the 1960s there was an official acknowledgement that not much had been done at Jamaat or Federation level to recognise their voice and cater to their needs.

3.7 Qur'an Reciters

Zanzibar with all its Arab influence over the years was bound to be a town in which reciters of the Qur'an thrived. Over time, some individuals emerged within Khoja Shia Ithna-Asheri community whose recitation was so engaging that locals of all faiths would listen and appreciate their talent. The most famous of these was Mu'aalim Abdulrasul Bandali. He had a distinctive accent and a melodious voice that used to be broadcast all over Zanzibar on '*Sauti Ya Unguja*' (Voice of Zanzibar) radio.[134] Many tuned in to listen to his Qur'an recitation and his rendition of the famous supplications of Kumail, Iftitah, Waritha and Arbaeen. Every year, on Ashura (10th day of Muharram), during the lamentation describing the massacre of the grandson of the Prophet in Karbala, he would get up to call the traditional "last adhan" that never failed to move the masses to tears.

Beyond having a mellifluous voice, Maalim Bandali was a compassionate man. Both the community and the British Government appreciated his services, the latter awarding him a Coronation Medal in 1953. He also received the Order of the Brilliant Star (*Wisam al-Kawkab al-Durri*) from the Sultan of Zanzibar for his services to the government.

Mu'allim Abdulrasul Bandali receiving the Order of Brilliant Star by the Sultan of Zanzibar, Sayyid Sir Abdullah bin Khalifa bin Harub for his services to the Government.

His son, Murtaza - famously known as Maalim Murtaza - followed in his father's footstep. Over decades he has provided melodious Qur'anic and religious renditions on countless occasions for the appreciation of the global Shia community. Amongst the Asians of Zanzibar, Maalim Bandali and his son were the only father-son pair to have recited *Barzanji* (a rhythmic narration in praise of the Prophet) during the Prophet (pbuh)'s birth celebrations (*Maulidi*) at Mnazimoja.[135]

3.8 Activism and Media

The history of Zanzibar media began when Sultan Bargash established the Sultanate Press (*al- Matba'an al-Sultaniyya*) in the 1880s. The first paper in East Africa was a small Swahili quarterly booklet, *Msimulizi* (The Reporter), edited and printed in October 1888.[136] The first issue of the weekly *The Gazette for Zanzibar and East Africa*, popularly known as *The Gazette*, appeared on 1 February 1892. It was published by a British trading company in Zanzibar and became the official channel of communication to the public.

A new Swahili monthly newspaper, *Habari za Mwezi* (Monthly News), appeared in October 1895 and lasted until 1910.[137] On 9 July

1899, the Indian community launched a Gujarati paper, the *Zanzibar Vepar Samachar* (Zanzibar Business News). It was published every Sunday and quite popular within the Indian community leading *The Gazette* to comment that 'judging from the first number, we think it is likely to be a success'.

Zanzibar Akhbar (The Zanzibar News) was established in 1900 in a house in Shangani by Bhairamji Hormasji Mory. It was published in Gujarati and English, starting as a weekly, becoming a daily before finally going back to a weekly. It was published by the Mori Press and was still in print in 1917.[138] It is in this context that Fazalbhai Janmohammed made an attempt to fill a valuable niche in the media industry of Zanzibar and succeeded admirably.

Born in 1873 in Hyderabad, Fazalbhai came to Zanzibar in 1890 when he was 17 years old. After working in the Customs authorities for a while, he joined Sir Euan Smith Madressa as a teacher. He was so popular and likeable that he was soon accorded the title "Master" which has since become his synonymous surname. A suitable opportunity to express his passion came in 1895 when he bought a printing press in partnership with Mr Saleh Chagpar and another member of the community. This partnership lasted for a short while during which time Fazalbhai learnt the art of printing. The chance to own a printing press came his way again when Valabhdas Kalyanji and Gokaldas Hansraj provided him with the facilities of one. It was here that he published the first issue of *Islam Samachar* - a single-sheet purely Gujarati paper[139]- on 28 July 1901. This historical event is preserved in the Zanzibar archives.[140]

FAZAL JANMOHAMMED MASTER

Mr. Yusufali A. Karimjee Jivanjee, a prominent member of the Bohora community, assisted Fazalbhai both in his personal capacity and through his company. This support was invaluable and *Islam Samachar* continued to print appearing every Sunday until 30 July 1903. It changed its name to the *Zanzibar Samachar* in August 1903 and became a daily on 30 July 1906. Circumstances, however, were not favourable for a daily newspaper. In addition, Fazalbhai's efforts to incorporate English columns in the paper were not successful and circulation diminished. The paper did not go to print in October 1911 when Master went to India. On his return, the *Zanzibar Samachar* resumed first as a daily, then a weekly under a new name: *El Islam & Samachar*. At this time, there were five presses in Zanzibar: the Union, the Meher, the Najah, the De Lord Press, and the Husseni Printing Press (Master's).[141]

By 1913, the media industry in Zanzibar was fading. Fazalbhai Master shut down the paper, took his press to Mombasa and started a daily paper there called *East African Samachar*, its first issue being released on 29 January 1914. His press and paper flourished[142] and with successful marketing, he was able to sell the paper in parts of Uganda, as well as Mwanza and Bukoba in Tanganyika. In these years, his was the most important Indian newspaper in East Africa. Indians wrote to it frequently to present their grievances and make pleas for justice to the colonial authorities.[143]

Fazalbhai Master was committed to the truth and championed the just cause. In November 1911, a mass meeting was held to show sympathy towards the empire of Turkey and declare contempt against the cowardly step of Italy in occupying Libya. The leading members of almost all sects were there, amongst them Janab Ali Sayyed Abbas, from the Khoja Shia Ithna-Asheries, who chaired the meeting. Naser bin Suleman bin Naser Lemki was also present; as the son of the Governor of Dar es Salaam and a respected personality in his own right, his presence added weight to the protest. A sub-committee was formed to raise funds for those rendered helpless by the war, the aged, widows, and orphans and Fazalbhai was an active member of it[144]

At the beginning of the First World War in 1914, Fazalbhai Master published a daily Gujarati translation of Reuter's cables. This attracted

Indian readers eager to know of developments in the war. After a while, as wartime martial law began to monitor media activity, he stopped the publication as it was too risky to continue.

Fazalbhai Master returned to Zanzibar in 1916 and restarted *The Samachar* as a Gujarati weekly on Sunday, 1 May 1917 at an annual subscription of Rs. 10 and sold about 300 copies. He tried to introduce English columns to bolster the circulation but was unsuccessful again and so it remained a Gujarati-based newspaper.

His publications addressed public welfare and matters that were of benefit to Zanzibari society, paying particular attention to Islamic matters and specifically those relating to his own community, the Khoja Ithna-Asheries.[145] Despite this focus, by all accounts, he supported just causes without discrimination and his publications exposed injustices to any section of Zanzibar society.

A particular example is when Mr. Saleh Vali Dharsi, then President of the Ismailia Council, filed a libel case against Fazalbhai when he wrote a series of articles in support of those members of the Ismailia community, who used to attend the Muharram lectures. Fazalbhai lost the case in the Magistrate Court and was sentenced to four months in prison and a fine of Rs 750.00. On appeal, the case was heard in the High court, where Judge Murison stated that he could not see anything libellous except the use of the word "uneducated" in one place with respect to Mr. Saleh Vali Dharsi for which Fazalbhai was fined Rs 10.00.

There were other similar cases against Fazalbhai mostly brought about because of his firmness in standing his ground on causes he believed in.[146] After having firmly established Samachar over a strenuous and demanding quarter of a century, Fazalbhai decided to go on a pilgrimage to Karbala, Iraq. **In July 1920,** he and his wife Sat-bai left Zanzibar by sea. After arriving in Bombay, on the way to Kachchh, he had a heart attack and died on 18th August 1920 at the age of 48.

His son, Hassanali F. J. Master, took over the paper and although the news of his father's death overwhelmed him, it did not deter his zeal to preserve and improve the newspaper. He enlarged the size, increased the number of pages, and once again introduced English columns. By 1922, the circulation began to increase and it **became the most popular newspaper in East Africa, barring** *East African Standard* **and** *Tanganyika Standard*.[147] On Sunday, 27th December 1936, the paper took out a Silver Jubilee edition that contained historical photographs and interesting articles on the past of Zanzibar and other fascinating articles written by prominent people. The paper, its owner and staff received several letters of commendation and congratulations on publishing this edition.

For his media work and innovation in publishing a unique special edition, the Sultan of Zanzibar conferred upon him a Jubilee Medal. Encouraged by this positive response from the public to the Silver Jubilee edition, Hassanali went on to publish a coronation edition to celebrate the crowning of King George VI and Queen Elizabeth, which appeared on 11th May 1937. Hassanalibhai died suddenly due to heart failure on 19th December 1937, evoking widespread sincere sympathies from all quarters in Zanzibar as well as from all neighbouring territories. Sir J. Hathorn Hall[148] wrote that 'Hassanali will be very greatly missed in the realm of journalism and public affairs' expressing the widely held sentiment of the Zanzibar community.[149]

The burden of running the press and paper now fell upon Sat-bai, wife of Fazalbhai Master and mother of Hassanalibhai. From 1st January 1939, the newspaper began publishing under her name. Media was a special science requiring particular knowledge and experience, yet when the time came, Sat-bai took over and met the challenge head-on. Her handling of the situation must have been inspirational for the women of the community. At the time, it was unheard of a female in the Khoja Shia Ithna-Asheri community to possess media skills, let alone run a press. At a time when she could have chosen to enjoy a quiet retirement under the care of her family, Sat-bai boldly decided to take over the control of the newspaper to honour the work of her husband and her son.[150]

Mr Kashiram Khimdas, the Head Compositor and Manager, and Mr. Mohamedali A. Rahim, the Chief Editor, assisted her in this endeavour. During the Second World War, a shortage of materials led to reduction of the paper from 24 pages to 18 pages and then down further to just 12 pages. The popularity of the newspaper survived, but it suffered from a lack of advertising revenues. Such was the determination from Sat-bai and her staff that despite these setbacks and the constraints placed by the war, the newspaper did not miss a single publication. Sat-bai passed away in 1944.

With the death of Sat-bai, the responsibility fell to the next female head in the family - Sakinabai, the wife of Hassanalibhai. With the continued support of Mr Khimdas and Mr Rahim, she took control of the newspaper in 1944. With the war ending, trade began to expand and the economy improved, leading to advertisement revenue once again. The circulation of the newspaper began to increase and now it reached as far as India and Pakistan. Sakinabai expressed a desire to publish the Golden Jubilee issue, after which she intended to visit holy sites in Iran and Iraq. Sadly, Sakinabai passed away in 1952 after a short illness without fulfilling either of her desires. Her and Sat-bai's contributions as female proprietors of a highly-successful, international newspaper remain as an inspiring legacy in the history of Khoja Shia Ithna-Asheries of East Africa.[151]

With passing away of Sakinabai, the business now came into the hands of the children of Hassanalibhai and Sakinabai. Initially, Mohamed Rafik, her eldest son, took over the management of the press and the editorship of *The Samachar*. Due to his ill health shortly after, he passed on the editorship to his younger brother Roshanali who chose to continue to circulate the newspaper under the ownership of his older brother. He modernised the printing press by replacing the old metal types with a semi-automatic Heidelberg Machine.

In May 1952, he published the Golden Jubilee issue of *The Samachar* in memory of Mr and Mrs Fazal Master and Mr and Mrs Hassanali Master. This Golden Jubilee issue currently exists in the Zanzibar National Archive.[152]

The Samachar continued being published until August 1967 when the Zanzibar army confiscated the business and imprisoned Roshanali when he refused to run the press under their authority. After a sustained personal plea by his wife, Rubab Master, his younger brother, Anverali, and a prominent member of the community, Mustafa Rajabali to the

President Abeid Amani Karume, Roshanali was released. He and the family then moved to Dar es Salaam while the press remained in the hands of the army and some small printing-work continued there until the machines were decommissioned. In late 1975, Roshanali suffered a major heart attack and passed away in Dar es Salaam in 1976

One other literary personality in Zanzibar who is noted in records is Gulamhussein Mohamed Valli Dharsi, who was instrumental in the publication of Islamic religious books in Gujarati. The popular periodical - *Salsabil*[153] - in Gujarati was edited and produced by him, MohamedJaffer Sheriff Dewji and Mohammed Jivraj with the intention to awaken the faith of the community.[154]

GULAMHUSSEIN MOHAMMED VALLI DHARSI (1887-1961)

Popularly known by his pen-name SALSABIL, he was the eldest son of Mohamed Valli Dharsi. He was born in Zanzibar and received his early education at Sir Euan Smith Madressa. He was extremely well-versed in Urdu, English, Farsi, Gujarati, Arabic and Kiswahili such that by 1910, he contributed articles to Indian Journals and publications like "Rahe-Najat", "Noore-Iman", "Chaudmi Sadi" and "Muslim Review" often using the pen-name of MUNTAZIR and SALSABIL.

He had his own private library of some 2000 books, which included rare and valuable collections as well as several important literary and classical works.

He was among the founder members to establish the "Muslim Sahitya Karyalay" in 1938 that published many useful booklets on socio-religious subjects.

In 1943, the society published a popular monthly journal 'Salsabil' that had readership in Africa and India. He was also the Gujarati editor of the "Zanzibar Samachar". Among his publications in Gujarati are "Life history of Allama Qantoori", "Fascinating History of the Holy Mausoleums in Kerbala", "Islam and the Caliphs of Divine Kingdom", "The Worldwide Memorials of Ahlul-Bayt", "The Martyr of Kerbala" and "Life of Imam Sadiq A.S.".

For his valuable publications and religious services, he was conferred the title of "Hamiyul Islam" (The Defender of Islam). He regularly corresponded with many religious and literary luminaries such as Allama Qantoori, Haji Gulamali, Valimohamed C. Momin and Jafferali Aseer. Deeply religious, Gulamhuseinbhai regularly attended majalises and was always available to anyone seeking his advice or assistance. Gulamhuseinbhai died in Zanzibar on 11th March 1961 leaving behind four sons, three daughters and grand-children.

(Source: Africa Federation Archives)

3.9 Commemorations and Celebrations

Muharram in Zanzibar was commemorated by Shia Ithna-Asheries with the raising of black flags and the donning of black clothes as a mark of respect for the martyrdom of Imam Hussein (pbuh) and his family. The air surrounding the Imambada was filled with the strong, musky fragrance of traditional *oud* and *attar* used to scent the environs and mourning symbols. The programs in Muharram were always emotionally charged.

Muharram Azadaari in Zanzibar in the 1950s

From the second night of the new month, white flag poles of varying sizes were fixed to the two embroidered horizontal black velvet banners in such a way as to project a semi-circular shape, and placed on either side of the *mimber* (pulpit).

On the fifth night, bigger flags of different varieties,[155] resembling those seen in Hyderabad Imambadas (probably brought over from there), were brought out. These were wrapped in colourful satin or velvet, and embroidered with silver and golden threading to give them a lush, elegant look.

The grandeur of these symbols, the banners with their inspirational messages/imagery and the fragrance created the perfect atmosphere of awe and honour for the fully packed Imambada. The audience would sit spell-bound, listening to poetic lamentations of the tragedy that befell the martyrs and the heartrending wailing would gain fervour as the day of Ashura approached.[156]

Arbaeen Procession (Juloos) in Zanzibar proceeding from Kiponda KSIJ Imambargha to Cemetery (Kabrastan in Raha Leo area) in year 1950s

Chehlum[157] night activities attracted many from outside of Zanzibar to participate in the commemoration.[158] The Zanzibar *Julus*[159] assumed a pattern of its own that was adopted by other Khoja Shia Ithna-Asheri communities all over East Africa. "Hussein Day" where dignitaries from other communities were invited to express their opinions on the Tragedy of Karbala was another event which began in Zanzibar that was subsequently adopted by other Jamaats in East Africa.[160]

The tradition of holding a Hussein Day started in the 1940s in Zanzibar. It was first held in Victoria Garden by an ad-hoc Jamaat committee. The aim was to create awareness in the general public about Karbala, that it was not an event unique to Shias, but one that addressed the issue of justice within human society as a whole.

1950s Hussain Day organised by the Volunteer Corps of KSI Jamaat, Zanzibar. Seen are Prince Sayyid Abdullah bin Khalifa, the British Resident, dignitaries, religious and community leaders.

In Zanzibar, high government officials, diplomats, non-Muslims and Muslims of all denominations attended the annual Hussein Day. The chief guest was usually the Sultan of Zanzibar whilst speakers were mostly non-Shia who presented their views about the events in Karbala. A popular venue was the Portuguese Fort (Ngome Kongwe) at Forodhani, which exists until today and is now a Cultural Centre.

Hussein Day, Zanzibar, 1957 at Old Fort, Forodhani.
L-R: *Akber Jessa, Abbas Chatoo, Mulla Ahmed Lakha, unknown, Mohamedhusein Ahmed (Kokoni), unknown, Murtaza Bandali, Unknown.*

In Mombasa, this event was organized by Ithna-Asheri Young Men's Union and often held at the Ithna-Asheri Sports Club. In 1952, the Governor of Kenya, Sir Phillip Hitchell was the chief guest. Hussein Day used to be a well-known important annual event and many dignitaries would free up their schedules to attend the program.

Hussein Day, Mombasa, 1952 under chairmanship of Sir Philip Hitchell, Governor of Kenya.
L-R: Officer, Mohamedali Meghji, Sir Philip, Dr Rana, Officer. Side: Officer, Hon. A. B. Patel, Govt. Officer. Right: Waras Fatehali Dhalla. Left: Aga Sayyad Imam Molvi Sadiqali Rear: Volunteer, Jaffer Janmohamed, H. A. Jeevraj, Akbarali Karim (Hon. Sec), (extreme right) Hassan A. M. Jaffer

In Dar es Salaam, the first Hussein Day was held in 1945, on the open ground outside the present mosque. Later in 1948, a residential building (Kanji Damani) was constructed on this plot and the venue was shifted to the Bohora School on Ring Street (now Jamhuri School on Jamhuri Street). Alhaj Mohammedbhai Dhirani who served as Hon. Secretary of this Society for many years, penned the following reflection

> We commemorate "Muharram" in Imambarghas, demonstrating with black flags, delivering lectures, organize processions and reciters present their grief and sorrow through effective poems on the massacre of Karbala relating Islamic history as well as giving examples from the Holy Qur'an. Believers attend 'Majlis' (lectures) throughout the 40 days where Imam Hussein's pure characters are mentioned in the lectures; one tries to ponder upon to rectify to be a better Muslim. However, we have to reflect and contemplate, do these lectures change our etiquettes, our lifestyles or not? Or are we just attending the sermons as rituals and traditions? In addition, if there are no changes for the betterment then it's not the true 'Azadari' it's just for name sake. If after weeping, beating chests and grieving inside the Imambargha we forget and don't ponder on what was recited then it's pointless, we have gained nothing.[161]

The other event which was unique to the Khoja Shia Ithna-Asheri of Zanzibar is the celebration popularly known as *Khushali Bankro*. Here, the celebration of Prophet Mohammed (pbuh)'s birthday was observed by laying long wooden benches (*bankro*) and chairs spread along an entire street on which the participants sat. The entire Muslim community of Zanzibar joined in for this special celebratory program.[162] In other places, such as Dar es Salaam,[163] the celebrations of the birthday of the Prophet and other prominent members of his family were known as *Malavado* or *Melavdo*.[164]

In the history of *azadari* amongst Zanzibar Khoja Ithna-Asheries, the contributions of many personalities are valued and remembered with great appreciation. Amongst them, name of 'Golo Saleh' (Gulamhusein) repeatedly comes up in most smost conversations. Gulamhusein was born on 10th Muharram (Ashura) and his devotion to religion and service to the community are matter of record. From as early as the 1930s, he is associated with being an integral part of the procession of *Matam Njiani* (Julus), Khushali Bankro, Hussein Day and any community-related event. He was also a teacher much-loved and admired in his classroom, making him a prime role model for the youths. Mostly seen dressed in a coat and red tarboosh cap (Turkish cap) that projected an imposing personality, he was often observed recording lectures and lamentations that would be later relayed at community gatherings.

GULAMHUSEIN SALEH ALARAKHIA

"... as a result of fear arising from these events, unmarried girls living in Zanzibar were secretly evacuated. The young girls huddled in small canoes, known locally as ngalaw or ngarawa, - mostly at night - sailed from the southern tip of Zanzibar to mainland Tanzania…They landed near Dar es salaam and Bagamoyo. The touching accounts of their frightening experience are difficult to comprehend and may sound like unbelievable fairy tales. But such were the agonizing moments that many families had to live through." (Relentless Endeavours, p.84)

Gulamhussein Saleh Alarakhiya throughout these difficult times that Zanzibarians were going through, in his capacity as Hon. Secretary of the Zanzibar Kuwwatul Islam Jamaat remained determined to assist the community members and others in Zanzibar. He maintained close contacts with the Dar es salaam Jamaat and Africa Federation. From Dar es salaam, Hussein Nasser, the Jamaat President, Fidahusein Hamir, Hon. Secretary and Mohamedali Janmohamed formed the nucleus team that coordinated the efforts to ease the difficulties of the community members in Zanzibar. Sadly, in 1970, Gulamhussein was adversely reported to the Zanzibar authorities. As a result, he was detained for the entire month of Ramadan. When the investigations conducted by Zanzibar authorities revealed that nothing untoward was found, Gulamhusein was released on the order of President Abeid Karume. (Source: Africa Federation Archives)

Marriage within the Khoja Shia Ithna-Asheries called for elaborate preparations, as they blended both Islamic tenets and ceremonies based on the Gujarati culture. At the marriage events, one was likely to hear words like '*veeaji*' (wedding), *majlis*, *mandvo* (pre-marriage party), *maulud* (celebration), *doodhpino* (tasting of sweet milk by the groom), *vannai* (bride leaving ceremony), *sargas* (wedding ceremony), *cheracheri* (tricks played on bride and groom), *ponkhnu* (confetti ceremony), and *sattaro* (dinner party for the family). Bridal parties had to have a fish dinner that was supposed to be a good omen.

From the late 19th century to the middle of the 20th century, the groom traditionally wore a *sherwani*[165] and golden satin *pagri* (turban); he would have a sword tied around his waist and ride a horse to the wedding ceremony. Jamaat elders would also wear *pagris*, especially on the wedding nights.¹⁶⁶ This manner of dressing and conducting the marriage ceremony was amongst the traditions that were brought over from Kachchh and Kathiawad and retained within the Khoja Shia Ithna-Asheries in East Africa for a number of years afterwards.¹⁶⁷

After setting up their own Jamaat in 1877, the Khoja Shia Ithna-Asheries began to evolve their own unique socio-religious identity. They promoted Shia religious tenets and defined their community with a unique blend of Khoja and Swahili ethos. For many who came to Zanzibar, this first port of call provided the prefect ground for learning about the local culture. After enduring the harsh ocean-crossing, they knew there was no going back - not soon anyway. The only choice before them was to adapt and they did - extremely well.

They quickly realised that maintaining a good social relationship and mutual dependency were essential for survival. Most of them worked hard; some thrived, others prospered and along their journey, they were not afraid to challenge their beliefs and re-evaluate them. Nothing had come easy to them and they took nothing for granted - not even their faith. Instead, they took every opportunity to learn through their struggles, failures and successes. Soon they were able to put these experiences to effect as they traversed the interior of East Africa and other coastal towns seeking new and even better frontiers.

Early 1900s - Mombasa Khoja Shia Ithna-Asheris. Note the Union Jack flying in the background. (Courtesy A A Khatau)

PART 4A
Socio-Economic and Socio-Religious Change: Settlement Patterns in East Africa

4A.1 Overview of Settlement in East Africa

In 1844, there were 800 Indians in Zanzibar. By 1870, their number was 3,901, a rise of almost 500 per cent. The composition of the Indian population in 1870 was as follows: Muslims (mainly Khoja) - 3,396, Hindus - 474 and the rest were Christians (mainly Goans).[1] A British official confirmed that 'thirty years ago (1859) there were here only 165 families and 20 married women, showing that the members of this sect have multiplied six-fold in the last 30 years, and married or settled part have increased in a still greater ratio.'[2]

According to official British records, this increase was entirely owing to arrivals from Kachchh.[3] In 1890, Khojas' had numerically overtaken all the other Indian sub-groups combined. The same British source reveals that 'the British Indian colonists or traders in the Zanzibar dominions come under the following designations: Hindus, who number about 1000, Parsis[4] about 100, Khojas, who are the most numerous, reach probably a total of 4,000'.[5]

The Khojas thus formed the majority of the Indian settlers in Zanzibar and the impression gleaned from community sources is that they were wholly engaged in small businesses. The merchants and shopkeepers mainly employed fellow Khojas. A few of the more successful entrepreneurs had extensive business connections with almost all the ports on the East African coast.[6]

From 1890 onwards, there was a sudden shift of interest from the coast toward the interior regions of East Africa. This change came about because of the new economic opportunities that had become available as a result of colonial activism and increased military infrastructures. European missionaries had also concentrated on influencing the interior communities and by this time, Britain and Germany had a lot of influence over East Africa. Zanzibar was a British protectorate, whilst Uganda was under the British "sphere of influence".

In 1894, the East African Protectorate[7] was declared. As soon as this happened, plans for infrastructure and transportation systems to reach the interiors - such as the railway to Uganda - began to fall in place. Mombasa became an important coastal town attracting an influx of Indian immigrants who came either to provide labour for such projects or to explore the new trading opportunities that were becoming available.

Indians who came to East Africa during this time fell into one of four categories:
- Labourers for the construction of railways, drawn mainly from Punjab, Karachi, Sindh and Bombay. Many returned to India after the end of their contract, however, a few settled permanently in East Africa.
- Recruited soldiers, mainly from Punjab, that the government needed to provide security during the construction.
- Skilled workers, most from the Bombay Presidency, who came to help cope with the growing number of administrative tasks.
- Entrepreneurs who migrated, mainly from Kathiawar and Kachchh, for better opportunities and set up "start-up businesses".[8] Khojas belonged in this last category.

It is important to note that despite the relative success stories of the Khoja Shia Ithna-Asheries in Zanzibar and elsewhere in East Africa, poverty in varying degrees always haunted them as a community. Alhaj

Mohamedbhai Abdulla Khalfan of Dar es Salaam, Tanzania, produced a series of topical publications. One of them a remarkable 36-page book titled *Dastan* (meaning Sad Account). It included pictures and numerous sharp, shockingly graphic examples of poverty in Zanzibar.[9]

He observed that

> [In Zanzibar] there would be the segments of [the] community, varying in sizes, from time to time, struggling for their living in abject poverty. Basic poverty always produces dismal consequences like poor health leading to stubborn mental stress; bruise[d] family pride, more cases of divorce and fewer incidents of marriages for lack of affordable space of residence, [an] increase in the number of unmarried women and limited advancement in education, apart from others. Some aspects of poverty are so suffocating that relief comes about upon a last breadth(sic) of life only to make the poor wonder if there was life before death. Poverty is indeed a feature in human lives that test[s] the balance and stability in a society as a whole. It also tests the responsibility of the well-off and the powerful and holds them accountable for any failure in the test.[10]

The period between 1930 and 1960 was an ominous one for the community in Zanzibar. Poverty came upon many of the middle class and those who were not well-to-do settled into even more abject poverty. One of the main reasons for this is explained by Mohamedbhai Khalfan

> It all started when the League of Nations (the predecessor of the United Nations) appointed Britain as the Administrative Power over the then German Tanganyika, now designated as a Trust Territory, after the end of the First World War. The small Dar es Salaam port, developed by the new colonial power as an international commercial port for exports, imported and distributed goods to cater fully for the needs of millions of the people of Tanganyika and the eastern part of the Belgian Congo. Zanzibar Island, a small distance away across the sea, with some 1,200 business families, almost all of Indian origin, began to lose the mainland's huge lucrative consumers and exports market which was via Zanzibar for generations.[11]

It is clear from the Trade Directory (1960) that most of the Khoja Shia Ithna-Asheries settled initially in Zanzibar (or sometimes in Pemba). They would work for either a relative or one of the Indian traders for a short time, or set up their own business and put down roots. After acquiring local trading knowledge and becoming familiar with the Swahili culture, some ventured into the interior of East Africa and beyond. This pattern of a short stop in Zanzibar before venturing into other parts of East Africa was established well before the construction of the railways began. When other towns began to supersede Zanzibar, Khoja Shia Ithna-Asheries settled directly at coastal towns (Mombasa, Tanga and Kilwa) or moved to the interior venturing as far west as Mwanza, Bukoba and the areas around Lake Victoria.

Daily earnings and economic opportunities were central motives that drove the Khoja Shia Ithna-Asheries to take these generally calculated, but sometimes unknown risks. Their goal was always to better their own and their families' situation. Those who decided to explore the interior underwent a number of hardships: they were prey to thieves and wild animals, some died of disease and others faced unimaginable difficulties on their way. However, from historical studies, it seems that they knew that the unexplored territory also meant unrivalled opportunity. In this sense, whilst economic opportunities were the main attraction, these early Khojas were also explorers and adventurers in their own right. Their migration - during this period at least - was free, voluntary and economically motivated.[12]

What stands out in the case of Khoja Shia Ithna-Asheries is the remarkable extent of their resilience towards preserving their faith. The pattern is a familiar one that was replicated throughout East Africa; whenever two or three Khoja Shia Ithna-Asheries families came together in a village or town, they held religious functions in each other's homes. When more families joined them, they would form a *jamaat* (community) and build relevant institutions around it to preserve their socio-religious identity. Faith determined many of the behaviours, attitudes and social practices that formed an important element of their identity in East Africa and elsewhere.[13] This model of setting up communal institutions among Khoja Shia Ithna-Asheries is observed to this day.

BAGAMOYO

Bagamoyo[14] was a bustling trading town in the 1860s, which also served as a rich base for slave trade.[15] For Khoja Shia Ithna-Asheries, it was an easily accessible forward option from Zanzibar; from Bagamoyo, they could use a well-marked trading route to the interior of Tanganyika that led to Ujiji on the shores of Lake Tanganyika. By the 1880s Bagamoyo already had a settled Khoja Shia Ithna-Asheri population.

Early settlement in the Bagamoyo began in the mid-18th century with the Shomvi, a local variant of the Shirazi[16] who inhabit the East African coast. In Bagamoyo, the Shomvi and Zaramo[17] were closely connected and often interacted with each other.[18] Before the colonial occupation of Bagamoyo, these two groups ruled Bagamoyo. Apart from Shomvi and Zaramo, there were also other large numbers of Africans from the interior: the Doe, Kami, Kwere, and Zigua, as well as the Nyamwezi and Sukuma. The first four groups traded in agricultural products, rubber, and copal; the latter two groups came from a much further distance and traded principally in ivory, livestock, and hides.

In Bagamoyo, like other ports on the coast of East Africa, the exchange of goods took place between those that arrived via the Indian Ocean and those that arrived from the interior. The porters sold their ivory and other products to local wholesalers who, for the most part, shipped them onwards via Zanzibar.[19]

In 1840, when Sultan Seyyid bin Said (1804 - 1856) of Oman and other Omani Arabs invested in caravan trade, Bagamoyo actively transformed with a Customs Master being put in place to levy duties on all goods being traded. The Sultan protected his authority to collect taxes at the port by stationing a troop of approximately 30 soldiers from Baluchistan, a region that had come under the influence of the Omani Sultan.

The Indians who came to Bagamoyo were not a cohesive group. They were divided by religion into several communities, the most numerous being the Hindus (often referred to by Europeans as Banyans or Banians) and the Khojas (Ismailis and Ithna-Asheries). Although the

Indians were the minority, they were influential by virtue of being the principal financiers of the caravan expeditions. In the economic life of Bagamoyo, from the mid- to the late-19th century, Indians played the roles of the wholesalers and petty merchants.[20]

In the 1870s, there were about 22 families made up of a combination of Khoja Shia Ithna-Asheries and Khoja Shia Ismailis living there. Nasser Virji & Co established his business in Bagamoyo and attracted many Khoja Shia Ithna-Asheries for employment. In addition to the Nasser Virji family, there were also the families of Ladha Damji, Lalji Datoo (who had a shop as well as 100 acres of coconut farm), Mulla Mohamdali Moloo, Ismaili Dossa Thaver, Ismail Bandali Muraj and Fazal Mohammed.[21]

By the mid-1880s, Bagamoyo was the Sultan's highest earner among the coastal ports in terms of levying customs duties. This naturally attracted foreign curiosity. Germans began to take interest in Bagamoyo and it caught the attention of Carl Peters of the Deutsch Ostafrikanische Gesellschaft (DOAG German East African Company). The company went on to acquire 140,000 square kilometres of territory in Bagamoyo's hinterland. The Germans also needed control over coastal ports to serve as trading outlets[22] and in April 1888, they signed an agreement with the Sultan of Zanzibar, allowing them to levy customs duties in seven coastal ports between the Umba and Ruvuma rivers.[23]

Because the local rulers and townspeople had not been consulted for this agreement, tensions and skirmishes began in the settled communities of Bagamoyo and the coastal ports, which led to a full-scale rebellion in Pangani and spread to other areas. As a result, the Germans were chased out of every town except for Bagamoyo and Dar es Salaam. Once the Germans re-established their firm control over these two ports, they made Bagamoyo the administrative and commercial capital of Tanganyika. As soon as stability was established and business could resume, more Khoja Shia Ithna-Asheries began to move to the town.

To accommodate the growing Khoja Shia Ithna-Asheri community, a mosque and *imambada* were constructed under the supervision of Alhaj Saleh Jagsi (Jacksi) and completed in 1889. Alhaj Saleh would bring a *zakir* (religious reciter) and about 20 Khoja brothers from Zanzibar regularly during the month of Muharram to Bagamoyo and would especially commemorate the *Chehlum* (40th day after the martyrdom day) of Imam Hussein (pbuh) with local Khoja community. This passion to commemorate the *Chehlum* day was replicated wherever Khoja Shia Ithna-Asheries settled in East Africa.

Bagamoyo Imambada - built 1889

Imambada   *Shelter for madrasah*

By 1918, Germany had lost the War and the capital shifted to Dar es Salaam. Khoja Shia Ithna-Asheries moved out of Bagamoyo, there were no activities in the mosque and Imambada of Bagamoyo since then. In 1960s, Alhaj Amir Kanji, Alhaj Amir Walji and Alhaj Jaffer Dhirani began organizing annual Muharram gatherings there under the Ithna-Asheri Union Volunteers Corps - a committee under Ithna-Asheri Union of Dar es Salaam.
(Africa Federation Archives, 26 October 2018)

DAR ES SALAAM

Dar es Salaam began its life as a small fishing village called Mjimwema. In 1856 Sultan Majid extended this village and re-named it Mzizima. Sachoo Pira (Sachedina Pirani Mawji) and Nasser Mawji were among the first Khoja Shia Ithna-Asheries to settle in Mzizima[24]. Shaykh Amiji Musaji, a Bohora, arrived in 1860. Sultan Majid further extended Mzizima in 1866 and once again changed its name: this time to Dar es Salaam. For the greater part of the 20th century, Dar es Salaam remained the capital of historic Tanganyika (now Tanzania).²⁵

Although Hindu, Christian, Sikh, Buddhist and "traditional" African religious communities always exerted differing degrees of influence on the area, by far the strongest influence was from Islam and the very name "Dar es Salaam" carries heavy Muslim connotations. Historically, the vast majority of Indian Muslims in Dar es Salaam have tended to belong either to the Shiah community or one of the Sunni Sufi brotherhoods, each party assuming a dynamic role in the propagation and institutionalization of their faith in the town.²⁶

Muslims of Indian origin in Dar es Salaam, as with many other places in East Africa, were mostly members of Shia communities - either Ismaili, Ithna-Asheri, or Bohora - having ancestral links with the western coast of India, especially Kachchh, Gujarat, Kathiawar, and Sindh. In 1873, from a total general population believed to number close to 5,000, Bartle Frere found 107 Indians - 47 Khoja, 45 Bohra, and 15 Hindus. Subsequent estimates from 1898 show 600 Muslims and 200 Hindus, and by the turn of the 19th century, the village had between '900 and 950 Asians'. This diverse 'Asian' community co-existed well with most Hindus preferring to travel to and from India on a seasonal basis, while Muslims chose to stay on and were encouraged to settle in groups, particularly in the case of Khojas.²⁷

GULAMALIBHAI JIVAN PANJWANI (D. 1967)

He was President of Dar es Salaam Jamaat (1939-40). He married Sherbanu daughter of Bhanji Kurji. His children were Akberali Panjwani (former Hon Secretary of Dar es Salaam Jamaat), Alihussein, Hassanali, Shirin Hassanali Virjee, Rubab Pirmohammed Walji, Fatima Habib Chagani and Amina Akber Chagani.

Dr Sibtain Panjwani, past Secretary General of The World Federation (1996 -2003), is his grandson.

Gulamalibhai passed away in Dar es Salaam on 26 July 1967.

(Africa Federation Archives, 20 Oct. 2018)

In 1902, Gulamali Jivan Panjwani[28] came to Mombasa from Hariyana, Gujarat and initially stayed with Walji Bhanji for 22 days before setting sail for Dar es salaam He describes the Dar es salaam of 1902 as a small village surrounded by jungle. Animals freely roamed the area and in the rainy season, the streets would get flooded. The only mode of transportation used was walking. In the following years, however, this little village rapidly developed into a major town under German administration. During the First World War, there was a fluctuation of movement because people stayed away from the town when there was fear of imminent attack and return whenever there was peace.[29] Panjwani narrates that

> The Khoja Shia Ithna-Asheri Community of Dar es Salaam was small and the *imambada* was made of corrugated iron sheets. In 1902, Kilwa and Bagamoyo were the main trading centres. There was also a lot of trade between Dar es Salaam and Zanzibar Island. Dar es Salaam began to develop after the construction of the railway line and as it did, the importance of Kilwa and Bagamoyo diminished gradually. In 1918, there was an influenza epidemic, which killed many people amongst the native population. Dar es Salaam began to develop after the First World War and the development was very quick after the Second World War. Our community also grew very fast and a new *imambada* was constructed in 1942.

POPAT BHAI RAWJI
(1881-1962)

Popatbhai Rawji was born in Sadodar, Jamnagar, India. He married Rehmatbai, d/o Pirbhai Thawer.

His children are Mohamed Rawji, Hussain Rawji, Sugra Haji, Fatma Premji, Sherbanu Alibhai and Khairun Haji (all deceased).

Marhuma Fatmabai Premji and Marhuma Khairunbai Haji used to teach Qur'an to children in Dar es Salaam.

Popatbhai passed away on 28 June, 1962 and is buried at Dar es Salaam KSIJ Cemetery.

Africa Federation Archives,
2 November 2018

Popat Rawji[30] who arrived in 1904 describes our community in Dar es Salaam as a small *jamaat* (community). He says

> at the time, Sachoo Pira and Nasser Mawji were influential people. Sachoo Pira had influence with the German colonial government and was able to procure a plot on which a mosque was built together with a *musafarkhana* by its side. Sizeable contributions also came from Nasser Mawji for the mosque and Hemani Trust contributed towards the *musafarkhana*. The mosque was opened in 1907 by Agha Kushakshah, a relative of Aga Khan III. Versi Advani contributed a great deal towards the construction of the first *imambada*.
>
> From 1907 to 1918, Musa Ali Hussein of Maswa taught children Qur'an recitation. The new *imambada* was built following efforts by Br. Gulamhussein Virji to call upon the community for financial contributions. The first donors were Versi Advani, Rajabali Alidina, Alibhai Ebrahim, Daya Walji and Suleman Daya. The donors also helped collect contributions from the wider community. This resulted in the new *imambada* being built by 1942 entirely from the contributions of the members.
>
> Daya Walji donated the **madrasah** building and Alibhai Ebrahim donated the *bewakhana* in memory of his deceased wife. Br. Juma Haji built a dispensary in the memory of his deceased brother, Br. Ebrahim Haji (still operating under Dar es Salaam Jamaat by the name of Ebrahim Haji Charitable Health Centre). Mehfile Abbas was constructed through the efforts of Fatmabai Haji Mohamed Sheriff with the cooperation of Br. Haji Jiwan and Br. Gulamhussein Virji and through the collection of donations from women.
>
> Electricity was introduced in Dar in 1916 and running water in 1918. With the advent of tap water, water wells fell out of use. Motor vehicles were introduced in 1918. The local natives were very peaceful and faithful people and trade caravans went to Bagamoyo, Ujiji and Tabora mainly on foot.[31]

By 1907, there were 200 Khoja Shia Ithna-Asheries in Dar es Salaam. Amongst them Nasser Rattansey, Molu Kanji, Nasser Molu, Merali

Muraj, Pirbhai Rattansi, Dhalla Nanji, Alibhai Walli, Alibhai Ibrahim and Nasser Walji.

The railways came to Dar es Salaam in 1906 and soon after, the city began to boom. Once electricity became widely available in 1918, more economic opportunities drew the Khoja Shia Ithna-Asheries. Many of them settled there and the community continued to grow.

ALIBHAI EBRAHIM/ALI TOTO/ALI MAZIWA (1889-1962)

Alibhai Ebrahim sailed from India for Dar es Salaam in 1902. He was 13 years old when he joined his brother in Lindi. In 1904, he returned to Dar es Salaam, where he started hiring out handcarts and rickshaws to move merchandise from the port. Most of the businessmen were in Bagamoyo and Dar es Salaam was a very small town.

Alibhai had a dairy business selling milk as he had many cows in the farmlands beyond Ilala. Dar es Salaam Jamaat allowed him to build a Bewakhana above Ebrahim Haji Ithna-Asheri Dispensary in memory of his wife and name it Jenabai Alibhai Ebrahim Ithna-Asheri Bewakhana.

(Africa Federation Archives, 20 Mar 2016)

(L) This three-storey building on Uhuru Street was donated by Haji Alibhai Ebrahim to Dar es Salaam Jamaat. The building was recently demolished to pave way for the new housing development project of Dar es Salaam Jamaat Bewakhana.

(R) Bewakhana built on the first floor of the dispensary by Haji Ebrahim in memory of his wife Jenabai Haji Alibhai Ebrahim.

Gulamalibhai Damji was approached by many members to take the helm of the community in Dar es Salaam. He stood up for President and was elected unanimously. He came into the position at a time when there was no proper structure in the community and many legal matters were pending. It was under his leadership that the first constitution of the Jamaat was drafted and approved.

GULAMALIBHAI DAMJI

The Constituition was in two languages: English and Gujarati

The constitution was passed on 4 September 1937 and referred to the community as "the Khoja Shia Ithna-Asheri Jamaat".[32] It is interesting to note that the word "Muslim" was missing. Perhaps the community at the time felt that "Khoja Shia Ithna-Asheri" provided sufficient clarity about their identity to distinguish them from other ethno-religious communities. A large number of East African Khojas later migrated to Europe, Canada and the United States of America where they felt the need to include the word "Muslim" after "Ithna-Asheri" to identify themselves with the broader Muslim communities in their new homelands.

The 1937 Dar es Salaam Jamaat constitution had just 13 clauses, expressed clearly in Gujarati and English. The clauses indicated how rules could be made and by whom, who would execute them and who the final arbiters would be if any rules were broken or evaded. This simple but effective constitution served the community well until it was amended in the 1980s. The community that now called itself

"Khoja Shia Ithna-Asheri" made it clear in the constitution that it existed to serve according to the tenets and doctrines of the Ithna-Asheri faith with the following aims and objectives:

a) Work for the general upliftment of Jamaat members in all directions.
b) Buy property and organize institutions for the above objective.
c) Assist members of the Jamaat by providing such means as are available.
d) Do all such things for the above purposes as are consonant with and not repugnant to the doctrines and tenets of the Ithna-Asheri sect of Islam.

Membership was confined to Khoja Shia Ithna-Asheri male persons above 18 years of age, with a yearly subscription of Sh. 1/- payable in advance, but exempted if an individual was unable to pay. Once accepted, a member had a clear duty to honour the laws and by-laws of the Jamaat and a right to vote and discuss his concerns at meetings.[33]

The management comprised of 12 members equally split between office-bearers: President, Secretary, Joint Secretary, Treasurer, Mukhi, and Kamadia (note the absence of a Vice President) and six committee members. The duty of the management was to convene meetings, maintain discipline, fill up any vacant post - except that of the President – and arrange the celebration of religious holidays. It had the power to frame by-laws that would be put before the first General Meeting for approval and come into force after approval. The general body elected all 12 members of the committee to serve for a period of two years.[34]

The Jamaat properties were vested under the Trustees, who had 16 clauses governing their duties. In 1937, the Trustees had to manage six properties: the mosque, *imambadas*, burial ground, *musafarkhaana*, the *shamba* (farm) of Merali Muraj and the house built on his plot, that were all under the Jamaat. Their task was defined as follows: [35]

- Collect rents from the properties of the community.
- Lease the properties and keep the properties in repair.
- Submit accounts to the Managing Committee, together with the balance. They would be entitled to retain 10% of the cash in hand for current expenditure.
- Deposit all the money in one of the Dar es Salaam banks and make all payments by cheque.

On 23 October 1939, Nurmohamedbhai Jessa, Jumabhai Haji, Pirbhai Alibha, and Shivjibhai Somji, all residing in Dar es Salaam were appointed trustees for managing all matters concerning the acquiring, holding, conveying, assigning or disposing of any land or any interest in land held in trust for the Khoja Shia Ithna-Asheri Jamaat of Dar es Salaam. The Clerk of the Council duly registered the Trust document under the *Tanganyika Territory - The Land Of Perpetual Succession Ordinance - (Cap. 72 Of The Laws)* on 13 November 1939.[36]

Thus, the Dar es Salaam *jamaat* began to function as a rule-based community under a constitution whose checks and balances both its members and leadership were comfortable with. In doing so, they set in motion a process of discussion, debate and consensus-building that became a template for major decisions that needed approval by the general body. Such templates were brought over by early arrivals, who were part of the Khoja community before the break and are now practised in many *jamaats* in East Africa and the community beyond.

THE MAN BEHIND A MASK
(A frank profile of Mr. Satchu. G. Abdulrasul of Dar-es-Salaam, Tanzania)
By: ABBAS ALLOO

Beyond mere gratification of public curiosity, there lies people's right be acquainted with the achievements and the character of those who serve them in public life. This leads us to the introduction of Mr. Satchu. G. Abdulrasul. Many admired him for his keenness, courage, and stubbornness. He epitomizes what it takes to be a reformer or a minor prophet. Through his long and continued services as a Councilor at no time, did he hold any post. For he always chose to challenge the conventional and traditional. He is not equipped for compromise. He would rather shun away than give in. To many he was a symbol of a rebel without a cause.

Feared that he might become a leader of a rebel group within the council, but he resisted any such attempt. When he spoke, his main theme was the need for communal unity and his argument did little to disturb the unity of the community. He remained loyal to the Federation. In doing so won respect among all sections of community. He does not conceal himself behind any personality. Human weakness and failures are there. Rarely in his speeches and writings have personal touch or confessions been there. He has preferred to be a man behind a mask. It is not due to shyness, but lack of concealment of his character and mind that attributed to the individual behind a mask. Behind the composed exterior is a character that is singularly varied and rich in human feelings. The Satchu of public life is not lacking in human feelings.

The Satchu behind a mask often feels too much. To survive the kicks of life a man must be a tough hide, but Satchu is not well protected. He is basically an artist and an idealist. He has the artist's sensitivity and idealist's dreams. Throughout his public life, he has ridden himself under a light rein. He has fought his temper down and has established control. It has become a conviction with him that it is wrong to allow the weakness of temper to escape and is bad taste to display one's feelings. Years have now mellowed him. Grey whiskers add dignity to his features and an intelligent face. His eyes lit up when a pet subject of 'misconceived Azadari' or 'hypocritic religious' broached. He wants instant reformation and no compromise. Open, a warm and luminous face, Satchu was born in Dar-es-Salaam on 17-9-1920 in the prominent Satchu Peera family. His all education was in Dar-es-Salaam. After schooling, he remained attached to family aerated water bolting business of Abdulrasul & Sons. During 1966 branched off from family business and joined Tanzania Fishnet Manufacturers Ltd as Project Manager and became its General Manager in 1968 he conducted an experimental enterprise as Industrial Consultant. Towards the end of 1970, he has joined NATEX as planning Manager.

The father of Satchu Peera, that is great, great grandfather of our present Mr. Satchu was born in Kilwa/Southern coast town of Tanzania. Kilwa was then an important seaport and a town, which fell on the safari route to the south. He was an import merchant of various commodities such as grey cloth, cutlery, etc. In 1851, the family decided to fulfill the obligation of going to Hajj. They went to Zanzibar first to leave their only male child in the custody of an aunt. Having fulfilled the Hajj pilgrimage they were returning to Africa. The vessel met a storm and the family capsized with the ship, leaving in Zanzibar an orphan child, Satchu Peera who grew up in Zanzibar. The child at the age 18 went to Mjimema. The first thing he did on reaching the place was to build a mosque for indigenous Muslim community. The mosque in bank of ruins still stands witness.

He started a duka (shop) selling the local requirement and buying produce and ivory. When Germans, later on, moved to Dar-es-Salaam and made the place their headquarters Satchu Peera also moved from Mjimema to Dar-es-Salaam. He also took German citizenship. He is perhaps the first Indian Asian to have settled in Dar-es-Salaam. Many other people from Bagamoyo followed. Abdulrasul Satchu Peera was born in Dar-es-Salaam in 1874 and died in 1930 at the age of 56. In 1899, Abdulrasul Satchu Peera and brothers went into aerated (soda) and coconut oil extracting industry. This was among the earliest in the country. Later the brother expanded into other industries such as copra crushing, and soap making industries.

By 1925, the Abdulrasul Satchu Peera and his sons were among the first Asians in Tanganyika to go into sisal industry specifically invited by the local government. Also at about the same time they went into Cotton Ginning 1924 (Abdulrasul & Sons). Father of Satchu, Gulamali Abdulrasul Satchu Peera was born and died in Dar-es-Salaam in 1896-1971, expanded the Abdulrasul business to Lindi and Zanzibar. Zanzibar factory nationalized and Lindi factory had to be closed down. The sons of Gulamali Abdulrasul Satchu Peera continued the business in style of Abdulrasul & Sons bottling aerated water. Satchu. G. Abdulrasul is the eldest of the sons. (*Extracted from Federation Samachar 1974*)

Under the leadership of Gulamalibhai Damji, many trust properties were acquired and many buildings were constructed. The Daya Walji Madressa building donated by the Daya Walji Family was established during his time. The famous case of the Ali Walli Trust Building[37] was resolved by him through court proceedings. His foresight regarding economic stability paved the way for the community to acquire properties for investment which would benefit future generations. By 1942, the community had grown sufficiently large that a new *imambada* became a necessity.

Led by Gulamhussein Virjee and supported by Versi Advani, Rajabali Alidina, Alibhai Ibrahim, Daya Walji, Suleiman Daya, and many others from Dar es Salaam, the community built this new *imambada*, a part of which still exists today. Before the 1950s, the new *imambada* had a seating arrangement that followed an unwritten protocol; only bearded elders in long frock coats and caps or leaders of the *jamaat* sat against the walls on the sides; along the middle children in short pants sat right in front and behind them were the youngsters in long trousers - but without jackets; bringing up the rear were the jacketed youth. By the mid-forties, the frock coats had disappeared and in the fifties, the ubiquitous bush shirt typical of African fashion came into vogue.[38]

MULLA KERMALLI ALIBHAI (1889-1958)

Marhum remembered for his zeal in serving the community. Born in Hadiyana, Kathiawar, he migrated to Africa at the age of 16 and soon showed his business acumen which he used to handle Jamaat expenses.

He was an advocate of accountability. His important contribution includes purchasing Jamaat properties and increasing revenue for the Jamaat. He was the President of Dar es Salaam Jamaat for many years and his services as a trustee during the last few years of his life were very valuable.

He was also instrumental in the construction of Kanji Damani building opposite the mosque on Indira Gandhi Street. He had two brothers Esmail and Pirbhai Alibhai.

His wife was Kulsumbai and his children were Allarakhia, Mohamedhussein, Yusuf, Fatma Kassamali Panjwani, Sherbanu Kassamali Panjwani, Laila Hassanali Lakha and Rubab Gulamhussein Bandali Damji. (Africa Federation Archives, 2 June 2017)

ALHAJ JUMABHAI HAJI (1890-1976)

Born in Lalpur, Kathiawad, he led a simple life style. He was the owner and director of one of the major business entities in Tanganyika - Messrs Juma Haji & Co Ltd, owning several rice mills, sisal plantations and cotton ginneries. In 1921, he opened branches at Kindu and Albertsville in Congo.

He was the Honorary Secretary of Dar es Salaam Jamaat in 1930 and Jamaat Trustee from 1938 to 1956. He was the first President of newly-created Tanganyika Education Council in 1953 and held the post until 1957, he was also Vice-President of the Indian Chamber of Commerce for two years.

A generous man, Haji Juma left many legacies such as the Ebrahim Haji Charitable Dispensary, a donation of Shs 42,000 to the Supreme Council for the construction of Ebrahim Haji Ithna-Asheri Assembly Hall in memory of his brother and a 12-storey residential apartment building (Juma Haji Residency). He also laid the foundation stone of Mehfile Murtaza in Karachi in 1976. He passed away in 1977 and is buried in Karachi. He was married to Jena Bai. Mohammed son of Ebrahim Haji was his adopted son. (AFED Directory/Family source)

ALHAJ EBRAHIM HAJI (1892-1947)

Born in Lalpur, Kathiawad, he was the younger brother of Jumabhai Haji. He travelled to Dar es Salaam in 1910 and joined his elder brother's business. Due to his adventurous and enterprising nature, he played an important part in establishing their business in the Congo. As a result, some families followed him and settled there.

He was President of Dar es Salaam Jamaat from 1943 to 1946 and held the position of Hon Secretary. He was the Vice-President of the Indian Chamber of Commerce at its establishment. He passed away in Dar es Salaam in 1947 leaving eight children.

Amongst his children, Hussain (Sheny) was instrumental in building the first Khoja mosque in Toronto in 1980 with funds donated by community members and the Ebrahim and Juma Haji families. (Trade Directory/Family source)

This was a period in which philanthropists came forward and financed important projects. The Suleiman Daya Walji family gifted the religious school (Haji Daya Walji Ithna-Asheri Madarasa), Sachoo Pira presented the burial ground (Chungani), Alibhai Ibrahim sponsored the residence for widows and Jumabhai Haji donated the Ibrahim medical dispensary and built the Ibrahim Haji Ithna-Asheri Assembly Hall at the Muslim Institute (Mombasa).

Ebrahim Haji Assembly Hall, Mombasa   *Ebrahim Haji Dispensary, Dar es Salaam*

DAYA WALJI FAMILY

Daya bhai Walji, one of the oldest pioneers and pillars of the community and his son Murrabi Suleman bhai Daya arrived in Tanzania when the son was very young. Suleman bhai was in business with his father and during this time, he gave voluntary services to Dar es Salaam Jamaat by serving as Secretary and Trustee for some years during which he physically and financially struggled for the betterment of the Jamaat. His tireless efforts and financial contribution led to the success of the Jamaat in many spheres.

His services towards Dar es Salaam were noteworthy. In 1936, Suleman Daya was a member of the committee that was appointed to draft the constitution of the Jamaat and he served as Secretary of the Indian School and Chairman of the Indian Education Board for a number of years. He also served on the management committee of the Indian Association for many years. Suleman Daya was a strong believer in educating future generations. He donated to the Jamaat prime real estate during his life including the plot across the Aga Khan Hospital where the rental income used to finance an annual meal at the mosque. This plot and the adjacent plot were subsequently donated by his descendants to Dar es Salaam Jamaat for education purposes. This is where the Al Muntazir Boys Primary School now stands. In 1937, both father and son donated a building described by archives as 'magnificent' to be used as a Madrasah. This is the well-known Daya Walji Madressa where Husseini Madressa conducted its classes.

In addition to the madrasah building, they donated the adjoining two-storey flats to generate rental income to finance the administrative and operating costs of the madrasah. The construction of the proposed madrasah began at a slow pace. It is reported that to expedite work, Daya Walji started a hunger strike that led to a quick implementation of the project. Dayabhai passed away and was buried in Dar es Salaam in 1950 while his son Suleman passed away whilst on a Ziyarat trip on 21 June, 1945 and was buried in Jamnagar.

Amongst the earliest teachers of the Daya Walji Madressa were Mulla Gulamhussein, Manji Dhirani (father of Marhum Mohamed Dhirani), Maulvi Alimohamed Jaffer Dewji, Alihussein Munshi, Murad Kanji and Mohamedali Ratansi, formerly of Tanga. Teachers Alihussein Munshi and his wife lived in the rear portion of the madrasah building. Then, during the 1960s, this rear portion was occupied by Maulana Aqa Haider Saheb.

In the 1980s, it was used as the Principal's office of the newly-established Al Muntazir School. In the evenings it served as the office of the Principal of Husseini Society later renamed Husseini Madressa.

During the Presidency of Marhum Nurmohamed Nasser (1952-60), Dar es Salaam Jamaat had a small office room located in Kanji Damani Trust Building opposite the mosque. This room was then allocated to Mukhi Gulamhusein Manek who helped members of the Jamaat in complying with new statutory requirements for registration of Tanzanian citizenship. The Jamaat office was moved to the Daya Walji Madressah building and occupied almost half of the madrasah building while the other half continued to be used as a madrasah for boys. In the 1960s, Allama Sayyid Saeed Akhtar Rizvi was in charge of the overall classes which were held in three different premises: for boys, at Daya Walji building, girls and younger boys at the Ebrahim Haji Dispensary premises and the building opposite the dispensary (known as Esmail Alibhai Trust Building - which later housed the Jamat office. The Union Nursery also had its first classes at this premises.

The earlier Daya Walji Madressa teachers were Maalim Rajab Ali Hassanali, Zainab bai A.K. Shivji, Masumabai Versi and Mulyani Fatmabai (Mrs. Hussein Mohamed Walji) who also taught the Qur'an at home. Qur'an teachers who taught at home included Fatmabai Premji and Khairunbai Haji. When the Dar es Salaam Jamaat opened a madrasah branch in Upanga in the 1970s, the Qur'an teacher was Kassamali Abdulla, formerly of Zanzibar.

When Sayyid Allama Akhtar Rizvi was in charge, the Madrasah was held every afternoon. He followed the syllabus prepared by the Supreme Council. The students sat for common central examinations prepared by the Africa Federation. Apart from afternoon Madrasah, the Husseini Society provided training for boys in Namaaz and Dinyat during Maghribain. Boys therefore had two religious classes to attend daily. In the 1960s, the government introduced once-a-week religious classes in primary and secondary schools. Allama Rizvi prepared Dinyat books in English called "Elements of Islamic Studies" to be used in schools. The books gradually replaced the former Gujarati Dinyat books by Marhum Mohammedjaffer Sheriff Dewji which were common in all our madaris in the 1950s.

During the 1970s, the number of students attending the Daya Walji Madressah diminished as Qur'an teaching was done in homes. The boys also attended the Husseini Society in the evenings so the usage of Daya Walji Madressa was only for senior classes. The remaining Husseini Society boys used the two Imambadas. The Tabligh Subcommittee of the Jamaat, under the chairmanship of Roshanali Fazal came up with a proposal to add three floors to the Daya Walji Madressa building and move the Husseini Society classes from the two Imambadas there. The new 3-storey building was opened in 1980 by the then AFED Chairman, Abdulrasul Lakha. The Husseini Society operated from this new building six days a week and on Sundays at the Imambada where namaaz sessions were held.

The reconstruction of the Haji Daya Walji Madressa from a ground floor structure to a 4-storey Tabligh Centre was undertaken by Mohamed Dhirani when he was President of Dar es Salaam Jamaat. Thus, the building continued to serve the purpose that the family had defined.

(Africa Federation Archives + Various sources)

ALHAJ DAYA WALJI   **ALHAJ SULEMAN DAYA**

Daya Walji Madressa Building

Fatmabai Mohammed Sherriff (popularly known as Fatumumbai), with assistance from Haji Jivan Panjwani and Gulamhussain Virjee, as well as financial contributions from the community women built Mehfile Abbas to hold functions for ladies.[39] Haji Mohammedbhai Jaffer built a boarding house (Haji Mohammed Jaffer Khoja Shia Ithna-Asheri Tanganyika Boarding House) to provide for the young men who came to Dar es Salaam from towns and villages throughout East Africa to further their education.

Such philanthropic support for the community remains the hallmark of Khoja Shia Ithna-Asheri communal development to this day.

MOHAMEDALI JANMOHAMED (1908-1975)

Mohamedbhai grew up in Dar es Salaam and was known as humble and accommodating person to young and old, rich and poor.

From the 1920s, he assisted in many jamaat projects and took keen interest in the affairs of Africa Federation from its inception. During its 1945 preliminary conference, he was Secretary to the reception committee and subsequently in 1949 elected as the Hon. General Secretary to the Central Council of East Africa for a full term with Haji Abdulrasul Nasser Virjee as the President.

Reserved by nature, he listened to all points of view very carefully and spoke persuasively to move deliberations forward. He took an active interest in the affairs of Africa Federation and was a trusted advisor to Haji Ebrahim H. Sheriff and Haji Mohamedali Meghji during their respective leadership.

(Federation Samachar, Volume 15, No 1, 1975)

Because of the efforts of its members and the generosity of successful individuals, the Jamaat continued to thrive and by 1960, the number of Khoja Ithna-Asheries in Dar es Salaam had reached 1,696.

TABORA

By 1900, Khoja Shia Ithna-Asheries reached Tabora via Dar es Salaam and Bagamoyo. They used the busy Bagamoyo-Ujiji trading route that served caravan traders in ivory and slaves. As ivory prices rose in India and Europe during the 19th century, Arab traders pursued new sources of the commodity in the interior of East Africa, moving further and further west in search of more abundant herds.[40] Tabora became a principal way station for caravans coming from Zanzibar and coastal towns.

The town was originally a series of hamlets in the Unyanyembe region. Groups of Arabs and coastal traders established a base for themselves in Unyanyembe in the 1830s - 40s. They allied with local chiefs and intermarried within the tribe. The best-known example is Muhammad bin Juma al-Murjebi, whose son Hamed - also known as Tippu Tip - was one of the most famous traders in the interior during the late 19th century. Muhammad bin Juma married Karunde, the daughter of a Nyamwezi chief in the 1840s and in so doing, established a base for himself and others who came from the coast to that vicinity.[41]

In the early years of the town's history, the size of the community varied seasonally as traders arrived and departed with the caravans. Increasing numbers of Arabs and coastal Muslims settled there in the latter half of the 19th century, making Tabora the most important Muslim town in the interior. Men of Omani descent controlled important sectors of the economy and, through business partnerships, linked the Congo River basin with the Indian Ocean.[42]

By the 1890s more than 80,000-100,000 porters were passing through Tabora every year, and with them came more people from the coast - a variety of Arabs and Swahili people - as well as Africans from all parts of the interior.[43] From Tabora the routes continued north to the Kingdom of Buganda, west to Lake Tanganyika and the Congo, and southwest to the slave-hunting regions along Lake Tanganyika.

From 1850-1891, Tabora was a lawless town. Order was established with the arrival of German administration.[44] The prominent Khoja Shia Ithna-Asheri trading family in the area was that of Nasser Virjee. Their businesses extended as far as Kigali and Bujumbura[45]. By the late 19th century, Nasser Virjee family had an active trading base in Bagamoyo from where goods were brought to Tabora by porters who travelled on foot. This journey usually took 20 days and was rife with risk, often involving theft and looting.[46]

Even under these challenging circumstances, Nasser Virjee and others like him extended their trade from Tabora to Bukoba and elsewhere. By 1922, Nasser Virjee and his family were in a strong enough position to purchase a sizable sisal estate of around 450 acres in Mwanza. They were the first family to open a ginnery there. For his acumen in entrepreneurship and having extensive business infrastructure, Nasser Virjee was accorded the title of "King of Business in Tanganyika" by his compatriots within the Khoja Shia Ithna-Asheri community.

The Merali Remtullas were another prominent Khoja Shia Ithna-Asheri trading family in Tabora. They initially had businesses in Bagamoyo that had been established at the time of Sultan Barghash well before the occupation of Tanganyika by the Germans, as well as connections in Ujiji and Bujumbura. They moved to Tabora at the turn of the 20th century.

JERAJ JIWA — SHARIFF JIWA — NAZARALI JIWA

Shariff Jiwa came to Africa by dhow from his hometown Tithwa in 1899. He moved to Tabora in 1902 with his brother, Jerajbhai where they worked with Alidina Visram for two years. Then they started their own retail business before moving on to wholesale business with branches in Kondoa, Bukoba, Mombasa, Mwanza and Ujiji. His brother Nazaralibhai and his son Mohamedali established a soft drink factory in Tabora.

In 1926, Shariff Jiwa moved to Kisumu, leaving his elder son Kermali to look after the Tabora business. He set up a maize mill and a cooking oil factory in partnership with a Hindu friend in Kisumu. In 1930, Daya Premji joined in the Kisumu branch with his elder son Mohamadali. Karmalibhai lived in Kisumu up to 1938, and then left for Mombasa, leaving his paternal uncle, Nazaralibhai together with his son Mohamadali Nazarali to continue the business.

After the death of Jerajbhai Jiwa in 1953, the business was divided. Bukoba, Kisumu and Mombasa businesses were taken over by Nazeralibhai's family whilst the family of Muhamadali Shariff Jiwa took over Moshi Trading Company Ltd. The heirs of Late Shariff Jiwa built a masjid in Nairobi for the ithaale thawab of their late father. Brother Muhamadali Shariff Jiwa's wife had also donated a musafirkhana in Moshi.

(Extracted from Community Directory 1960, Trans. F. Ali.)

Ruins of the Shariff Jiwa coffee factory

One of the old staff quarters

Tabora Imambada

The Abdalla Alarakhia family were the other family that moved from Bagamoyo to Tabora around 1900 as well. Like the Remtullas, they too had thriving businesses in Ujiji and Bujumbura.

Sheriff Jiwa and his brother Jeraj Jiwa came from Tithwa in Kathiawad in 1899. They then travelled from Bukoba to Tabora via Biharamulo, arriving in 1902. Initially, Sheriff Jiwa worked for Alidina Visram. After one year, the brothers started their own small business and with their honesty, business acumen, friendly nature and hard work, they soon became part of the major business firms of the time and had branches in Mombasa, Bukoba, Mwanza and Ujiji.

There were other families present in Tabora whose names are not recorded in archival material, including seven Ismaili families and two Hindu families. These families owned small retail/artisan shops. From Tabora, Khoja Shia Ithna-Asheri traders carried goods to Mwanza, Bukoba, Ujiji, Kigoma, Kigale, Congo and Bujumbura.[47] Arabs were the main buyers and the community members the main suppliers.

The early pioneering families went on to build the Shia Ithna-Asheri *imambada* in Tabora. Over time, due to various reasons, the Khoja Shia Ithna-Asheri community began to leave the town and by the 1970s, there were only two families left and after their departure from Tabora, the centre was left to the Bilal Muslim Mission of Tanzania.

MWANZA

In 1923, 40 Khoja Shia Ithna-Asheries lived in Mwanza and those who come from there fondly remember the place for its charm and the beautiful scenic shores of the imposing Lake Victoria.

One of the most prominent members of the community was Ladhabhai Meghji. He was born in Nagalpur, Kachchh in 1890, arrived in Zanzibar in 1903 at the age of 13 and worked for seven years in Nasser Virjee & Co. By 1912, records show that he had already settled in Mwanza where he started a small business. Success followed and with time he was trading in commodities such as grain, rice, wax and animal hides. He then expanded his businesses to include rice mills, coffee mills, a cotton ginning factory, and a mill producing cottonseed oil.

Whilst most businessmen at the time were just interested in cotton ginneries, Ladhabhai was greatly involved in the actual growing of cotton. He was keen to improve the quality of the crop by promoting better agricultural methods. He used to travel to all the districts including Ukerewe and reward the farmers who produced the best cotton. Because of his efforts, Mwanza became the foremost producer of high-quality cotton.

Ladha Meghjee (1890-1951)

Ladhabhai was born in Nagalpur, Kutch, India and migrated to Zanzibar at the age of 13.

In 1911, at the age of 21 he married Sakinabai, daughter of Janmohamed Ravji of Zanzibar. Sadly, Sakinabai passed away in 1923 during childbirth. In 1925 Ladhabhai got married to Fatmabai Alibhai in India.

He was keen in Jamaat and public community affairs. Ladhabhai donated land for the construction of the mosque in Mwanza and the musafarkhana was built under his leadership in 1937. He was the President of Indian Association of Mwanza for many years and trustee of Mwanza School Board. The Mwanza public library bears his name due to his significant contribution.

Soon after his death, a large piece of land was given to the Holy Family Church at a nominal price. The Holy Family Primary School, now Nyakahoja Primary School, was built on this land. He passed away in Mwanza at the age of 61. He left behind a widow, 9 sons and 3 daughters. (Africa Federation Archives, 4 November 2016)

His business adventures also led him to purchase two gold mines around the Buckreef region not too far from Geita. Today, these mines - although no longer in his family - are the second-largest gold mines in Africa.

From all the accounts available, Ladhabhai's practice of making all the communities in Mwanza stakeholders in their development provided a model for emulation. Known for the quality he espoused and practised, he set a standard for others to follow. His interest in and promotion of cotton farming earned him a prominent status within the cotton industry.

A visionary man of many diverse abilities, his aptitude for leadership was recognised and respected by both the Khoja Shia Ithna-Asheri and other Indian communities. He was involved in setting up the public library and sports club, both of which greatly benefitted the general population of the town. Because of his contributions, he was awarded the King George V Silver Jubilee Medal in 1935. After the Second World War, Ladhabhai was once again recognised by the British Government and awarded the coveted Defence Medal.

He was elected as the President of the Mwanza Indian Association as well as appointed a trustee of the Mwanza School Board. A philanthropist at heart, he donated a plot of land to the Khoja Shia Ithna-Asheri community and in 1937, oversaw the construction of a *masjid* and *musafarkhana* for the community there.

Many came to know of his personal charity only after Ladhabhai passed away. Individuals from all of Mwanza's different communities: Africans, Europeans, Asians, Christians, Hindus, and Muslims, attended the burial ceremony. The Asian community arranged a memorial service in his honour and the British authority in Mwanza honoured him with a 7-gun salute.

Nasser Virjee and his family finally settled in Mwanza in 1923. There, he purchased a 45-acre piece of land where he grew coffee and cashew nuts. He also started a new business - the Mwanza Cotton Company Trading Company Limited. It had two cotton ginneries and an oil mill. Nasser Virjee had ten children; seven sons and three daughters, two of whom passed away at a young age. The oldest child was Fatmabai, followed by Mohamedali, Abdulrasul, Hassanali, Gulamabbas, Abdul Hussein, Ebrahim and Mohammed Jaffer. Mohamedali also passed away at the age of twenty in Kuchchh.

Abdulrasul Virjee served the Africa Federation in the 1950s as its Chair. He was also the chair of several societies including the Association of Mwanza, and was awarded an MBE by Her Majesty, Queen Elizabeth II in 1953. He passed away in 1955.

Abdul Hussein Virjee spent most of his life in Mwanza and eventually retired to England. Ebrahim spent most of his life in Karachi, taking care of the Virji business there. Mohamed Jaffer was the most active and hardworking of all the siblings. He served the Mwanza Jamaat for more than five years, was a member of the City Council of Mwanza and was Chairman of the Muslim Association.

Hassanali Virjee was the Mayor of Mwanza between 1957-1958 and played a major part in expanding the Nasser Virji business with the help and cooperation of his younger brothers. He migrated to Canada in 1976.

Mayor Hussein N Virjee delivering a speech

Alhaj Mohammed Jaffer at Arusha Conference Centre minutes before his death

ALHAJ MOHAMMED JAFFER NASSER VIRJEE (1922-1985)

Alhaj Mohammed Jaffer was born in Mwanza and received his primary education there. He went to Mombasa for his secondary education and then joined the family business (Mwanza Cotton Trading Company) aged 18 years. In 1940, he became its director and of United Stationers & Printers, and Msumari Ltd all in Mwanza.

He was a member of TANU and after Tanganyika got independence, the party nominated him to become a Member of Parliament. Due to family commitments, he could not take up the position.

He served as a nominated member of Mwanza Town Council and the Vice-Chairman of Mwanza Chamber of Commerce. He was a member of East African Posts & Telecommunications and the BAKWATA Council. He served as the President of Mwanza Jamaat for 20 years as well as a Councillor to Africa Federation. He was also on the board of Governors of Schools, Governing Board of the local prison and a valued member of British Red Cross Society.

He was married to Kubrabai who served Mwanza Jamaat for 35 years by taking the responsibilities of the Muharram Tazia and Tabut. In 1970, Mohammed Jafferbhai health suffered a set back but continued to give services to the community. Sadly, he died minutes after making observations on the Chairman's address at the opening session of the 43rd Supreme Council Session held at Arusha in 1985.

(Federation Samachar, Vol 21, Issue No. 1, 1985)

Apart from Nasserbhai Virjee and Ladhabhai Meghji, there is also mention of Gulamalibhai Jetha from the Khoja Shia Ithna-Asheri community who held trusteeship of various community organisations in Mwanza.[48]

GULAMALI JETHA
(1901 - 1985)

Alhaj Gulamalibhai Jetha was born in Lalpur, India and migrated to Tanganyika in 1920. After working with Messrs. Nurmohammed Jessa and sons for a few years, he established his own business in Lindi.

From Lindi, he moved to Tabora and then to Mwanza. He was a pioneer in business and a leading industrialist. He established a ginnery and a rice mill in Masaka, Uganda.

Gulamalibhai served Mwanza Jamaat in various capacities, was its President for 25 years, and contributed substantially to the upliftment of the community. He was a staunch supporter of the Africa Federation and recipient of a special citation by the then Chairman of the Federation, Haji Ebrahimbhai Sheriff Dewji for his efforts in raising the Federation Foundation fund. (Africa Federation Archives)

Records show that the Mwanza Jamaat was small, consisting of the families of Manji Pirbhai, Jiwa Hasham, Nasser Virjee, Ladha Meghji, Gulamali Jetha, Mohamedali Karim, Pyarali Hasham, Bandali Damji, Khanmohamed Hasham, Fazal Visram Hassanali Pirbhai, Mohan Pirbhai, Gulamali Dewji, Anandi Khimji, Walli Kalyan, Hussein Ibrahim Railey, Mohamed Hussein Rehmtulla Mawji, Ahmed Jaffer, Sherali, Zawar, Suleman Manji and Pirbhai Rawji.

Around Mwanza, there were several small villages where Khoja Shia Ithna-Asheries had shops. Below is the list as provided by records:

- *Misungwi:* Mohamed Jaffer Harji
- *Malampaka:* Abdulhussein and Company, Gulamhussein Daya, Yusuf Alibhai, Mohamedali Kermali, Hassanali Alibhai, Kermali Dharamsi
- *Nansio:* Shahabuddin Alibhai, Sherali Mohamedtaki, Noorali Ladha Meghji, Haji Khimji
- *Ibaraginnery:* Bandali Damji, Mohamedali G.A. Satchu, Jafferali Abdulrasul Noormohamed, Ali Hassan Ahmed, Haji Juma
- *Magu:* Nazarali Jetha, Rashid Tarmohamed, Sherali Rajabali Ismail
- *Ngudu:* Fidahussein Manji, Hassanali Manji, Pyarali Valimohamed, Abdul Karim Merchant
- *Kisasa:* Rajabali Gulamhussein Sumar

- *Luguru:* Shariff Khimji
- *Shanwa:* Habib Pirbhai Dhanji, Kassamali Dev Karan, Ladha Jivraj
- *Kome:* Mohamedali Haji Somji, Bandali Walli Kalyan
- *Sengerema:* Rashid Dhalla's elder brother Hussein Dhalla
- *Buyombhe:* Jafferbhai
- *Katunguru:* Rashid Dhalla, his son Mohamedrafiq and family

KHARUMWA

Situated 18 miles from Lake Victoria, Kharumwa was another place where Khoja Shia Ithna-Asheries established a community. The settlement there began during the German rule in the 1900s and its pioneers were the Nasser Virjee family who started wholesale and retail shops in the area.

Kharumwa had local farmers producing peas, gram seed, chickpeas, *moong* (green gram), mustard, wheat, rice and cotton in relatively large quantities as well as thriving livestock and dairy farming practices. The Nasser Virjee Company invited and employed many Khojas to take advantage of these favourable conditions, advising them to invest in buying agricultural and dairy products.

However, living conditions were austere; Kharumwa did not have electricity or a water supply. For fresh water, the community had to employ a carrier who would transport water from Lake Victoria in drums carried by donkeys. During the rainy season, the roads would become flooded and remain impassable for several weeks. During these periods the community would have to harvest and store rainwater for measured use until the roads were accessible again.

In 1953, the British government dug wells which alleviated the water problem. Today, Kharumwa is a town in north-western Tanzania. It is the administrative centre for Nyang'hwale district, which is one of the five districts of the Geita Region.

According to the Africa Federation Archives, Suleiman Manji was the President and Treasurer of the Jamaat at Kharumwa and Hassanali Abdullah Dhirani was its Secretary. After Suleimanbhai Manji, his brother Fazal Manji became President and Treasurer and Gulamabbas Ladha Damji took over as Secretary.

In the 1950s, the Kharumwa Jamaat built a primary Indian Public School with adjoining quarters for the teachers.[49] In 1959, when the Chairman of Africa Federation, Alhaj Ebrahimbhai Sheriff Dewji visited Kharumwa to raise funds for the education and tabligh foundation, there were 15 families there.

KHARUMWA JAMAAT RESIDENTS
Sitting L-R: *Suleman Manji, Mawlana Sayed Sayade Akbar, Sherali Zaver.*
Standing L-R: *Amir Mohammed Manji, Fazal Manji.*

These were the families of Suleiman Manji, Mohamed Manji, Fazal Manji, Gulamhussein Ebrahim, Hassanali Abdullah Dhirani, Rashid Murji, Hassanali Rajabali, Jaffer Fazal, Gulamhussein Bandali, Ebrahim Sherali, Rajabali Zaver, Sheralli Zaver, Hussein Dawood Pardhan, Gulamabbas Ladha Damji and Jivraj Kunverji. Alhaj Ebrahim was able to raise Shs.16,000 from this small community.

By 1961, Gulamhussein Ebrahim had built a mosque with two shops aimed at bringing in rental income for Jamaat expenses. Around Kharumwa, there were several villages where Khoja Shia Ithna-Asheries ran retail businesses[50]. These families would attend Kharumwa Mosque and Imambada for Muharram and Ramadhan religious ceremonies. Amongst those who provided religious services to the Khoja Shia Ithna-Ashries of Kharumwa were Maulana Sayeed Sayade Akbar, Maulana Sayeed Azizul Hassan Naqvi, Hassan Abdulla Dhirani, Gulamabbas Abdallah Sumar, Mulla Ramzan Sumar, Mulla Nisar Chandoo, Jaffer, Ramzan Alimohammed Meghji, and Gulamabbas Ladha Damji.

The community continued to thrive until the 1970s when its members gradually began moving out of Kharumwa in pursuit of prospects elsewhere. In the present times, there is no longer a Khoja Ithna-Asheri presence in the town and the Sunni community looks after the *masjid, imambada* and *madrasah* properties. The fate of the school and teacher's quarters is unknown.[51]

BUKOBA

The history of the Khoja Shia Ithna-Asheries in Bukoba goes back to 1900 when Gulamabbas Visram first came from India. He arrived at the port of Mombasa and travelled inward to Kisumu, before finally settling in Bukoba town in 1901. In that same year, two cousins - Rashid Moledina Asser and Ahmed Jaffer Asser - also settled there. Within the decade, records show that almost 150 Khoja Shia Ithna-Asheries were living in Bukoba, amongst them the families of Nasser Mawji, Valji Bhanji, Pirbhai Gulamhussein and Amersi Sunderji.

Pirbhai Visram[52] writes that by 1914, the following families had already established businesses in Bukoba: Nasser Mawji (est.1904), Nasser Virji, Sheriff Jiwa, Walji Bhanji (est.1907), Pirbhai Gulamhussein, Amarsi Kurji, Abdulla Khimji (est.1908) and Amarsi Sunderji (est.1913). When the German Colonial Government opened up the borders with Rwanda and Burundi, four Khoja Shia Ithna-Asheries expanded their businesses with new branches in Kigali; these were Nasser Virji, Pirbhai Gulamhussein, Walji Bhanji and Abdulla Khimji.[53]

Gulamhussain Visram writes that before 1910

> there were three shops owned by Khoja Ithna-Asheri families in Bukoba. The owners were Jivraj Khatau, Valji Bhanji and Nasser Virji. There was one Khoja Ismaili shop belonging to Alidina Visram. Religious gatherings were held at the shops of Jivraj Khatau and Valji Bhanji and all the Indian Muslims who lived

in Bukoba used to attend these gatherings. After 1910, with the assistance of local Khoja Shia Ithna-Asheries, an *imambada* was built for the use of the community and an African religious teacher was employed to teach religious instructions to the children of the community.

At this time, Khoja Ismailis also used to attend the religious gatherings organised by Khoja Shia Ithna-Asheries. After the First World War, Ismaili missionaries came to Bukoba and instructed the Khoja Ismailis to disengage with Khoja Shia Ithna-Asheries. Relationships between the two communities began to deteriorate soon after.[54]

It seems that until 1910, all Indian Muslims observed their faith as one community in Bukoba and it was only after this period that the dynamics in the larger Khoja community in Gujarat and Bombay began to infiltrate and disrupt the unity of the Indian Muslim community there. Bukoba is just one example of such unified observances by all Muslim communities. The Khoja Shia Ithna-Asheri archives mention similar gatherings being held in many other places in East Africa.

By 1925, the Khoja Shia Ithna-Asheri community membership had increased as more families came to settle in Bukoba. Under the leadership of Gulamhussein Visram and with assistance from Pirbhai Visram (Kaka), Rashid Moledina and donations from communities in Mwanza, Kampala and Mombasa, the project to build a more accommodating *imambada* to cater for the needs of the growing community was started. Due to the ongoing war depression, it took them 15 years to complete the building. Pirbhai Visram finally laid the foundation stone in 1934.[55]

In the early 1940s, Kassamali Haji Alarakhiya collected funds to extend the local school which was previously named the Indian Public School and is presently known as Grewal Primary and Secondary school. He donated a number of buildings in Arusha too. His son, Gulamali, established one of the biggest industries in Bukoba - a coffee factory called "M/S BUKOP Ltd." in 1930. When the Alarakhiyas left, Abdallah Fazal purchased the factory.[56]

RASHID MOLEDINA   **FIDAHUSSEIN RASHID**

Born in Mombasa, at the age of 33, Rashid Moledina was a capable managing director of M/s Rashid Moledina & Co. [Mombasa] Ltd, and director of Rashid Moledina & Co.[T] Ltd] Bukoba. He had a good experience in the coffee market. He traveled to Europe, Middle East, Sudan, India, Pakistan, and Ceylon for business to meet clients who used to import coffee from him. Well-respected in the business community, he was a member of the managing committee of hard coffee - the Association of East Africa. He also served in the managing committee of Mombasa coffee Exchange.

He personally went out of his way to raise funds and contribute as much as he could for the community. He was Trustee for the Council and President for 3 years for "Hussayni Faiz" as well as Mombasa Ithnasheri Sports Club. He also served as a Trustee of the Khoja Shia Ithnasheri Education Board as well as 'Murtaza Ali's [a.s.]" 1400 years memorial trust. Haji Rashid Moledina was the Honorary Treasurer as well as trustee of the Mombasa Jamaat. After he passed away, his role of Honorary Treasurer given to his only son Fidahussein. (Extracted from The Community Directory 1960. Trans. F.Ali.)

BUKOBA - INDIAN PUBLIC SCHOOL

In 1920, the Indian Public school at Bukoba was an ordinary school located in a rented, corrugated-sheet building and only one teacher used to teach all the students. By 1924, the government approved a grant from which the new school was built. Pirbhai Visram laid the foundation stone of this school. I recall from my memories and what was related by my father that I joined this school some time in 1942.

At that time, a few teachers from India had been recruited. Every year, a new class was added. When I completed school in 1954, the 12th standard (metric) was introduced and I remember we were hardly 12 students. Due to lack of students, boys and girls shared the same class. Every morning we used to have religious prayers before proceeding to our classrooms. We sang the Indian national anthem. We used to utilize other facilities next door at the Hindu Union including the playground.

> The library had a good stock of Indian books and magazines.
>
> The following teachers are remembered for their dedication:
>
> [1]] M.D Bakre: The head master who served for about fifteen years; he was very strict when it came to discipline. By the Grace of Almighty, I had the opportunity to meet him in 1968 in Pune, India. He was a Brahmin so he never married until his death. He used to take us to Kashura hills and would sit for long hours admiring the nature. His hobbies included stamp collecting; after his death his collection was donated to one of the schools in Pune.
>
> [2] Zaverbhai Patel: Our math teacher whom I last met in London.
>
> [3] Mr. Sivasubramanyam: Our head master who encouraged the students and their parents to go for further studies and quite a number opted to go overseas, mostly to India
>
> [4] J. C. Haji: He introduced the activities of Scouting and Girl Guides. The first troop leader of scouts was Roshanali N. Ladha. We used to camp at Chamnene, cook our own food, sleep in the tents and spend even up to four days in camp.
>
> During all these years, a committee managed the school with representatives of different communities. Only the Chairman, Abdulla Fazal and the Secretary, Habib Halari secured their permanent seats for 33 years. The same committee also managed the Indian Public School in Kamachumu. As the number of teachers, arriving from India with their family increased, three residential blocks were built for the teachers, which presently serve as a hospital managed by the Asian Community.
>
> During the colonial rule a local prominent businessperson, P. S. Gerewal was nominated as the member of Lagco (Council) representing West Lake region. He built a new wing for the primary school with more facilities and the school was renamed Gerewal Primary School and managed by the Indian community.
>
> After independence, the second wing was built by the government to provide facilities for a secondary school and renamed as Gerewal Primary & Secondary School. Today, the Education Department of Tanzania manages the school.
>
> (-Roshan Abdullah Fazal, Past Chairperson of Africa Federation Archives. Ed. F. Jaffer.)

KIGOMA AND ENVIRONS

Ujiji is the oldest town in western Tanzania, located about 10 km south of Kigoma. In 1900, Ujiji was considered an important trading town with an estimated population of 10,000. Kigoma, situated in north-western Tanzania, was the other town that had a lake port on the north-eastern shores of Lake Tanganyika. It was also close to the border with Burundi and Congo.

Karmali Hansraj and Ladhabhai Damji have narrated and recorded their perilous journey from the East African coast into the hinterland of western Tanzania where they both eventually settled in Kigoma.

In 1909, Karmali Hansraj[57] arrived from India with his five-year-old son, Gulamhussain. They disembarked at Dar es Salaam and stayed at the Ismaili Musafarkhana. After a week, they set out in search of economic opportunities and decided to venture to Tabora and beyond. They took a train to Iglula and from there walked for two days covering the 60 miles to reach Tabora.

Once there, they rested for a month before trekking for 70 miles over another couple of days to reach the town of Manakurwa. In Manakurwa, there were four small trading shops. Three belonged to Khoja Shia Ithna-Asheries: Shariff Jiwa, Nasser Virjee and Wali Omar and one belonged to an Arab, Khalil bin Nasser. Karmali Hansraj stayed in Manakurwa for one year working for Wali Omar but the place did not suit him and he decided to go back to Tabora.

From Tabora, he went out again, this time first by train to Malagarasi and then on foot 120 miles to Ujiji, a hub of economic activity. At Ujiji, there were 15 shops, all most likely belonging to Khoja Shia Ithna-Asheries. Nasser Virjee & Co. employed Hansraj and he writes that at the time, all the religious gatherings were held at Nasser Virjee's house. After working for three months in Ujiji, he was transferred to a trading branch of Nasser Virjee & Co. in Bujumbura.

GULAMHUSSAIN KARMALI HANSRAJ (D. 1961)

Karmalibhai passed away in Bujumbura, Burundi while his wife Labbai is buried in Kigoma.

Gulamhusseinbhai Karmali passed away in Dar es Salaam in 1961 after suffering a heart attack and is buried in Kigoma. His wife Roshanbanu passed away in 1977 and is also buried in Kigoma.

Their children were Mohamedtaki, Sultan, Kassamali, Noorbanu Dhalla, Maryam Shamji, Fatma Gulamali Rajabali and Nargis Jagani.

(Africa Federation Archives, 15 April 2016)

Apart from Nasser Virjee's shop, there were four other Indian and eight Arab shops there. In 1915, **Nasser Virjee & Co.** closed down their business in Bujumbura which was under German rule at the time. Two years later, Belgian authorities took over the control of the town. Due to the uncertain circumstances during World War I, Karmali Hansraj moved to Ujiji for two months, but upon his return, he opened a shop with his son in Bujumbura and remained there until 1936. During their years there, the family of Kermali Hansraj provided their residence to the community to hold all religious functions. After they left Bujumbura, they settled in Kigoma and transferred their business there.[58]

Ladha Damji[59] was born in Nagalpur. In 1905, aged 17, he came to Zanzibar by ship and was first employed by Hasham Merali. He then met Nasser Virjee and got a position in Nasser Virjee & Co. for three years with the condition that he would be willing to travel to wherever the company required him to. Ladha Damji recounts that he began his employment in Bagamoyo and after a short time there, was sent to Kilimathi which was 450 miles away. Accompanied by a group of 20 local African helpers who carried the trading stock, he made the 20-day journey on foot. He stayed in Kilimathi for 12 months before being assigned to Tabora at a distance of 200 miles, which he again covered on foot.

Six months later, he was transferred to Ujiji, a further 200 miles away. Ladhabhai walked there to meet with Bandali Esmail Muraj who managed the Ujiji branch and stayed on to work there for 18 months. Upon the completion of the contracted three years, he continued for one more year. At the end of this period, Nasser Virjee, impressed with Ladha's loyalty, gave him a ticket to India where he went to get married. Upon his return, he once again joined the employ of Nasser Virjee & Co. He travelled by train to Tabora, then by foot to Kigoma where he worked under Ali Hasham, who was the manager of the Kigoma branch.

By 1912, there were 40 Khoja Shia Ithna-Asheries living in Kigoma. There was also an Ismaili community, the most renowned member being a man called Dosa Thaver. Religious celebrations and commemorations were held at his house and attended by both Khoja Ismailis and Khoja

Ithna-Asheries.⁶⁰ At the time, there were tensions in Zanzibar, but in Kigoma these two groups lived side by side without tension. It appears that their daily challenges surpassed any religious differences that the communities may have been aware of. Such camaraderie was observed in many other small towns in the interior of East Africa, where each group had a small number of adherents and needed their united efforts to overcome the constant obstacles they faced.

In 1914, Ladha Damji was transferred to Kasanga (near Kulugu) 600 miles away where he worked for about five months. When World War I broke out, the small town was vacated on the instruction of the German colonial authority. As a result, Ladhabhai had to travel with his family by dhow to "Sultanfema" 50 miles away. After two months there, he moved 200 miles into the interior to "Kirodo" to further avoid the effects of the war. At Kirodo, his wife delivered a baby who passed away within a few days. This was a sad time for Ladhabhai, but times were tough for everyone due to the ravages of war. When he finally made his way back to Ujiji, he continued to work for Nasser Virjee despite the tough work conditions of the time.

In 1917, Ladha Damji moved to Kigoma, which at the time was a small town where lions lurked the streets in the late evenings. He built his own clay brick house and settled there. Kigoma slowly began to prosper as a port and the 40 Khoja Shia Ithna-Asheries living in Ujiji began to migrate to Kigoma one by one. As they increased in numbers, there was a need for an *imambada* that could accommodate the growing community in Kigoma.

Kigoma mosque, built 1935

In 1922, a house was purchased and converted to accommodate religious gatherings. Daily prayers were held there and a *madrasah* was set up to impart religious instruction with an African religious teacher being employed to teach Qur'an to the children of the community. One of the rooms in the house was allocated to accommodate travellers and visitors to the area.

By all accounts, the Asian community co-existed well in Kigoma and lived together co-hosting and attending many functions.

Celebration by Asian Community of the Independence of India and Pakistan (1947) on Kigoma club ground

Guard of Honour by scouts at above celebration (1947)

From the accounts of those who resided in Kigoma at the time, the community appears to have been equally loyal to the British Government, to India and Pakistan and to the Government of Tanganyika following its independence from British rule in December 1961. Their loyalty, perhaps, was shaped dynamically by the geopolitics of the time.

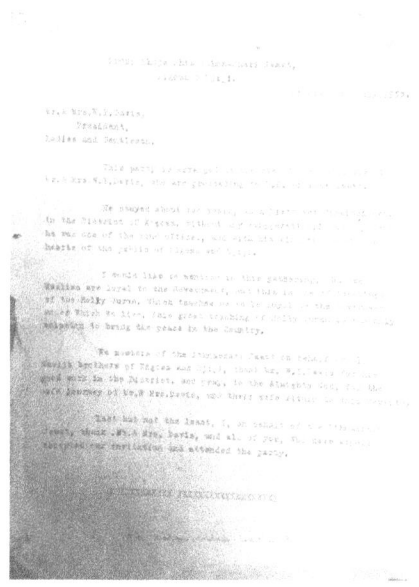

Party 23rd July 1955

LADHABHAI DAMJI
(1890-1963)

MOHAMMADALI LADHA DAMJI
(1915-1963)

Mohammadali bhai was born in Ujiji-Kigoma. After his primary education, he went to Zanzibar for his secondary education, where he also attained his religious education. Upon his return to Kigoma in 1930, he joined his father's business and expanded it, opening several branches all over the district. They dealt in agricultural produce mainly dry fish (dagaa). Later, they expanded into transport, sundries, hardware, and motor spares. Ladha Damji & Sons was the first company to build a rice mill and became the sole exporters of processed rice to other regions of Tanganyika. Later on, Remtulla Alibhai Panju, G. R. Ladak and Hussein Dhalla also built rice mills to cater for the huge production of paddy in the region. Ujiji became the main centre for milling paddy rice, which was now the main export from Kigoma region.

Mohammadali bhai married Mariambai, daughter of Hasham bhai Shivji of Ujiji and they were blessed with two sons, Akberali and Mukhtar. He has a record of honorary services both and some of them were: President of Khoja Shia Ithna-Asheri Jamaat of Kigoma in late 1950s, Chairman of Chamber of Commerce, Councilor of Kigoma Jamaat in Africa Federation in 1950s, Senior member of East African Muslim Welfare Society, Founder and Trustee of Khoja Shia Ithna-Asheri primary school of Kigoma Jamaat in 1950s, Chairman of Suleiman Premji Sports Club, Chairman of the organizing committee of celebration of India and Pakistan independence.

In 1953, he represented Kigoma region in celebrating the Coronation Ceremony in Dar es Salaam. He led the delegation for raising funds to build two houses for the Jamaat. In 1954, Mohamedali bhai took Mwalimu Nyerere in his car for TANU campaign trips in the region. On 23 July 1955, he organized a farewell party, on behalf of Khoja Shia Ithna-Asheri Jamaats of Kigoma and Ujiji, for Mr and Mrs W. B. Davis (District Commissioner) who were going back to UK.

(Africa Federation Archives, 13 February 2018)

MBALE

Once Khoja Shia Ithna-Asheries reached Mwanza and Bukoba, they were then able to cross Lake Victoria into Uganda and settle in Kampala, Bukakara and Masaka. Others used the northern coast that linked Mombasa and Tanga with Lake Victoria and chose to settle in towns like Mbale, Tororo, Iganga and Jinja.

Mbale is a picturesque area surrounded by mountains and beautiful waterfalls. When Walji Bhanji[61] came to Mbale in 1906, there were already 16 shops there belonging to Khoja Ismailis and Hindus. Historically, Asian traders who came via Jinja and Budaka by road were already in Mbale before the construction of the Uganda Railway.[62] In this sense, Asian traders were already established before the influx of traders that came with the construction of the railway.[63] Historical accounts show that Asian and African traders were already active before the British Administration had full control of Mbale.

In particular, Alidina Vasram had connections with one of the largest African trading establishments of Kakungulu belonging to the chief of Mbale. The latter's diary reveals that on 27 December 1904, he bought cloth worth 349 Indian Rupees and four days later, on 31 December, he made a deal with Alidina Vasram to build a permanent home paying 4900 Indian Rupees in advance.[64]

Walji Bhanji bought a plot of land, built a house and a shop and began a wholesale business. In 1919, he opened a cotton ginnery in partnership with Remtullah Rawji. Lalji Rawji,[65] manager of the ginnery, recalls the arrival of Walji Bhanji in 1906 and how he applied to the District Commissioner Perryman for a plot. In the beginning, Mbale was very much an undeveloped area surrounded by forest on all sides. Houses were made of mud and iron sheets and wild animals would roam around in the evenings hunting for prey. By 1922, however, more Khoja Shia Ithna-Asheries were coming to settle in Mbale as shopkeepers.

The community already had a cemetery given to them in 1906 by the government. An Iranian Shia Ithna-Asheri, Mohammed Baqir who was already a resident of Mbale assisted the newly-arriving Khoja Shia Ithna-Asheries in their times of need. He had built an *imambada* that held regular religious gatherings. Once more families began to settle in Mbale, the community acquired two plots from the government and in 1926, built a new *imambada* on one plot and a house on the other plot to generate rental income for the community. Ali Mohammed Nanji, Remtullah Rawji and Vasanji Gangji assisted and contributed their time and wealth generously for the benefit of the community.

Lalji bhai Rawji

Laljibhai Rawji recalls the arrival of Waljibhai Bhanji, who started a wholesale business in Mbale. Waljibhai used to trade with Mombasa in crop produce. Remtullabhai Rawji was his manager.

In 1919, they jointly opened a cotton ginnery at Budaka, a town near Mbale. In 1922, he constructed buildings and warehouses at Ladoto (22 miles from Mbale) and appointed Laljibhai as manager.

There were four or five Ithna-Asheri shops at Mbale. An Iranian called Mohamedbaqir who was a hunter and a trader in ivory, built two rooms on land adjacent to his mud house where he held regular religious lectures for the community.

He was very pious and helpful and instilled great interest in religion among our brothers. An influenza epidemic once resulted in many deaths and it was Br. Mohamedbaqir who arranged for free medical treatment and general aid. Other brothers who served the Jamaat were Alimohamed Nanji, Vasanji Gangji and Remtulla Rawji.

Laljibhai recalls that in 1906, DC Perryman gave the community a plot for the cemetery. In 1926, a public procession was planned for Ashura night, however, the District Comissioner of Mbale was not in favour for fear of riots.

He also recalls an incident in 1914 when he was travelling from Jinja to Mbale in a cart pulled by four men. Two wild buffaloes suddenly appeared and the four men ran away leaving Laljibhai alone. Fortunately, at the same time some wild animals started howling in the nearby valley and their noise drove the buffaloes away. Laljibhai started pushing the cart himself and soon the four men re-appeared and they continued the journey.

The other prominent method of transport during this period was 'machera" where others would carry people in a litter. The DCs preferred this mode of transport. He recalls that in 1919, there was a worm infestation and farms destroyed leading to a famine.

(Africa Federation Archives, 24 February 2017)

Vasanji Gangji[66], who came to Mbale from Mombasa by foot (a distance of 710 miles) writes that in the late 1920s, he approached the Khoja Ismaili community leaders to accommodate Khoja Shia Ithna-Asheri children in their school, but he was met with refusal. After this rejection, he worked with Ibrahim Ladha, Remtulla Rawji and Mohammed Jamal to raise funds for a community school.

Over time, children from other communities also began to attend this school. In 1933, the government granted the community a new plot of land and a new school was built to accommodate the increasing number of children in the community. By 1956, the Khoja Shia Ithna-Asheri community had established itself and as the numbers grew, the community decided to collect donations for a bigger *imambada*.

Alimohamed Nanji, Mohamedali Hansraj, Abdulrasul Vasanji Gangji and Rajabali Khimji collected Shs.155,000 from the communities throughout East Africa and the Chair of Africa Federation officially opened the *imambada* for functions in 1957.

Imambada in Mbale, Uganda

MUHAMADALIBHAI G. R. HANSRAJ (1923-2009)

Muhamadalibhai was born in 1923. After completing his basic education in Soroti, he joined Allidina Visram High School in Mombasa. In 1940, he joined his father's business and came to Mbale to expand the business.

At the age of 20, he was elected as the Secretary of the Indian public school in Soroti and served the committee from 1942 to 1945. From 1946-1947, he served in the Mbale Indian Association committee and the Mbale Muslim Association. He served as the Secretary of the East African Muslim Welfare Society from 1955-1958 and thereafter as its Vice President.

He was the first mayor in 1959 and served as the first Secretary of its Chamber of Commerce. At community level, he was a committee member of Mbale Jamaat from 1946 until 1956 and served as President thereafter.

(Trade Directory 1960, Trans. F. Ali)

SOROTI

Ngoro[67] and Soroti[68] are the cotton towns of Uganda. By 1912, Ngoro had 13 shops, three of them belonging to Khoja Shia Ithna-Asheries: Habib Daya, Mohammedali Daya and Gulamhussain Daya. Although there were only three families, they had an *imambada* where

Gulamhussein Daya conducted religious ceremonies that all the Indian Muslims of Ngoro attended. Whilst the community remained small and some eventually migrated to Soroti and Mbale, preservation of faith and children's primary education was a priority for them. The community in Ngoro built a primary school and an *imambada* that they opened in 1959. Ramzanali G. R. Hansraj, Rajabali and Mohammed Sumar assisted in this project.

Moledinabhai Merali[69] writes that when Haji Merali Nanji arrived in Soroti in 1914, there were only four shops in the small town. Soroti like its neighbours was not yet developed and wild animals lurked within the human settlements. When Moledina Merali arrived in 1919, circumstances had improved and there were twelve shops, four belonging to Khoja Shia Ithna-Asheries. Once settled in Soroti, Moledinabhai began to hold weekly religious functions at his house.

In 1926, the Indian Association of Soroti started a school under a tree and later bought a plot of land on which they built a primary school. In 1931, the government granted the Khoja community a plot of land on which an *imambada* was constructed with the assistance of Gulamhussain Hansraj and members of the community. As the community grew, a new *imambada* - with a *musafarkhana* - was built in 1949. Moledina Merali, Gulamhussain Hansraj, Juma Ramji, Alibhai Merali, Hassanali Khaki and Abdalla Nurmohammed were influential in getting this project completed.

For the community of Soroti, the name of Gulamhussein Remtulla Hansraj[70] is synonymous with service. His life was spent helping others. He arrived from Kachchh at the age of 12 and was employed by Ismail Haji Khimji who had a business in Lindi. Upon completion of his three-year contract, Ismail Haji Khimji was so impressed with the young man that he extended the contract for a further 30 months. Gulamhussein showed such responsibility that Ismail Khimji went for pilgrimage and left him in charge of all the businesses when he was just 15 years old. Some years later, Gulamhussein went to Kachchh to get married and when he came back, he settled in Soroti.

His services were not reserved for the community alone; he also contributed to the well-being of the general population. He served the

Muslim Association of Soroti and the Indian Association of Soroti and held a position as trustee of the Soroti school board. When he finally got a chance to perform pilgrimage, his passion for the Qur'an was ignited when he saw pilgrims reciting and discussing it. He was greatly saddened by the fact that he could neither read nor understand it. Upon his return, he made a disciplined effort and was able to learn and understand the Qur'an within three months. Such was his love for the holy text that people often saw him reading it in his spare time.

His humble disposition to serve humanity began from a young age and continued throughout his life. Incidents of Khojas such as Gulamhussein Hansraj and their dedication to service are mentioned repeatedly in community literature and conversations with elders. Individuals such as these are the people who shaped the early history and left legacies to be emulated.

Gulamhussein Hansraj

Gulamhussein bhai arrived in Africa at the age of 12 and joined Ismail Khimji in Lindi. He had a three-year contract at a salary of 1000 kodis, which was equivalent of 300 rupees for 3 years. At that time, the community's population was 200.

He recalls fellow traders as Ali Walli, Ismail Khimji, Jaffer Najak, Moledina Waaras, Alidina Khaki, Gulamhussein Pardhan, Alidina Sajan, Moledina Mohamed, Gulamali Jaffer, Moledina Sumar, Allarakhia Sumar, Murji Moledina, Hirji Merali, Talib Dossa, Jaffer Premji, Pirmohamed Janmohamed and Mulla Esmail Gulamhussein. Traders from nearby villages regularly came to Lindi for Muharram.

Four-wheel 'rukwama' carriers transported merchandise from rural areas such as wax, ivory, rubber and grain. Goods going out from Lindi were mainly clothing, salt and tobacco. Two prominent Arab traders were Bashir bin Ali and Bwana bin Haji who mainly dealt in lime (chokaa). There were also two Liwalis namely Ali bin Athmani and Mohamed bin Zubeir.

Having gained some experience, Gulamhussein bhai travelled to Antalaha, Madagascar where his uncle lived. He stayed there for six months but was not impressed so he left for Zanzibar. After staying a month there, he returned to India in 1914 and got married. He came back to Jinja in 1920, worked for Haji Merali and later transferred to the shop's branch in Namasagali. Haji Merali was a partner with Jumabhai Ramji. After the death of Jumabhai Ramji, Gulamhusseinbhai took charge of their shop in Bugondo. Later on, he opened his own shop in the same town.

Due to the challenges of educating children in Bugondo, Gulamhusseinbhai moved to Soroti in 1927. The school in Soroti consisted of 20 children studying under a tree. In 1930, a school was constructed and 60 pupils enrolled. Over the years, more classes were added and the student body reached 600. Gulamhusseinbhai passed away in Soroti and is buried there. His children are Mohamedali, Ramzanali, Pyarali, Roshanali, Kulsum Somani, Sughra Mehrali, Rukia Fida Ladha and Shirin Khimji (all deceased) and Anwarali. (Trade Directory 1960)

JINJA

Lake Victoria is Africa's biggest lake and on its northern edge of the lake, there is a waterfall which some people believe is the source of the River Nile. The locals who have been part of the landscape for centuries call this river Kiyara which means "water breaking upon the river's rocks".[71]

Situated on the shores of Lake Victoria is a town called Jinja, which became the main town of the Eastern province of Uganda. When Nasser Pradhan[72] arrived in 1908, Jinja only had huts and houses mainly built of mud. There were four Khoja Shia Ithna-Asheries living there already. They were Walji Bhanji, Haji Merali, Abdalla Nathoo and Juma Muman, each having a trading shop.

Abdalla Nathoo had built a dedicated space behind his house to hold religious gatherings where Bohora, Ismaili and Sunni Muslim faithful gathered. It is interesting to note that in Jinja, a Sunni brother used to recite the religious lectures for the whole of the congregation. During the commemorations of Imam Hussein (pbuh), Sunni, Bohora and Ismaili families participated and contributed just as the Khoja Shia Ithna-Asheries did. As each community increased in numbers and set up their own centres, such egalitarian religious gatherings ceased. The impact, if any, that this separation had on the religious unity they had built over the years would be an interesting subject to study.

Jinja Imambada

In 1927, the Khoja Shia Ithna-Asheri community built a new *imambada* in Jinja with the help of financial contributions from all over East Africa. Haji Merali and Suleiman Ismaili assisted in raising these funds. Habib Kassamali Jaffer paid for the construction of the mosque. The other important personality who left his mark in Jinja was Hassanali Rashid[73]. He served the community from 1928 until 1941. He also participated in interfaith activities between various Muslim communities encouraging them to gather together at events.

With the advent of electricity, telephone, railways and mechanised transportation, Jinja prospered. In 1960, it boasted cotton ginneries, sugar factories, oil factories and cotton mills. The community benefited from and thrived on this success.

MOHAMED MANEK

NASSER PARDHAN

After a long sea journey from India, Nasserbhai Pardhan arrived in Zanzibar in 1900. He lived in Zanzibar, Pemba and Tanganyika before opening a shop at Changamwe, a suburb of Mombasa. After spending four months at Changamwe, he travelled to Kisumu by train and onwards to Jinja by boat. He recalls that in Jinja Abdulla Nathoo had constructed a special room made of iron sheets for holding religious gatherings. A famous Sunni Aalim, Molvi Abdulla Shah used to give religious lectures. Haji Tamachi Turk, another Sunni brother had very friendly and cordial relations with our members and used to sponsor nyaz (Sacred food) and majlis (religious lecture and lamentations). The nyaz on 12 Muharram was regularly sponsored by him. Four Bohra families were close to our community and the nyaz on 9 of Muharram was regularly sponsored by one of them - Abdulhussein Kadarbhai. After 1958, the Bohra community started having their own programmes due to an increase in their numbers.

In 1910, some European families opened businesses in Jinja. The main agricultural produce was chillies (pilipili hoho) and simsim. At first, cotton produced was little and of poor quality. Mr. Burkell, a European, used a manual spinning wheel (charkha) to gin cotton.

Due to encouragement from the government, cotton production increased and by 1923, cotton became the main agricultural produce. In 1918, there was an outbreak of influenza, which led to many deaths. Up to 1926, bicycles were used as the main means of communication. Postal services started in 1906 when Haji Suleman Turk offered his guarantee that he would sell stamps worth 500 rupees every month. Telegraph services also started in 1906. Local telephone services started in 1910 and extended to nearby areas in 1940. The Rupee was the currency in vogue until 1920; the florin introduced in 1921 and shillings and cents in 1922.

Mohamed Manek migrated from India to Mombasa in 1905. He came to Jinja via Kisumu by train and then Entebbe by boat. After working for 15 years, he bought a farm near Bujuta, 14 miles from Jinja. He grew rubber, coffee, sugarcane and maize at this farm as well as produced jaggery (coarse brown sugar) from sugarcane. Mohamedbhai also kept cows and goats. Mohamedbhai and his family lived in a house made of mud. Once a group of bandits, armed with bows, arrows and spears attacked his home while he was away. His wife, Fatmabai took a rifle and started shooting in the air. On hearing shots, the bandits ran away and thus, Fatmabai - who had learned how to use a rifle from Mohamed - was able to avert disaster.

Jinja had its share of raids. Once, fifty bandits armed with weapons, their faces covered with mud and charcoal, raided two Indian shops at Bujuta, seven miles from Jinja. One of the shops belonged to Nasser Pardhan. On learning of the raid, Mohamed Manek arrived at the scene with his pistol. The bandits fled but the loot was not recovered. A similar incident happened in 1917 at Kaberamaido at a shop where Nasser Pardhan was manager when 15 people stormed in and demanded free cigarettes; he refused and they attacked him with sharp long sticks. Nasserbhai immediately got hold of a long knife (panga) and a rhino whip and confronted them with the help of the others in the shop. The bandits fled.

In 1926, there was an outbreak of plague and an Ismaili brother, Rashid Khamis, his wife and his daughter all got it. When Rashid's wife died, no one was ready to give ghusl due to the infectious nature of the disease. Fatmabai, Mohamedbhai's wife, and an African woman carried out the rites. On the second day, Rashid passed away and Mohamed gave him ghusl and handed over the body to the Ismaili community. On the third day, the daughter passed away and once again, Fatmabai carried out the ghusl rituals. (Africa Federation Archives, 5 May 2017)

KAMPALA

Rashid Nurmohammed[74] and his brother arrived in Zanzibar from India in 1905. From there, Rashid went to Mombasa, then to Nairobi and then via Kisumu before finally reaching Kampala[75] in 1907. After five years of employment, he opened his shop there. According to him, among the Khoja Shia Ithna-Asheries in Kampala were Walji Bhanji, Khimji Bhanji, Bahadur Mawji and Jetha Damji, all of whom had large businesses and employed many people.

Rashid recalls that the combined number of shops that Walji Bhanji and Khimji Bhanji owned in Kampala as well as in the interior of Uganda was around 45. This can be compared to Alidina Visram, an Ismaili entrepreneur, who had around 100 shops all over Uganda. Within the Khoja Shia Ithna-Asheri community there were also the families of Jamal Ramji, Jamal Walji, Ladha Kassam, Jaffer Pradhan,

Rashid Nurmohammed, Amersi Sunderji and Kurji Jetha, who were all progressing in their respective businesses.

By 1912, the community in Kampala had an *imambada* that was built and donated by Khimji Bhanji. They held their religious functions there as well as the religious instruction classes for community children. Khoja Ismaili's and Bohora's also joined in the ceremonies. Rashid Nurmohammed gave the lectures.

When Kara Walli[76] arrived in Kampala in 1912, aged 12, there were 100 Khoja Shia Ithna-Asheries in Kampala. He noted how the community, whilst persevering with the difficulties of life in the new land, still took on any economic opportunity available to them. At the same time, they were actively holding religious functions to preserve their Ithna-Asheri faith.

KARABHAI WALLI

Karabhai arrived in Africa, in 1912 aged 22. He travelled by train from Mombasa to Kisumu then via Fort Bell to finally reach Kampala. In Kampala, he worked for Walji Bhanji. At the time there were 100 community members there and 10 shops belonging to them.

From 1913 to 1915, Karabhai lived in Barara. In 1925, he established an institute for children under the Indian Association. In 1930, this institute was awarded a government grant.

Car transport in Kampala started in 1915/16 and by 1920, the telephone lines had connected Kampala, Jinja and Entebbe.

In 1935/36, railway lines were introduced and by 1940, electricity was connected. Gradually our community members increased and by the grace of the Almighty, a big imambada was built in 1959. (Trade Directory, 1960)

In 1915, Alidina Visram established the first cotton ginnery in the area. Amongst the Khoja Shia Ithna-Asheries, Jamal Ramji installed a cotton ginnery in 1922 and by 1925 owned a coffee factory as well. In 1932, Hasham Jamaal established a cotton ginnery. By 1944, Jamal Walji, Ladha Kassam and Merali Dewji had also established cotton ginneries. As with all the surrounding areas, electricity, telephone lines and mechanised transport changed the face of Kampala and brought prosperity. From 1920, the Khoja Shia Ithna-Asheri community began to increase in numbers.

KHIMJIBHAI BHANJI

The Kampala Jamaat was formed in the 1920s and the first constitution drafted and registered in 1926.

The then President of the Jamaat, Khimjibhai Bhanji offered a roofed structure in his home to be used as imambada by the jamaat.

(Africa Federation Archive, 11 April 2020)

At this time, Kampala also saw a larger presence of other Indian caste communities such as Lohana, Vania and Patidar who began to establish their trading position in Uganda. To accommodate the increased social and religious requirements, a new *imambada* was built in 1919 and then extended in 1929 and 1945.

The old Kampala Imambada and Baitussalaat (1930) Presently Wilson Mall, Wilson Road - still owned by Kampala Jamaat

The Old Imambada building (the third one), part of which was also a *Baituassalaat* (prayer hall), was built in 1930; its foundation stone was laid by Kurji Jetha, (grandfather of Dr Jafferali Asaria). Before this, Kampala Jamaat had an *imambada* made of corrugated iron sheets, a common feature in those days. Jamal Ramji donated the plot for the first mosque on Wilson road in 1919/20. Khimji Bhanji, Rashid Nurmohamed, Nasser Virji, Ladha Kassam and Bahadurali Mawji among others contributed to the cost of the mosque complex itself.[77]

Under Alarakhia Kassam,[78] who served the community with passion, extensions were made to the *imambada* and eventually a new religious centre built. He was assisted by many others including Jamal Ramji, Jamal Walji, Ladha Kassam and Jaffer Pradhan.

1960 saw the completion of a well-designed Kampala Mosque, situated at an elevation, overlooking open grounds and with a new *imambada* on one side. Mirza Ahmed Hassan Kazmaini had laid the foundation stone for the construction of the mosque in 1959. Upon completion of the mosque in 1960, Maulana Seyed Tahzibul Hassan Saheb formally opened it. The Africa Federation Chairman Haji Ebrahimbhai opened the *imambada*. By this time, the community also had their own primary and secondary school with boarding.

Kampala Imambada 1959

Kampala Mosque 1960

ALI BHAI RAMJI

Alibhai Ramji came to Africa in 1896 and started a business with his brother Jamalbhai. In 1904, Jamalbhai established a business in Jinja, Uganda. In 1921/22, he started a cotton ginnery, and then in 1927 opened a coffee industry. His son donated the wonderful masjid (drawings next page) in his father's name in Kampala in 1974.

Kampala's old imambada (Neat Drawing)

Kampala's new imambada (Neat Drawing)

NURMOHAMED HASHAM JAMAL

Hasham Jamal Khoja Shia Ithna-Asheri Kampala Boarding

> **WAQF NAMU for the New Mosque and Imambada, Kampala**
> **Sunday 18 August 1963**
>
> With greetings and by the Almighty's *taufiq* on behalf of Haji Alibhai Ramji Charitable Trust, the Masjid built on Plot 108, Nakivubo, North Road, Kampala has been given as *Waqf* and for this we are really thankful to the Lord.
>
> We are greatly indebted to the Mumineen who sincerely assisted in bringing this task to a completion and by making it (the masjid) neat, attractive and beautiful. The full authority of running and managing the religious activities at the Masjid is handed over to the K.S.I. Jamaat of Kampala, which is fully responsible for the same, neither Haji Alibhai Ramji Charitable Trust, its trustees, nor any of its family members has the right over it, they remain as normal community members participating only in functions at the Masjid.
>
> Furthermore, we will be obliged to the Kampala Jamaat to solemnize the sanctity of the Masjid by having the *sigha* recited, announcing the Masjid as *Waqf* and conducting its inauguration.
>
> A Masjid being the Lord's house, our earnest request is that its sacredness remains at all times and may the Almighty grant us all the *taufiq* for the same. We are overtly grateful to the Kampala Jamaat for accepting to shoulder this responsibility wholeheartedly. In the blessings that He grants us, in it being a share of the 14 infallibles, we praise HIM and with the *Wasila* of the *Panjatan*, may these services of ours be accepted in the realm of the All Powerful. Ameen.
>
> On behalf of Haji Alibhai Ramji Charitable Trust: Mohammedali Haji Alibhai Ramji – Trustee, Pyarali Mohammedali Haji Alibhai – Trustee.
>
> *(Africa Federation Archives, Trans. by F. Ali)*

Past Presidents of Kampala Jamaat 1920s -1955

- *Marhum Khimjibhai Bhanji - 1920s*
- *Alibhai Jeraj - 1920s to early 30s*
- *Rashidbhai Noormohamed - 1930s*
- *Alarakhia Kassam - 1935s*
- *Mohamedbhai Alibhai Ramji - 1940s*
- *Akbarali Abdulla Nathoo*
- *Haji Habibhai Walji - 1949*
- *Hajibhai Merali - 1950's*
- *Sultanali Gulamhusein A. Datoo - 1954*
- *Gulamhusein Kurji Jetha -1955*

(Africa Federation Archives, 11 April 2020)

Haji Habibhai Walji
Longest serving trustee and a renowned philanthropist, he contributed a great deal to Jamaat activities.

Ebrahimbhai Kassam
(Past President and Trustee) Noteworthy devotion to Jamaat. He started serving when he was only 10 years old.

Growth of the KSI community in Uganda
Excerpt from 'Sustained Struggle-on the life and times of Mohamedjaffer Sheriff Dewji (1889-1961)'
by Hassan A. M. Jaffer
(Reproduced with permission of the author)

In 1961, I was visiting Kampala when I went over to see a friend, Gulamali Manji, who introduced me to his father, Manjibhai Walji. When Manjibhai recognized me, he asked, "How is your grandfather?" Before I could respond, Manjibhai quipped, "Tell him to come back to Kampala. There is Allah in Kampala now!" The words used in Cutchi were '*Toje Dade ke cho, bhale pacha ache. Hane Allah hida achi vyo aae*'. I was stunned at this comment and did not know how to react. As I stared at Manjibhai in utter disbelief, with a smile, Manjibhai beckoned me to sit down and explained.

"Your grandfather came here once for the month of Muharram (in 1942). We had our old Imambara then, part of which was used as *Baituassalaat*, since we did not have a proper Masjid."

"In his Muharram Majalis, for ten days, your grandfather lectured us with stress on one subject only – *Salaat*. He talked about the importance of *Salaat*, the need for offering *Salaat* on time and the importance of offering *Salaat* in a Masjid. He talked about *Sawab* for building a Mosque and the *ajr* (reward) of *Baaqeatussalehaat* for such charity. He also stressed on the importance of paying religious dues, Zakaat, Khums and for making donations for good causes. He made a sarcastic remark about Kampala in Gujarati: '*Imam Hussein che; Khuda nathi!*' This comment irked.

"In Kampala there are many well-to-do businessmen. He cautioned us about the consequences of not paying religious dues. His was not the usual traditional type of Majalis that we were accustomed to for the months of Muharram. He gave lectures in Gujarati and drove home his points well. Ladies also took much interest in his Majalis as they could also understand him well in Gujarati."

"Mohamedali Alibhai Ramji and Nazerali Jamal Ramji approached your grandfather requesting him to stop labouring the point as they promised to build a proper mosque soon. On behalf of Haji Alibhai Ramji Charitable Trust, Mohamedali Haji Alibhai Ramji and Pyarali Mohamedali Haji Alibhai as trustees handed over the newly-built Masjid to the Jamaat."

With sardonic humour, Manjibhai concluded, "Ask your grandfather to come back. We have since found Allah in Kampala!"

Haji Mohamedjaffer did not live long enough to visit Kampala again. His death took place in Zanzibar towards the end of the same year, on 18 December, 1961 at the age of 72.

(Archive Section of Africa Federation, 8 September 2017)

Picture shows participants attending a Majlis organised by the Volunteer Corp to mark opening of "Sabile Hussein" on 9 Muharram, 1361 A.H. (Monday, 26 January, 1942).

Identified in the photograph are: Marhum Mulla Mohamed Jaffer Sheriff Dewji (on Mimber), Marhum Haji Esmail and Marhum Mulla Jaffer Pardhan (standing on each side holding Alam) Among those seated are, Marhum Haji Mehrali, Marhum Alarakhiabhai Kassam, Marhum Karabhai Walli, Marhum Rajabalibhai Salemohamed, Marhum Gulamhussein Remtulla, Marhum Shariffbhai Mawji, Marhum Bachubhai, Marhum Alibhai Kaba, Marhum Jamalbhai Walji, Marhum Abdulrasulbhai, Marhum Moh'dalibhai Haji Mehrali, Marhum Nazeralibhai Jamal Ramji, Marhum Ahmedbhai Mulla Najafi, Marhum Husseinbhai Jetha Damji, Marhum Gulamhusseinbhai Dataredina, Marhum Mohamedbhai (Bagamoyo), Marhum Rajabalibhai Rashid, Marhum Mohamedali Ahmad Kassam, Marhum Gulam (Babubhai) Manji Walji, Marhum Husseinbhai Mulla Najafi (Late father of current AFED Chairman, Shabir bhai Najafi), Haji Ebrahimbhai Ladha Kassam (current AFED Trustee from Uganda), Haji Amirbhai Ahmad Kassam, Haji Mohamed Taqi Jeraj.

(Photo + identified by Mohamed Taqi Jeraj, Toronto, Ebrahim L. Kassam and Hussein H. Kara (Africa Federation Archives, 8 September 2017)

FORT PORTAL

Beyond Kampala, there are small towns such as Fort Portal, Hoima, Masindi, Kaberamaido and Arua. Khoja Shia Ithna-Asheries began settling in these places in the early 1900s.

Fort Portal[79] is in western Uganda in Toro kingdom situated between the Rwenzori Mountains and National Parks. Today, it is a significant market town and tourist resort. According to Suleiman Kaba[80], he arrived at Fort Portal (198 miles from Kampala) in 1903. He described the place as being a fertile land with abundant greenery. Housing was mud huts and people travelled everywhere mostly on foot.

Hassanali Suleiman

Born in India, Nangalpur, he migrated to East Africa at the age of 16 in 1928. After working in Mombasa, Bukoba and Kampala for 10 years, he settled down in Fort Portal, Uganda in 1939.

Hassanalibhai was a person with great feelings for the community. In Fort Portal, he converted part of his house for 10 years into an Imambada for religious functions. He was the Mulla of Fort Portal. He pioneered the purchase of a small mosque in 1959 and was instrumental in the acquisition of a larger mosque for the same town in 1965. There were about 40 families in Fort Portal at that time. Political upheaval in 1972 forced Hassanalibhai to come to the United Kingdom where he lived in Bath for seven years, and attended religious functions in Peterborough.

In 1977, he moved to South London. Murrabi Hassanalibhai Suleman affectionately known as "Chacha" in the Community was the founder member of Hyderi Imambargha in South London, United Kingdom. (Africa Federation Archives, 20 July 2018)

At the time, there were three shops belonging to Khoja Shia Ithna-Asheries which increased to six by 1910. Among those who settled there were the families of Bahadurali Mawji, Pradhan Jivraj, Ahmed Bhimji, Fazal Bhimji, Suleiman Ismail, Nuralli Chagpar and Ismail Manji. Fort Portal went through considerable hardship as the Spanish influenza epidemic and famine hit the area and took many lives. By 1929 however, the community had overcome the influenza epidemic challenges. Prosperity came to Fort Portal in the 1930s, and the Khoja Shia Ithna-Asheries helped to improve the condition of the town by contributing financially towards the upliftment fund.

Initially, Suleiman Kaba held religious gatherings at his house. Later on, with the building of the first *imambada*, people began to become more aware of the importance of religious instruction. The communal record shows that from 1929 until 1957, religious gatherings were held at the houses of Abdulrasool Alarakhia, A. A. Moledina, Ahmed Bhimji and Hassanali Suleiman.

Until 1938, Khoja Ismailis used to attend the religious gatherings organised by Khoja Shia Ithna-Asheries. Once the Khoja Ismailis built their Jamaatkhana in 1938, they decided to conduct their religious ceremonies there. In 1958, Ahmed Bhimji and Pradhan Jivraj built an *imambada* and donated it to the Khoja Shia Ithna-Asheri community.

Until 1935, Fort Portal had 18 shops: 8 belonging to Khoja Shia Ithna-Asheries, 7 to Khoja Ismailis, 2 to Goans and one to a Hindu. In 1938, the shopkeepers raised funds to build a community primary school, which was upgraded to a more accommodating and fully-functional public school in 1959. After 1947, Fort Portal grew economically and by 1960, it had 75 shops: 20 of which belonged to Khoja Shia Ithna-Asheries, 55 to Khoja Ismailis, 4 to Hindus and 1 to a Goan.

HOIMA

Hoima[81] is a city in the western region of Uganda. It is the main municipal, administrative, and commercial centre of Hoima District. It is also the location of the palace of the Omukama of Bunyoro.[82] When 13-year-old Habib Kassam[83] joined his father in Hoima in 1918, there were five shops there owned by Khoja Shia Ithna-Asheries. They belonged to Kassam Mohammed, Jamal Datoo, Nasser Daya, Merali Rattansi and Jiwa Rattansi. He recalls that Hoima was a small gathering of mud huts surrounded by forest and wild animals.

Kassambhai Mohammed

1918 was a challenging time as the Spanish Influenza epidemic was rife and took so many lives that dead bodies lay on the roadsides. After the epidemic, famine followed which lasted for nine months and devastated many areas.

Khoja Shia Ithna-Asheries living in Hoima used to hold regular religious gatherings at each other houses and the annual martyrdom of Imam Hussein (pbuh) was commemorated at Jiwa Rattansi's home. Bohora families joined these gatherings until 1927 when they opened their own centre. In 1931, Khoja Shia Ithna-Asheries built a primary school for the community children and on recommendation by the government, the school was converted from a community school to an Indian Public School. In 1948, a house was converted into an *imambada* for communal social and religious gatherings.

COMMUNITY HISTORY:
NARRATED BY HABIB BHAI KASSAM MOHAMMED

Kassamalibhai Mohammed, aged 13 left India in 1918 for Africa. From Mombasa he travelled by train to Kisumu then by boat to Jinja and train to Namasgali. He crossed Lake Kiyoga to reach Masindi where he hired 20 labourers and travelled about 64 miles by cart. The labourers would make turns to carry the cart.

The main business in those days was mats, onions, hides and butter. Hoima was a small town, with houses made of raw bricks and surrounded by a thick forest. Nobody dared go out further than 500 feet from their shops during the evening for fear of wild animals. Thursday night sermons and other gatherings were held people's homes. Muharram *majalis* were held at Jiwabhai Rattansi's residence and Bohora community members joined in.

In 1927, when the Bohora's increased, they started organizing their own gatherings. There was one common graveyard for all Muslims. There was a small shelter with an iron-corrugated roof there and sermons were held every Thursday. In 1918, the influenza epidemic killed many people. In 1920-21 drought hit the area for 9 months and the Government ordered rice from India for the affected people.

People commuting to and from Kampala would normally go by foot. The currency used was Rupees and Kori. A Rupee was equal to 100 Koris. Daily postal mail was carried by natives on their heads and escorted by two Indian soldiers. For any money transfers to Kampala, people used to pay through the government accounts. In 1922, the "German flooring" was a common currency in use; later on shillings and cents were introduced.

The motorcar business began in 1920 and telephone lines in 1939; the latter were confined to Hoima, Masindi port and Butiyaba. In 1931, an Ithna-Asheri school was built and Mulla Rizwi Hussayn Saheb used to teach religious education as well as Gujrati. After 2 years, the school was changed into an Indian public school. In commemoration of 1300 years since Imam Hussein (pbuh)'s martyrdom, funds were raised to buy a house and since then all religious activities were conducted there. Merali Rattansi, Mohammed Merali, Pyarali Lalji and Hassanali Datadina organised the delivering of sermons. In 1948, following the imambada purchase, the Jamaat was officially established.
(Trade Directory, 1960. Trans. by F. Ali)

KABERAMAIDO

Kaberamaido is located approximately 163 kilometres by road northwest of Mbale, the largest city in Eastern Uganda. It is part of the Kaberamaido District, which is part of the Teso sub-region an area inhabited by the Kumam people[84]. Today, Kaberamaido is considered a medium-sized town and has a population of 5,100 as of 2020.[85]

Hassanali Salehmohammed was born in 1917 in Mundra, Kachchh. At age 12, he left India and came to Mombasa and from there travelled to Kaberamaido where he worked for six years in his maternal uncle's Gulamhusssein Ladha's (*batabata*) shop. When he arrived around 1929, Kaberamaido was a village that had five to seven retail shops owned by the Turkish community and five owned by Islamilis.

After working for his uncle, he worked for two years in a shop owned by his brother. Then he went back to India to get married and returned to Kaberamaido in 1937, joining his brother's business as a partner. He recalls during those days that Ismailis and Ithna-Asheri were one community attending religious functions together.

HAJI HASSANALI SALEHMOHAMED (1917-1972)

The Thursday religious gatherings, commemorations and celebrations were held at everyone's residence in turn, except for Muharram gatherings which were always held at his residence. Gradually the Khoja community increased[86] and in 1949, a plan was prepared to construct the Quaide Azam Memorial Hall Muslim School.

At first, only a small donation of Shs. 254 was collected. Seeing no progress for some time, Hassanalibhai went to Kampala and collected Shs. 75,000. The hall was finally constructed in the memory of Quaide Azam at a cost of Shs. 95,000 and the then Pakistan High Commissioner, Janab Subhan Saheb, conducted the opening ceremony in 1958. About 125 children studied in this building.

During this period of construction, Hassanali converted from Ismaili beliefs to Ithna-Asheri beliefs in 1954. He provides the basis for this conversion as follows:

> In 1954, Agakhan sent a verdict (*farmaan*) that required me to believe in Agakhan and sign on the form, where I and my brothers Rajabali Salehmuhammed and Yusuf Salehmuhammed decided to leave Ismaili sect and embraced the Ithnaasheri sect. At that time I was holding the post of "*Mukhi*" in the Jamatkhana, for the sake of faith, I sacrificed myself towards the truth thus my brothers and I abandoned Ismaili faith.

Years later, these three brothers travelled with their mother to India. From there, they proceeded to perform pilgrimage in Mecca and then visited the holy cities in the Middle East before finally returning to Kabiramaedo in 1955. On their return, they were met with the need for a new *imambada* for the growing community.

With passion, confidence, and an enterprising spirit, Haji Hassanali took full responsibility for providing the funds for the construction of the *imambada* at a cost of Shs. 120,000.

After the foundation-stone laying ceremony was held in 1958, Haji Hassanali and Haji Gulamhussein visited several Jamaats in East Africa to collect donations. As a result, they surpassed their expectations and a sum of Shs. 150,000 was collected. The construction of the *imambada* and *musafarkhana* was completed by the end of the same year and both buildings were officially opened by Haji Rajabali Salehmohamed. Hassanalibhai Salehmohamed also served as President of the Kaberamaedo Jamaat for a period.

Imambada - Kaberamaido

MULLA HAJI GULAMHUSSEIN LADHA (1896-1964)

Mulla Ladha's family was the first Ithna-Asheri family in Kaberamaido. He arrived in 1938 from Soroti. He was a Zakir-e-Hussain and used to recite majlises in Kutchi and Urdu that the Ismaili Community would attend too.

All religious programs were held at Mulla's house. Members of the Ismaili Community later on requested turns to hold majlises at their houses as well which Mulla recited.

Mulla Ladha used to recite majlises in Atuboi (a town 15 miles away) as well where all the residents were Ismailis and the majlises were held at the Jamatkhanas.

(Africa Federation Archives 18 December 2015)

ARUA

Arua is a city and commercial centre in the northern region of Uganda. The first Khoja Shia Ithna-Asheri to settle there was Nurmohammed Jivraj. He was 19 years old when he arrived in Mombasa in 1905. From there, he took the train to Kisumu, then a boat across Lake Victoria and finished his journey by walking the last 21 miles to Kampala where he stayed for five years. In 1915, he was the first Khoja Shia Ithna-Asheri to open a shop first in Arua and then another in Khoruma in Congo.

He went back to India after a few years and upon his return in 1928 to Uganda recalls that by then, Arua had ten shops owned by Indians.

In 1933, another Khoja Shia Ithna-Asheri, Janmohammed Teja joined him in the small town. According to Nurmohammed Jivraj, under the supervision of the Indian Association of Arua, a primary school was established in 1937 to cater for the education needs of the children of the community. As the community grew, this school was expanded with government aid. In 1949, Hirji Alibhai[87] and in 1952, A. S. Kaba came to Arua. After their arrival, religious gatherings were held at A. S. Kaba's residence. The religious understanding within the Khoja Shia Ithna-Asheri community was so basic that the community needed to seek assistance from the African Muslim community in Arua. Nurmohammed Jivraj relates that in 1954, a child aged under two died and no one had sufficient knowledge about the burial rites and had to rely upon African Muslims. They also buried the child in their burial ground.

As numbers slowly grew, with the financial assistance of Rajabali Nurmohammed and contributions from the Arua community, an *imambada* and *musafarkhana* project was initiated in 1957 and officially opened by the then Chairman of Africa Federation, Alhaj Ebrahim Sheriff, in 1960. The community in Arua already owned a separate burial ground for Khoja Shia Ithna-Asheries.

NOORMOHAMED JIVRAJ

In 1915, Noormohamed Jivraj was the first Ithna-Asheri to settle in Arua. He worked for 5 years at Datoo Damji. In 1910, he went to Masindi, 130 miles from Kampala to start his own business. After five years in Masindi, he moved to Arua where he opened a shop. He also opened another shop in Karuma, 14 miles away in the Congo. The area was primitive and the locals hardly covered their bodies until after 1950. Motor vehicles introduced in 1928. It was only in 1956 that Arua enjoyed running water.

Janmohamed Teja came to Arua but passed away in three years. Hirji Alibhai came in 1949 and Alibhai Suleman Kaba in 1952. By 1957, the number of members of the community had risen significantly.

They decided to build an imambada and musafarkhana. Br. Rajabali Jivraj donated Shs. 50,000 for the benefit of his Marhum father Noormohamed Jivraj. Shs. 15,000 was collected from other members, Shs. 28,000 from the Congo and Shs. 25,000 from different Jamaats. A teacher was hired, under the aegis of the Indian Association, to run a class for educating the children. Later the school became a grant-aided government school. Currently (1960) there are a hundred Asian shops in Arua, 12-13 belonging to the Ithna-Asheri community.

(Africa Federation Archives, 25 March 2016)

Arua Imambada - 1960

LAMU

Lamu Town on Lamu Island is Kenya's oldest continually inhabited town. It is one of the original Swahili settlements along coastal East Africa estimated as having been established in 1370. The original name of the town is Amu, which the Arabs referred to as Al-Amu. In 1506, the Portuguese took control of the entire island and mispronounced the name as Lamu, which stuck. Transferring to the Omani protectorate in 1652, Lamu soon became a centre of poetry, politics, arts and crafts as well as trade. This was the golden era of Lamu.

The first Khoja to arrive in Lamu was Dewji Jamal. He came in 1870 when Lamu was the chief port of Kenya and established a branch of his company, Dewji Jamal & Co. there.

Communal records show that the decade between 1880 -1890 witnessed a large number of Ithna-Asheri arrivals to the town. Most of the new Khoja Shia Ithna-Asheries came from Kachchh or Kathiawad, but some also came from Bagamoyo, Zanzibar and Kilwa. In 1883, seven sons of Kanji Asani left Jamkhambadia (near Jamnagar) in Kathiawad for Lamu. The journey took them forty days by dhow. Of the seven sons, five were Ithna-Asheries. These were Dewji Kanji, Daya Kanji, Panju Kanji, Samji Kanji, and Ramji Kanji and together they started their own import/ export business.

Photo Credit: Zahir Bhalloo

At the time, Lamu did a great deal of trade with Somalia and India. The main export from Lamu was palm-mat bags for packing cloves as well as mangrove poles. Lamu imported rice, sugar, wheat and spices.[88]

In 1885, Nazerali Dewji (a son of Dewji Jamal) arrived with his family in Lamu from Zanzibar. He had a handwritten letter from John Kirk, the British Consul in Zanzibar, to his deputy in Lamu that read:

> I have been asked to mention to you that Nazerali Deoji [sic] and his family have gone to settle in Lamu, and to say that he is the Agent of Deoji [sic] Jamal of this place, a British Indian. In addition, I would say that the family of Deoji [sic] Jamal, including his Agent now at Lamu, have formally left the Khoja sect and joined that of the K.Shias. They are still however British subjects. For leaving the Khojas the family has sometimes been annoyed by their former co-religionists.[89]

The population of Khoja Shia Ithna-Asheris increased to about 300 by 1895. Initially, they met at individual homes for religious and communal observances. In 1896, the Lamu Jamaat started a special fund to build a mosque and *imambada* to cater for their social and spiritual needs. They already had the land donated by Dewji Jamal, and Nasser Dewji supervised the construction and played a leading role in the collection efforts. Sadly, in 1901, he died on board a German ship while returning from a pilgrimage to Mecca and was buried at sea.

Shortly after the mosque and *imambada* were completed, the Khoja Shia Ithna-Asheri community of Lamu fell into a decade of communal discord. There was some sort of internal factionalism which gripped the jamaat - although there is no record of its exact nature - and appears to have been deeply entrenched by how long it lasted.

It has been implied, as is often found in communities, that the conflict was social in nature or related to strong differences of opinion about the issue of land and property acquisition. By all accounts, shortly after the conflict began, one of the factions built another mosque (in 1900) with contributions coming from Zanzibar as well as from Jivraj Khatau and Jivraj Meghji. This splendid mosque stands to this day with a scenic seafront view.

Khoja Shia Ithna-Asheri Mosque, Lamu, Kenya (Photo: Zaheer Bhalloo)

MOMBASA

From the 1920s onwards, the Khoja Shia Ithna-Asheries began to migrate mainly to Mombasa. Having become the chief commercial port of Kenya, Mombasa now had a lot to offer economically and attracted them in large numbers. Another important reason was the lack of adequate higher education facilities in Lamu, although, in this regard, there was some effort on the part of Jiwan Visram who established a primary school to teach reading, writing and arithmetic to the children of the community.[90]

WALJEE HIRJEE

Mombasa[91] is a coastal city in Kenya along the Indian Ocean. Its rich history dates as far back as 900 A.D. It was a prosperous trading town in the 12th century with considerable Islamic influence. Khoja settlement in Mombasa dates back to 1867 when Waljee Hirjee, a prominent Khoja merchant from Zanzibar opened a shop at the Old Port.

Abdalla Datoo[92] Hirjee arrived from Zanzibar in 1882[93] when he was only 15 years of age. He joined the firm of Tharia Topan as an accountant and was responsible for 30 shops spread all over East Africa and Mozambique, travelling by foot or by mule to supervise the businesses. In those days Mombasa was not yet the thriving port it would become. Ndia Kuu and Vasco Da Gama St (now Mbarak Hinaway St) were the two main streets.

The town boasted a few stone buildings but most of the rest of the island was covered by jungle infested with puff adders. Leopards roamed about the town at night and every so often lions would walk over the ford at Makupa when the tide was low. In this sense, it was a small place surrounded by wild growth despite the existence of a port by 1880.

The seaport led to increased business activities and Mombasa began to attract more Khojas. In 1887, the combined Khoja population (both

Ismailis and Ithna-Asheris) on the island was estimated at only 25 compared to around 1,900 in Zanzibar and 385 in Bagamoyo at the same time. After the British administration took over in 1895 and made Mombasa the capital of the British East Africa Protectorate, things began to change.

Mombasa, Ndia Kuu, 1895

A mere year later the town already boasted a sea terminal of the Uganda Railway. With the establishment of the Imperial British East African Company (IBEA) in 1888, Mombasa became the chief commercial port of East Africa. Large numbers of Khojas began to arrive from the old mercantile centres of Zanzibar, Bagamoyo, Lamu and Kilwa; others came directly from India. Khojas who had already established firms in smaller towns decided to open branches in or shift altogether to Mombasa.

Dharamsi Khatau was born in Nagalpur, Kutch in 1865. He had four brothers Jivraj Khatau, Manji Khatau, Kassim Khatau and Killu Khatau.[94] In 1880, two years after the death of Killu, Dharamsi Khatau left Bombay with his parents, taking along Killu's widow and daughters. The journey to Mombasa by dhow took about a month and on the way, his father - Khatau Nanjani - passed away and was buried at sea.

Dharamsi first arrived in Zanzibar where he established Dharamsi Khatau & Co. In 1893, he called his brother, Jivraj, from India to manage one of the branches of the family business that he had opened in Mombasa.[95] Jivraj extended the company's business deep into the interior.[96] The company quickly grew into a successful import business with 40 branches scattered in many towns across East Africa. Many Khoja Shia Ithna-Asheri pioneers worked for Dharamsi Khatau & Co before establishing their own businesses including Rashid Moledina, Abdalla Kanji, Rashid Nurmohammed of Kampala, Moledina Virji, and Ali Mohammed Jagani.

At this time, two famous Bagamoyo merchants, Allidina Visram and his Ithna-asheri nephew, Nasser Virji, also decided to shift their businesses to Mombasa and opened branches there in 1895 and 1900 respectively. With all this thriving commerce, the town grew substantially bigger over the next ten years. Abdalla Datoo recalls that at that time, Bohoras were in the foremost position as traders, followed by Memons; Khoja Shia Ithna-Asheries were at number three and then came the Hindus and other communities. Such was the fame and prominence of these merchants that some even had streets named after them like Sherriffbhai Street.

By the time Walji Bhanji[97] arrived in Mombasa in 1896, almost sixteen years after Abdalla Datoo, there were 20 families there. Amongst these early settlers were the families of Issa Thawar, Jivraj Meghji, Dharamsi Khatau, Jaffer Dewji, Ismail Kalyan, Janmohammed Advani, Saleh Mohammed Dhala, Saleh Lakha, Abdala Janmohammed Jaffer, Jaffer Kassam, Meghji Mulji, and Zainul Abedin.

Jivraj Meghji[98] opened his business in 1896. The business was looked after by family members, Molu Meghji and Ladak Meghji. Mombasa was now thriving and had a good port with the ability to dock large ships bringing a variety of goods from overseas. Trading became more profitable as goods flowed to and from the interior of Kenya and Uganda via the railway network. As trade opportunities increased, Khoja Shia Ithna-Asheries began to establish themselves both socially and economically in the town. Among the Indian business fraternity generally and Khoja Shia Ithna-Asheries particularly, Isabhai Thaver[99] and Dewji Jamaal were well-known and respected businessmen.

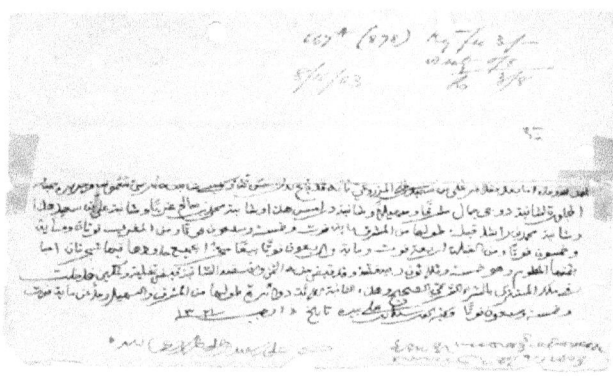

Original Arabic Deed of Sale of a plot of land for the cemetary to Dharamsi Khatau & Co. next to the shamba of Dewji Jamal.

HAJI ABDULLA KANJI (1881 - 1944)

Hailing from Kutch, Bhuj (India), Haji Abdulla Kanji, was known as "Bapu", pioneer of Mombasa and a passionate philanthropist. He arrived in 1902 on a dhow along with other Indians. Soon after he became a successful merchant along with his brother, Bandali Kanji. Over the years, he established himself in the business world, setting up and managing a flourishing real estate company and an import-export business until his death at the age of 63.

A visionary with great hopes for the future of Mombasa, Haji Abdulla was instrumental in shaping the community. He made decisions based on ethics and morality rather than finance and self-serving reasons. He believed in equitable allocation of business commodities and wealth. He imported products and shared them with other businessmen within and outside the community with the condition that the selling price of goods remain the same without undercutting on price. Haji Abdulla invested much of his savings in land, building residential homes and commercial properties. A great deal of the city's planning and construction was done under his personal supervision. To attest to this, the road comprising of houses which he built, was named Abdulla Kanji Road (now Tewa Road off Moi Avenue).

Abdulla Kanji was an individual who helped people. His concern for the youth led to him sourcing employment opportunities for them in the local shipping companies and banks through his contacts. For those struggling financially, he offered free housing. In September 1926, he and his associate, Fazalbhai Ladak Shivji donated a musafarkhana. In his lifetime, Haji Abdulla earned the nickname "Bwana Judge" as he was known and respected for resolving disputes of all sorts. While he never took any official position in the community, leaders and elders always sought advice from him. He always remained in the close company of Aalims – often hosting them and taking religious advice from them. In the community, he was well known for continually upholding principles and ideals without reservation and his charitable contributions to various communities were in confidence.

In 1944, An idea was floated by Haji Hussein Amersi Sunderji Jethbhai to establish a fully fledged Primary School up to Class VII for which necessary funds had to be raised and a Trust established. A team consisting of Haji Abdul Hussein Nurmohamed, Haji Husein Amersi Sunderji Jethabhai, Haji Mohamedraza Abdulla Kanji, Haji Abdulrasul Merali Dewji, Haji Ramzanali Valli and Haji Ali Mohamedjaffer Sheriff Dewji approached the most elderly person of the community: Haji Abdulla Kanji for advice and blessing.

Haji Abdulla Kanji volunteered to head the fund-raising committee and nominated Haji Ali Mohamedjaffer Sheriff Dewji as his Secretary. The fund was floated and fully backed by Molvi Alimohammed Jaffer Dewji in his sermons from the pulpit. Necessary funds were soon raised with the major contribution being made by Haji Nazerali Panju in the memory of Alibhai Panju. The Alibhai Panju Khoja Ithna-Asheri School Benefit Trust was thus established.

(Mombasa Jamaat Chronicle, 4 January 2002)

By 1897, the Khoja Shia Ithna-Asheri population in Mombasa had grown to about a hundred individuals. The social and spiritual needs of the community began to increase. Dewji Jamal & Co bought a *shamba* (a small farming land) called "Kitumba" and donated it to the community for religious purposes, including a cemetery.[100] Two years later, in 1899, the community built a mosque-*imambada* facility on the shamba (*bustan* in Persian) which became known as "Bustani" (now Hyderi).[101] Sadly, in the same year, the community was caught up in internal communal discord.

The Old Bustani (Courtesy: A. A. Khatau)

Communal antagonism in Zanzibar and Lamu fuelled the situation in Mombasa; for a time it seemed that conflict was the only way to settle differences in the Khoja Shia Ithna-Asheri community.[102] According to Sadak Jivraj Meghji, differences arose soon after the purchase of a small bungalow near the Bustani. The exact nature of the circumstances that led to the conflict needs exploring as the facts are not available in the archives. Nonetheless, the disaffected party decided to acquire their own cemetery and build a new mosque-*imambada*.[103]

1904, Mombasa. Visiting dignitaries from Zanzibar at the opening of the Kuwwatul Islam Mosque on Old Kilindini Rd. (from Sayyid Muhammad Redha Shustary).

Sitting L-R second row: Sayyid Muhammad Ali (first l), Sayyid Muhammad Al (third l), Sayyid Abdulhussein Mar'ashi (center), Sayyid Jaffer Mar'ashi (second r), Sayyid Muhammad Taqi Mar'ashi (first r). Standing (third row R-L): Alimohammed Jagani, unknown, Ismail Kalyan.

From this time onwards, the Khoja Shia Ithna-Asheri community of Mombasa had two jamaats: "Bustani" and "Kuwwatul Islam", each with its own facilities. The two *jamaats* were eventually reunited on 28 October 1966 under the famous slogan '*ek bano nek bano*' (be united and virtuous) and the wall between the two cemeteries (nicknamed the "Berlin Wall" by the local community) was finally brought down.

The "Berlin Wall" being brought down by representatives of the two jamaats. Abdulhussein Dharamsi Khatau and Sadak Jivraj Meghji (Courtesy A A Khatau)

In 1926, a *madrasah* was built with the funds donated by Dharamsi Khatau Trust[104] to impart religious instruction to the community's children. In the same year, a *musafarkhana* was built by Abdalla Kanji[105] and Fazal Ladak with donations from the community. In later years, the community was able to build their own school donated by the family of Alibhai Panju. An entire generation was educated in this institute and it is held in fond memory by many.

Foundation-stone laying Ceremony of Alibhai Panju Jaffery Primary School, 1951. Pictured: Haji Nazerali Panju laying the stone. (Standing behind, L-R): Gulamali Kassamali Merali Dewji, Syed Mohamed Husein Murawwij, Abdulrasul Merali Dewji, Rashid Moledina, Abdul Husein Nurmohamed, Mohamed Sachedina Kalyan. (Far Right): Mulla Hassamali Kermali.

As the Mombasa Khoja Shia Ithna-Asheries began to establish themselves economically and socio-religiously, they replicated three other important institutions that already existed in Zanzibar. Pyarali Rustamali Ladha[106] recalls that he and his friend felt that there was a need to create a sense of voluntary service within the youth. The idea of a "Husseini Fauj" (Army of Hussein (pbuh)) was put forward and implemented in 1927 by Gulamraza Rashid, Gulamali Kaka and Pyarali Rustamali Ladha with support coming from Gulam Kassamali, Asgerali Rashid, Asgerali Kaka, Hassanali G Virjee, and Jafferali Dewji. This was in line with the tradition of voluntary service to the community that had already been put in place over the decades in various other *jamaats* across the region.

The Elders of Mombasa - A Reflection and Devotion in the Development of Volunteerism and Tabligh.
Pyarali Rustam, reminiscing about his childhood

In 1927, at the age of 8, there arose in me an interest and desire to volunteer for services to the community. My friend Gulamraza Rashid and Br Gulamali Kaka joined me in this. The three of us established the "Husseini Foj" (The Army of Hussein) - an organization of volunteers to serve the community. Like all our other organizations, our membership kept on changing like a tide - sometimes going up to 50 and sometimes down to 5. Since it did not have a place to call its own, it sometimes became difficult to gather the youth at one place. Realizing this problem, in the year 1932, a prominent philanthropist in the community Marhum Bahadurali Mawji came forward and offered us a spacious room at his property near the Old Customs.

We also started "Mehfile Husseini" at this location. Majlis was held at this location every Friday night and during Muharram and *wafat/khushalis*. Marhum Bahadurali always attended these Majalis and also offered financial help. We would like to pay tribute to Marhum for his unrelenting support. Other regular attendees and supporters were Allama Haji Mohamedjaffer Sheriff Dewji, Marhum Alibhai Sachedina and Gulamhussein A Datoo (Bishon), They also helped us financially.

In 1935, due to increase in attendance at Majalis, Haji Mohamedjaffer Sheriff Dewji offered us the ground floor of his residence near the sea shore at a token rent of Shs. 10 per month. Mehfile Husseini has been conducting its programs at this premise for the last 27 years. During the month of Muharram, *Shabih* and *Taboot* for both Imambadas are prepared there. Those helping in this preparation include Br Hussein Lalji, Br Hussein Visram, Br Mohamedtaki Noormohamed and Br Noorali Mohamedali. In keeping with the name of the Mehfil, the birthday of Imam Hussein (pbuh) is celebrated on 3 Sha'ban every year.

The memories of this annual great celebration are still vivid among the residents of Mombasa. The attention of the organization focused on two distinct facets of *tabligh*. One was the formation of Night School where religious education and *masaels* were imparted to the youths. The other was the introduction of Ashura Procession (*Juloos*) in remembrance of the martyrdom of Imam Hussein (pbuh).

The Night School was established in 1934 and continues to-date (1960). *Juloos* could not be introduced early enough due the objections it came across. However it finally started in 1938 and it continues to-date (1960). The most note-worthy contribution in Night School was from Mulla Mohammed Jaffer. His boundless efforts and appealing teaching led to the rapid growth of the Night School. It stood out as one of the most successful institutions of the community. The benefits derived from the religious knowledge obtained from the school have made people successful in both their secular and religious life.

In order to encourage the offering of prayers and the quest for religious education, one of the famous elder personalities, Marhum Jaffer Dewji, nicknamed "Baba" used to give gifts to

> children who regularly offered prayers. Baba also visited the students regularly and showed a deep interest in their studies.
>
> Reminiscing of the old days, Br. Pyarali Rustam also recalls the excellent Majalis by Mulla Kassamali in fine Kutchi language and the wisdom-laden Gujarati Majalis by Allama Mohamedjaffer Sheriff Dewji.
>
> In Mombasa of today, the enthusiasm for religious knowledge, the upholding of prayers, the love towards Majalis, the respect towards elders, in short, the religious awakening that we see - all of this - attributed to the contribution of these great personalities.
>
> *(Trade Directory 1960)*

The second institution was a night school for adults, similar to the one in Zanzibar. Its main purpose was to impart religious education to the adults of the community and in Mombasa the classes were conducted by Mulla Mohammed Jaffer.[107]

The third institution was the setting up of an evening gathering at somebody's house, a regular event in the life of the community popularly known as *Mehfil* (a gathering for the purpose of religious discussion and poetry). This culture still exists in various Khoja Shia Ithna-Asheri communities throughout the world. Mehfile Husseini was first formed and held at the house of Bahadurali Mawji.

Senior community personalities of Mombasa Jamaat such as Jaffer Dewji, Bahadurali Mawji, Allama Haji Mohammedjaffer Sherriff Dewji[108], Alibhai Sachedina, Alimohammed Jagani, Gulamhussain Datoo (Bishon) and others supported these three institutions by regularly attending the organised functions. They gave moral support, advice and religious lectures when requested. There were also varieties of trusts set up within the community in Mombasa to cater for the financial needs of the community in this regard.

Amongst many who contributed towards the upliftment of the socio-religious state of the community, the role played by Allama Haji Mohammedjaffer Sheriff Dewji[109] is renowned and documented. Born in 1889, he was one of three sons of Sheriff Dewji;[110] the other two being Hussein Sheriff Dewji and Mohammedali Sheriff Dewji. He migrated to Mombasa where he established a successful business under the name of Sheriff Dewji & Sons.

Apart from being a successful businessperson, he had a passion for learning Islam and sharing it with others. He spoke Urdu, Farsi, Arabic, Gujarati and English fluently. His sermons were well-liked, delivered in Gujarati as well as Urdu. At his own expense, he would travel to other places in East Africa and beyond, to spread the message of Islam. He was also an avid writer, mainly on religious topics.

In his lifetime, Mulla Mohammedjaffer wrote and published 26 books in Gujarati including popular *madrasah* textbooks such as *Sham-e-Hidayat* (The Light of Guidance) and *Diniyat* (religious studies) Parts 1, 2 and 3, which were used in almost all the Khoja Shia Ithna-Asheri *madrasahs* of East Africa. Additionally, his published titles include *Al-Musawat, Tohfah-e-Rizviyyah, Tohfah-e-Jafferiyah, Rooyat-e-Hilal, Al-Mahasin, Yadgar-e-Husein, Dalil-ul-Zaireen, Najasat-ul-Mushrikeen, Rooh (Aatma), Kamli-Waale, Shaheed-e-Islam*. His book *Imam-e-Zamana* was translated into Urdu and later also into English by Barrister Alhaj Murtaza Ahmed Lakha.

ALHAJ MOHAMEDJAFFER SHERIFF DEWJI

Haji Mohamedjaffer lived and had a business in Mombasa, Kenya. Of his own volition, he learnt the languages of Urdu, Farsi, Arabic and English. Marhum was a lucid and fluent Zakir who delivered majlises in Gujarati and masaeb in Urdu.

His lectures were effective and enjoyed by men, ladies and children alike. In 1928, he wrote "Shaheed-e-Islam', in which he submitted a strong rebuttal to the opposing school of thought which ridiculed Azadari of Imam Hussein (pbuh) and also reinforced the institution of the commemoration of his martyrdom. In 1940, he established the Husayni Night School, also known as Madrasah-tul-Faiz-e-Husayni (now known as Husayni Madrassah).
(Africa Federation Archives, 6 April 2015)

Mulla Mohammedjaffer lived in Mombasa, Kenya for several years while conducting his business. He died in 1961[111], aged 72, and was buried in Zanzibar.[112] He dedicated his life to awakening the religious understanding of the Khoja Shia Ithna-Asheries. *Shamme Hidayat* (Light of Guidance) became a well-known household reference book, as well as a text for teaching at the *madrasah*. He left a positive legacy in the community, not only through his work but also through his offspring, who continued to serve in his footsteps.

Personalities who played important roles in the establishment of Bilal Muslim Mission

L: *Ayatullah Seyyid Mohsin al-Hakim*   R: *Allama Syed Saeed Akhtar Rizvi*

L: *Alhaj Ebrahimbhai Hussein Sheriff Dewji*   R: *Alhaj Mohamedalibhai Meghji*

In December 1959, as fate would have it, Syed Saeed Akhtar Rizvi[113] happened to meet Mulla Mohamedjaffer for a few hours on board the ship State of Bombay. This brief meeting resulted in a long-lasting association between them. Together with Alhaj Ebrahimbhai Hussein Sheriff Dewji - then the youngest ever Chairman of the Khoja Africa Federation - they championed and initiated the idea of *tabligh* (propagation) beyond the Khoja Community in Africa under an organization that later became known as Bilal Muslim Mission.

Ebrahimbhai spoke good Farsi and when he visited the *Marja* (most knowledgeable scholar) of the time, Ayatullah Al Udhma Seyyid Mohsin Al-Hakim, he raised the idea of extending *tabligh* beyond the community. Ayatullah gently admonished the leaders for being self-centred and directed them to preach Islam according to Ahlulbayt (pbut) to the Africans with whom they co-existed; this was their sacred responsibility.

Alhaj Mohamedalibhai Meghji who took over the next term as chairman of the Africa Federation supported and worked to realise this idea. Bilal Muslim Mission was the result of a historical resolution adopted at the Africa Federation Triennial Conference of December 1964 in Tanga.[114]

Alhaj Mohamedbhai Khalfan of Dar es Salaam, the Vice Chairman of the Africa Federation in the 1990s and ex-officio member on the Committee of Bilal Muslim Mission of Tanzania at the time, relates the following:

> Allama Seyyid Saeed Akhtar Rizvi was offered the enrolment as Dar es Salaam Jamaat Resident Alim while he was still in India. He applied for the appointment and was successful mostly because he knew English relatively well, a rarity [at] the time for the Islamic Scholars from India. However, as he was being delayed catching a passenger ship for Dar es Salaam and while the month of Muharram was only a few weeks away, the Dar es Salaam Jamaat had made an alternative arrangement for a Zakir. In the meantime, the Lindi Jamaat requested the Dar es Salaam Jamaat to find it a Zakir for Muharram. I, as the Hon. Secretary of the Dar es Salaam Jamaat, [was] directed by the Management Committee of the Jamaat, to get Allama Seyyid Saeed Akhtar Rizvi who had already arrived in Dar es Salaam to agree to go to Lindi and accordingly, I booked him a flight to Lindi to arrive in time for the Muharram Zakiri.
>
> The Lindi Jamaat liked him and therefore he continued to serve it. The most praise-worthy [quality] of the Allama was his resolve to learn Kiswahili, when others like him in the engagement of *tabligh* did not choose to learn any new language, even Gujarati or English, after living for years with a local Jamaat. Allama's zeal in tabligh soon caught the attention of Ebrahimbhai Sheriff, the Chairman of the Africa Federation based in Arusha.
>
> Allama Rizvi was posted in Arusha to handle the new desk set up for recruiting Resident Alims for Africa Jamaats under a centralized system of appraisal and a standard form of contract. With this new position and already well-known among the leaders of the Africa Federation, he was appointed by the Africa

Federation as the First Chief Missionary of [the] newly-formed Bilal Muslim Mission in Tanzania. He saw the Mission growing in performance for a number of years. His knowledge of English and Kiswahili proved a great asset to the Bilal Muslim Mission.

As the Vice-Chairman of the Africa Federation in [the] 1990s, I was the ex-officio member on the Committee of Bilal Muslim Mission of Tanzania when Allama was still in the Bilal as the Chief Missionary while [the] Committee's leadership rotated based on periodical appointments by the Africa Federation. We were fortunate here in having a Chief Missionary for the Bilal Muslim Mission like the Allama, who in addition to having the knowledge as an Islamic scholar had also the knowledge of the locally-used languages. He also had a congenial disposition working as a team with others and more importantly, he was a prolific writer.[115]

Haji Alibhai Mohamed Jaffer was another such personality. He was fondly known as "Ali Chacha" and came from the distinguished family of Haji Dewji Jamal. Just like Allama Rizvi, he left his mark in the communities he served. His personal legacy is the establishment of the Bilal Muslim Mission of Kenya and Tanzania in collaboration with Allama Seyyid Saeed Akhtar Rizvi, their main aim being to spread the faith of the Ahlulbayt (pbut) to the indigenous people.

Haji Ali was compelling when countering opposition and awakening the conscience of the Khoja Shia Ithna-Asheri Community. He was the driving force behind the Bilal Muslim Mission in Kenya, an establishment that was close to his heart for much of his life.

He dedicated 34 years of service to this institution until the end of his days, tirelessly conveying this message of faith to the local populace. He not only worked to ensure that religious knowledge reached them, but made provisions for secular education by establishing schools in various local regions.[116]

Both Allama Rizvi and Haji Ali had noble ideas that they strove to implement in their own unique ways and in the process made history.

MURRABBI HAJI ALI MOHAMMED JAFFER SHERIFF (1912 - 1998)

Haji Ali Mohamed Jaffer was born in Zanzibar and later migrated to Kenya and then to Tanzania before finally settling in Mombasa. He studied at Alidina Visram High School and upon completion of his secondary education, joined his father, Mulla Mohamed Jaffer Sheriff in the family business.

His charismatic personality endeared him to young and old alike. He was pious, hardworking and devoted to the spread of Islam from a very young age. He was also a gifted linguistic and orator, fluent in Gujarati, Kutchii, Urdu, Punjabi, Kiswahili, English, Farsi and Arabic and used to translate Arabic and Farsi speeches of visiting Ulemas into Gujarati and Kiswahili.

His communal services began at a young age when he became a member of Faize Huseini (a Welfare Organization) in Mombasa. In 1942, as Secretary of the Committee, he assisted in establishing the School. Haji Ali served various institutions of the community with a high level of integrity. His vast portfolio of accomplishments included being President of The Ithna-Asheri Sports Club, President of the Ithna-Asheri Young Men's Union formed in 1945, and President of The Khoja Shia Ithna-Asheri Kuwwatul Islam (Bostani) Jamaat several times. After the formation of The Federation of Khoja Shia Ithna-Asheri Jamaats of Africa, he served as its Hon. Treasurer and Vice President.

His philanthropic undertakings stretched to the Kenyan Government Public Sector during World War II in 1940 – 1945, where he served in the Asian Police Reserve. Appointed by the Kenyan Government, he served as a member of the Asian Education Advisory Council and Mombasa Muslim Association from 1945 to 1948. Together with Marhum Hussein Allarakhia Rahim, he translated Dua-e-Kumail with its commentary in English. The impressive office building of Bilal Muslim Mission and the twelve flats for members of our community on it, were built as a result of his untiring efforts. For years, he served as a member of Mombasa Jamaat's Matrimonial Committee. Haji Ali was a co-author (with Marhum Al-Haj Hussein A. Rahim) of "Guidance from Qur'an" and "Uongozi wa Tabia Njema".

(The Light Magazine,, Vol.33 No.2, April 1999)

Haji Ali Mohammed Jaffer at a Bilal Muslim Mission of Kenya meeting in Mombasa Kenya. On his left is Syed Akhtar Rizvi and on his right two sheikhs of Bilal Muslim Mission.

NAIROBI

Nairobi[117] was originally a swamp inhabited mainly by the herding community of the Maasai.[118] When Khoja Shia Ithna-Asheries came there in 1896, work on the Kenya and Uganda railways had already begun. In 1899, a supply depot was created halfway along the Uganda railway line and the small town that grew surrounding it was named Enkare Nyirobi meaning "cool waters" in Maasai, because of a nearby watering hole. Nairobi soon began to grow as a town.

Walji Bhanji,[119] originally born in Malia Hatina in Kachchh in 1869. He had two brothers, Khaku Bhanji and Karim Bhanji. After Khaku's death, Walji Bhanji married his brother's widow, Kaiserbai, and raised his brother's children, Suleman and Bachibai. Kaiserbai bore him two sons, Alibhai and Valimohammed. In 1898, Walji Bhanji left Kachchh and arrived with his family in Mombasa. He stayed with Ladha Kanji and opened a small shop selling matches and tobacco.[120]

In 1899 (or 1900), he decided to go to Nairobi. He travelled by train to Voi and then by donkey to Nairobi. Walji Bhanji was able to establish a successful import-export business with sixty branches all across East Africa. The family firm (Valimohammed, Alibhai and his stepson Suleman were all partners) would import salt from India and sugar from Mauritius, while exporting raw cotton and ivory to India and the Far East. Cotton ginneries were set up in Mbale and Butiaba. Walji Bhanji himself stayed mostly in Mombasa, working from his home.

Walji Bhanji (1912 - 1998)

Walji Bhanji came to Mombasa and set up a business. A while later, he branched out and in Jinja he soon became a leading cloth merchant. Walji Bhanji controlled the cloth business and prices declared by his firm were considered as the genuine current prices.

Walji Bhanji gradually expanded to Kenya and Uganda. Due to lack of family supervision, it became difficult to control the business. The recession following the First World War made things difficult and W. Bhanji had to close his business in 1932.

After its closure, Suleman Khaku opened a new company in the name of Valimohamed Walji Bhanji, which is currently active. The company made strong inroads in ivory trade for which it was famous. When Walji Bhanji arrived in Mombasa; there were 20 families of our community. Majlises were held at the house of Haji Jaffer Dewji. Walji Bhanji passed away in Mombasa in 1932 and his son Valimohamed passed away in Zanzibar in 1938.(Africa Federation Archives, 26 November 2016)

When Walji Bhanji started his retail business selling tobacco, matches and other small items in Nairobi, the town was just recovering from an outbreak of plague. From communal records, there was no adverse impact upon the small Indian community living there at the time.

By 1903, there were 75 Shia Ithna-Asheries settled in Nairobi. They held religious gatherings at the house of Nurali Dhanji. Communal records show that Jaffer Dewji bought a plot of land just outside Nairobi and employed four Khoja Shia Ithna-Asheries.

By 1905, Nairobi was already a humming commercial centre and had replaced Mombasa as the capital of British East Africa. The city expanded quickly, supported by growth in administrative functions. More Khoja Shia Ithna-Asheries began to settle in Nairobi and by 1912 there were eight families there: Nasser Mawji, Nurali Dhanji, Sher Mohammed, Pirbhai Jivraj, Sunderji Pradhan, Dharamsi Pradhan, Gulamhussein Nurmohammed and Alimohammed Jagani. Out of these, six owned their own shops.[121] There were also 25 Punjabi Shia Ithna-Asheries settled in the town.

After the Great Depression of the 1930s hit Africa, Walji Bhanji lost a lot of his wealth. Smith Mackenzie advanced him a large sum to purchase some cotton crop, but unfortunately, locusts devoured the entire harvest. In 1932, he declared bankruptcy and all his properties were sold.

When he passed away, he left behind many who remembered him fondly. He had a good relationship with the local African communities to the extent that his colleagues and employees remembered him in their folk songs. Passers-by frequently heard these eulogies as they pushed their handcarts bringing cotton and ivory to the depots.

The religious gatherings in Nairobi were at first held at the houses of Sunderji Pradhan and Jamal Din. With funds gathered from Khoja Shia Ithna-Asheries throughout East Africa, an *imambada* and attached *musafarkhana* were built in 1939 (the Parkroad complex). The construction of the local mosque was completed in 1945 and donated to the community by the family of Shariff Jiwa.[122]

NAKURU

In the late 19th century, Nakuru was one of the major places of settlement for Europeans. Its name, as with many others in Kenya, originated from the Masaai language. Nakuru, established by the British as part of the White Highlands, was reserved for European immigrants during the colonial era. It became a township in 1904.

In 1927, the family of Walji Bhanji arrived in Nakuru and opened a trading shop. He employed four Khoja Shia Ithna-Asheries in his trading business and these families remained in Nakuru for six years. The communal records show that they closed the business and moved out in 1933. In 1934, Akber G. A. Datoo settled in Nakuru.[123] Not much is known about the community there after that, but the trade directory mentions that by 1960 there were around 50 Khoja Shia Ithna-Asheries in the town.

Nakuru Mosque

Nakuru Imambargha

Alhaj Mumtaz Kassam[124] recalls what Nakuru was like when he migrated there from Mombasa in 1980:

> All religious functions were held at Alhaj Datoo's residence. A faraway derelict Railway Mosque of colonial times was cleaned up and set up for Fajr and Maghribain prayers. The members felt that there was a need to encourage more families from Nairobi and Mombasa to settle in Nakuru for various business opportunities and thus a mission started to accomplish the same. It wasn't easy to convince and uproot already settled families to take up fresh challenges. Alhamdullilah, through determination, a total of seventeen families migrated to Nakuru within a span of two years.[125]

KISUMU

According to the trade directory, the first Khoja Shia Ithna-Asheries to arrive in Kisumu in 1926 were the family of Sheriffe Jiwa.[126] Kisumu, which means "a place of barter trade" is believed to be one of the oldest settlements in Kenya dominated by diverse local communities at different times.

In 1898, the British identified Kisumu as an alternative railway terminus and port for the Uganda railway and in 1901, the railway line finally reached the town. By 1920, Kisumu had become an important commercial centre.[127] For Indian traders, Kisumu was a hub from which imported goods could be distributed to the surrounding areas and into Uganda. Pioneer Khoja traders in the interior of Kenya mainly conducted their business from Kisumu. These trading activities only expanded when the railway arrived and port facilities were built there.

The most notable Indian trader was a Khoja Ismaili called Allidina Visram, who operated dukas (shops) in Kisumu and other places well before the Uganda Railway was completed.[128] The pattern of commerce adopted in the interior by Alidina Visram and the other Khoja traders, including Shia Ithna-Asheries, revolved largely around the exchange of an increasing variety of imported goods and local produce of every description.[129]

In the 1930s, Sheriffe Jiwa's eldest son, Kermali, arrived in Kisumu and was later joined by Daya Premji and his sons, Gulamhussain and Abdul Hussain.[130] These Khoja Shia Ithna-Asheries came to set up shops at a time when there was a conflict of interest between established Asian businesses and new African entrepreneurs. The Indian traders were witnessing the emergence of African small traders who opposed their dominance in Kisumu.

Despite these political and economic conflicts, the Jiwa and Premji families stayed until 1953. Communal data remains vague about the community history after this period. The trade directory simply mentions that there were around 50 Khoja Shia Ithna-Asheries in Kisumu in 1960.

PANGANI

Many Khoja Shia Ithna-Asheries used the northern coast route that linked Mombasa and Tanga to travel to, and settle in Moshi and Arusha by way of Pangani and Tanga. Around 1895, Shermohammed Sajan[131] arrived in Pangani on his way to Moshi and Arusha.

Pangani is a town in northeast Tanzania and lies 45 km south of Tanga. It came to prominence in the 19th century. During this time, under nominal Zanzibari rule, it was a major terminus of caravan routes, including slave trade, to the deep interior of Tanganyika (Tanzania). During his visit in 1857, Burton, the British explorer, found twenty Indian merchants from Kachchh in Pangani. They were the main importers and exporters of trade goods, as well as the primary financiers of the caravan trade. These merchants made a vast profit by lending money and imported goods to Arab and coastal Swahili traders who handled much of the caravan trade between the coast and the interior mainland.[132]

From the 1860s onward, the people of Pangani established large plantations of sugar and coconut. After the Sultan of Zanzibar signed treaties with Great Britain outlawing the ocean-going trade in slaves in 1873, Pangani became a center for smuggling slaves across the narrow channel to Pemba to evade British warships.

Siwji (or Shivji) Alarakhia[133] with his wife and children: Salehmohammed, Nurmohammed, and Virbai arrived in Pangani in 1897 (or 1898). He recalls that Pangani was a small but busy port controlled by the German colonial government. The settlement was mainly made up of mud huts with roofs of dried coconut leaves. There were 100 Khoja Shia Ithna-Asheries already settled there. They had a mosque and *imambada* catering to their socio-religious needs.

Slave trade was still prevalent and construction work was mainly done by slaves. Lime was used to build houses, being a strong ingredient almost equal to cement and it allowed the buildings to remain sturdy for a long time. Due to Arab influence, the doors and windows were designed to reflect Arabic architecture, which can still be seen around the town centre. At the time, **there were 25 houses of Khoja Ismailis** and one belonging to a Hindu. About eight miles away, on the bank of river Ruvu, a German had set up a small sugar factory and was called Bwana Sukari meaning "Mr Sugar". **Communal records show that amongst the Khoja Shia Ithna-Asheries who had settled in Pangani were Gulamali Dhirani, Abdulrasul Haji Kassam, Hasham Ladak, and Rajabali Hasham.**

In 1907, Siwji (Shivji) Alarakhia travelled from Pangani to Tanga. There were no motor vehicles and it took him 10 hours to travel by mule. From Tanga he went to Korogwe[134] by train and once settled there, he started up a shop. He remembers the main communities in Korogwe were Bohoras; there were also about 25 Hindu families. The houses were made of mud and had roofs thatched with straw or banana leaves. In 1909, his son, Salehmohamed, was the first Asian to open a shop in nearby Mombo.

At that time, Tanga was the main port from where goods would be transported by train to Mombo. From Mombo, Salehmohamed used to travel extensively. He would go with four local people, two to help him carry his personal belongings and food and two to handle the mules. They usually covered 10 to 15 miles a day. This is how he managed to establish his trading business in the Usambara area around Mombo.

In 1911, Salehmohamed arranged for the marriage of his younger brother, Nurmohamed, in Zanzibar. Unfortunately, Nurmohamed died in Mombo in 1914 and left behind a widow and a six-month-old son, Hassanali.

By 1917, Salehmohamed had 20 small shops **in the surrounding districts.** A punctual and disciplined individual, Salehmohammed would prepare a schedule of all his travels for the year and send it to his agents and business colleagues. Those who wished to see him would try to meet him according to this itinerary.[135]

Siwji (Shivji) Alarakhia initially named his business "S. Alarakhia". When Salehmohamed took over, he changed it to S. S. Alarakhia, which became the trademark and identity of the family business. They had branches in Mombo, Lushoto, Soni, Bumbuli, Mlalo, Malindi, Shume, Gare and Magamba run by Asian and local (Wasamba'a) staff.

After Salemohamed passed away, his nephew, Hassanali, took over as S. S. Alarakhia & Co and in 1948, he transferred the business to Lushoto where it continued to run until 1979 when it finally closed.

The first President of Africa Federation Alhaj Abdulhussein Noormohamed, referred to S. S. Alarakhia as the "Uncrowned King of Usambara". Salehmohamed was a religious, kind-hearted, hospitable person and his generosity was always deeply appreciated. He always had four to five guests at his table for meals. He would go to the train station with food to offer to strangers and would welcome them to his home to rest.

THE KHOJA SHIA ITHNA-ASHERI PIONEERS OF LUSHOTO

SHIVJI ALARAKHIA KHIMJI
(1864-1945)

SALEHMOHAMED ALARAKHIA
(1886-1943)

HASSANALI ALARAKHIA
(1914-1995)

THE PANGANI MOSQUE & IMAMBARGHA PRESENTLY UNDER BILAL MUSLIM MISSION

Suleman Khimji arrived in Pangani in 1899, at age 14. In 1901, he journeyed 330 miles by foot to Kondoa. At that time there were 11 Khoja Shia Ithna-Asheries living in Kondoa, amongst them Jaffer Khimji, Nasser Virji and Juma Lakha who each had a shop. Religious gatherings were held at the house of his brother, Abdallah Khimji, who had already established his business in the area. Suleman worked for him before starting his own business selling goats and sheep. For his trade, he needed to travel to Singida 100 miles away, a journey that took five days on average.

During those days, the value of a goat was Rupee 1, Rs 5 for a cow and Rs 12 for a milk-giving cow. Travelling by foot became too much and Suleiman decided to buy a Muscati donkey worth Rupees 300, an expensive investment for the time. He travelled on it for two years and then traded it for 70 cows. At the end of 1909, he travelled by foot to Pangani taking 400 bulls and 200 donkeys with him. There he got married and settled.[136]

After a period in Pangani, Suleman sailed to Dar es salaam by steamer. His brother, Abdalla Khimji who was in Dar es Salaam joined him and they both travelled by train to Saranda via Dodoma. Once there, they constructed a house and opened a shop to join the six Ismaili shops already there. Abdalla Khimji returned to Dar es Salaam and Suleiman looked after the new shop in Saranda. Due to the ill health of his wife, Suleiman had to close down the Saranda business and return to Tanga. He started his own business in Kohuwi, 45 miles away from Tanga. The climate was not conducive however and after a short period, he left for Pangani to seek medical treatment for his wife. After five months of treatment, he travelled on foot to Kondoa and restarted the business of selling cattle.

In Kondoa, he use to deal with herds of cattle with over 600 animals and shepherd them to Singida and Pangani on foot or mule. He would commute from Kondoa to Singida and Karama all the way up to Korogwe, a distance of 365 miles which would take him about 40 days to cover.[137] He recounts encountering many challenges on his journeys, ranging from the plague epidemic, attacks from wild animals as well as having to deal with hostile intentions from the colonial authorities.

Suleman and Abdallah Khimji were brothers who travelled from India facing difficulties through the Arab population and going through tough times to arrive at Pangani in 1888.

Sulemanbhai was only 14 years old.

(Trade Directory 1960)

SULEMAN KHIMJI   ABDALLAH KHIMJI

HAJI MERALI KASSAM (1916-)

Haji Merali Kassam was born in Mariya. After acquiring basic education, he left for Dar es Salaam at the age of 14. He worked for a year and a half in Dar es Salaam and Kondoa Irangi. He then went to Kampala and lived there with three of his elder brothers for a year. He then roamed for six years in the jungle of Toro (Fort Portal) and the thicket of Congo. He lived alone without a family. In this period, he tried hard to teach the natives about religion and quite a number of them embraced Islam. He was Hafiz-e-Qur'an and earned himself the title of Sheikh Merali. After six years of total devotion to his Creator, he went to Mwanza where his sister and cousin lived.

After a few months, he took off again travelling to Dodoma, Kondoa, and Morogoro and then to a small place called Boma between Mombasa and Tanga. In 1939, he planted a sisal estate single-handedly. He also planted coconut, beetle nut, banana and sugarcane plantations and fruits such as pineapple, oranges and tangerines. Later he started a twine business using the coconut husks. He made copra and sold it to Pangani Industries and a buyer in Madagascar for making soap. Due to his selflessness, he earned trust and respect within the Khoja and Pangani community at large. The workers he employed on his four farms cried on his demise for a long time lamenting that they had lost a godfather.

Haji Merali served as a secretary of Pangani Jamaat. He was the kind of person everyone depended on for assistance during sickness, major disaster or a shoulder to cry on. He hosted elaborate Hussein Day Programmes for many years on his premises in Pangani where more than 2000 people converged from Tanga, Mombasa, Zanzibar Moshi, and Arusha. Prominent speakers from Zanzibar and Mombasa invited to give inspiring lectures everyone loved to listen. Marhum and his family hosted the Resident Aaalims for many years even after his death. He married Aminabai Abdrasul Rashid of Mwera in 1952.

He passed away at the age of 44, six months after he had an encounter with a cheetah when he tried to save a friend who was brutally attacked. Marhum Merali was a farsighted and a visionary individual who believed in education for all regardless of gender and status. He believed in progress and unity, supported the Africa Federation, and was a regular generous contributor towards the Federation. On his death he bequeathed 20% of his property to the Federation which his wife handed over the funds to the Federation without hesitating despite the fact that she was widowed at the age of 33 with four young daughters to raise.

(Africa Federation Archives)

In 1916, Sulemanbhai returned to Kondoa with 70 porters carrying goods that he sold. With the profits from these sales, he bought cattle. Unfortunately, on his way back his cattle were infected with red water fever[138] and quarantined; out of 325 oxen, only 125 survived. Tired of the risks of his business of choice, he decided to take a break and instead bought two farms at Mandera and Mkonde, 12 miles from Gombezi Station. He eventually settled in Tanga in 1930.

Trading and travel ran in his blood though and in 1934, he went to Arusha and spent a year there trying to trade. He did not succeed and returned to Tanga, this time to finally settle and concentrate on educating his children. Suleman Khimji's resilience is not an exception, but simply one of many examples of how the early pioneers of the Khoja community toiled to achieve a comfortable and sustainable standard of living.[139]

TANGA

The earliest documentation about Tanga[140] comes from the Portuguese who controlled this seaport for over 200 years between 1500 and 1700. From the mid 1700s, the Sultanate of Oman gained control of Tanga along with Mombasa, Pemba Island and Kilwa Kisiwani. Tanga town continued to act as a trading port under the Sultan's rule. When the Germans bought the coastal strip of mainland Tanganyika (Tanzania) from the Sultan of Zanzibar in 1891, Tanga became the centre of German colonial administration and a military post before the establishment of Dar es Salaam in the early 20th century.

In 1900, Fazal Alarakhia Khimji, younger brother of Siwji (Shivji)[141] arrived in Pangani, aged 20 years. In 1909, when Tanga increased its trading activities with the arrival of the railway, Fazal opened a shop there. According to his accounts, Tanga was a very small town, resembling a big plantation with houses made of mud and roofs thatched with palm fronds. Being a coastal town, **Tanga was a fishing village under German control with a** substantial population of fishermen.

In 1914, Fazalbhai left Tanga for Mombo and then went to Mazinde, eight miles from Mombo, to start a business of extracting soda ash (*magadi*) for sale to the Dar es Salaam markets. In 1916, he went to Mkumbara where he continued in the same vein. In Mkumbara, there were five Indian shops with an Indian population of about 20. During the First World War, the British army invaded the area and the Indians had to hide in huts belonging to the local African population in the hills of Sumena, 2.5 miles away.

11 days later, when they returned to Mkumbara they found their houses had been broken into and looted. As a result, Fazalbhai, his wife and three daughters returned to Mombo. Upon reaching Mombo, Fazalbhai succumbed to pneumonia, and after five days of illness, passed away in 1916. He is buried in Tanga. Fazalbhai's grandson, Marhum Hassan Abdulrasul Fazal, served Tanga Jamaat in various capacities including as President for five years.

ABDULRASUL FAZAL ALARAKHIA   HASSANALI ABDULRASUL FAZAL

Among the Indian community settled in Tanga, Bohoras were in the majority numbering 50 heads. They had their own religious centre, including a mosque. There were four Khoja Shia Ithna-Asheri families in Tanga; these were the families of Shermohammed Ladha, Fazal Alarakhia, Siwji (Shivji) Alarakhia and Nazerali Ratansi. In 1910, records state that this small Khoja Shia Ithna-Asheri community held socio-religious functions in their own *imambada*. Tanga being a coastal town was of strategic interest to British East Africa (Kenya). After the First World War, Britain gained control of Tanganyika (Tanzania) and continued to develop the town and by 1919, it had become one of the largest towns in the region.

After the establishment of British rule in Tanga, news reached Zanzibar that the people in Pangani and Tanga had been looted and their condition was pitiable. As a result, Ali Nathoo, a philanthropist in Zanzibar sent a dhow full of clothes and foodstuff for all those affected. Additionally, in 1918, the local population suffered severely because of the spread of infectious diseases. Rebuilding at Tanga only started gradually from 1920. It was under German occupation that Tanga finally saw rapid and planned growth. A tramline was developed within the city to facilitate domestic transport and a new port built for exports. As usual, prosperity began to attract more Indians to Tanga.

By 1924, Khoja Shia Ithna-Asheri families were arriving in Tanga, amongst them the families of Habib Kassam Manji, Gulamhussein Datoo and Jaffer Khimji.[142] Habib Kassam Manji[143] was only 24 years old when he came and he recalls that within the Khoja Shia Ithna-Asheri business persons, four were in prominent positions at the time. The foremost was Mohammed Tharoo, who had sole agencies to sell tea, sugar and tobacco. The others were Jaffer Khimji (clothing), Nazarali Rattansi (African clothing) and Juma Ibrahim (farming).

The community already had an *imambada* and in 1925, Jaffer Khimji donated the mosque building. By 1945, a more accommodating *imambada* was needed as more families had come to settle. Salehmohamed Alarakhia used to make frequent visits to Tanga, took a deep interest in the affairs of the Jamaat there and was a trustee on the committee. He provided Shs. 12,000 in his will for the construction of a new *imambada* to replace the old one, which at the time was made of tin sheets. Tanga Jamaat collected another Shs. 12,000 in donations from its members at the initiative of Habibbhai Kassam Manji and the construction project began.[144]

The community of Tanga needed more donations and it had to seek help from other Khoja Shia Ithna-Asheri communities in East Africa. There was still a shortfall after the fundraising run which was made up by Habib Kassam Manji. The opening ceremony of the new *imambada* was performed by Marhum Haji Dawood Nasser of Karachi and Marhum Nazerali Rattansi in 1952. Habibbhai was a great philanthropist, donating funds towards the boarding house in Dar es Salaam as well as the Hindu temple in Tanga.

Later, in co-operation with Pangani Jamaat, Mohamed Jaffer Peera and Hidayat Hassanali Hasham Dhalla, he repaired the whole *imambada*, whose re-opening was conducted by Marhum Mohamedali Sheriff Jiwa - then Vice President of Africa Federation. Working with his nephew, Sheralibhai Abdulla Kassam Manji, he organised and installed benches at the Dar es Salaam cemetery and a water pump at the mosque.

ALHAJ HABIB BHAI KASSAM MANJI - (1902-1991)

Habib bhai Kassam Manji moved to Tanga at the age of 24. There he joined employment as a broker and later started his own business. He concentrated on the timber business and formed a company called "Timber Concessions Limited" owning sawmills in Pandeni (near Muheza) and at Mkumbara (now a cocoa farm). He later purchased a warehouse and timber yard called "Tanga Timber Sales" located on airport road. He also acquired Mtibwa - Msowero under the name of Tanganyika Timbers Ltd. Most of the business was local with some product exported to South Africa (soft timber) and Japan (hard timber). Some also shipped to Kenya and Europe. He started a company called Habib Kassam Manji (Tanga) Ltd. which dealt with items used by the timber industry and sisal estates.

They had agents in Moshi, Arusha and Lushoto and in agreement with D T Dobie, took over their tire sales Division in Dar es Salaam. Later on he went into the quarry business with Dr Abbasi. In 1949 he purchased a schooner named "Al Hassanain" and later renamed it "Mkoani" (after a town in Pemba). Later he formed a company called "East African Navigators Ltd" - the first such shipping company in East Africa owned by the locals. The company expanded and owned Sea Gull and Sea Horse (both purchased from Tanganyika Railways).

Other schooners purchased included Sukarimawe (from Italy), Diolinda (later named Almasi and purchased from Seychelles) and Maymoon. He also built a ship "Twiga" at Dar es Salaam and a "dock yard" in Dar es Salaam (presently Birth No 5 and 6). His ships would ply between the coastal towns of Mombasa, Tanga, Pemba, Zanzibar, Lindi and Mtwara, carrying passengers and local produce. The ships also carried aviation fuel from Mombasa to Dar es Salaam for the UN army stationed in (Belgian) Congo.

In partnership with his brother Ibrahim and a local businessman, M D Kermalli in Zanzibar, he started Habib Industries Ltd, which imported rice paddy from the mainland, cleaned it and resold it locally. The company also installed a modern factory to make coconut oil for export to soap manufacturers in Aden. He also started Habib Properties Ltd, investing in real estate and later built his residence in Raskazone in Tanga. In 1956, he started transporting timber for local sales. In 1960, he purchased Kimativi Sisal Estate in Naitivi, Lindi from the Karimjee Group, where besides sisal, he planted and sold cashew nut trees. In 1963, he purchased Njianne Sisal Estate, 50 miles south of Dar es Salaam. In 1970, He purchased 50 percent of Afrimetals (a company manufacturing office and school furniture) and started a coir factory in Bagamoyo in partnership with a local. He also formed Tanganyika Cone Factory - producing paper cones for the textile industry. At the same time, he set up a new company Tracparts Ltd formed in Tanga, in cooperation with an Italian company Berco, selling parts for Caterpillar tractors.

In 1978, he donated the factory owned by his family in Nazimabad, Karachi now known as Mehfile Zainab. Habib bhai moved to Dar es Salaam where he passed away at the age of 89.
(Africa Federation Archives, 3 March 2017)

Habibbhai Kassam Manji's son, Alhaj Kassam Manji who lives in London, explains:

> There arose the need to have a cemetery for the community. Until then marhumeen were buried at the farm of an Ibadhi Sheikh, Alhaj Umar Istambuli. One of our members Habibbhai Sheriff had very good relations with the Sheikh and because of his efforts, Sheikh Umar donated a piece of land measuring 25 ft x 25 ft. The Jamaat also purchased two other pieces each of 25 ft x 25 ft from the Sheikh considerably extending the size of our cemetery. Br Suleman Khimji then built a shed (*banda*) at this plot.
>
> Adjacent to our cemetery, there was a 75 x 75 ft plot. Habibbhai offered the owner of the plot his four plots on 8th Street adjoining the Jamia Mosque in exchange for the said plot. As a result, our cemetery was extended. Br Gulamhusein Datoo constructed [a] water well at the cemetery and donated two buildings on 14th Street to [the] Jamaat so that the rental income of Shs. 500 per month would help cover Jamaat expenses. Br Kermali Mohamed Tharoo also donated two buildings whose monthly rental income, Shs 125 and Shs 150, would cover majlis and Imambargha [sic] expenses. Br Jaffer Khimji donated a building [to be] used as [a] Musafarkhana. Habibbhai also donated two buildings located on 14th Street - under Lailabai Trust - for education.

Habibbhai hosted religious scholars who visited Tanga and, as President, represented Tanga Jamaat in Africa Federation Conferences and Supreme Council Sessions. A far-sighted leader of the community, a generous man and a public servant, Tanga Town Council appointed him as a councillor and soon he became Chairman of the Finance Committee, Hospital Committee and Governor of the Education Board. He also became a trustee of Tanga Muslim School built by the Karimjee Jivanjee family.

Another interesting personality, Fazal Remtulla[145], was 16 years of age when he arrived in Tanga by steamer from India in 1908. His journey and what he relates about his journey to Pangani, then on to Singida, Korogwe, Iringa and Hendeni, Metema, Kitengeri and finally

Chingutwa reveals that by 1910, Khoja Shia Ithna-Asheries had already settled in most of these places and settlements. This shows the pioneering spirit of the early Khoja Shia Ithna-Asheries. It reflects their willingness to migrate and adapt, but also shows that once settled, they worked hard to instutionalise themselves socio-religiously to preserve their faith.

ARUSHA

Arusha[146], situated south of Mount Kilimanjaro, is a pleasant serene place facing Mount Meru. Business in this little town increased substantially during the 1860s when the Pangani Valley trade route extended through Old Moshi to Arusha and beyond. Shermohammed Sajan[147] walked for a month from Pangani and reached Arusha in 1898. On his way, he encountered life-threatening challenges from wild animals and robbers. His courageous travails were inspirational to many of his compatriots and are vividly described in the trade directory.[148]

He was an independent-minded, principled man and records show he was jailed by the authorities in Pangani for supplying food to those who were suffering from hunger during the food shortages at the time of the First World War. It also seems that he was the first Khoja Shia Ithna-Asheri to open shops in Moshi, Arusha and Pangani and then encourage others to move to Moshi and Arusha.

Shermohammed's honesty and trustworthiness were so famous that both community and non-community members used to deposit money with him for safekeeping. Even the government establishment honoured his words, cheques and contract notes. He was a community bank before the first financial institution - The Standard Bank - was set up in Arusha in 1928.

When Shermohammed arrived, Arusha was under German Colonial control. The Germans had a strong presence; they built a military fort (*boma*) in 1900 and had soldiers garrisoned there. One constant feature of the German colonial policies was the segregated pattern of planning that clearly divided townships into African quarters, Indian quarters and European quarters. This policy created separate quarters that were seamlessly taken over by the British when the Germans left.[149]

ALHAJ SHERMOHAMED SAJAN (1852-1951)

The family of Sajan Somji was prominent in the city of Nangalpur, India. Sajan was known as an honest businessman with qualities of humility, generosity, and leadership. His first son, Shermohamed (Sher) was born in 1870. As a teenager, Sher was head of the Ismaili youths of Nangalpur.

Sajan and Sher travelled to Zanzibar via Oman. From Zanzibar they first went to Pangani and then to Arusha on foot with a party of 25 people. They carried foodstuff and gifts like beads, cigarettes, matches and candles to give to tribal leaders for permission to march ahead. Arusha impressed them with its beauty and cool weather. The German officials who met them convinced them to abandon their trip to Nairobi and stay in Arusha. As an incentive, they could choose any plot near the Boma and construct their houses there. They were allowed to set up any business related to food, strategic products and import and export of most goods. Shermohamed chose a piece of land of roughly 20 acres about 200 meters south of the Boma. They built a large six-bedroom house with plenty of space at the back for a vegetable farm and living quarters for their workers. The construction of the house was completed and the family moved in in 1903. This was the settlement of the first Indian family in Arusha, Tanganyika.

Shermohamed made trips to Tanga to buy food and other imported goods from India. Locally, they visited Maasai villages to sell them beads in return for products which were produced by the Maasai, such as hides and skins, vegetables and agro products to export to India, UK and Germany. Besides trade, they assisted the Maasai community in whatever way they could. An important tradition among the Maasai was the Circumcision Ceremony. Generally, only the Maasai were allowed to attend. Sajan and Shermohamed understood the great importance of the ceremony and offered the families whose boys were circumcised medications from India to help speed up the recovery and healing process. Maasai men did not cover their bodies and the women wore skirts made of hides. Shermohamed had a working knowledge of their language - Kimaasai. The Germans and the British therefore used Shermohamed to play a significant role in convincing the Maasai men and women to cover themselves.

In 1912, the Germans introduced the use of motor vehicles which resulted in a major change in the distribution system of goods, especially food products. It enabled Shermohamed to double the volume of business in a few months and continue to increase rapidly. As their business grew, they needed a work force to sustain it and gave first preference to relatives and friends. Those people included his closest friend, Murabbi Mohamedali Ladak Kanji who set up a hardware store in partnership with Shermohamed in Moshi in 1937. Others were Suleman Ramji (transport business in Arusha), Gulamhusein Moledina (clothing shop in Moshi) and Suleman Jivraj (Ismaili cousin) (retail shops) and others. There were many also who were recruited directly for his business or assisted in other ways and among them were Remtulla and Gulam Ladak (brothers), Gulamhusein Kanji, Sajan Ladak, Husein Karim, Nazarali Karim, and many others.

Shermohamed was able to generate the profit from his business, expand, consolidate his existing business empire and diversify into other sectors. Soon his business empire was the largest in

Tanganyika, if not the whole of East Africa. By 1932, the Shermohamed Empire included retail shops selling all daily groceries, provisions and textiles, hardware, motor spares and agricultural items. He also owned coffee plantations and petrol pumps in Arusha and Babati and was a major supplier to the central procurement department of the British Government.

When the Standard Bank opened its first branch in Arusha in 1928, Shermohamed was the only non-European allowed to open a bank account. Prior to that all banking services were provided by the Shermohamed companies (in Arusha, Moshi, Pangani and Mbulu), which enabled their customers to deposit and withdraw money, and to transfer money from one customer to another. Government offices would readily accept and cash bills of exchange signed by Shermohamed. Sometimes customers would end up at Shermohamed's door in the middle of the night to draw money from their accounts, but he never turned them back.

Shermohamed became a household name in Arusha, Moshi, Pangani and other cities, including Nangalpur. The first non-European house to be supplied with electricity and piped water was the Shermohamed house. The first 3 cars that came to Arusha belonged to the three Shermohamed brothers – Hassanali, Mohamed-Taki and Jafferali.

Note: Company was established in 1904. Descriptions of elephants and rhinos, and Arusha as a half-way point between Cape Town and Cairo can still be found in advertising material today.

His business activities were seriously interrupted by the onset of World War 2 and he sustained huge losses. The youngest brother, Jafferali, passed away which was a major personal tragedy suffered by the whole family, but especially by Shermohamed himself, who had lost his wife some years earlier. The company managed to survive but with difficulty. In 1948, the family suffered another personal tragedy with the death of Nasim, a young daughter of Mohamed-Taki Shermohamed who was hit by a truck.

In addition to being a successful businessman, Shermohamed believed strongly in doing good, keeping a close family, and giving to charity. He made large amounts of charitable donations, including to the building of local mosques, but preferred anonymity. For those individuals whom he found had no religion, he would teach them about Islam and ask them to learn and adopt the practices of the religion whilst they worked within his enterprise. This practice may have led to the conversion of hundreds of people (especially the Fyomis of the Babati-Mbulu Area) to the religion of Islam.

Shermohamed went for his first Hajj in 1905 under very difficult circumstances. In 1950 he expressed the desire to go for Hajj one more time before his death. He went for Hajj accompanied by his youngest son-in-law, Hussein Ibrahim. He was a very happy man when he returned from Hajj and passed away peacefully in 1951. Around 700 people, of all faiths, attended his funeral the next day. Arusha had never seen such a large funeral gathering. For a simple ordinary human being from Kutch, India, Shermohamed's life and times is one of immense courage and inspiration, and a rare tale of adventure and pioneering.

(Africa Federation Archives, 11 May 2018)

By 1902, Khoja Shia Ithna-Asheries had begun to steadily stream to Arusha. By 1908/9, among those who had settled there were the families of Nanji Damani, Mohammed Damani, Ismail Ibrahim, Hasham Ibrahim, Jaffer Pradhan, Sachoo Jivraj, Nasser Lila, Suleiman Ramji, Bandali Ladak, Ali Damani, Sajan Ladak, Hussein Karim, Remtullah Ladak, Alimohammed Pirbhai, Nazerali Karim, Gulamhussein Kanji and Remtulla Pirbhai. These were the pioneers of the Arusha Khoja Shia Ithna-Asheri community. There were also 12 members from other Asian communities residing in Arusha at that time.

Suleiman Ramji joined the employment of Shermohamed Sajan in 1904. After working for him for eight years, he opened his own shop at Mbulu. He operated this shop for 14 years and then moved back to Arusha where he started a transport business, which is going on well to this day.[150] At that time, travel was mainly on foot and merchandise was transported by porters. In 1909, the German authorities started the use of bullock carts for transportation. From 1923, motor vehicles came into use and this made trading much easier.

Mohamed Damani used to live at Boma la Ng'ombe, 35 miles from Arusha. In 1904, he moved to Arusha where he constructed a mud house with a grass thatch roof. His early encounter with the colonial authority was not a pleasant one. Story has it that one day, a German official entered the shop and when Mohamed did not immediately stand up and greet him, he became angry and began swearing at him. Mohamed, a man with self-respect did not take this lightly and ended up slapping the officer. A skirmish broke out and although Mohamed won the fight, he was jailed for two years for assaulting an officer.[151]

After his release, he started his shop again and did some farming as well. He grew onions and garlic to sell in Moshi. In 1912, the government issued a directive that all mud houses had to be replaced by sturdier structures. The following year, Mohamed built a brick house to replace his mud hut and a year after that, he bought a plot across the road and built a tin house that served as a shop for his son Gulamhussein to run. However, the ensuing war had repercussions for everyone and soon after Mohamed Damani had to close the second shop and both father and son worked in the main shop.[152]

At this time, the Arusha Khoja community did not have a cemetery. When Nanji Damani passed away in 1913, he was buried in the African cemetery behind Standard Bank. Upon witnessing this, Mohamed made a will request to Juma Lakha that he wanted to be buried in the land behind the tin house where he once had a branch shop and the entire land be donated as a cemetery for the community. He also informed the government about this will. When he passed away, he was buried according to his will and the land was donated as he requested.[153]

After the railway service began in 1929, Arusha grew very fast. The Khoja community witnessed an economic transition and huge trade expansion after the First World War. When the British took over Arusha from the Germans in 1916, they established a civilian administration that reflected the German colonial policy of division and discrimination. The German farmlands surrounding the towns of Arusha and Moshi were passed on to settlers from the United States, Britain and Greece. Undeterred by this obvious prejudice towards the non-White, Khoja Shia Ithna-Asheries took up whatever opportunities came their way. Most of them went into trade and some succeeded in setting up small factories.

There was no established *jamaat* in the beginning and *majlises* were initially held at the home of Hasham Ebrahim, then at Shermohamed Sajan's and finally at Gulamhussein Kanji's residence. By 1930, the community had reached 75 members and they obtained a piece of land for a 33-year lease to construct an *imambada* on, which was completed in 1931. On the land across from the *imambada*, a shop was set up as an investment and the rent was used to fund the expenses of *imambada*.

Arusha's temperate weather attracted many visitors and there was a lot of movement of community members to and from the town. The family of Remtulla Pirbhai generously constructed two rooms above the shop to be used as a *musafarkhana*. Over the next few years, the community continued to grow and to meet its increasing needs, the Jamaat embarked on a project to build a mosque, *imambada*, *musafarkhana* and **madrasah** by 1957. The funds for the mosque were donated by the families of Jamal Ramji and Remtulla Pirbhai and the rest of the funds were raised by community members.

ALIBHAI DAMANI

Alibhai Damani, Mohamedbhai's brother, lived in Kondoa-Irangi. He came to Arusha in 1912 for five months and then went to India to get married. After his marriage, he returned to Kondoa-Irangi in 1913 and stayed with his brother Kanji Damani. Initially, Alibhai was working as a tailor and had a small shop near the Malala River in Meru. Then Mohamed asked both his siblings to move to Arusha.

After the death of Mohamed, Alibhai finally moved to Arusha. In May 1916, he wanted to go to India again. This time, he went by train to Mombasa where with the help of a police officer called Abdulla Budha he was able to obtain a temporary passport to travel to Mumbai. Once in India, he went to his home town of Dhandhuka where he stayed for 18 months. He finally left Mumbai for Mombasa on 20 July 1917.

When Alibhai arrived in Mombasa, he was charged Shs 200 by the immigration officer, which was the standard deposit for new arrivals. He immediately informed Juma Ebrahim in Moshi and Jaffer Lakha in Arusha about the payment, who both sent telegrams to Mombasa Immigration officials through Major A. D. Brown confirming that Alibhai was a resident of Arusha and had only gone to India for a visit.

Alibhai was thus able to regain his residency rights and go back to his small shop at Meru-Malala. It was only because of the close network of the community and the inextricable links that the members had with each other that they were able to influence and help each other - even remotely - in such situations.

MOHAMMEDTAKI REHEMTULLAH PIRBHAI (1919-1964)

A compassionate man by any standard, Mohammedbhai was born in Mombasa. After acquiring his education there, he joined his family business in Arusha at a very young age dealing in produce and transportation.

An active worker, he dedicated his time to the betterment of the community. In 1956, he became the President of Arusha Jamaat. With passion and zeal, he began the construction of the Mosque, Imambargha & Madrasah, his family being the main contributors.

In 1959, he was appointed as the Deputy Treasurer of Africa Federation where he served under Alhaj Ebrahimbhai Shariff Dewji. In 1961 Mohammedtakibhai took a lot of responsibility of The Africa Federation due to Ebrahimbhai's ill health. Outside of the community, he also was an active member of Arusha Farmers Association from 1958-1960.

(Africa Federation Archives, 26 May 2014)

By 1960, Arusha municipality had a population of about 10,000 out of which 233 were members of the Khoja Shia Ithna-Asheri community.[154] The entrepreneurial trading trends in this town were no different to those mirrored all across East Africa. Khojas arrived, worked for fellow Khojas while studying the market and environment for a couple of years and then ventured into their own businesses.

MOSHI

Moshi[155], situated on the lower slopes of Mount Kilimanjaro, is home to the highest mountain in Africa. It had a very small settlement surrounded by jungle and wild animals and housed a military camp established by the German colonial government in 1893.

Hasham Ibrahim[156] and his brother, Ismail Ibrahim, came from Jamnagar and arrived in Zanzibar in the late 1890s. After working in the employ of Hajibhai Khaku and Ladhubhai Lalji, they came to settle in Moshi around 1905/6. Their brother Mohammed Ibrahim also joined them after a while and Shermohammed Sajan came to set up his shop too. The railways reached Moshi in 1912 and was followed by Khoja Shia Ithna-Asheries settlers.

In 1921, when Mulla Gulamhussein Kanji[157] arrived in Moshi, Shermohammed Sajan, Hussein Karim, Mohammedali Ladak and Hasham Ibrahim were already well settled. Mohammedali Sheriffe,

Walli Jaffer Dhanji, Mohammedali Dhanji and Gulahussein Moledina joined them later. These were some of the pioneers of the community.

Trading in Moshi began to boom as transport and administrative infrastructures improved with the coming of British Colonial rule. Trading companies, small factories and mills were set up. The community was at the forefront of the small business sector, working with the local Chagga tribe and they dominated the retail arena.

Hasham Ebrahim Mamdani (1882-1964)

Born in Changa Chela, Jamnagar, Hashambhai migrated to Zanzibar where he worked for about two years and then travelled to Pangani where he joined the employment of Hajibhai Khakoo for 6 years, followed by one year with Ladhubhai Lalji, before moving to Moshi.

The area where Moshi is currently situated was desolate woodland. He migrated to German Moshi, known as Old Moshi. He and his brother Esmail were the first Ithna-Asheris tin this area. After the establishment of British rule, the new Moshi town started being populated. Shermohamedbhai Sajan and Mohamedbhai Ebrahim joined them.

Hashambhai opened a shop dealing with clothing and grocery provisions at Machame. After seven years in Machame, he moved to new Moshi. Later, he opened a shop in Arusha and ran it for five years. In 1919, he went to India where he stayed for two months before returning to Moshi. In 1960, the population of Khoja Shia Ithnaasheris in Moshi was 344. Moshi Jamaat population grew to about 600 in the early 1980s, presently the population of Moshi Jamaat stands at 110 men, women and children, a drastic drop.

(Africa Federation Archives, 14 November 2016)

Before 1926, religious gatherings in Moshi were held at the house of Shermohammed Sajan. After 1926, they were held at Mulla Gulamhussein's house. The first *imambada* was built in 1932 and a second one in 1942 to cater for the expanding community. The *musafarkhana* was constructed soon after, funded by Mohammed Sheriff Jiwa. The rental income from a building donated by the family of Valli Jaffer Dhanji was used for Islamic *tabligh* work. All these projects were undertaken in the 1920s under Moshi Jamaat's first president, Mohammed Ladak.[158]

Mohammedbhai remained at the helm for a long time and the connections he made whilst working for the colonial administration gave him great influence. With his experience, he was able to assist

Muhamadalibhai Ladak

Muhamadalibhai Ladak was born in Kutch Nangalpur. At the age of 12, he arrived in Pangani and lived with Hasham Ladak, whilst working for Shermohamed Sajjan and Remtulla Mulji. He also worked in Bhullu, a small village in north Tanganyika. In 1918, he was employed as an interpreter for the army, travelling to Babati and Kondoa. Having gained a lot of experience, he started his own business in Mbugwe in 1917. The following year, he came to Arusha and established a shop R. Muhamadali Ladak. Due to his rapport with the army, most of his business came from them. Until 1927 the area was underdeveloped, there were no transport facilities and people travelled on foot passing through thick wild jungle. He often used to travel from Bhullu to Singida on foot.

Muhamadalibhai still remembers one of his trips when journeyed to Singida with his goods tied on a Muscati donkey. Their halfway camp was quite far and they ran out of water. When they finally reached the camp that evening, they found the pond there had dried up and could only get a little bit of water by digging for it. They set up camp and unfortunately, soon after nightfall, a thirsty lion attacked the Muscati donkey. The local workers who were with him didn't know what to do, but Muhamadalibhai took command of the situation, lit a fire and scared off the animal. Everyone in the camp took turns to patrol the camp throughout that night.

Muhamadalibhai recalls that he got only 2 cups of water as his ration and he made tea with one of them, it was according to him the most delicious brew he had ever had. The lion attacked again at dawn, but this time the camp was alert they were able to chase it away once more. That particular journey was rife with adventure as they encountered a massive python as well as a pride of lions before they reached their destination.

In 1920 Mohamedalibhai travelled to India and when he returned to Africa, he established a business under M. Ladak Kanji and opened a branch in Nairobi. His main trade was selling Shanga(beads), Panga (big knives) and Khanga(traditional East African cloth). In 1935, he started the business of coffee. In those days, travelling from Moshi to Arusha took 5 days on a bell cart, 3 days on foot and 5 hours by car. As his business scope grew gradually, Mohamedalibhai established an industry of talcum powder and geru (geru is red soil which the native Masaai applied on their entire body). Later he closed down both these industries and bought a 175-acre piece of land in Moshi on which he built a house to his personal specifications with a hardware shop on the ground floor. This shop still exists in the middle of Moshi town.

The Jamaat of Moshi was established in 1920 and elected him as its President. He also served 12 years as Vice President of the Indian public school and 5 years as President of the local sports club. In 1952 he travelled throughout Tanganyika collecting for Nairobi Masjid and its guest house. He also personally conducted a collection for the Kutch-Nangalpur Masjid; a property was bought in Mombasa with the funds and its income sent to Nangalpur. In 1958 he travelled with Ebrahimbhai, President of the Council for the Federation Fund.

(Trade Directory, 1960)

many in dealing with colonial bureaucracy. He was respected by the Indian community and made chairman of the Indian Public School and Sports Club in Moshi. Apart from working for the local community, Mohammedbhai helped raise funds for community projects outside Moshi including the Khoja community in Nagalpur, Kachchh.

Mohamedali Sheriff Jiwa (1909-1990)

Mohamedalibhai was born in Mombasa and studied upto London matriculation level. In 1931 he moved to Moshi where he established a successful business called Moshi Trading Co. Ltd. He had a deep interest in community service and was awarded the MBE by the British Government in 1955.

He was instrumental in the formation of the Indian Public School, which he led as President for 18 years. He was President of the Muslim Association and served Moshi Jamaat as Honorary Secretary, Vice-President and Trustee over the years. He also served as Vice President of Africa Federation, President of Tanganyika Territorial Council and Tanganyika Boarding House.
(Africa Federation Archives, 23 June 2017)

Hassanali Mohamedali Ladak (1926-1967)

At young age, Hassanalibhai held a respectable position in the business community. He managed the family business called M Ladak Kanji Company and at the same time took a keen interest in community and public service.

He was a committee member of Moshi Indian Public School and an Honorary Treasurer of the Jamaat. He was the Hon Secretary of Moshi Ithna-Asheri Club, KSI Tanganyika Territorial Council and Tanganyika Boarding House. He was an ardent supporter of the Africa Federation. The community lost a dedicated prominent leader when Hassanalibhai died in car accident in 1967 while serving as Vice President of the Africa Federation.
(Africa Federation Archives, 23 June 2017)

Haji Dostmohamed Moledina (1921-2000)

Born in Moshi, Haji Dostmohamed Moledina was a well-known social worker in the service of the public and in our community. He was a dynamic Councillor representing Moshi Jamaat at the Africa Federation Supreme and Territorial Councils for many years. He was a very active member of Moshi Jamaat with great wisdom and dedication. He made many friends by his amiable nature.

Alhaj Dostmohamed (fondly known as Dost) was consistent in attendance of the Africa Federation Supreme Council Sessions and Conferences. He was also Vice President of Moshi Club and Hon. Secretary of the Jamaat. Dostmohamedbhai passed away in Nairobi in 2000.
(Africa Federation Archives, 23 June 2017)

Khoja Shia Ithna-Asheri Mosque, Moshi

Jaffery Charitable Medical Service (JCMS), Moshi

Khoja Shia Ithna-Asheries in Moshi began to achieve such a level of economic prosperity that in 1947, Gulamhussain Lakha chartered a plane for the community members to travel to Mecca for pilgrimage. This, according to the Trade Directory, was the first such initiative, to take community members for pilgrimage.

SINGIDA

Singida is another place where Khoja Shia Ithna-Asheries settled. It is accessible from Arusha, Dar es Salaam and Mwanza. Hasham Dewji[159] was 18 years old when he arrived in Zanzibar from India in 1902. He worked for three and a half years for Ismail Sumar and then for two and a half years with Hasham Hirji in Zanzibar.

In 1907, he migrated to Pangani and worked for Ahmed Shermohammed for one year before becoming a partner in the business for two years. In order to verify the accounts of upcountry branches, Hashambhai used to travel quite often to the interior. It was very normal for him to walk a distance of up to 50 miles a day.

In 1909, he travelled by dhow from Pangani to Dar es Salaam, boarded a train to Morogoro and then to Kilosa where he took over the responsibility of all the business branches. In 1910, he left the partnership and opened his own shop in Kitete, which he left to his brother to run. The following year he went to Pangani, got married and then moved to Dodoma where he stayed until 1918.

Over the next 12 years, he moved to Dar es Salaam, Zanzibar and Machoni in succession, trading in retail goods. It was 1930 when

Alhaj Hasham Dewji

he moved to Singida and opened a shop selling food crops. At that time, there were only two Khoja Shia Ithna-Asheri families residing in Singida. The religious functions were held at Hasham's residence.

After the demise of his mother, Hasham and his two brothers decided to build an *imambada* from their late mother's fund. This was completed in 1935 and served the community for the next 15 years. In 1940, the Indian community united to establish a school that served

Alhaj Hussein Hasham Dewji

Husseinbhai was born in Dodoma, Tanzania in 1917. His late father was a proficient businessman and Husseinbhai took over his father's business - "Hasham Dewji & Sons" - at the tender age of 16, operating it efficiently.

Husseinbhai was a humble and social individual. He served Singida Jamaat with great zeal and dedication. He was also the President of the Jamaat for many years. Those who had a chance to meet him could immediately sense how he deeply committed to the Jamaat he was. He would warmly welcome anyone visiting Singida for business or any other purpose.

Husseinbhai was courteous and philanthropic by nature and an outstanding figure in the public. He served as a trustee of the Muslim School and Manager as well as Trustee of Indian Public School. He also served as the Chairman of Indian Association.

all and in 1945, the Ismaili community opened their own school as well. A new *imambada* was built in 1950 with Mombasa and Dar es Salaam community members contributing Shs. 20,000 and Singida Jamaat members raising the deficit.

KILWA

The route linking the coast and the south of Tanganyika connected Kilwa to Lake Malawi passing through the town of Lindi. By 1910, Khoja Shia Ithna-Asheries had already settled in Kilwa, Lindi, Masasi, Tunduru and Songea, some arriving by boat and some by train, but almost all completing the final leg of the journey by foot.

Haji Siwji Somji[160] arrived in Zanzibar from India in 1910 at the age of 18. After working in Zanzibar for 16 months, he travelled to Kilwa and then walked 320 miles to Songea where his brother Jaffer Somji had a shop. He recalls that his brother had arrived in southern Tanganyika at the time of the Maji Maji rebellion (1905-1907) by the Africans against the German colonial government. The rebellion was triggered by a German policy that forced the indigenous African population to grow cotton for export.

The policy - introduced in 1898 - was brutal. It levied taxes on the Africans and relied heavily on forced labour to build roads and accomplish various other tasks. In 1902, the authorities ordered villages to grow cotton as a cash crop (for export). Each village was charged with producing a quota of cotton and the headmen of the village left in charge of overseeing the production were set against the rest of the population. These harsh measures had a negative impact on the social fabric of African village society and strained the resources of the village. There was a lot of animosity against the German government which resulted in an uprising that began from the southern coast and spread into the interior until Lake Nyasa.

Khoja Shia Ithna-Asheries who had settled in Kilwa, Lindi, Masasi and Songea must have been affected by it, but to what extent is not recorded. The end of the rebellion was followed by a period of famine, known as the Great Hunger (*njaa*), caused at large by the scorched-earth policy of the Germans.

Historically, Kilwa was important on the East African coast described by explorers as "one of the most beautiful towns in the world". Although Kilwa had been trading peacefully for centuries, the city's gold trade attracted the Portuguese who were in search of the mineral. During the period of Portuguese subjugation, trade essentially stopped in Kilwa. When the Omanis overthrew the Portuguese in the late 17th and early 18th centuries, Kilwa experienced an economic resurgence. It later became the capital of German East Africa.

By the time Jaffer Siwji Somji arrived in 1906, Kilwa was already under German rule. He noted that there was already a strong presence of Khojas there and also intra-communal tension within the community

ALHAJ SIWJI SOMJI (1882-1963)

Siwjibhai Somji was born in India. At the age of 18, he travelled to Zanzibar by dhow. Once there, he worked for Gulamhussein Somji Lilani at a salary of 100 rupees a year. After that year passed, he found employment at Remtulla Allarakhia Tejani's where he worked for four months.

Siwjibhai left this job and travelled to Kilwa on a ship named 'Governor'. He then travelled from Kilwa to Songea on foot taking with him tents, labourers and food. He used to walk 6 hours every day. It took them 24 days to reach Songea - a distance of 320 miles.

He started working at Jaffer Somji's shop in Songea. In 1905, the African population carried out the "Maji Maji Rebellion" against the German rulers.

The revolt continued for three months and subsided when the Mayor Mr. Johannes brought German army to quell the rebellion. In 1906, Jaffer Somji moved from Songea to Kilwa where he opened a shop. In 1923, Jafferbhai passed away in India and Siwjibhai brought his brother's family from India.

Siwji Somji, Rawji Somji, Esmail Rawji and Fazel Rawji opened a partnership business under the name of Jaffer Somji & Co. in Lindi and the business was operational up to 1934 when they split. Thereafter, Siwji Somji and Hassanali Jaffer Somji ran a joint business called Somji Store up to 1957 when they split up.

Siwjibhai recalled an interesting incident that took place in 1934. He had gone to Mbwera (Rufiji) from where he loaded a ship destined for Dar es Salaam with dried coconuts. Due to a fierce storm, the ship ran aground and broke into pieces. They were not very far from the shore, but because of the turbulent waves, people could not swim and had to cling to the wooden planks to avoid drowning. The small rescue boat on the ship was used by some, but it also capsized leading to the drowning of an Arab woman. Siwjibhai, two Arabs and the ship captain decided to use one of the rafts to go ashore. When Siwjibhai saw that the raft could not take the weight of all of them, he decided to jump into the sea and swim to the shore. His three colleagues finally made it to the shore as well. (Africa Federation Archives, 7 April 2017) regarding the religious status of Aga Khan III.¹⁶¹ Whilst the court ruled on some claims, it suggested that clarity on the theological and religious issues be sought from Aga Khan who was due to visit Kilwa. In 1905, Agha Khan III arrived in Kilwa. He held a number of question and answer sessions under the directive of the local German court. The main participants were Sherriff Nurmohamed, Suleman Walji, Haji Suleman Bhimjee and Agha Khan. A perspective on what happened at the meeting can be gleaned from the document published by Adelji Dhanji Kaba.¹⁶² This publication was in response to the booklet published by Mr Verteji titled *Hazar Imam's Guidance*.

When Sherriff Nurmohammed arrived in Kilwa in 1883, there was already a well-established Khoja community. He describes the harshness of the German court against the Khojas, which is corroborated by the report of a group of Indian businessmen accused of acting against the German sovereignty in 1895. The Indian businessmen were alleged to have supported a rebel movement and found guilty. The entire community had to pay a hefty fine, but the three individuals accused received a much more severe sentence in being expelled from Kilwa.¹⁶³

With the assistance of Lakha Kanji, Pirani, and Aliya Jumani, Sherriff Nurmohammed was able to open his own shop. At the time, there was cohesiveness within the Khoja community in that they use to meet up on social occasions, hold religious lectures, carry out lamentation rituals, recite *salawat* on the 14 *Masumeen* and perform *ziyarats*. The majority of the congregation was from Kachchh and the rest were from Jamnagar and Junagadh. At the time, everyone in the Khoja community was a firm supporter of Agha Khan III.

Just before 1905, *farmans* came from Aga Khan III seeking to restrict those who were professing the Ithna-Asheri beliefs and branding them as disloyal to Agha Khan III. The Khoja Jamaat began to divide along lines of dispute. Agha Khan III issued a *farman* that 'those who signed allegiance to Ismaili faith were the only ones allowed into the Jamaatkhana'. Following this *farman*, the Khoja community of Kilwa split up with 40 families following the Ismaili faith and 22 families becoming Ithna-Asheri. At the request of the German court, Aga Khan III agreed to meet with the representatives of those who held Ithna-Asheri beliefs, however nothing was resolved.

The two groups began to drift even further apart and the Khoja Shia Ithna-Asheries subsequently formed their *jamaat* of 25 families. They had a mosque, an *imambada*, a *musafarkhana*, and a burial ground. Within the *imambada* building, there were two shops for the poor and needy as well as a *madrasah* to provide religious instruction for the children of the community.

Community archival sources show that around 1900, among the Khoja Shia Ithna-Asheris present in Kilwa were Haji Nanji Kara, Nurmohamed Mulji, Jaffer Somji, Siwji Somji, Kermali Dhanji, Bandali Bhimji, Bachubhai Meghji, Ramzanbhai Hassam, Ahmed Walji, Gulammohamed Jivraj Bhojani, Kassamali Bhimji, Hassanali Dharsee, Kassamali Chagan, Hussein Dewji, Merali Mawji, Jaffer Aladin, and Suleiman Walji. These were the pioneers of the Khoja Shia Ithna-Asheri community there. Many others from the surrounding villages such as Njinjo, Miteja, Muhoro and Mbawara joined them during Muharram commemorations.

KILWA 1929

Standing L-R: Driver Sadiki & Rajabu, Bandali Bhimji, u, u, u, Mohamedali J Visram, Gulamali Bhimji, Tailor Mohamed Juma.

Sitting: Hassan Merali, Asian postmaster holding Akber K Bhimji, Malaika Chatoo, Kermali Dhanji, Merali Mawji holding his daughter Fatma, Kassamali Habib, Nanji Kara w. Yusuf, Mulla Yusuf holding two daughters. Standing near pillar in turkish cap is a servant. Near feet of Kermali Dhanji is his nephew Raza Jaffer Somji.

Last two rows: Kassamali Bhimji Nayani, servant Nassoro holding child, Laila J Somji, Zainab Merali Mawji, Rubab Merali Mawji, Rubab J Somji, Zahra Mulla Yusufali, Kulsum M Mawji, Maryam Bhojani, Gulammohamed M Mawji, Mohamed Hussein J Somji, Mohamedjaffer Kara.

Haji Merali Mawji (1888-1960)

Haji Merali Mawji was born in Khandna, India. At the age of 12, he left his parents to vie for better prospects by sailing to Kilwa where he worked at Esmail Bhalloo. In 1906, he went to India to get married and on his return went to Njinjo, a village near Kilwa where he opened a small shop. In 1909, he moved back to Kilwa.

In 1923, he went to Iraq and Iran for Ziyarat. In 1946, he went for Hajj. In 1948, he closed his business in Kilwa and moved to Monduli. He rendered invaluable services to Kilwa Jamat and was trustee of Arusha Jamat. Alhaj Merali Mawji died in Mumbai, while on a Ziyarat trip.
(Africa Federation Archives, 6 October 2017)

Kilwa Jamat in Perspective
Nurmohamed Manekia

Nurmohamed Mulji Manji Ukka Manekia was born in Mahuva, Kathiawar, India. His grandfather Manji Ukka Manekia was a pious man. Nurmohamed and his uncle Shamji Manji used to go to their neighbour Majnamia Saheb of Kodinar for training in *Namaz*, *Majlis* and *Salam*. In 1860, he travelled to nearby town of Ghogha for a trade fair. From there he took the sea voyage to Zanzibar in 1864. In Zanzibar Hassan Gulamhussein of Bhavnagar employed him.

They used to have *majlis* at the business premises every Thursday and Hassanbhai would recite *Rozatush Shohada* in his characteristic manner and style. Nurmohamed then joined Mohamed Walji whose pious nature and strong faith impressed him and inspired him to seek a more spiritual life too. In 1883, he opened a shop in Kilwa with the help of Lakha Kanji, Sachedina Pirani (Sachoo Peera) and Aliya Jumani. At the Kilwa Jamatkhana, there was no limit on duration of *majlis* and *matam*. They also used to recite Salawat on 14 *Masumeen* and *Ziyarat* at the Jamatkhana. The *majlis* session would take 2-3 hours. Most of the members were from Kutch, a few from Jamnagar and one from Junagadh.

In matters of faith, Mohamed Walji Harji of Zanzibar influenced Nurmohamed. Although he participated in rituals at the Jamatkhana like *Majlis* and *Dua*, he also prayed *Namaz* at home. He finally converted to "Subhaniyya" (Ithna-Asheri), although after his conversion, he offered to increase his contribution to Jamatkhana. There was an argument about conducting *majlis* at home, the Jamaat having been against it. The Jamaat was asked to get an opinion from Zanzibar Jamaat. In Zanzibar, Haji Peera Walli, Nasser Lilani, Versi Advani and Lakha Kanji requested the Waras to write a letter giving permission for *majlises* to be held at home. After some time a letter by the Waras was sent, but without signature of the Mukhi. This led to a division in Kilwa Jamaat with some in favour and some against having *majlis* at home. At this time about 40 people converted to Subhaniyya (Ithna-Asheri).

Around 1899, there were 40 Ismaili families and 22 Ithnaasheri families in Kilwa. Members used to go to both Jamatkhana and Imambada. An important incident in the history of our community is the meeting between Aga Khan III and Sheriff Nurmohamed, Suleman Walji and Suleman Bhimji during Aga Khan's visit to Kilwa in 1905. During this 24-hour visit, the Aga Khan visited Kilwa Jamatkhana and met government officials. He spent 6 hours on land during which the rituals of presenting shawl, *paghramni* and *kangwa* were carried out.

The most common community magazines during that period were *Rahenajat*, *Rafeeq* and *Baghe Najaat*. Community news were sent to these magazines that had a global reach including Mumbai, Zanzibar, Mombasa, Bhavanagar, Mahuva, Jamnagar, Dar es Salaam, Bagamoyo and Lindi.

The foundation stone for the Kilwa Imambada was laid in 1899. A drive was started for contributions to construct it and it finally was at a cost of 7500 rupees. The three main contributors were Nurmohamed Mulji, Alidina Dhalla and Esmail Bhalloo. Four *mutwallis* (trustees) were appointed including Nurmohamed Mulji. After the passing away of two of the *mutwallis*, Esmail Bhalloo and Alidina Dhalla were appointed. It was also agreed at the time, that after the passing away of Nurmohamed, his son Sheriff would take his place. In 1900, land was obtained behind the Imambada for a graveyard.

By 1914, there were 25 Ithna-Asheri and 35 Ismaili families. By then, the community had a big portion of land comprising of gardens, a mosque, a large *sahan* (courtyard), *Hawz* (water fountain), a two storey Imambada and a *musafarkhana* (guesthouse). There was also a *madrasah*. The first President of Jamaat was Nanji Kara. To cover expenses, income was derived from a farm. The total cost of all this construction was about Rupees 18,000 to 20,000, 99% of which was raised locally. The cost of the *madrasah* and *muallim* was borne by members at the rate of 2 Anna per household.

The above history of Kilwa was extracted from a letter written by Sheriff Manekia on behalf of his father Nurmohamed to Adelji Dhanji Kaba, dated 3 April 1914 and printed in the book "Kilwa na Sawal Jawab" At the end of the letter, Nurmohamed requests that relevant points should be relayed to the son of Sheth Mohamedali of Bhavnagar (Magistrate) who had requested for a history of Kilwa.

The families that had settled in Kilwa include Haji Nanji Kara, Nurmohamed Manekia, Jaffer Somji, Siwji Somji, Kermali Dhanji, Mulla Yusufali Abdullah, Bandali Bhimji, Bachubhai Meghji, Ramzanbhai Hasham, Ahmed Walji, Gulammohamed Jivraj Bhojani. Kassamali Bhimji, Hassanali Dharsee, Kassamali Chagani, Hussein Dewji, Merali Mawji, Jaffer Aladin, Suleman Walji and Abdulla Damji.

Between 1930 and 1960 the population of Khoja Ithna-Asheris reached about 200. The mosque complex was about a mile from the town and members of the community would reach it by walking or by rickshaw. During the month of Muharram, those staying in small villages such as Njinjo, Miteja, Muhoro and Mbawara would come to Kilwa to take part in *Azadari*. About four Bohora families attended too. Sermons were recited by Haji Habib Sheriff Manekia, Haji Gulamabbas Merali Mawji and Haji Pyarali Hassanali Rahim of Zanzibar. Before 1930, Mulla Yusufali Abdullah used to recite *majlis*.

The last community members left in Kilwa were Haji Gulamali Kermali Dhanji and Haji Anverali Manekia. The last family to leave Kilwa was

Kilwa Cemetery

Kilwa Mosque

Kilwa Kivinje Khoja Masjid/Imambada Ruins

Husseinali Manekia who moved out in September 1971. Husseinali (Motabha) is the son of Habib Sheriff Manekia.

Habib, a prominent trader and Zakire Imam Hussein (pbuh) was born in Kilwa in 1909 and passed away in Dar es Salaam in 1980. His other children are Alhaj Anverali Manekia, Shirinbai Aunali Mohamedhussein Khalfan, Amirali Manekia and Zainab Fazelhussein Fazal. The properties in Kilwa are under the care of Africa Federation and being managed by Bilal Muslim Mission of Tanzania. The families of Gulamabbas Hussein Dewji, Kermali Dhanji, Habib Sheriff Manekia, Gulamabbas Hassanali Dharsee and Jaffer Aladin continue to support the mosque and *madrasah* in Kilwa.There is a plan to carry out major renovations of the Kilwa Mosque, *imambada* and *madrasah* in the near future.

(Africa Federation Archives, 29 April 2016)

| HABIB MANEKIA | HUSSEIN HABIB MANEKIA | ANVER HABIB MANEKIA |

LINDI

Lindi has a long history that goes back to the 11th century when it was just a small fishing village. Over the centuries, the settlement expanded and by the 18th century, it was one of the final destinations of slave caravans from Nyasa. When the Germans arrived, they built a fort (*boma*) at the seafront. It was during their rule that the first Khoja came to Lindi.

When Gulamhussein Remtullah Hansraj[164] arrived in 1906, there were already 200 Khoja Shia Ithna-Asheries settled there. Amongst them were the families of Ali Walli, Kassamali Walli, Ismail Khimji, Jaffer Najak, Moledina Karim Visram, Alidina Walli Khaki, Gulamhussein Remtullah Pradhan, Alidina Mohammed Sajan, Moledina Mohammed, Gulamali Jaffer, Moledina Sumar, Alarakhya Sumar, Murji Moledina, Hirji Merali, Taleb Dossa, Jaffer Premji,

Pirmohammed Janmohammed and Mulla Ismail Gulamhussein. The community already had a *masjid* and *imambada* (built in 1901) as well as a burial ground.

Mustafa Yusufali Pirmohamed narrates[165] that Pirmohamed Janmohamed Dosani, born in Mundra, Kachchh migrated to Zanzibar after the death of his wife Fatmabai, only six months into their marriage. Pirmohamed's only sibling, Remtulla Janmohamed, was *Mukhi* at Mundra Jamatkhana and while he did not migrate to Africa, his only daughter, Fatema, was married to Musa, son of Jaffer Najak of Lindi.

Pirmohamed's second wife was Jibai - also called Chagbai - and sister of Nasser Kurji. He had two children with her, Abdulla and Sakina (who later married Abdulla Hameer). After the death of his second wife, Pirmohamed travelled to Lindi around 1900 and married Sakina, sister of Rashid Alidina. Sakina had three children, Abdulrasul, Jenabai (who later married Mukhtar Moledina) and Kulsum who died at a young age.

Pirmohamed's son, Abdulla, migrated from Zanzibar with his father when he was a child of six years. When he grew up, he worked for Esmail Khimji for a short period. During the First World War, Abdulla, his family and other community members had to leave Lindi and seek a safe haven in the nearby port village of Mingoyo as the battles raged in nearby areas. Around 1916, at the age of 23, Abdulla went to Zanzibar to get married to Sugra, daughter of Jaffer Hameer. After his marriage, Abdulla lived in Zanzibar and worked for his father-in-law.

ABDULLA PIRMOHAMED (1893-1959)

A few years later, in 1920, he decided to return to Lindi where he started a small shop in the Ndoro area near Mpilimpili. Abdulla had ten children: the first three Mohamedrafiq, Fatma Kanji and Zehra Dinani were born in Zanzibar. Fizza, Mohamedhussein, Yusufali, Nargis Jaffer, Gulamabbas, Kaniz and Haiderali were born in Lindi.

In 1933, Lindi Jamaat offered Abdulla the chance to move one of its properties: a newly constructed one-storey house (Golfa House) at the corner of Gold Coast St/Queen's Avenue (now Ghana St/Uhuru St). The lower floor shop was previously rented to Lindi Stores while the residential upper storey had been reserved for Jamaat guests, especially visiting Aalims. Over the years, a total of four generations of the Dosani family had lived on these premises.

Abdulla originally started a provision shop on the lower floor that became famous as the Bachupira shop. It gradually grew until it was selling a variety of groceries e.g. sugar, rice, soap, ghee, flour, all kinds of nuts, dried fruits, tinned food, imported fresh fruits including pomegranates from Spain and apples from South Africa, *desi* herbal medicines, chocolates from the UK and Belgium, as well as hand-woven Muslim caps from Singapore and fishing gear. The shop had a huge credit base and things like a kilo of potatoes, a bottle of paan chutney, or an ounce of saffron were often invoiced monthly.

In his younger days, Abdulla was a frequent reciter of *marsiya* as he had a melodious voice. **He served as Honorary Treasurer and carried out the** *nyaz* **(food) duties of the Jamaat.**

Yusuf Pirmohamed (1927-1991)

Zawar from Lindi on a Ziyarat trip to Iraq (1954)

Gulamhussein Kalyan recalls that when he came to Lindi in 1924, Haji Hamzaali Noormohamed was the President of Lindi Jamaat and Abdulhussein Sachedina was the Honorary Secretary. The membership fee at that time was Shs.1.

GULAMHUSSEIN KALYAN (1903-1987)

Gulamhussein Kalyan was born in Kutch Mundra. He learned Qur'an and Dinyat from Mulla Haji Mohammed Khaki. Then he went to Bombay to study at Khanmohamed Habib School. He stayed at Sir Karim Ebrahim Baronet Orphanage.

In 1922, he travelled to Zanzibar with Bande Khoryo and worked at Ladha Meghji. In 1924, he accompanied Rashid Versi to Lindi where he worked at Razahussein Pardhan's business. Gulamhussein Kalyan was a very pious person. Even in his old age he could be seen walking the long distance from his home to the mosque to attend every Jamaat namaz. He used to recite majalis as well. In 1956, he moved to Rwangwa and to Mtama in 1975. In 1984, he returned to Lindi where he died. (Africa Federation Archives, 12 October 2018)

Gulamhusseinbhai relates that during the end of the First World War, the British navy came to Lindi and there was a lot of looting. All Indians were sent to Chibubu for their protection amongst them a rich merchant, Fateh Fazal Chandoo and his father-in-law Rashid Mohamed Chandoo.

Gulamhussein was transferred to Songea by his employer, Razahussein Pardhan and remembers that the Songea airport was constructed in 1934, three years before his son, Hussein was born. His sister, Kanbai, was married in Songea as well and she was the mother of Abdulhussein Mohamed Samji. He lived in Songea from 1934 to 1941 when he moved back to Lindi because of his children's education.

The *musafarkhana* and *madrasah* in Lindi were donated by Haji Mohamed Jaffer Hassam in the 1930s. Some of the early teachers of Dinyat at Lindi included Mulla Gulamali Ladha, Mulla Abdulhussein Remtulla, Mulla Abdulhussein Mulji and Mulla Jafferali Nazarali. After his death, Mohamed Jaffar Hassam left his house to the community for communal use.

Rashidbhai Versi is another luminary who served the Lindi Jamaat as President for 27 years with zeal and dedication. He was instrumental in raising funds for the local boarding house constructed to help visiting students from upcountry to acquire their education in Lindi.

RASHID VERSI (1893-1963)

He was born in Kachchh, India and had five siblings: Remtulla, Bandali, Gulamhussein, Fatmabai and Sakinabai. Remtulla was the first to migrate to Zanzibar and then to Lindi. Remtulla's first wife, Virbai Manji Sumar, died in Lindi and is buried at the cemetery near PC House at the seashore, as there was no community cemetery at that time. Remtulla died during a visit to Kachchh, India.

Rashid first arrived at Mombasa where he worked for some time winnowing grains (kupepeta). He then moved to Zanzibar and finally to Lindi with Gulamhussein Kalyan in 1924.

(Africa Federation Archives, 22 November 2019)

In Lindi, Rashid first started a business selling clothes. Then he opened a garage which turned out to be a thriving venture. He also owned a sisal plantation at Narunyu about 40 km from Lindi. Around 1933, he constructed the house in which he lived to the end of his life.

In 1959, despite his ill health, Rashidbhai together with Fazalbhai Ladha Dinani, visited 10 Jamaats to raise the Foundation Fund for Africa Federation. The team visited these towns – some with established *jamaats* and others without - in the Southern region: Newala, Kitangari, Mkunya, Luatala, Lulindi, Songea, Tunduru, Namtumbo, Matemanga, Mbinga, Chiungutwa, Masasi, Nangomba, Lindi, Mingoyo, Ndumbwe, Mtwara, Mahuta, Mnero, Mikindani, Mtama, Ruangwa, Kilwa, Pande, Mbwera and Muhoro.

Rashidbhai was honoured with citations for his role in raising these funds. The Jamaat President, Alhaj Gulamabbas Haji Jusab and the Honorary Secretary, Alhaj Fidahussein Haji Mohamed Khaki showed their appreciation to Rashidbhai for his dedication to the Jamaat and especially for being instrumental in the construction of the Haji Mohamed Jaffer KSI Trust Building and KSI Students Hostel.

Honorable Sir, Rashidbhai Versi
Lindi, Tanganyika

Salamun Alaikum,
As a servant of the community and its President, it is an honour to present to you this Citation on behalf of the Federation of Khoja Shia Ithna-Asheri Jamaats of Africa, for your role in serving the community with utmost zeal, untiring physical efforts and great financial contribution.

Financial constraints had started to curb the activities of the Federation and there was a great possibility that these activities would halt at any time. There was despair all around. There were people who confidently said that the current financial situation did not give hope of raising more than Shs 100,000 if a collection was started. During these difficult times, you encouraged us and stood shoulder-to-shoulder with us. I wish to pay tribute to your enthusiastic encouragement with gratitude and deepest appreciation.

Despite physical challenges due to age and business commitments, you left the comfort of your home and join the team at your own expense, in the lengthy and arduous journey to collect funds. Due to your important contribution, the Foundation Fund was able to collect Shs. 725,000 and the Scholarship Fund Shs. 65,000. The Council would also like to note your considerable personal contribution.

As a result of your selfless efforts, the community has attained great respect for which I wish to congratulate you sincerely. I pray to Allah (SWT) that He continues to give you strength to serve the community with your physical efforts, great spirit and financial contribution.

I hope and pray that your efforts will be a source of encouragement to others in the community to follow suit.
Your servant, Ebrahim Hussein Sheriff
President, Federation of Khoja Shia Ithna-Asheri Jamaats of Africa
20 Jamadil Akher 1376/21 December 1959

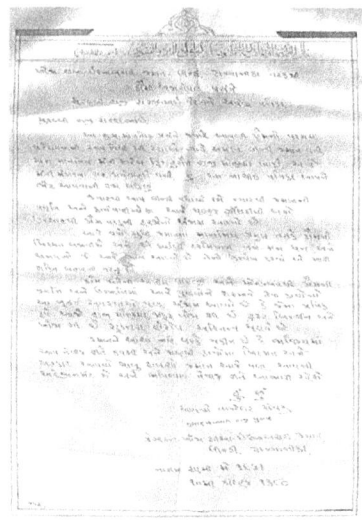

Translation of Citation Awarded by the Khoja Shia Ithna-Aasheri Jamaat, Lindi to Murabbi Haji Rashidbhai Versi on the occasion of Flag Raising Ceremony.

Murabbi Haji Rashidbhai,

On this auspicious occasion during which you will be raising the Flag of the Community, I am honored to humbly present to you this Citation on behalf of the all members of Lindi Jamaat, the Honorary Secretary, Br Fidahussein Haji Mohamed Khaki and the Jamaat Secretariat.

Since your arrival in Lindi, the Jamaat has attained steady progress. You have infused new energy in the Jamaat activities which you have carried out with utmost zeal.

You have served this Community for a very long period as President of the Jamaat. The sacrifice that you have made through your physical efforts, in spirit and in financial contribution is enormous, beyond description.

You have shown great affection towards the community and carried out your duties with love and dedication at an old age which would put younger generations to shame. As a result of your hard work, we have the Haji Mohamed Jaffer KSI Trust Building and KSI Students' hostel.

The Jamaat not only hopes, but is certain that in the future you will continue to serve and assist the community in communal and religious activities. The Jamaat would like to express its deep appreciation and is ever thankful.

I am,
Your obedient Servant, Gulamabbas Haji Jusab,
President, Khoja Shia Ithnaasheri Jamaat, Lindi, Tanganyika
25th May 1961/10th Zilhajj 1380

TUNDURU

Tunduru, situated in Ruvuma Region in southern Tanzania, was one of the other areas that Khoja Shia Ithna-Asheries settled in. From conversations with elders of the community in Dar es Salaam as well as private family archives, the earliest settlement of our community in Tunduru is believed to have been in the year 1915. At present, more than 100 years later, the beautiful Masjid constructed in 1957 still stands as a legacy of the once vibrant community, but only three families remain in the region. The 70 Marhumeen buried in the cemetery are another testimony of the community's footprint.

The history of Tunduru Jamaat began when Lalji Datoo migrated to Kilwa and from there headed to Tunduru with Virji Walji Somji

(Bapa), finally arriving in 1915. Once settled, they encouraged other relatives to join them. Jessa and Jadavji Dhanji came soon after. By 1940, there were 10 families (45 individuals) and a mosque had already been built. In 1950, the British Government moved the Tunduru settlement to a more pleasant area, about 2 kms away in Majengo.

Among the pioneers in Tunduru were the families of Lalji Datoo, Jafferali Jadavji Dhanji, Yusuf Jadavji Dhanji, Rajabali Jaffer, Kassamali Moledina, Mulla Hussein Jaffer, Abbas Merali, Fazal Premji, Mohammed Premji, Jaffer Fazal Premji, Razabhai Premji, Kermalli Premji, Ahmed Hassam, S. S. Ahmed (Masi Mumbai), Shariff Esmail Rawji, Gulamhussein E Rawji, Hussein Kanji, Fidahussein Panju, Abdulrasool Juma and Hassanali Rajani.

With more families coming to settle in Tunduru, a new mosque had to be built in 1957. The funds for this project were collected entirely from the local Khoja Shia Ithna-Asheries, with bricks and timber for the mosque donated by the family of Laljibhai Datoo. Local community members like Hussein Jaffer, Shariff Esmail Rawji and Gulamhussein E. Rawji conducted the religious ceremonies.

The Lalji Datoo family also established the Datoo Primary School (1963). This small community contributed a hefty - for the time – Shs. 17,000 towards religious propagation and educational scholarships for the community.

A BRIEF HISTORY OF TUNDURU JAMAAT

The earliest settlement of our community in Tunduru is believed to be in 1915, when Lalji Datoo migrated from Malia in Gujarat, India to Kilwa where he met his cousin Virji Walji Somji (Bapa). From Kilwa he proceeded to hinterland towards Tunduru, an area infested with lions and other wild animals. After settling down, Laljibhai Datoo invited other relatives to join him. In the 1940s the Jessa Family of Dar es Salaam established a cotton ginnery at Kitanda, 10 miles from Tunduru and Jafferali Jadavji Dhanji started employment there. These two families established themselves and later on many other community members moved and settled in Tunduru. Early Khoja Shia Ithna-Asheries in Tunduru opened small shops and some even ventured into interior villages like Nalasi, Mbesa and Matemanga. Lalji Datoo built the first *masjid* in Tunduru around 1940 and at that time, there were 10 families (45 heads).

The religious activities performed there such as daily *Namaaz*, *Majlises*, *Azadari* and *Dinyat* classes were the focal point of the community. The Jamaat had local *mullahs* like Hussein Jaffer who had a melodious voice in reciting *Majlis* and *Duas*. Shariff Esmail Rawji and Gulamhussein E Rawji were the stalwart *Mullahs* who steered the community ahead. The Premji family members were at the forefront in *Azadari* as well. Mehralibhai Premji was among the dedicated members of the community who served as Secretary of the Jamaat for many years. In 1957 a new *masjid* was constructed on a new plot (Majengo). All community members contributed funds generously and built their residences near the *masjid* as well. The families of Laljibhai Datoo contributed bricks and timber for the entire *masjid*. Maulana Haroon and Sayyed Sharafat Hussein from India served in Tunduru in 1960s.

Following the resolution at the Conference held in Arusha in 1958, a special committee was formed to visit Jamaats in East Africa and Belgian Congo to collect funds for *tabligh* and scholarships. Fazalbhai Ladha Dinani and Haji Rashidbhai took charge of visiting Jamaats in Southern Province of Tanganyika. Tunduru Jamaat members contributed Shs. 17,000 - a hefty amount during that period. In 1960, Haji Ebrahim Sheriff (President of Africa Federation) visited many Jamaats, including Tunduru in appreciation of their support. Fazalbhai Ladha Dinani provided the transportation for the visit. In 1963 Datoo Primary School was established by the Lalji Datoo family providing secular education to children up to the age of 12. The teachers were recruited from India. Children later on proceeded to Lindi for secondary education.

(Africa Federation Archives, 27 September 2018)

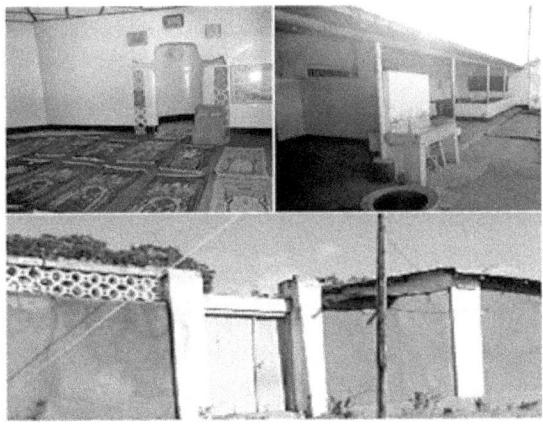

Clockwise from top left:
Inside Tunduru mosque, ablution area and fence around the mosque.

SONGEA

Songea appears to have been the major last stop for the Khoja Shia Ithna-Asheries as they ventured into southern Tanganyika. There is a need to research the history of the Khoja Shia Ithna-Asheri community here as records are not easily available. What is available is a document about the opening ceremony of a new mosque and *imambada* on 24 Zilhaj 1384 (April 1964). This project was accomplished with generous donations from the families of Ladhabhai Dinani and Jadavji Dhanji.

The Honorary Secretary of Songea Jamaat, Alhaj Fidahussein Haji Mohamed Khaki spoke on this occasion saying that the community had finally been able to fulfill the need for these institutions after having settled in Songea 35 to 40 years ago.[166] He also mentioned his appreciation towards the Dinani family for having met the full cost of the mosque, recalling their frequent contributions towards the Council's Foundation Fund and the Dar es Salaam Boarding House.

4A.2 Distinctive Settlement in East Africa

I have tried to provide as much detail in this book about the various initial settlements and their development. More extensive and comprehensive data needs to be collected to complete the history of the Khoja Shia Ithna-Asheries in East Africa. However, from the descriptions above, a distinctive pattern or a model of development emerges about the preservation of unity and faith that the Khoja Shia Ithna-Asheri Community strove for.

The first phase always began with two or three families settling in one place. These trail-blazing Khoja Shia Ithna-Asheries would venture into the interior and set up a trading base. Soon, others followed and bring their families too. They would meet at each other's houses for religious gatherings. Amongst them, those with the most religious

Laying of foundation stone for the Songea Mosque by Jafferali Jadavji Dhanji in 1961

Opening of Songea Jamaat (1964)

Group Photo inside Songea Imambada, Opening in 1964
In this photo: Mohamed Iqbal Nasser, Fidahussein Karmali Rajani, Ladhu Bhimji, Sherali Kassamali Jeraj, Fidahussein Somji, Shabbir Jeraj, Ramju Jadavji, Abdulhussein Rajabali Alidina, Jawad Khaki, Ramzan Moloo, Gulamali Jadavji, Mohamed Gulamali Abdulla, Haiderali Khaki, Aziz Karmali Rajani, Somji Tarmohamed, Anver Kipara, Nurmohamed Jadavji, Azad Khimani, Hassanali Jeraj.

awareness would pass on their knowledge to others. These small closely-knit groups were the first pioneers who shouldered the responsibility of establishing an institutional community.

Once the "community" existed as a decently-sized entity, an *imambada* and *masjid* would be built. Where possible a *madrasah* would be included to impart religious instruction to the children of the community. This would then be followed by the construction of community schools to provide a set standard of education at a primary level and beyond it. The two strong core objectives that fuelled these developments were the need to achieve economic self-sufficiency and preserving their faith.

Early Khoja Shia Ithna-Asheries realised that in order to survive they needed a stable base underpinned by religious values. Without this spiritual base, the community was at a higher risk of fracturing and depriving the Khoja Shia Ithna-Asheries of their vital ingredient: cohesive communal support and networking. The pattern adopted by the early pioneers shows them continually striving to achieve the right balance of faith and financial prosperity.

They sought to achieve this by setting up a rule-based community (*Jamaat*), a concept they were familiar with, having experienced the same system in the larger Khoja communities in Kachchh, Kathiawad and Mumbai. They understood the advantages of communal living with its strengths and weaknesses and chose to adopt this model of functioning - with some modifications - to achieve their objectives in their new home. This ability to adapt dynamically was a major factor in sustaining the community.

This cycle described above replicated itself, phase-by-phase, wherever Khoja Shia Ithna-Asheries settled in East Africa. In a sense, the creation of a continually evolving rule-based community (Jamaat) has become their hallmark wherever the Khoja Shia Ithna-Asheries have settled to this today.

Tanganyika Territorial Council Meeting (1954)

Seen above are members of the Tanganyika Territorial Council at a meeting held in 1954.
L-R: *J M Jaffer (President), Bashir Rahim (Hon. Secretary), Dost Mohamed Moledina (Moshi), Ebrahim Hussein Sheriff Dewji (Arusha), R R Jaffer (Dar es Salaam), Hassanali Alarakhia (Lushoto), Gulammehdi K Haji (Dar es Salaam), Hassanali Ladak (Moshi), Mohamedali Sheriff Jiwa (Moshi).*

PART 4B

Socio-Economic and Socio-Religious Change: Evolution into a Distinct Community in East Africa

4B.1 Communal Development: A Singular Rule-Based Community

While analysing the process with which the Khoja Shia Ithna-Asheries established and nurtured their newly found identity, it is imperative to remember that this evolution was happening in the challenging environment of the colonial era. Apart from the daily obstacles they faced from the colonising authority, there were three main ideological challenges they had to deal with under German and especially under British rule.

Firstly, there was the tendency on the part of the colonial administration to treat the Indian population as if they were a single, homogenous "community". The most reiterated explanation by communal scholars for this policy is that the colonial governments lacked insight into the complexities of social organization within the Indians. Personally, this feels like a lackadaisical explanation as the British in particular were well acquainted with India and Indian ethnography having ruled over that region for over 200 years. They must, therefore, have already been intimately aware of the vast varieties of cultures that existed in British India.

A more practical explanation appears to be that the authorities found it too laborious to have to deal with each of the Indian communities and their cultural needs separately in administrative matters. They simply could not be bothered with their brown subjects who, in the British colonial mindset, were easily dispensable when not serving its collective interest and objectives.

Secondly, as a matter of political expediency, both German and British colonial governments divided the subjects they ruled into three categories, namely: "European", "Asian" (which included the Indian as well as the Arab communities) and "African", dealing with each on an ad hoc basis. In doing so, the colonial government created a social structure based on skin colour throughout East Africa, with the British or German (its white subjects) at the top, then Asians (its brown subjects) and lastly the Africans (its black subjects) at the bottom.[1]

This was the constant feature recognised both during German as well as British rule. Their policies created a segregated pattern of urban planning and construction, which also reflected the socio-economic hierarchies in colonial East Africa. Places such as Dar es Salaam, Tanga, and others were clearly divided into African quarters, Indian quarters and European quarters. This policy of creating artificial separations also gave more credibility to "racial" differences based on the assumption of European superiority paralleled by the inferiority of all other "races". Under this arrangement, the White European expatriates had the largest slice of whatever budget was allocated for development. The remaining amount was shared between Asians and Africans. Khoja Shia Ithna-Asheries faced this reality along with all the other Indian communities.

Thirdly, by choosing to ignore the magnitude of differences and complexities present between the various Indian communities and using this system of simple segregation, the colonial administration created and fuelled tensions that had adverse effects. Indians were a heterogeneous group composed of sub-communities differentiated by religion and caste, each with its internal organization, social structure, and norms.[2] Insensitive decisions on the part of colonial masters made the Indian communities apprehensive about the long term preservation of their social identity and culture. One such issue was the question of communal burial grounds in Zanzibar covered earlier, which turned out to be a source of marked friction and bitterness.[3] This incident was one of many that demonstrate that a strained atmosphere existed in East Africa between the British authorities and the Indian communities.

The reality was that under both the Germans and the British, Indian communities in East Africa had to live according to colonial rules and practices. Non-white residents and Africans in East Africa did not have any choice in the discriminatory practices that had legal force and inevitably, got on with their lives the best they could. Each Indian community fell back on its own resources to provide basic services and amenities to its members. Most chose to institutionalise separately to preserve their cultural practices as well as build educational and social infrastructures. What is noteworthy here is that they had to pay for their development, with hardly any assistance from the colonial government. This challenge of financing progress steered Muslim Indians into organising themselves along sectarian tendencies whilst Hindu Indians coordinated according to their inherent caste system.[4]

The word "caste" (lineage), commonly used as an equivalent to the term *Jati* (by birth), simply denotes the various social groups within the general four-fold division of Indian society.[5] In East Africa, Hindus coming from different districts in India but belonging to the same wider *jati* or "caste category" formed affiliations and in this way, various Hindu "communities" emerged in East Africa.

The Muslim divisions on the other hand corresponded to the various sects within Islam, especially in the case of the Shias. The Indian Sunnis were too few to organise institutionally compared to the Indian Shias. Within the Indian Shias, their numbers allowed them to set up distinct institutions based on their communal experiences in India. They were already well disposed towards the use of the term "communities" that had existed in India. The retention of the word 'Khoja' by Shia Ithna-Asheries from Kachchh and Kathiawad is an interesting, but deliberate variation probably kept as a mark of their identity, given the history of their split from the majority Khoja Ismaili community.

Broadly speaking, the Muslims in East Africa fell into one of three categories. Firstly, the coastal Swahili population and Arabs who had their distinctive Islamic sub-culture; secondly, the African Muslims and thirdly, the Indian settlers groups, a majority of whom belonged to the Shia sects.[6] In the case of the Africans residing in the interior who embraced Islam, a great many elements of indigenous African beliefs can be seen to have been retained alongside those of Islam.

The Indian Muslims were widely different. The bulk of the Sunni Indian Muslims followed the Hanafi School of thought. The majority of the Indian Muslims, however, were Shia belonging to one of the three important sects: the Ismailis, the Khoja Shia Ithna-Asheries and the Bohras - who are descendants of those Hindus who converted to the Musta'lian form of Ismailism in India.[7]

From the above, what emerges is that Islam in East Africa expressed itself through heterogeneity. Whilst the presence of Islam was entrenched institutionally within the coastal Swahili people in early 20th Century East Africa, it did not organise to form a united Islamic front to represent the Muslim interest. Sensitivity to the sectarian differences amongst themselves did not allow for any coordinated Muslim endeavour towards building united infrastructures or forums. This changed in the decades following the Second World War.

There was some attempt by Muslims in East Africa to devote serious attention to how Islam could unite them and support their sense of identity during the uncertain post-war period. Muslim communities urgently felt the need to sustain the fast-vanishing traditional framework of Islam as a reaction to the threat of Western ideas and their impact on Islamic values.[8] Sadly, these well-intentioned attempts did not withstand the test of time because the bonds forged were on a social, superficial level. As a result, they were unable to formulate a long-term plan that could become a united, sustainable voice against any challenges to their way of life.

The Khoja Shia Ithna-Asheries who settled in various towns and villages in East Africa had to adapt to the circumstances brought about by the segregation policy of the colonial governments. Their immediately relevant social environment was the presence of various

Indian groups, both Hindu and Muslim (notwithstanding the Goans, and Zoroastrian Parsis), who settled alongside the Khoja Shia Ithna-Asheries. Despite their differences, the challenges that all these communities faced were remarkably similar and naturally, compelled them to work together to achieve a common goal.

A matter that provoked strong feelings among the Indians was that of education. Education for their children failed to receive the attention of the British Colonial government on anything like the scale the Indians felt it deserved. Hence, we observe from the reports of early settlements from the Khoja Shia Ithna-Asheri Trade Directory (1960) that the setting up of educational institutions was mainly due to the initiative of Khoja Shia Ithna-Asheries or accomplished jointly with various Indian communities.

These early Indian schools ran on a basis of self-help and/or through the philanthropy of individuals. In some rare cases, the colonial government did show sensitivity to the educational needs of Indian children. For example, in the 1920s, the British were willing to sponsor schools for the general Indian community in Zanzibar and elsewhere in East Africa, with promised grants-in-aid.[9]

Whilst the various Indian communities in East Africa shared many cultural traits and a common language, there were marked religious and caste differences that separated them. Overall, they co-existed as separate entities, each community maintaining its unique identity. At times, they would work together when their interests converged, but for the most part there existed - alongside a peaceful economic rivalry - a sense of being distinct from one another. Thus, the Khoja Shia Ithna-Asheries, like all the Indians who settled in different places within East Africa, organized themselves into independent and socially exclusive societies and developed their own communal, religious, educational and health institutions.

The early Khoja Shia Ithna-Asheri pioneers established the foundational base for a "community" in their respective towns. Later on, this core developed into a distinct group that needed to build mosques, *imambadas*, schools, dispensaries and sports facilities. The colonial governments were not readily supportive of these needs as their primary concern was the interests of the European settlers and, very remotely when it suited them, those of the indigenous Africans. Therefore, along with other Indian communities, the Khoja Shia Ithna-Asheries were left to their own devices to build nearly all the social, cultural and welfare institutions they required.

4B.2 Communal Development: Philanthropy

The community looked to their philanthropists for assistance to set up their social, religious and educational infrastructure. Both archival and oral records show that whenever the community requested it, their patrons responded generously. The financial backing and support of these individuals was fundamental to the survival of the young Khoja Shia Ithna-Asheri community.

It was because of their unfailing support that the young sapling of a society was able to establish its roots even in the face of opposition from the wider Khoja community. The prime motivation of these benefactors, according to the records examined in the communal archive of Africa Federation, was not only to perpetuate their faith but also because they understood the immense value to the community in having a strong framework to support the social, educational and health requirements of its members.[10]

The emphasis on philanthropy within the Khoja Shia Ithna-Asheries can be explained partly by religious responsibility,[11] but also by their cultural background that played a huge part in shaping their philosophy of selfless giving. The Khojas who came to East Africa brought with them long-standing traditions of benevolence from Kachchh and Kathiawad.[12] This buttressed Islam's emphasis on sharing one's wealth with the needy, augmented by their customs of living in harmony with joint families and local communities.

It has been a tradition amongst Muslims to make donations or bequeath one of their properties in their lifetime to create a *Waqf* (Trust) for charitable purposes. This is in obedience to the Prophetic injunction of leaving behind *Sadaqatun Jaariya*[13] that would help to perpetuate *thawaab* (Divine reward) for the donor even after his/her death. This spirit has sustained the development and growth of the KSI community globally.

Hassan Jaffer relates a typical example of philanthropy within the Mombasa community that repeats in some form or other throughout the history of our community. The story showcases how good intention, charity and the foresight of community elders cohered so well that it multiplied the donation manyfold for the benefit of the community.[14] He recalls the story of Molubhai Remtulla who lived in Mombasa around the 1920s.[15]

Molubhai was an elderly widower with one child - a daughter, who lived with him. He owned a piece of land on Salim Road, opposite Mackinnon Market, on which stood a small cottage. In 1927, Molubhai approached Haji Abdulla Kanji, Haji Kassamali Jivraj and other elders of the community with an offer to bequeath his only property to the Jamaat and for its income to be utilized for making tea as *Nyaz* (offering) after the weekly religious gathering on Thursday nights. He was advised that, while the community appreciated his noble gesture, it would not be appropriate for him to give away his only asset and deprive his daughter of any inheritance.[16]

In an unexpected turn of circumstances, the daughter passed away the following year. After her demise, Molubhai once again presented the same offer to the leaders of the Mombasa Jamaat. This time around, faced with his sincere detemination, the elders had no choice but to accept. In a hand-written note - in Gujarati - on a small piece of paper, Molubhai bequeathed his lifelong savings to the Jamaat and thus the famous Molubhai Trust came into being.

Due to his advancing age - he was approaching 70 years of age - Molubhai moved to a small room near the Husaini Mosque in Mombasa. In 1929, a year after his daughter, he too passed away.

Initially, the donated property fetched a monthly rental of KShs. 10. With inflation, this amount steadily increased and in 1956 the rental income was recorded as being KShs. 75 per month. Decades later, in 1974, Shell Company of Mombasa showed an interest in the property; the Chairman of the Mombasa Jamaat at the time, Haji Mohamedhusein Gulamhusein, assisted by Haji Mohamedraza Abdulla Kanji, a Trustee of the Jamaat, negotiated a five-year lease with Shell Company at the rate of KShs.1,500 per month plus a lump sum gratuity of KShs.150,000. The contract also required Shell Company to pay the entire rent in advance.

Accordingly, Shell Company paid out KShs. 90,000 and to this amount, the Jamaat Trust Board added KShs.45,000 as a loan from other Trust Accounts. They used the total amount to invest in a property which was leased out at a monthly rent of KShs.1,600. This income was then proportionately credited to the respective Trust Accounts based on the capital amount invested.

After the lapse of the five-year lease, the Shell Company renewed its lease, this time for KShs. 5,000 per month and only for a portion of the plot. The remaining land fronting the main road lay dormant. The Trust Board of the Jamaat resolved to once again borrow money from other Trusts and at a cost of almost KShs. 3,000,000 built a property on that small piece of land. This was then leased out at KShs. 30,000 per month. In less than a decade following 1974, Molubhai's seedling of a good intention i.e. to offer tea to those who attended the Thursday night gatherings had grown exponentially into a self-sustaining Trust that served the community in ways beyond his imagination.

After all the outstanding loans and dues were repaid, the building reverted fully to the Molubhai Trust which in 2015 earned a monthly rental of KShs. 30,000. The market value of the land in 2015 was estimated at around Kshs 4.5 million. Its capital value and ensuing income continue to increase for utilization to the cause it was initially bequeathed for.[17]

Molubhai's grave in Mombasa with Gujarati inscription

Molubhai Trust Builing on the main Mombasa thoroughfare, now known as 'Digo Road.' The two floor building has been leased to 'Pwani Forext Bureau'. Note the "wafer thin" width of the building on one side.

This is just one example of philanthropy where the donor and community worked together in a symbiotic relationship that benefited both. This is how *barakah*[18] is understood by Muslim philanthropists. This principle is defined as 'what is given in the way of Allah and is accepted by Allah, survives'. In this way, *thawaabe jaari* (perpetual benefit) for those who have departed this world continues unabated for them in their new abode. The community as a whole accepts this Divine precept absolutely.

According to the Trade Directory, many early philanthropists responded to the needs of their respective jamaats. Their contributions are existential for Khoja Shia Ithna-Asheries of East Africa. Had they not responded in the way they did, the evolution of the Khoja Shia Ithna-Asheri community would not have taken the course it did.

Amongst these early philanthropists was Datoo Hemani who left money for a girls' school in Zanzibar, fondly remembered by locals as Datoo Hemani Girls' School. Nasser Nurmohamed left a charitable dispensary in Zanzibar. The Panju family constructed Alibhai Panju Jaffery Primary School in Mombasa. Dewji Jamal donated the tracts of land for the mosques, *imambadas* and *kabrastan* in Mombasa, Nairobi, and Lamu. In addition, there are also investment-related trusts that bear the name of Dewji Jamal and his family members.

Satchu Peera, another great benefactor, secured land for the mosques in Dar es Salaam and personally supervised their construction. He also donated land for the kabrastan there. Jaffer Khimji and his brother Abdulla, along with Nasser Virji, donated plots for the mosque and *imambada* in Tanga. Ladhabhai Meghji gave land for the mosque in Mwanza. Mohamed Jaffer of Lindi built a boarding house for students in Lindi and Dar es Salaam. Jeevraj Meghji, together with Jeevraj Khatau and Dharamsi Khatau, gave substantial endowments for mosques, *imambadas* and *kabrastans*. Abdulla Kanji and Fazal Ladak Sivji gifted the *musafarkhana* in Mombasa. Khimji Bhanji helped establish the first *imambada* for the Kampala Jamaat.

In the interiors of Uganda, names like Kassam Mohamed (Hoima), Ahmad Bhimji (Fort Portal), G. R. Hansraj (Soroti), Allarakhya Kassam, Jamal Ramji, Karabhai Valli (Kampala), Gulamhusein Ladha and Hasanali Salemohamed (Kaberamaedo), Haji Merali, H.K. Jaffer and Suleman Esmail (Jinja) and many others are mentioned as selfless and dedicated benefactors.

Whilst this list is not in any way exhaustive, it gives a fair idea of the extent of philanthropic spirit within the Khoja Shia Ithna-Asheries of East Africa. Their charitable endeavours were geared towards fulfilling whatever needs the fellow community members had in the new environment they had chosen to settle in.[19]

4B.3 Communal Development: Entrepreneurship and Permanency

Apart from the crucial role philanthropy played within the Khoja Shia Ithna-Asheries in East Africa, other noteworthy factors also influenced and accelerated the institutional development of the community.

The first point to note is that in common with other Muslims, Khoja Shia Ithna-Asheries did not have the same kind of link with India that the Hindu communities did. The prevalence of the caste system within the Hindus had resulted in deeper, inseparable bonds to their communities back home. In this respect, the Khoja Shia Ithna-Asheries were not as entrenched in their cultural heritage as their Hindu counterparts, which in turn gave them the freedom to explore and cultivate a new identity based on their personal ideals and circumstances.

The second point, gleaned from conversations with the elderly within the community, is that the Khoja Shia Ithna-Asheries migrants came to East Africa intending to pursue economic prosperity and with a clear goal of permanent settlement if things worked out. They were willing to move to remote and unexplored regions to achieve these goals; as evidenced by the reports in the Trade Directory.

The early pioneers faced considerable hardships; with their few personal belongings, these daring pioneers ventured into unknown areas well before the construction of roads and railways. Pursuing dreams of opportunities and the thrill of adventure, they travelled on foot or pack animals, facing up to life-threatening encounters with wild animals, looters and even ruling authorities on the way, to set up small shops in the interiors of East Africa.

Their enterprising nature meant that they did not pause at this achievement and the majority of them began expanding at the first opportunity. From shopkeepers, they ventured into retail, wholesale, distribution, transport, insurance and construction. Some went on to specialise in the ivory trade, cotton ginning, coffee, sisal production and other basic industries.

Their determination to seek the betterment of self and community meant that when opportunities did not present themselves in one region, they were willing to uproot themselves and moved to another. This semi-nomadic tendency to find greener pastures before deciding to settle led to many of them exploring more than one area of trade and becoming wealthy merchants in the process. This wealth was then inevitably shared with the community and used to help it grow and succeed.

The Trade Directory is a rich treasury of information regarding these early entrepreneurs and their achievements. The Sachoo family, for example, were trading since 1851. In the years 1893-94, they mainly traded along the East African coast and in Dar es Salaam. They established the first soap industry in German East Africa using camel-powered machinery to extract the oil for the soap from copra. Five years later, they went on to build a soda water factory.

At about the same time, Abdulla Khalfan began the first soap factory in Mombasa and then moved to Zanzibar. In the rest of Tanganyika, Abdulla Fazal was the leading coffee buyer, establishing two coffee factories after World War II and earning recognition as the "King of Coffee". Similarly, Jaffer Somji was called the "Uncrowned King of Kilwa" because of the large number of businesses he owned there.

Among the Khoja Shia Ithna-Asheries who purchased sizable tracts of land were the Nasser Virjee family who in 1922 purchased 450 acres of a sisal estate in Mwanza. In 1957-58, the family uprooted all the sisal to plant cashew nuts. They were the first family to open a ginnery in Mwanza.

In 1931, Jamal Ramji began to process coffee in Uganda and formed Jamal Ramji & Co. He was also prominent in the cotton trade. While many were cultivating sugar, Jamal Walji explored other options. After coming to Entebbe in 1904 and starting up a retail store, he then moved to Hoima and invested in ginneries. In 1941, forming a subsidiary of his original firm, Jamal Walji & Co. Ltd, he bought large coffee and tea estates in Jinja.

Other entrepreneurs included Habib Walji and Jaffer Pradhan who were in the motor spares business, Hasham Jamal who owned sawmills, Ladha Kassam who was in the cotton and dairy business, Alibhai Sunderji who was in oil and soap, and Mohamed Manek who started as a farm manager and went on to own a major bus transportation network.

In 1907, the Sheriff Family formed Sheriff Jaffer & Co. to build a copra factory in Mombasa and began to produce "blue mottled" soap. In 1924, they added a maize mill to their Mombasa copra and soap factories. In Arusha, Ebrahim Sheriff and his nephew, Yusuf, imported machinery to process beans grown by local Dutch farmers.

They soon partnered with these farmers to raise French beans. The Sheriff's started in 1953 with 300 acres of beans and by 1964, had 90,000 acres producing over ninety varieties of beans.

Overall, the Khoja Shia Ithna-Asheries preferred to set up their businesses wherever they could and began enticing their sons and other family members to join it and expand. This trend of owning businesses that provided a comfortable living for more than one generation was seen as the standard of "success" such that Khoja Shia Ithna-Asheries who chose to excel on a professional level were scarcely recognised.[20] We find four extremely prominent examples from communal archives.[21]

In Zanzibar, one of the most distinguished Khoja Shia Ithna-Asheries in the legal profession was Hussein Alarakhia Rahim. Born in 1900, he started as a clerk in the police department at the age of 15. He rose to the position of Chief Inspector and after studying law became a public prosecutor and acting crown counsel; in 1952 he was appointed as a first-class magistrate. The communal record notes that he was the first Asian to preside in the High Court in Zanzibar. After retiring in 1962, he left Zanzibar to act as Secretary of the Tanzania Law Society in Dar es Salaam. He received an M.B.E. as well as three medals for police and military service.

ALHAJ MULLA HUSSEIN ALLARAKHIA RAHIM (1900-1979)

He was born in Zanzibar in 1900 and was a famous and well-known personality. He was the President of the Kuwwat ul Islam Jamaat (Juni) of Zanzibar for many years. He served in many other institutions including as President of the Faize Ithna-Asheri. After the Second World War, he introduced the Ithna-Asheri Volunteer Corps with Alhaj Ebrahim Hussein Sheriff as its Chairman, Ali Ebrahim Jivraj as Secretary and Abbas Tejani as Treasurer.

Marhum was a popular Zakir-e-Hussain (pbuh) renowned for his Urdu majalis. Community members specially looked forward to his majalis on the 9th, 10th and 11th nights of Muharram during Julus at Mehfile Abbas and Mehfile Shahe Khurasan (Kiwanjani). He regularly spoke at Hussain Day programs in Zanzibar, Mombasa and Tanga. He held an immense love for Ahlulbayt (pbut) and Azadari. During Ashura eve one year, there was a danger of Julus being attacked. While Mulla Saheb was reciting majlis at the Kuwwat Imambara in Kiponda, the Police Commissioner Colonel A. M. Bell came to advise him to cancel the Julus.

After the majlis he went home, changed into his Public Prosecutor uniform and led the Julus. The attackers fled on seeing this. When the Julus reached Mehfile Abbas, he wore his black sherwani on top of his uniform and recited his scheduled majlis!

Mulla Rahim reciting majlis in Hujajtul Islam Jamaat (Nai Misid) in Zanzibar. Seen L to R: Agha Murawwij, Aqa Raza and Agha Najafi. (Photo courtesy: A. S. Fazal)

Mulla Rahim reciting majlis during Chehlum Julus outside the doorstep of Mehfile Abbas in Zanzibar - 1959

Mulla Hussain Rahim started his career in Zanzibar in the service of British Government as a Public Prosecutor and was a Crown Counsel on various occasions. He was Registrar of the High Court and held the position of Resident Magistrate (First Class). He was responsible for editing the Zanzibar Law Reports and was instrumental in drafting and the adoption of Muslim Laws and Acts in the Judiciary. He was awarded MBE by the British Government due to his exemplary services. He was also decorated with the Coronation Medal and Order of the Brilliant Star. Marhum was also the Chairman of the Zanzibar Broadcasting Corporation.

In the year 1961 a farewell party in honour of Mulla Hussein was held when he retired from the Residents Magistrates Courts of Vuga, Zanzibar.

Sitting L-R: Alhaj Huseein M. Nazerali (Tabora), Sheikh Mohamed Salum Ruwehy, J, S, Balsala, MR. G. M. Mohan, Alhaj Hussein Allarakhia Rahim, Honourable Judge G. J. Horsfall, Mr. V. N. Carvalho, Sheikh Abdalla Saleh Farsy and Mr. Ahmed Idi.

Standing L-R: Mr. Abdulrehman Bajuber, Mr. M. R. H. Rahim, Mr. S. Lalji, Mr. H. S. Datoo, Mr. J. Gopal, Sheikh Mtoro Taqdiri, Mr. M. M. Versi, Mr. M. A. Dhalla, Mr. Maulid Ali, Sayed Mohamedtaqi al Marashy, Mr. Anver H. A. Rahim, Mr. H. G. Allarakhia, MR P. F. Billimoria, Mr. Mohammed Dungersi, Mr. G. I. Mohammed, Mr. Abbas A. Mirza, Mr Gouth A. Bawazir.

Back row, L-R: Mr. Mohammed, Mr.Ameir Haji, Mr. Hellam Nassor and Mr. Tahir Nassor.

Marhum contributed articles in various magazines, among them Samachar (a Zanzibar weekly), Salsabil (monthly) and The Light Magazine published by Bilal Muslim Mission. He authored an English commentary on Dua Kumayl and co-authored Guidance from the Qur'an. He was one of the architects of the Africa Federation, drafted its first constitution, and opened the first conference of the World Federation in London in 1976. Marhum passed away in London in 1979 at the age of 79 and buried at Brookwood Cemetery.
(Africa Federation Archives, 25 August 2017)

Habib Kassamali or H.K. as he was popularly known, was born in 1890 in Pangani, Tanganyika, which was then still a German colony. His family later migrated to Mombasa, Kenya where he completed his secondary education and began working for Standard Chartered Bank. Through dedication and hard work, he rose rapidly in his career both in banking and insurance.

In 1921, he took up a job in and moved to Uganda where he established an agency called The South British Insurance Company Ltd. and soon became the principal representative in the territory. His agency grew to become one of the largest personal insurance agencies in the world and his name became synonymous with quality, responsibility and trust.

In 1935, he was appointed as a member of the Legislative Council of Uganda where he served until 1962 when Uganda attained independence.

For his services, he was awarded the title of "Father of the House" and Commander of the Order of British Empire (CBE) in 1947 and later in 1953 he represented Uganda at the Coronation of Queen Elizabeth II in London.

ALHAJ HABIB KASSAMALI (H.K.) JAFFER (1890 – 1973)

Habib Kassamali or H.K. as he was popularly known was born in Pangani. Later, his family migrated to Mombasa where he completed his secondary education and began working for Standard Chartered Bank. Through dedication, responsibility and trust, he rose rapidly in the Bank. In 1921, he moved to Uganda and established 'The South British Insurance Company Ltd'.

In 1947, he organized joint celebrations of the India and Pakistan Independence. Both Hindus and Muslims participated at the celebration to maintain unity amongst the Asian community. He was a renowned philanthropist and supported many families on a monthly basis. As a member of the Legislative Council, he obtained land for the mosque and imambada in Kampala for a peppercorn sum of 1 shilling. He also built the mosque in Jinja on Iganga Road. (Africa Federation Archives, 7 February 2020)

Habibbhai Kassamali seated second left with fellow members of the Legislative Council, Uganda

Habibbhai Kassamali addressing the 4th Triennial Conference as Councillor for Kampala, 1955

In Tanganyika, among the distinguished advocates was Mahmood Nasser Rattansey. He was born in Dar es Salaam in 1916 and studied law first in Bombay and then at Lincoln's Inn, London, UK. He began his practice in 1948 in Tabora and later moved to Dar es Salaam where he quickly became active in politics. Whilst President of the Asian Association, he was nominated to the Legislative Council and then to the Central Legislative Assembly. He also served as Nyerere's counsellor in organising TANU; at independence, he was one of the country's most influential Khoja Shia Ithna-Asheri politicians.

From Kenya, there was Abdulhussein Nurmohamed Kalyan whose father Nurmohammed travelled to Zanzibar from India in 1880 at the age of 10. Nurmohammed had two brothers, Esmail Kalyan and Sachedina Kalyan. The Kalyan family was one of the first families to settle in East Africa. After 10 years in Zanzibar, they moved to Kenya. Abdulhussein was born in Zanzibar in 1901 where he grew up and obtained his primary school education . He moved to Mombasa in 1913 and after two years, established the famous A H Nurmohamed & Co Ltd. that later had several branches in East Africa.

ABDULHUSSEIN NURMOHAMED (1901-1967)

Murrabbi Abdulhussein has an enormous record of service to the community. He was President of the Federation of Khoja Shia Ithna-Asheri Jamaats of Africa from 1946 to 1949 and from 1952 to 1958. His efforts to unite and bring about progress in the community are well known. Owing to his noble and great service, the Council awarded him an honorary membership. Some of the first steps taken during his first term were to carry out the census of the community, introduce Birth and Marriage Certificates issued by the Council, award education grants and scholarships for higher education, and obtain scholars for tabligh and grants for acquisition of higher religious education. Murrabbi Abdulhussein passed away at the age of 66.
(Africa Federation Archives, 21 July 2017)

In 1926, he entered public community service and became an executive member in both the Indian National Congress and the Indian Association, positions he held for 13 years before taking up the role of Hon. Secretary in both institutions. After two years, he became the President of the Indian Association, a post that he held up to 1948 serving the Indian community in Mombasa.

He was also a member of the Mombasa Municipal Board from 1939 to 1955 during which time, he was Vice-President of the Board for the years 1950 - 51. He was a member of the Kenya Board of Commerce & Industry for Copra and Coconut Oil production from 1945 to 1948 and President of the highest organ of the business community of East Africa called the Federation of Chambers of Commerce of Eastern Africa from 1948 to 1950. After serving in the Municipal council for 16 years, he retired due to ill health.

In addition to all these roles, Murrabbi Abdulhussein was President of Pandya Memorial Society and served as an executive committee member of Coast Subsidiary Hotel, Kenya Maize Marketing Board, East African Tourist Travel Association, and Board of Governors of Mombasa Muslim Institute. In 1958, he was appointed as a member of the Kenya Legislative Council and in 1960, he was appointed to the Kenya Council of State. He also served on the Education Board of Mombasa Jamaat.

JAFFER ALLARAKHIA RAHIM

He is remembered for his notable services to the Supreme Council and also served as President of Kuwwat Jamaat of Zanzibar and as President of Education Board of the Federation. After completion of his school education in Zanzibar, Jafferbhai joined a teachers' training college.

In 1943, he went to the School of Economics and Political Science at Cambridge, UK with a scholarship from the Zanzibar Government. On completion of his studies, he was appointed as Welfare Officer. He also served as Chief Commissioner of Zanzibar Boy Scouts Association. He worked as a scout for more than 36 years. He was given several awards, including "Wood Badge" and Silver Award and "Guild Cross" in 1935 for saving a drowning person in Zanzibar harbour.

As part of his work in the field of social services, Jafferbhai had an opportunity to travel worldwide. He visited many countries in Europe, Turkey, Middle East, India, Pakistan, Ceylon (Sri Lanka) and various African countries. Jafferbhai had an excellent command of the English language and his analysis of issues during Council meetings were inspiring and effective. He was known for regularly using the motto "March with Time".

(Africa Federation Archives, 15 September 2017)

These personalities excelled in their fields and it was due to individuals like these that most Khoja Shia Ithna-Asheries had a sense of economic and professional entrenchment in East Africa. They felt at ease in a country that had offered them so much despite the harsh,

> **RECOGNITION OF COMMUNITY MEMBERS - 1953**
>
> In June 1953, during the Coronation Ceremony of Her Majesty Queen Elizabeth II, as the Queen, she had the pleasure in honouring the following:
> - Br. Fazal Haji Nasser Mawji, Zanzibar – OBE Title
> - Br. Ahmed Abdulrasul Lakha, Zanzibar – MBE Title
> - Br. Abdulrasul Nasser Virji, Mwanza – MBE Title
>
> **CORONATION MEDALS**
>
> Br. Abdulhusein Nurmohamed (Mombasa), Br. Hassanali G.A. Datoo (Mombasa), Br. Mohammedali Shariff Jiwa (Moshi), Br. Ahmed A. Moledina (Uganda), Br. Abdullah Fazal (Bukoba),, Br. Gulamhussein Remtulla Hansraj (Uganda), Br. Abdulrasul Bandali (Zanzibar), Br. Hussein Dewji (Zanzibar), Br. Anver Hassan Virji (Zanzibar), Br. Akbar G. Dharsee (Zanzibar), Br. M.D. Kermalli (Zanzibar), Br. Hussein A. Rahim (Zanzibar).
>
> Br. Hassanali G. A. Datoo of Mombasa was appointed the Police Reserve District Commissioner, a post that no Asian had been given before. The Central Council in its 11th Session held in Mombasa in March 1954 recorded its congratulations to the above named personalities.
>
> **1954**
> - Br. Mohamed Shariff Jiwa of Moshi was honoured an M.B.E title by the Queen for his services to the public in Tanganyika. The Central Council in its 12th Session held in Mombasa in April 1955 recorded its congratulations to Br. Jiwa.
> - Br. Jafferali A.G. Versi (Manager of Messrs M. Suleman Versi Ltd), was appointed as Governor of the new Legislative Council of Southern Province i.e. Lindi Region.
>
> The Central Council in its 12th Session held in Mombasa in April 1955 recorded its congratulations to both Br. Jiwa and Br. Versi for their awards.
>
> *(Africa Federation Archives)*

discriminatory practices against the non-European population in the region. For Khoja Shia Ithna-Asheries, the acculturation to the East African landscape was such that no serious social or cultural link to speak of was maintained with their original communities in Kachchh, Kathiawad and Mumbai.[22]

The linkage to the birth land of the early pioneers weakened to such an extent that by 1960, for the generation born in East Africa and their children, India was understood mainly or solely through movies; there remained only a superficial understanding of their connection to it. They still knew that their father or grandfather was most likely born there but most, if not all, had no real understanding of their rich heritage as Kachchhi or Kathiawadi and sadly, in the process they had forgotten the sacrifices their ancestors made to preserve the faith and forge the identity they took for granted.

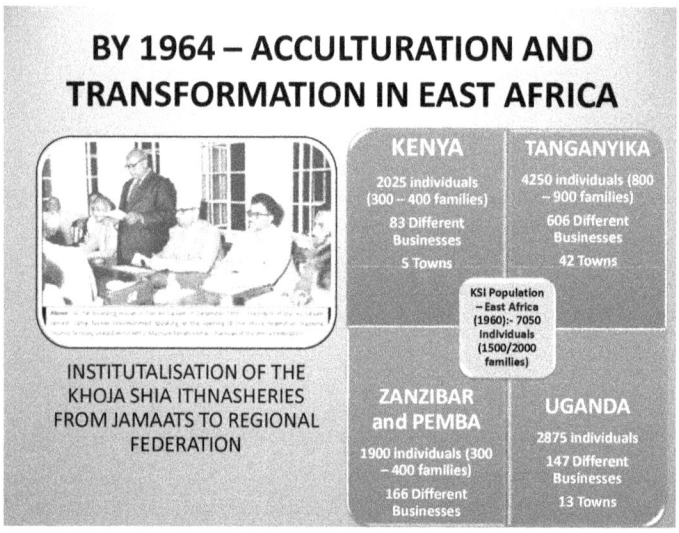

The third point to note is the extent of the spread of businesses that Khoja Shia Ithna-Asheries had invested in by 1960 and commensurate with it, the institutionalisation that had occurred in the community. By 1960, the Khoja Shia Ithna-Asheries had a combined estimated population in East Africa (Tanganyika, Zanzibar, Kenya and Uganda) of around 10,050 individual heads.

In Tanganyika, there were 4250 individuals and 606 different businesses in 42 towns. In Zanzibar, there were 1900 individuals and 166 different businesses. In Kenya, there were 2025 individuals and 83 different businesses in five towns. In Uganda, there were 2875 individuals and 147 different businesses in 13 towns. In simple terms, for every 10 individuals, there was one business or roughly one business per two Khoja Shia Ithna-Asheri families.[23] This shows the scale and depth of commitment to make East Africa their abode.

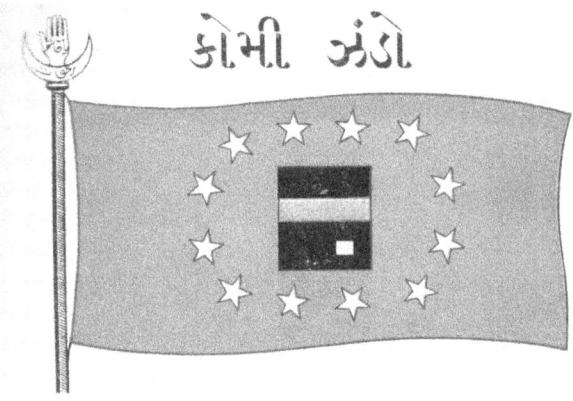

The Federation adopted its own Community Flag

HUSAINALIBHAI G. MERCHANT

Haji Husainalibhai G. Merchant JP of Bombay, India was the original designer of the Federation Flag. He initially designed the flag for Jamaats in India and Pakistan but later the Community in East Africa adopted the same design as its communal flag.

Haji Husainalibhai was one of the prominent industrialists of our community in Bombay and performed valuable social and welfare services. He was the trustee of several leading trusts in India.

The Government of Maharashtra made him a (JP) in 1965 in appreciation of his services to the State.

(Africa Federation Archives)

PART 5
The Structural Institutionalisation of the Khoja Shia Ithna-Asheries in East Africa

5.1 The Idea of Centralising

The structural institutionalisation of the Khoja Shia Ithna-Asheries began with a few families getting together for weekly religious gatherings; celebrating and commemorating important religious events. Coming from the main Khoja community that functioned as a *jamaat*, it was only natural that the new pockets of Shia Ithna-Asheri settlements in Zanzibar, Tanganyika, Kenya and Uganda would follow the same path in establishing themselves. As the number of families getting together increased, they began to form individual *jamaats* with constitutions and rules to govern their activities.

The idea of organising a central structure first began in 1927 amongst some Khoja Shia Ithna-Asheries residing in Mombasa. They were discussing the way forward for the community after having successfully established *jamaats* in many parts of East Africa. They felt that there was a need for a clear sense of direction for the future, however, their enthusiasm was not met with much support from the leadership and their attempts to garner interest in their theories bore no fruit.

Prior to the attempt to organise a central structure for Khoja Shia Ithna-Asheries in East Africa, Khoja Shia Ithna-Asheries in Kachchh also laboured a dream to establish a federation that would unite the community. It appears that among the leadership within Kachchh Jamaats, the discussion of setting up of central body did take place although no official record of such a discussion is found. What could be established is that the pressing task for the community in Kachchh was to establish and widen the network of *jamaats*.

In 1933 the leaders of Kachchh Jamaats agreed to hold a **conference in Mundra, Kachchh** to discuss the creation of a network of *jamaats* along with their mosques, *imambadas*, and *madrasahs* with the aim of establishing a federation in India to unite the community. This was the vision of Seth Dawood Haji Nasser who created the Kachchh Federation. Due to the War that ensued soon after, this project did not see fruition. The idea, however, was picked up in Africa where it flourished.[1]

The contribution of Haji Nasser towards the development and welfare of the community was immense and greatly appreciated even after his demise. Mulla Asgharali M M Jaffer reminisced about it to a packed audience at Mehfile Khurasan, Karachi. Paying tribute, he said that Marhum Nasser was a highly respected pioneer and that the community would declare school holidays in his honour during his visits to East Africa. He generously donated towards expenses of various schools and *madrasahs*.[2]

Haji Nasser served as President of the Bombay Khoja Ithna-Asheri Jamaat and in this capacity flew several times to Zanzibar with his eldest son, Mohammedali, to resolve issues between the '*Nai*' (New) Hujjat Jamaat and '*Junni*' (Old) Kuwwat Jamaat. He also took the initiative to build a huge guesthouse behind his mansion in Bombay. Here, travellers and visiting Aalims were provided with all the facilities and services they required. The guests, mostly from Africa and India, stayed from a few days to months on end completely free of charge.

Haji Nasser also opened and personally supervised an orphanage called *Darul Aaman* in Karachi; the beneficiaries of this institution went on to have successful careers worldwide. In recognition of his great service, the Karachi Jamaat conferred on him the title of "Fakhre Qaum" (The Pride of the Community).[3]

A HISTORICAL CHRONICLE
THE FIRST EVER KHOJA SHIA ITHNA-ASHERI CONFERENCE HELD IN CUTCH MUNDRA IN INDIA IN 1933

Seth Dawood Haji Nasser (1189-1975) was amongst the most active Cutchi Khoja merchants of his time. He had businesses in India, Burma, Japan and Africa. After severing the cord with the mainstream Aga Khani Khojas, the first pressing task of the leader of the Khoja Shia Ithna-Asheri community was to establish a network of Jamaats acquired or built. This was somehwat achieved between 1880-1933.

It was the vision of Haji Nasser to create a Cutch Federation. The first "All Khoja Shia Ithna-Asheri Conference" was held in Mundra, Cutch on 7-9 November 1933 under his Chairmanship. The Honorary Secretary was Hassanalibhai P. Ebrahim and the Assistant Secretary was Roshanali Nasser. 52 delegates from 14 centers of Cutch and four invited guests took part. The following Khoja Jamaats attended: Bhadil, Bharapur, Bhuj, Jarpara, Kapaiya, Kera, Nagalpur, Lakdia, Lakhapur, Mandvi, Mundra, Samagoga, Sinugara and guests from Mumbai.

Musabhai Jaffer welcomed the delegates and drew their attention to the need for unity in the community. He emphasized social/religious reforms and pursuing of education in order to uplift all areas of the community. To support education, there were community boarding houses in Jamnagar, Mahuva and Rajula, but none in Cutch. He therefore appealed to the community to pool its resources to build one.

In his opening address, Haji Nasser emphasized the need for education, a prerequisite if the community was to stand with other communities. He said if the conditions were unsuitable in India, then merchants could migrate to Africa. Since he had business offices in Africa, he offered to sponsor them all and let the Federation take root there. After much discussion, it was resolved that a boarding house be built in Mundra, Cutch. A resolution was also passed for the establishment of The Cutch Khoja Shia Ithna-Asheri Conference. Its objective would be to promote unity, economic, religious and social reforms in the community. Addressing social reforms, the Conference passed ten more resolutions aiming to regulate the *reet-rivaaj* (traditions and ceremonies) of marriages.

Soon after, the years of war as well as the formation of Pakistan led to large numbers of Khoja Shia Ithna-Asheris migrating. The Cutch Conference never saw the light of day although there is a boarding house in Cutch to this day that found its birth at that first meeting. Dawoodbhai Haji Nasser and his wife, Zainabbai are buried in Najaf, Iraq. They had 11 children; six sons and five daughters.

(Africa Federation Archives, 12 May 2017)
Photo: Alhaj Dawoodbhai Haji Nasser addressing the Africa Federation Conference held in Kampala in 1955)

In 1932, the editor of the monthly magazine *Munadee*,[4] Abdulhussein Sachedina (popularly known as Abdulhussein 'Azad'), who was based in Dar es Salaam, revived the discussion that had originally begun in Mombasa. He presented an intellectual argument for the need of a central organisation. He was amongst the first profound thinkers in the community who wrote about developing a clear sense of direction for the Khoja Shia Ithna-Asheri community under a unified platform.[5]

He inspired many through his various editorials in which he expressed his ideas with passion and lucidity. The following words demonstrate not only the clarity of his thinking but also his ability to move the community to action:

> [The] Ithna-Asheri Society today is overwhelmed by layers of backwardness and retrogression. These layers have been building up for the last several years, and continue even today. The horizon is bleak and dark, and nowhere is a ray of light to be seen. The ship of our community is drifting aimlessly and helplessly in a vast ocean, and none can predict when it will perish against the rocks. This is not a figment of imagination by a poet, or empty, fictional verbiage by a writer. Those who care to spare a moment or two to make an appraisal will agree that our words portray an exact and accurate picture of the prevailing situation.

He then proceeded to spell out the ills that had surrounded the community, condemning the time-worn traditions and social norms that they still subscribed to. He described the state of the Khoja Shia Ithna-Asheri at the time; how the community was scattered and disorganised. He pointed out that those in remote areas were losing contact with the mainstream Ithna-Asheri society. He held the leaders of major *jamaats* responsible and appealed to them to rise to the challenges of the changing times[6]. The formula he put forward was as follows:

> Progress without reform and organization is difficult. We need a strong, fortified set of laws, which should bring about order and discipline in all our Jamaats, big and small, and should open up the stifled path of progress and advancement. This has got to be our goal, and the easiest way to achieve this is to form a Central Council of the Shia Ithna-Asheri Community in East Africa.[7]

In response to this, Abdulhusein Nurmohamed wrote a letter, published in *Munadee* in January 1933 supporting the concept of establishing such a council. His letter showed that he understood the advantages of an organized, central body and he had a clear sense of the direction in which he thought the community could be led. It is no wonder then that when the council was finally formed twelve years late, he was elected its first President.[8]

ABDULHUSSEIN JUSAB SACHEDINA "AZAD" (1911-1957)

Abdulhussein Jusab Sachedina was born in Mundra, Cutch in India and lived in Dar es Salaam and Lindi. He was the first secretary of Lindi Jamaat. Being a writer, he took the pen name 'Azad'. He was amongst the first people to float the idea for the creation of a Federation of all KSI Jamaats in Africa and is thus one of the "Pioneers" of the Federation.

In his book on Khoja History, Marhum Mulla Asgherali writes the following regarding Marhum Azad Sachedina: 'Among the first thinkers who wrote about the need of a common platform was Marhum Abdulhussein Sachedina 'Azad', editor of the Gujarati monthly, "Munadee". In 1932, he wrote an editorial in his monthly, appealing to leaders of major Jamaats to rise to the changing times. He was among the first visionaries who saw an ailing society and suggested a remedy with clarity. His powerful pen heralded a new era. Marhum Azad had an appealing style. He wrote poetically, gracefully and with enviable coherence.'

Abdulhusein Sachedina passed away at the age of 46 in Dar es Salaam. (Africa Federation Archives, 28 December 2018)

Nurmohamed's efforts motivated many within the community to discuss and seriously consider the idea of centralising *jamaats* under one body to provide a platform for debate and develop purposeful consensus on community development.

Whilst these ideas were taking root, *Munadee* sadly stopped publication and the discussion about a central council fizzled out for a while. After some years, another community-based monthly magazine - *Salsabil* - picked up the discussion where it had been left. Under the editorship of Gulamhussein Mohammedwalli Dharsee the magazine reached out to its audience and invited opinion pieces regarding the future of the community.

Nurbhai H H Khaki, a resident of 'Belgium Congo', first mooted the idea to hold a competition and many submitted their thoughts as articles. The first four winners selected were:

1. A. H. Nazerali of Mombasa
2. Taslimbhai of Tanga
3. Haji Mohammed Jaffer Sheriff Dewji of Mombasa
4. Haji Mohammed Sherriff Jiwa of Arusha.

Brother A.H. Nazerali of Mombasa presents his views on Aims and Objectives For the forthcoming Conference

Within this period I came across a book "Two words" published in Dar es Salaam in which Molvi Alimuhamed Haji Jaffer had written about the need to have a "Conference" which was then published in Vol. 10 of *Salsabil*. I was glad to read about it and I hereby present my views about the aims and objectives in brief:

1. Kenya, Uganda, Tanganyika and Zanzibar to decide and make a province (Madagascar, Somali and Congo to be permitted to join).
2. Whoever wants to join should be permitted and all centers should have the same constitution.
3. To discourage community conflicts and establish unity and brotherhood within the members.
4. Any cases not resolved within the Jamaat should be presented to the Council and its decision should be accepted.
5. All birth, death (with its causes), marriages, divorces as well as population i.e. census to be presented every three months.
6. To initiate building of madrasah, schools, boarding houses etc. for imparting religious and academic knowledge to the community.
7. To establish maternity homes for ladies as well as drug stores (chemists) for the community
8. After the establishment of the Council all brothers above 18 years to take an oath of loyalty to serve the community; he with his family to fulfill the conditions according to our faith. Every responsible adult is obliged to be loyal to their community.
9. To establish a head office of "The Council" and the Secretariat to oversee and fulfill the needs of the centers.
10. Every centre (Jamwaat) to elect a delegate per 10 heads to represent them during annual meetings.
11. To run the day-to-day activities of the Council, main centres such as Mombasa, Dar es Salaam, Kampala and Zanzibar should contribute Shs 1000/-. Towns with 250-500 members to contribute Shs 500/- and those with 100-250 members to pay Shs 250/-.

The above written aims and objectives are for the information of our brothers and whosoever wants to contribute more, will be given a chance. The task cannot be accomplished only by these aims; some petty things need to be added to run activities smoothly. It is my suggestion that it is necessary to have a "Preliminary Conference" where these aims and objectives be sieved into a constitution where a program can be decided.

(Extract from Salsabil, October, 1944 - Trans. F. Ali)

Soon after this, widespread discussion began on the merit of establishing a central council for Khoja Shia Ithna-Asheri in East Africa. This idea began to percolate in the community.

Some passionate youth in Dar es Salaam took up the discussion, amongst them Satchu Gulamali Abdulrasul Sachoo (grandson of Sachoo Pira). A fiery speaker and visionary, he used to publish a magazine called *Inqilab*[9] and invited many to contribute articles including Bashir Rahim.[10] Satchu and Bashir organised the youths to form a club they called *Kumar Mandal* that met every other Saturday evening. They would have open discussions that often led to passionate arguments and once a month they would also get an external speaker to address them. Slowly, these events increased the credibility and prestige of their society.[11]

These youth of Dar es Salaam, supported by individuals like Habib Kassam of Tanga, took on the task of convincing Dar es Salaam jamaat leadership to call a conference for the establishment of a Central Council of Khoja Shia Ithna-Asheries. Dar es Salaam Jamaat leadership supported their plea and on 15 August 1945, Gulamhussein Virjee, the Secretary of Dar es Salaam Jamaat wrote to every jamaat in Zanzibar, Tanganyika, Kenya and Uganda. In his invitation, he explained the merits of and the need for the conference and invited each *jamaat* to choose and send delegates to represent them at the first-ever conference of Khoja Shia Ithna-Asheries that would tentatively be held in Dar es Salaam.

In his letter, Gulamhussein Virjee posed important questions to the scattered leadership: What was the real state of communities in East Africa? How important was it to call such a conference? He reflected upon these questions a great deal and finally concluded that if the community did not set up the Central Council and work to overcome their challenges together, they would fail the aspirations of all the Khoja Shia Ithna-Asheries who had settled in East Africa.

All the *jamaats* responded positively with the majority opting for Dar es Salaam to be the location for the first conference. The date of 10 November 1945 was set and agreed upon by consensus and the venue chosen was Anjuman-e-Punjabi Muslim Community Hall. All those who wished to add items to the agenda were requested to submit them by 31 October 1945. A letter outlining these details was sent out to all the jamaats and included with it was the request to nominate names for the position of Chairman for the first conference.

ABDULHUSSEIN NURMOHAMMED (1911-1957)

Murrabbi Abdulhussein (seen in photo addressing the Africa Federation meeting) was born in Zanzibar and after acquiring basic education there, went to Mombasa.

Within two years, he established "M/s A.H. Nurmohamed & Co. Ltd" which is well known in East Africa. In 1922, he got engaged and in 1926, he married.

He served for 13 years in the Managing Committee of National Congress and Indian Association, whilst serving as Secretary for the associations. He was one of the elected board members of Mombasa Municipality from 1939-1955. In 1950/51, he served as the Vice President of Municipality. He was also a member of Kenya's Board of Commerce and Industries. Furthermore from 1948-1950 he rendered his services as President of the Federation of Chambers of Commerce of East Africa. Abdulhusseinbhai was President of Pandya Memorial Society. He was also a member of the Managing Committee of Coast Subsidiary Hotel, Kenya Maize Marketing Board, East African Tourist Travel Association and Mombasa Muslim Institute. In 1958, he was nominated as a member of Kenya's Legislative Council, in 1960, he was elected to the Kenya Council of State.

He had served as the first President of the Federation of KSI Jamaats of Africa from 1946-49 and again from 1952-58. During these years, he improved the state of the community and devoted himself to the betterment of Africa Federation. The Federation honoured him as a lifetime Councillor. He is a member of the Education Board in Mombasa.

(Extract from Trade Directory 1960, Trans. by F. Ali)

Soon after, by a majority vote, it was suggested that Honourable H K Jaffer be the first chair, but due to important work that needed his attention, he was unable to attend the conference. By consensus, Abdulhussein Nurmohammed was nominated to take up this role.

Abdulhussein's credentials were uniquely tailored to this position. His parents originally came from Mundra, Kachchh and settled in Zanzibar where he was born in 1900. After completing his primary and secondary education, he moved to Mombasa in 1913 and established his own business. By 1926, he began the active contributions that would distinguish him as a dedicated public servant.

He served in various positions within The Indian Association of

Mombasa, eventually becoming its President in 1943. He held the position of Secretary of The East Africa Indian National Congress and went on to become its President as well. As a member of the Rent Control and the Building Control Boards, he represented the interest of the Asian communities in Mombasa in both areas. He also held various positions within the Khoja Shia Ithna-Asheri community: he was President of the Kuwwatul Islam Jamaat, Mombasa, member of the Education Committee, Life Member of the Ithna-Asheri Sports Club and Ithna-Asheri Young Man's Union. With such a wealth of experience, the community could not have asked for a better person to lead it as it met for its first conference in East Africa.

To ensure it met its responsibilities as a host, Dar es Salaam Jamaat set up a welcoming committee comprising of Ibrahim Haji, Hasanali Rahim, Fazal Pirbhai Thaver, Gulamhussein Virjee, Abdulrasul Rajabali Alidina, Mohammed A Khimji, Raza Suleiman Versi, Haji Jivan, Jafferali Nurmohammed, Gulamali Jessa, Abdulrasul Molu Chattoo, and Mohammedali Kassamali.

From 1 November 1945, delegates began to arrive using every mode of transport available. They were looked after by a dedicated group of volunteers who catered for every need that they reasonably could. One name that stands out in records is that of Mohammedali Janmohammed Hasmani; he dedicated every waking moment to ensuring the comfort of the delegates - some of whom had undertaken long, arduous journeys to arrive - such that he was singled out for a mention in the conference as well as in the review that *Salsabil* published.

Group photo before the address by the Chairman Abdulrasul Nurmohammed

5.2 The First Conference of Khoja Shia Ithna-Asheries of East Africa

The First Conference of Khoja Shia Ithna-Asheries of East Africa began at 3.30 p.m. on 10 November 1945 at Mnazi Mmoja, Dar es Salaam. The meeting opened with a beautiful recitation of verses from the Qur'an by Mohammedhussein Gulamhussein Virjee followed by *Hadith al-Kisa* (The Narration of the Cloak) by Habib Mulji.

Before the official opening, Shaykh Sadikali Saheb, a religious scholar, addressed the conference and advised all who were present at the conference that any progress for Khoja Shia Ithna-Asheries in East Africa depended on how united and serious they would be in implementing what they decided amongst themselves. Drawing lessons from the lives of the Ahlulbayt (pbut) and the sacrifices of Karbala, he lamented:

> Sadly, whilst we claim to be the followers of [the] Ahlulbayt (peace be upon them), we do not even try to follow in their footsteps in our conduct. As followers, what will beautify the community is to adopt fully their way of living and unless the community does that, it will not be able to achieve the right progress....

The East Africa Shia Ithna-Asheri Conference

Gulamhussein Virjee spoke next on behalf of the welcoming committee. He made a plea to the delegates not to expect the conference to produce quick-fix solutions for the challenges facing the community. On the contrary, he warned, the community would face a long road of struggles before it would see the fruits of its efforts. He pointed out that many examples throughout human history proved nothing long-lasting was ever achieved without sacrifices of time and resources. He encouraged the gathering by pointing out that they had a great resource of intellectual leadership available to them within the many East African jamaats who could steer the community towards the progress and development they sought.

When the Chair of the First Conference of Khoja Shia Ithna-Asheries of East Africa rose to give his first speech, the delegates welcomed him with a rising crescendo of clapping. After thanking the delegates for the opportunity to serve, he posed a simple question: 'What does this conference mean to us?'

He urged that the task for each person present was to answer that question and think deeply about their reason for being there and then warned:

> We cannot be here to just talk big, pass resolutions, eat, laugh, enjoy ourselves and satisfy our conscience that we attended the conference. If we only do this, then people will have a right to call the conference just a 'show'. However, if we take our presence seriously and put into effect whatever we decide at the earliest opportunity then we will have understood the real meaning of the conference.

He went on to explain to the attentive audience that

> our community in East Africa is moving chaotically. It needs a solid purpose and practical directions. Moreover, having one primary conference is not enough. It is a start. We will have to prepare not only a constitution and by-laws but also to inculcate the right mindset in the community. Whether you are poor or rich, in your heart you must be willing to sacrifice whatever you can afford to. If a rich person thinks that his rightful place in the community is to rule over the community whilst disparaging the poor or the youth of the community look at the leadership with rebellion, such a mindset will not benefit the community. Instead, it will take us into a blind hole.

> We are living in times of tumultuous change and we need unity at all levels of the community, compassion in our dealings with each other and rules that makes us an organised community. We must aspire for those things that can make each Khoja Shia Ithna-Asheri feel proud to belong to our community. At the same time, our community in East Africa must establish a central body that can create a long-term vision whilst also addressing the more immediate problem of false rituals, customs, arguments, fights and bad behaviour within the community with a loving communal spirit.

He went on to appeal to the youth to prepare themselves to take on the responsibilities of their communities. He exhorted them not to criticise the ongoing leadership or create division by passionate talk about their flaws. Instead, he told them to bring to light any negative traits by bringing them respectfully to the attention of community leaders and working together to address them. In doing so, he said, they would 'together bring goodness back into the community'.

He warned the community that brooding over past errors would not benefit anyone. Everyone was aware that mistakes had been made and lessons had been learned. 'If after 50 to 60 years of communal experiences, we are still not able to progress in the right way then we will go backwards as a community,' he stated. After enumerating the various religious, social, educational and economic challenges they had, he reminded the delegates that 'the success of this conference will depend upon how we progress our work in this conference as well as the level of support the Jamaats provide to our decisions.'

After his speech, the participants thanked the organisers and particularly Dar es Salaam Jamaat for the warm welcome. The delegate from Ujiji, Nasserali Merali, summed up the mood and the feeling of the gathering when he spoke:

> ...it is through this conference [that] the community will benefit and achieve a great deal. Our presence today shows that the Khoja Shia Ithna-Asheri Community is [a] living and moving community. Moreover, because we are a community that is alive, no worldly power can break our unity and our Jamaat...

our obligation as member[s] of this august community is [to] loyally and effectively implement the resolutions that are passed by this conference. Whilst blood continues to flow in our veins, we should never breach our constitution....

His words were applauded enthusiastically by all and this speech is just one telling example of the raw emotions of the Khoja Shia Ithna-Asheri community at the time. They had both a passionate urge and the self-confidence to take the community to greater heights.

The first three resolutions of the conference were then moved by the Chairman. These resolutions were emotionally measured and remarkably sensitive to the past struggles of the community. They also reflected an appreciation of the efforts of the past generation who made it possible for Khoja Shia Ithna-Asheries to prosper in East Africa and call it their home.

The first resolution stated:

'This First (Primary) conference sends [a] message of peace, love and exhortation to all Ithna-Asheri brothers and sisters settled in East Africa and assure[s] them of their heartfelt support in their religious progress. Furthermore, this conference recommends to all Ithna-Asheri brothers and sisters that they treat each other in the spirit of respect and cooperation because this conference believes that such feelings are the only true basis of happiness and progress of the Ithna-Asheri community.'

The second resolution stated:

'This primary conference pays a special tribute to those Khoja Shia Ithna-Asheri personalities and leaders who have provided their selfless services to the community and made its settlement strong in East Africa. For those who have left this world, we pray to Allah SWT to give them success and [to] those who are still serving, we record our deep appreciation.'

The third resolution stated:

'[The] Khoja Shia Ithna-Asheri Community as one of the primary settlers of East Africa contributed to its general upliftment, continues to add to its progress and regards East Africa as their home. We will contribute our reasonable share towards its progress. Furthermore, this conference recommends that we will work towards [the] future progress of East Africa by actively working in close relationship with other communities.'

These three resolutions were unanimously approved by the conference. Mohammedali Janmohammed was elected as General Secretary on recommendation from the Chairman and the stage was then set for deliberations to start in earnest. Discussions began about how to set up a central council and the processes that would then guide the community in overcoming its present and future challenges. There was a need to produce a governing document that would provide rules for setting priorities equitably and implementing all decisions. This meant a date had to be set for a constitutional conference.

After long deliberation, the fourth resolution was passed, stating:

'This first conference unanimously agrees that it considers [it] important to call a constitutional conference at the earliest. Furthermore, it authorises the central provisional council to choose any date in May 1946 that suits the majority of Jamaats to call for the first constitutional conference.'

This resolution was proposed by Honourable Ahmed Lakha, seconded by Mohammedali Sheriff Jiwa and unanimously passed.

The location of the constitutional conference was proposed in the fifth resolution by Mohammed Sachedina:

'This conference authorises the provisional central council to hold the constitutional conference at a place that carries the support of the majority from the Jamaat invitations that are received.'

Gulamhussein Virjee of Dar es Salaam seconded the proposal and the resolution passed unanimously.

Once these details for the constitutional conference were in place, there was a need to create a provisional body authorised to follow up on the decisions that would be made during this first conference. Mohammed Abdalla Khimji proposed the next - sixth - resolution:

'To progress the decisions approved by this first conference as well as oversee the work till the constitutional conference, a 16-member committee be appointed by this conference with the following remit:

- This committee will be known as "The East Africa Khoja Shia Ithna-Asheri Provisional Council".
- This Council will comprise 16 members: 4 each from Tanganyika, Zanzibar, Kenya and Uganda. The chairman of this Conference will be the chairman of this Council.
- The quorum for this Council will be [a] minimum of five members to be present and at least one member present from each of the territories. Only then will the deliberations and decisions passed be recognised as legitimate.
- The office of the Provincial Council will be based in Mombasa and the Chairman has the authority to appoint the Secretary of the Council.

This resolution was seconded by the Honourable Ahmed Lakha and passed unanimously.

The council then unanimously approved the following individuals as Chairman and members of the Council:

1. A. H. Nurmohammed – Chairman
2. Ahmed Lakha Kanji – Zanzibar
3. Husein A Rahim – Zanzibar
4. Abdulhussein Hassam Nasser – Zanzibar
5. Hussein Mohammedali Nazerali – Zanzibar
6. M S Kalyan – Mombasa
7. Jafferali Mohammedali – Mombasa
8. Rajabali G A Datoo – Nairobi
9. Abdulrasul Merali Dewji – Mombasa
10. H K Jaffer – Jinja
11. Mohammedali Alibhai Ramji – Kampala
12. Pirbhai Visram – Kampala
13. Mohammedali Remtullah – Mbale
14. Mohammed Haji Abadallah Khimji – Dar es Salaam
15. Abdulrasul Nasser Virjee – Mwanza

16. Habib Kassam Manji – Tanga
17. Mohammedali Sherrif Jiwa - Arusha

Following the appointment of the Provisional Council, Abdulrasul Virjee proposed the following resolution, which was the seventh:

> 'This conference recommends that a draft constitution be prepared and sent to all the Jamaats at the earliest and their views sought and presented at the constitutional conference.'

This resolution was seconded by Nazerali Nurmohammed and unanimously passed.

At this point, a strong plea was made by Haji Pirbhai Visram to remember that they were primarily a faith-based organisation and therefore when drafting any constitutional principles, the members should remain cognisant of the limits set out by Islam. The Chairman assured the conference that this would be abided by.

The Chairman then recommended that invitations be sent to Jamaats in Italian Somaliland, Madagascar and Belgium Congo. At the same time, the Chairman explained to carry out the work of the central council effectively, the community needed to have demographic data of all communities settled in East Africa. This recommendation was put in the form of a resolution and proposed by Mohammed Abdalla Khimji of Dar es Salaam. Thus, the eighth resolution stated:

> 'This first conference recommends that a census form be prepared and sent to all the Jamaats at the earliest and up-to-date demographic record be made available at the first constitutional conference.'

This resolution was seconded by M. Ladak Kanji and unanimously passed.

It appears from the reading of various documents that in 1945, education was a priority for the community. One pressing challenge that Khoja Shia Ithna-Asheries in the smaller towns faced was the lack of secondary educational facilities. Many delegates urged the conference that if secondary education facilities were not provided as a matter of urgency, there was a real danger that the intellectual standard of the community as a whole would be lowered. This would have profound consequences on the social and economic progress of the families involved. The conference took up this challenge seriously and after long deliberations, a ninth resolution was proposed by Abdulrasul Nasser Virjee:

> 'This first conference recommends to the Provisional Central Council that to cater for the educational needs of the children of our community, boarding houses be built in suitable places for them to receive an appropriate education. Furthermore, those youths of sufficient capabilities [be] sent overseas to receive higher education. A report [will be] prepared for the same and submitted at the forthcoming constitutional conference.'

This resolution was seconded by Hussein Nazerali and Nazerali Nurmohammed and passed unanimously.

Having passed these foundational resolutions, they adjourned and allowed the next day for the specially appointed and tasked constitutional sub-committee to prepare a draft constitution. Following a resolution, the constitutional sub-committee comprising of 10 members was chosen from among the delegates present at this first conference. They were:

1. A. H. Nurmohammed – Chairman
2. Honourable Ahmed Lakha - Zanzibar
3. Hussein A Rahim - Zanzibar
4. M. S. Kalyan – Mombasa
5. Abdulrasul Merali Dewji - Mombasa
6. Mohammed Abdal Khimji - Dar es Salaam
7. Abdulrasul Nasser Virjee – Mwanza
8. Bhai Jaffer Pradhan – Kampala
9. Bhai Pirbhai Visram – Kampala
10. Bhai Mohammedali Janmohammed – Secretary.

The constitutional subcommittee met on 11 November 1945 to prepare a draft constitution to send out to all the Jamaats for deliberations amongst their members. They were to submit their views and amendments for formal deliberation and adoption at the forthcoming constitutional conference that would be called by the Provisional Central Council. This draft constitution was placed before the first conference on 12 November 1945.

After some discussion, the following was approved and sent to all the Khoja Shia Ithna-Asheri Jamaats of East Africa:

1. On (Date) at (Place), the Jamaats in Tanganyika, Uganda, Kenya and Zanzibar held the first Constitutional Conference and passed a resolution to set up the Khoja Shia Ithna-Asheri Central Council of East Africa, which will be known as 'Central Council' in this constitution. The following are its objectives:
   a. To bring the general activities of all the Khoja Shia Ithna-Asheri Jamaats collectively under the Central Council.
   b. To protect the benefits, interests and rights of the Khoja Shia Ithna-Asheri Community.
   c. To take the necessary steps to uplift the religious, social and economical status of the Khoja Shia Ithna-Asheri Community.
   d. To encourage the establishment of religious and educational facilities for the Khoja Shia Ithna-Asheri Community.e. To undertake all such activities [that are] beneficial to [the] Khoja Shia Ithna-Asheri Community.

2. The Central Council will not undertake or participate in any activity or activities that are contrary to the Laws of Islam.

3. The election of Jamaats to represent in the Central Council will be according to the constitution passed at the first Constitutional Conference.

4.
   a. [The] Central Council will be made up of 25 members in total comprising the President, 4 Vice Presidents (one each from Kenya, Uganda, Tanganyika and Zanzibar) and 5 members from each of the territories of Kenya, Uganda, Tanganyika and Zanzibar). If in the future, neighbouring territories join the Council then such territories will also have a right to nominate 1 Vice President and 5 members to the Council.
   b. Each territory will have the right to choose the delegates to represent the territory at the conference and members to represent it at the Council.
   c. The quorum for the Central Council meeting shall be 9 members. At the minimum, a representative from each territory must be present.

5. The headquarters of the Central Council will be based wherever the President resides.
6. [The] Central Council shall meet once every six months at the minimum. In addition, if necessary, the Council can call a meeting, provided notice of the meeting together with the agenda [is] sent to all the members of the Council 30 days before the meeting.
7. Any decision made by the Council and passed by the majority of its members shall be binding on the entire member Jamaats.
8. Each member Jamaat will have the right to send one delegate per 100 of its population to the conference. A small Jamaat will have a right to send one delegate to the conference if its population is less than 100. These delegates will be chosen at their respective general meetings and they will have a right to represent their respective Jamaats at the session of the conference.
9. To be recognised as a Jamaat, [a society] must have at least 10 individuals residing in the place where the Jamaat is formed. If it has less than 10 individuals, it will have the right to join with the neighbouring Jamaat and be represented by it at the conference.
10. [The] Central Council will decide the date of the conference. It will send out notice of the date together with the agenda of the conference 60 days before the date of the conference. Every member Jamaat shall have the right to add item[s] to the agenda and [this] must be sent to the Council 15 days before the date of the conference.
11. [The] Central Council will seek [a] nomination for the post of President from each member Jamaat. The Jamaats will decide upon these nominations. The nominee who gets the majority votes of the delegates will be declared President.
12. [The] Central Council will have the authority to decide the place for the conference depending on the majority support of member Jamaats.

At the final session, many speeches - some funny, some visionary, and some audacious - were presented by the delegates. They thanked their host Dar es Salaam Jamaat profusely for organising the first primary conference. This conference had given the community a sense of direction and an outline of how to work together centrally to chart out the path ahead.

The Chairman of this first conference noted the crucial support provided by many in awakening the community to the need for centralising the Jamaats in East Africa. To that end, he proposed a final, tenth, resolution:

> 'This first conference takes note of all those who worked hard to make this conference a success, especially the community members of Dar es Salaam Jamaat as well as many community magazines, specially Salsabil, whose circulation awakened the community to the need for a conference to establish a Central Council.'

Volunteers at the First Conference of the KSI Jamaats of East Africa. Standing L-R: Mohamed Dhirani, Yusuf Nazerali Panju, Gulamabbas Suleman Mohamed and Akber Panjwani. Sitting: Gulammehdi K. Haji, Mohamed H. Rahim and Pyarali Rustamali Ladha. Front row: Mustafa H. M. Walji and Kassim Panju

These ten resolutions passed at the First Conference of Khoja Shia Ithna-Asheries of East Africa in 1945 show the determination of the community to chart out its destiny and its confidence in its communal resources. It is interesting to observe the manner in which the society leaned towards organising itself into a rule-based community.

The systemic manner in which it first called the Conference, chose its Chairman, and proceeded to adopt a constitution whilst always seeking the widest possible consensus can perhaps be attributed to the British political education that many of its members had received. It is an admirable part of the community history to see that despite a colonial influence, its members were able to balance out the best of both worlds by using their educational base to create a solid framework for their vision, whilst prioritising loyalty to their faith.

At the Central Council, Abdulhussein Nurmohammed was elected the first Chairman and served from 1946 to 1949.[12] This was not a surprise because he was a man of erudite disposition and well-liked in the community. Moreover, he was a public figure recognised by the colonial authorities and respected both within and outside of the community.

GULAMHUSEIN NASSER LAKHA

MOHAMMED ABADALLAH KHIMJI

Gulamhusein Nasser Lakha assisted him as Honorary Secretary. The Vice-Chairman was Mohammed Abadallah Khimji and the Treasurer was Abdulrasul M. Dewji. This initial Central Council body later on metamorphosed into Africa Federation.

The second Chairman of the Federation was Abdulrasul Nasser Virjee (1950-1953).[13] He hailed from the pioneer family of Nasser Virjee and had a towering figure, but was a man of few words with a philosophical attitude. Assisted by H. K. Jaffer (Vice-Chairman), Mohamedali Janmohamed (Hon. Secretary) and Juma Haji (Hon. Treasurer), his team introduced welfare and education as priorities at the Federation level. In the religious department, they started bringing maulanas (religious scholars) from India and Pakistan who were stationed as resident aalims in different jamaats in Africa.

For the next two terms, from 1953 until 1959, Abdulhusein H. Nurmohamed and his team returned to serve the community. The only change in the original team was in the post of Honorary Treasurer which was held by Jaffer Sherrif. During these two terms, unity and dedication were a priority and an emphasis was placed on religious as well as secular education. Spirituality and Islamic values took precedence over all other sectors of the Federation.

In 1952, at the opening of the Third Conference Abdulhusein H. Nurmohamed gave a speech[14] that provides a view of the thinking of the community at that time. They considered themselves loyal British subjects with their economic and political state being settled and positive. In 1958, a special propagation fund was set up and a team was appointed to tour all member Jamaats to collect the monies for it.

From 1959 to 1965, Ebrahim Sheriff Dewji took over as Chairman,[15] assisted by Mohammedali Sharrif Jiwa (Vice-Chairman), Hassanali P Visram (Honorary Secretary) and Mohammedtaki R Pirbhai (Honorary Treasurer).

Haji Ebrahim was one of the most vigorous and active presidents of the Federation. He came from a family known for its religious services to the community and in his term blazed a path of structural progress and vitality within the Federation. He had a charming personality and was able to come up with just the appropriate words required to sway individuals towards his point of view.

At the 1958 Conference he explained his obligations to the community as well to God on the Day of Judgement. He exhorted the community to support him in fulfilling these obligations in every way it could. He was able to pass the resolution at the Federation Conference to collect foundation funds for its projects, which stated:

> 'This conference makes a resolution to our community residing in East Africa and Belgium Congo. "The Federation" will collect money for the "Foundation Fund" from the community members of East Africa and Belgium Congo for which a committee consisting [of] five members should be elected to accomplish this task within six months.'[16]

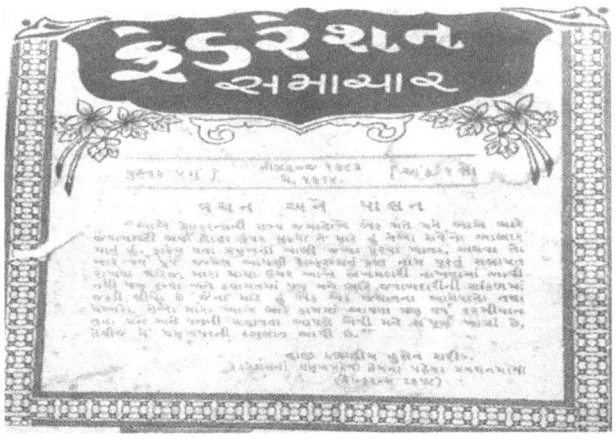

Ebrahim Sheriff Dewji's Gujarati statement

To implement this resolution effectively, he divided the implementation plan into four phases. The delegation responsible for the first phase included Haji Ebrahimbhai Sharif (Arusha), Haji Mohamedalibhai Ladak Kanji (Moshi), Molvi Professor Mohamedlatif Ansari Saheb (Mombasa) and Haji Hassanbhai Nasser Virjee (Mwanza).

This delegation travelled to Dar es Salaam, Zanzibar, Pemba, Mombasa, Uganda, Rwanda, Urundi and Belgium Congo. Many other members of the community joined them along the way such as Haji Mohamed Husseinbhai Merali Dewji of Kampala, Hussein Nazerali Panju, Mohamedtaqi Dewsi Manji and Mohamed Suleiman Khimji of Tanga. Others who assisted in various capacities included: Mohamedali Hansraj, Hussein Kassam Mohamed, Musa Alibhai, Mohamedjaffer Bahadurali Mawji, Merali Mulji, Kermali Esmail, and Mohamedali Alibhai.

The second phase covered Arusha, Moshi, Tanga, Pangani and Lamu. Haji Mohamedtakibhai Remtulla, Jafferali Mohamedali Merali, Anver Karim Mohamed Tharoo and Mohamedalibhai Sharif joined the efforts here.

The third phase covered the West Lake province of Tanganyika and Congo. The delegation responsible included Haji Ebrahim Hussein Sharrif, Haji Mohamedalibhai Ladak, Maulana Zawarhussein Saheb, Suleimanbhai Mohamed Bhimji. In addition, Abdallah Fazel, Mohamedjafferbhai Nasser Virjee, Karimbhai Remtullah, Amirali M. J Mulla, Ladhubhai Jaffer, Gulamali Fazal and Gulamali Jetha and Razabhai Karmali Pirbhai assisted the delegation.

The fourth phase included the Southern province (of Tanganyika) and the Eastern province in the Ifakara and Mahenge districts. The delegation there comprised of Haji Ebrahim Hussein Sharrif, Maulana Zawarhussein Saheb. Suleimanbhai Mohamed Bhimji, Haji Gulamabbasbhai Merali Mawji, Fazal Ladha Dinani and Rashidbhai Versi also helped in this last phase.

On these trips, Mohamedalibhai Ladak and Suleiman Mohamed Bhimji played a unique role in convincing people to donate. Their joint efforts, together with the eloquent sermons by Maulana Ansari and Zawwarhussein, inspired the community to donate a total of Shs 500, 000/- for the Khoja Shia Ithna-Asheri Tanganyika Boarding house.

The delegations travelled for 105 days by air, car and steamer covering 13,239 miles visiting 127 towns and meeting 1200 people. They visited 82 towns in Tanganyika, 20 in Uganda, 19 in Congo, Rwanda and Burundi, two in Kenya and four in Zanzibar and Pemba. This implementation plan was the first of its kind for the community and yielded other positive benefits apart from collecting funds.

The strategy devised by Haji Ebrahimbhai H. Sharrif brought awareness to the towns visited regarding the communal needs as well their responsibility towards fulfilling those needs and the benefits they would also gain from helping each other. Ebrahimbhai also undertook an analysis of the needs and requirements of the *jamaats* he visited. The following properties amounting to Shs. 810,000 were purchased

from the Foundation Fund. They were:
- 34 Plot Regent Estate in Dar es Salaam
- A four-storey building on Ring Street in Dar es Salaam
- A three-storey building on Station Road in Mombasa
- One house in Singida.[17]

The rental income from these investments was used for various activities, including much-needed scholarships for funding higher education.

Sheikh Gulamabbas was amongst the first batch of students sponsored by the Federation of KSI Jamaats of Africa (AFED) to go for higher religious studies overseas. He first enrolled himself at the *Darul Uloom Mohamediya*, Surgodha, Pakistan in 1959. Later, in September 1962, he moved on to *Jame Imamiyya Maddresatul Waizin*, Karachi, Pakistan.

SHEIKH GULAMABBAS M. K. S. VERSI (1937 - 1988)

Maulana Sheikh Gulamabbas Versi (was fondly known by the name of Maulana Abbas Pinji) was born in Zanzibar to the renowned family of Mohamedhussein Kassamali Versi. He was educated in Zanzibar and started reciting Majlises at a very young age.

He drew inspiration from eminent Aalims of Zanzibar like Alhaj Mulla Mohamedjaffer Sheriff Dewji, Alhaj Mulla Hussain Allarakhia Rahim, Alhaj Mulla Ahmed Abdulrasul Lakha Kanji, and Alhaj Mulla Raza Rashid Nathani. Maulana Gulamabbas Versi regularly attended Majlises and engaged in discussions with the visiting Aalims such as Allahmah Rashid Turabi, Maulana Gulamabbas

Rizvi, Maulana Seyed Aqa Raza and others Zakirs who came to Zanzibar during the Ayam-e-Muharram and Safar. Maulana Gulamabbas was the Resident Aalim of the Mikindani/Mtwara Jamaat. He died on a Friday at the age of 51 at the Nyangao Mission Hospital, Lindi Region, after a short illness.

Sheikh Gulamabbas returned from his studies in Pakistan in May 1963 and soon thereafter sent out on a tour of Tabligh to Zaire (Congo DRC). On completion of this tour, he was posted as the Resident Aalim of Tunduru Jamaat. His penchant for further religious knowledge saw him travel to Najaf, Iraq in June of 1965, where he studied until 1969. On his return to East Africa, he resumed his duties as a Resident Aalim, at Lindi and then Mikindani/Mtwara Jamaat where he remained until his death. Sheikh Gulamabbas Versi had an impressive record of dedicated services to various Jamaats in the southern regions of Tanzania. The loving care he took of the Mikindani Mosque and Imambada is living proof of his unpretentious nature and commitment to serving the community in very remote areas, often under difficult conditions.

By this time, the community had begun to regularly send students abroad for their higher education. The presence of Khoja Shia Ithna-Asheries from East Africa in the United Kingdom began in 1941. From conversations with past students, the first student to arrive was Jaffer Rahim who studied at London University. This was during the Second World War. Soon after, in the period 1945-1954, more students arrived from Zanzibar, Kampala, Dar es Salaam and Mwanza. By 1959, more than 18 students (male and female)[18] were studying in the UK. During this time, the family of Nazerali Jiwa migrated there from East Africa. Their arrival was a milestone for the small community of Khoja Shia Ithna-Asheri students.

The residence of Nazerali Jiwa family in Barnet, Middlesex, United Kingdom became the unofficial centre for religious gathering and networking. During one such gathering and in the presence of 17 people, a provisional committee was appointed to set up the East African Ithna-Asheri Union[19] with the Chairman of the East Africa Federation Haji Ebrahim H. Sheriff as its ex-officio patron. It was during his tenure that the Khoja Shia Ithna-Asheri students who arrived in the United Kingdom formally organized their Union. This indicates not only the close affinity they maintained with East Africa, but also an appreciation of the benefits accrued from the centralised efforts towards funding their education under the Federation.

At their meeting in May 1959, the Khoja Shia Ithna-Asheri students adopted a constitution. In this constitutional meeting, the question of membership was prominent in the minds of these students, just as it is in the larger established communities today. Whether to open up the membership to all or restrict it to Khoja Shia Ithna-Asheries elicited a lively debate. The general body, after due deliberation, resolved that open membership was not desirable and a geographical restriction was agreed up. Only those Shia Ithna-Asheries directly associated with or born in East Africa were eligible for membership.

Thus began the institutionalisation of Khoja Shia Ithna-Asheri Community in the United Kingdom which, over time, evolved into the London Jamaat. The London Jamaat, therefore, has the honour of being the first Khoja Shia Ithna-Asheri Jamaat in Europe.

The East African Ithna-Asheri Union was the first institution that held social and religious functions at a time when there was a cultural vacuum for these students. These functions - including marriage

---

FOND MEMORIES BY ALHAJ ANVER M RAJPAR
PRESIDENT, MEHFIL-E-MURTAZA

Though I now live in Karachi, my connection to the Khoja Shia Ithna-Asheri community of London dates back from my student days in the 1950s. In 1958, we students decided to form an organization to attend to the needs of Khoja Shia Ithna-Asheri of East African origin residing in London. A committee was formed to draft the constitution in which I took an active part. Within four months, a constitution was produced and the East African Ithna-Asheri Students' Union came into being.

I served as Secretary (1959-61) and then as President (1960-61). The union was dissolved upon the formation of the Khoja Shia Ithna-Asheri community of London. After my graduation, I left the UK but have always maintained contact with the London community. I have witnessed the development of the Husseini Shia Islamic Centre, Stanmore. Many people have contributed toward the development of this organisation and to all of them - living or dead - the community remains grateful.

FOND RECOLLECTIONS BY MOHSIN KAMALIA
PRESIDENT OF NASIMCO

When I last visited the Husseini Shia Islamic Centre, Stanmore in October 1988, I could not contain my joy at the development of our community in London. In the sixties when I was studying in the UK, I had the privilege of serving the Muslim Community of London. There was no Jamaat but we had an organization called the East African Ithna-Asheri union whose President I was from 1967-1968. When I recall those days and see the change today, tears of joy fill my eyes; many people have and still are contributing towards the

development of this Jamaat. We should not forget the pioneers whose contribution, is greater considering the difficulties they had to face and their own limitations in many fields.

ceremonies - were held in hired halls in different places until the formal physical set-up of London Jamaat.[20]

Ebrahimbhai was passionate about Islamic propagation outside the community. In 1962, under his leadership, Africa Federation received permission from Marja e Taqlid Ayatullah al Udhma Sayyid Muhsin al-Hakim to collect religious dues and spend the funds within Africa. On the recommendation of Ayatullah, work on Islamic propagation began soon after led by Maulana Sayed Saeed Akhtar Rizvi.[21]

In 1962, Maulana Rizvi prepared a scheme for *tabligh* and sent it to Ebrahimbhai. After some amendments, a pilot scheme was put into effect in 1963. Before the triennial Conference of the Africa Federation in Tanga in 1964, Sayed Rizvi's recommendations were circulated as a Secretariat paper and boosted following a resolution by Hussein Nasser Walji that called upon the Federation to become involved in *tabligh* activities among the local populace.

This 1964 memorandum on *tabligh* activities was ultimately adopted as a policy appropriately named as Bilal Muslim Mission, after the great African companion of the Prophet (pbuh) and first *Muazzin*[22] of

MOHAMMEDRAFIQ G SOMJI (1935-1989)

Born in Zanzibar, raised in Dar-es-Salaam, and having studied in India, MohamedRafiq received a breadth of exposure from a young age. His passion for serving the community began when he was appointed as Administrative Secretary of the Federation of KSI Jamaats of Africa at the age of 24, under the mentorship of Marhum Ebrahim Hussein Sheriff Dewji in 1959.

MohamedRafiq's witty nature and natural ability to connect with people from different lifestyles enabled him to establish good rapport with those that he sought to serve. His tenure with the community spanned most of his adult life. He was part of the Editorial Board of the Federation Samachar, and served as the Secretary of the Dar es Salaam Jamaat.

He was an active Secretary of Bilal Muslim Mission for more than 20 years under the patronage of Marhum Seyed Saeed Akhtar Rizvi. He served as Administrative Secretary for the Supreme Council under two former Chairmen: Marhum Ebrahim Hussein Sheriff Dewji and Marhum Mohamedali Meghji during which he often travelled on behalf of them to various jamaats. At the time of his death, he was serving as the Vice Chairman of Africa Federation under the leadership of Habib Mulji. MohamedRafiq dealt with community matters with the utmost presence of mind, especially during periods of conflict, which he resolved with grace. His interest in the well-being of the community never diminished even during the final months of his life when he was in poor health. He was an all round sportsman and had a great love for horse-riding. He was known for his jovial personality, and his death was a huge loss to the community.

Islam, Bilal. Maulana Rizvi was its chief missionary and his secretary for 20 years was MohamedRafiq Somji.

The setting up of this organisation under Maulana Rizvi[23] and the thinking that led to it brought about two changes. Firstly, a realisation that the function of a religious scholar could be much more than just lecturing and could be varied to take the full benefit of his or her knowledge. Secondly, it spurred and prompted the boys and girls from the community to engage in religious studies not only to better understand their faith deeper but also to explain their faith to others.[24]

During his term, Ebrahimbhai organized a special trip to visit the Jamaats of Madagascar, Mauritius and Reunion Island. These places were near each other geographically and had functioning Jamaats. He went in 1961, accompanied by Mohammedali Meghji, Sayed Amirhussein Naqvi, Gulamabbas Kassamali Bahadurali Mawji and Rafiq Somji. This was the first official delegation from the Federation visiting these places. They travelled by ship and their first stop was Mauritius.

From anecdotal oral sources, it appears that the aim of Ebrahimbhai's visit was to learn first-hand the state of Khoja Shia Ithna-Asheries there and how they could work together to fulfil their religious, economic and social needs. In Mauritius, they were received warmly by the community of 80 Khoja Shia Ithna-Asheries who regularly met in the small *imambada* of timber construction. They were hosted by the Pirbhouy family which was active in the community affairs. The delegation also visited Reunion Island where there was one functioning Jamaat.

In Madagascar, their first stop over was Majunga where they stayed for five days, hosted by Mohammed Bhalloo and Fazal Chennai. They travelled by road to Marwai and then to Maevatanana. In these places, the delegation met with the leaders of the Jamaats and the community members.

Their main destination was Antananarivo, the capital of Madagascar where there were 225 Khoja Shia Ithna-Asheries residing at the time (by 2022, the community had grown to 3000 Khoja Shia Ithna-

Asheries) and were hosted by Noormohammed Hiridjee. During this time, leaders from Antananarivo Jamaat and other Jamaats in Madagascar (15 Jamaats were known to exist at the time) met with the delegation to jointly chart out the way forward to mutually benefit all the communities.

Various challenges within the social, religious and economic fields were identified (broadly similar to what the Khoja Shia Ithna-Asheries of East Africa faced) and possible solutions on how to overcome them were discussed. One area that needed clarity was how best to institutionalise when communities are under two different colonial powers and subjected to different rules. Khoja Shia Ithna-Asheries of East Africa and Mauritius came under the British colonial rules whereas the Khoja Shia Ithna-Asheries of Reunion and Madagascar came under French colonial rules.

Time was needed for reflection on this as well as to develop the right constitution if Jamaats of Madagascar were to centralise. It was decided that the delegation return and a draft constitution be prepared in the meantime. Mohammed Amirali Bhalloo was appointed to coordinate contact and communication between the two leaderships. The delegation left Antananarivo and visited Tulear, Marondava and Belu Jamaats before returning to East Africa

In 1963, Ebrahimbhai and the delegation returned to Antananarivo and the other Jamaats in Madagascar. This time there were two aims in mind. Firstly, in their visit, many delegates had expressed difficulty in finding accommodation when visiting Antananarivo and requested that a musafarkhana be established to cater for visitors. During this visit, Ebrahimbhai went around the Jamaats in Madagascar to collect funds for this cause. He collected enough funds for the community to purchase a building in Antananarivo that was converted to a travellers' lodge. The community named it in his honour and to this day it is known as the Ebrahim Sherrif Dewji Musafarkhana.

The second aim was to chart the way forward for the two communities institutionally under a constitution. This time representatives from all Jamaats met in Tulear and a draft constitution was presented for discussion and adoption under the interim chairmanship of

Mohammed Amirali Bhalloo. Following the adoption of the constitution, the Territorial Council of Madagascar was established and Rajabali Sunderjee was elected as its first president. Soon after, the Territorial Council joined Africa Federation as a member.

Ebrahimbhai's plea to these Jamaats to join as members of the Federation to strengthen the resources within the community was a simple message and accepted and understood by the leaders and community members. At its core was a fundamental reality that working together with limited resources brings about progress and prosperity quickly for all; a united community benefits all the communities in Africa when in crisis.

The unity that was forged by Ebrahimbhai and his colleagues between the two communities endures to the present time. Today, this Territorial Council is known as Conseil Regional Des Khojas Shia Ithna-Asheri Jamaats De L'ocean Indien (CROI) with Mauritius as a member. In time, Reunion Island had four Jamaats that centralised and became members of the Africa Federation.

Ebrahimbhai was a visionary who was well ahead of his time. His presence as a leader of the community brought about a much-needed vibrancy and confidence in the idea that a community can achieve a great deal if its intellectual and material resources are directed correctly towards the objectives of the institution as agreed by the larger community

On the 10 of January 1964, whilst still at the helm of the community, Ebrahimbhai died suddenly in Zanzibar at a time when the community was facing profound political change.[25]

The shock of his premature passing away was felt deeply within and outside of Africa. He left a large vacuum and it fell to Mohammed Ali Shariff Jiwa to continue the mission of Marhum Ebrahimbhai in the interim until a new chairman was elected.

The community, suddenly deprived of a dynamic leader, needed to be reassured regarding both its stability and direction. Times were changing drastically and the community began to face nationalism

Marhum Ebrahim's final journey, 1964

Moving Tributes titled 'Tearful Remembrance' by Zinatali G Dewji of Singida, Tanganyika (Left) and 'Where Have You Gone, Our Leader' by "Anis" of Mwanza, Tanganyika (Right).

from the African majority who were taking over the control of their own destiny in East Africa. These changes presented challenges that were vastly different from those they had dealt with under German and British colonial governments. It was left to Alhaj Mohammedali Meghji, elected as Chairman in 1965, to provide this stability. He had a calm demeanour and mature presence which reassured the community.

DRAMA IN 1960 AT HAJI MOHAMMED JAFFER BOARDING HOUSE DURING SUPREME COUNCIL MEETING (NOW ALMUNTAZIR ISLAMIC SEMINARY)

Haji Mohammed Jaffer (pictured top left) Boarding House United Nations Road, Dar es Salaam

In 1960, Dar es Salaam Jamaat hosted the Africa Federation Supreme Council meeting. The president of the reception committee Murrabi N. M. Nasser delivered the speech to welcome the President, Councilors and Delegates for the Supreme Council Session. To honor the Councilors, Delegates and community members, boarding house organized a drama. The drama was in three in episodes of which the 1st episode was poetries, 2nd was Drama named *Sikandar-e-Azam* "Alexander the Great" and 3rd episode was about Akhlaq.

Student Poetry Session episode.
Front row, L-R: Mohammedhussein Bhimani, Firoz Kermali, Fateh Kermalli, Akber Alibhai, Akber Manji.

1st Poem	2nd Poem
*Aao bacho tumhe dikhae boarding bare shaan ki, jisme ilm milta hai ukhuwat aur iman ki, (Ithna-Asheri Boarding zindabad …*2)*	*Pratham Ali, bija Hassan, Hussein trija jaan, chotha Zainul Abedeen panjum Baqir naam*
*Haji Mohammed Jaffer ki hai Anokhi yeh sakhawat, Hai aur sakhi bhai or sakhawat ki alamat hai (Ithna-Asheri Boarding zindabad… *2)*	*che Jaffer Sadiq chatha, aadil apna Imam saacha jaano Saatma Mussa e kazim naam, Alireza che athma,*
*Ithni duniya hasil hai aur maarefat islam ki, iss boarding me ajayega aisa ek bacha jo, chand dino me banjayega sacha ek insaan jo, (Ithna-Asheri Boarding zindabad ….*2)*	*nawma Taqi nirdhar, daswa Naqi agyarwa, Hassan askari jaan, Imam chela barwa che Mahdi saheb Hukam khudathi haal che dunyama gayab,*
*Aao bacho tumhe dikhaye boarding bare shanki, jisme ilm milta hai ukhuwat aur iman ki (Ithna-Asheri Boarding zindabad ….*2)*	*teo bin dawo kare howano imam, jutho taddan jaanine taje tenu naaam.*

After the drama Murrabbi Ebrahimbhai Shariff Dewji (President of the Africa Federation) addressed the gathering to thank and appreciate the efforts of the boarding house for organizing such a wonderful drama. He also thanked the Councillors, Delegates and the Community members for attending.

Murrabi Ebrahimbhai Shariff Dewji, Sitting left to right: Murrabi N. M. Nasser (Chairman of organizing committee of host Jamaat) Murrabi Mohammedali Sheriff Jiwa (Vice President of the Africa Federation) and Murrabi Mahmood Rattansi (lawyer) from Dar es Salaam

DRAMA AT BOARDING HOUSE 1960
SIKANDAR E AZAM (ALEXANDER THE GREAT)
This photograph was taken after the Drama

Sitting L-R: *Mohammedhussein Kermali (Songea),Murtaza R Jivraj (Kigoma),Hussein Ladhu Jaffer (Kigoma), Asgher Rajani (Songea), Gulamali Noorali Rashid (Bukoba), Gulam Raza (Pangani), Hassan Ismail Lalji (DSM), Yusuf Ismail Lajli (DSM), Hussein Khatri (Kamachumu, Bukoba), Gulamabbas Dostmohammed (DSM), Mohammedraza Khimji (DSM), Mohammedhussein Bhimani (Bukoba), Sikandar Abdullah Fazal (Bukoba), Hassanali Abdullah Fazal (Bukoba), Hussein Mawji (Maya Maya), Mohammedhussein Mullani (Bukoba), Liyakat Khimji (DSM), Akber Manji (DSM), Hassan Karim Rehmtulla (Kigoma), Akber Alibhai (Malampaka, Mwanza), Mahmood Khimji (DSM), Aliraza (Ifakara)*

Standing L-R: *Asgar Karim Rehmtulla (Kigoma), Gulamabbas Sumar (Mwanza), Sultan Bhimani (Bukoba), Firoz Gulamhussein Kermali (Kigoma), Rustam Molledina (Bukoba), Yusuf Arab (Lindi), Hussein Arab (Lindi), Anverali Noorali Rashid (Bukoba), Mohammedtaki Mohammedali Kara (Bukoba), Ahmed Manek (Singida) as Sikandar, Amir Khatri (Kamachumu, Bukoba), Hussein Khimji (DSM), Hassanali Jadavji (Lindi), Fidahussein Noorali Rashid (Bukoba), Habib Esmail Rai (Mwanza), Esmail Jassat (Mbeya), Fateh Keramali (Masasi Lindi), Hussein Rajani (Songea), Akber Habib Jadavji (Arusha), Amirali Mohamedali Kara (Bukoba).*

By 1960, Africa Federation - with 50 *jamaats* unified under it - spoke for the Khoja Shia Ithna-Asheries of Africa. The organisation had grown in stature and rightfully earned the respect of its members. They now had a formidable voice to address their challenges and pursue the relevant paths to fulfilling their needs. Around this time, they also adopted a flag to embody their essential principles.[26]

The green background in the flag represented the hope that Islam gives to humanity, the twelve stars surrounding the Ka'bah represented the twelve holy personalities from the family of the Prophet (pbuh) through whom knowledge of Islam reached the community, the Ka'bah in the centre was for the belief in Allah (SWT) on which the entire community was founded, *Hajar al-aswad* (the black stone) stood for their objective which was to serve God and the crescent on the flag pole symbolised brotherhood. This flag, and its various elements was also a statement of the progressive elimination of any Hindu/Ismaili relics that may have been inherited from their origins. The community was now fully aligned to Islamic objectives according to Shia Ithna-Asheri tenets and were proud to proclaim this.

The Community Flag hoisted in Mombasa by Alhaj Ebrahimbhai, on his left are Fidahussein Rashid and Hussein Jeraj

FLAG RAISING CEREMONY

In early 1960s Africa Federation introduced the tradition of raising the Africa Federation flag on the occasion of Eid al-Fitr in all member Jamaats. This tradition was for solidarity and unity of the community, and members took great pride in this ceremony. Unfortunately, the tradition later stopped in the small Jamaats due to migration of the members and is now performed in some Jamaats only.

Flag raising ceremony, Mwanza 1962

Abdulrasul Muman reciting verse from the Qur'an before flag raising, Kigoma, 1964

Ladhubahi Jaffer raising the flag in Kigoma

Alhaj Pyarali Shivji hoisting the AFED flag in Dar es Salaam on the eve of Eid ul Fitr. Looking on are Alhaj Azim Dewji, Alhaj Anwarali Dharamsi, Alhaj Murtaza Jivraj, Alhaj Aunali Khalfan and community members.

Another important change brought by Khoja Shia Ithna-Asheries under the federation was the unification of resources. Together, the Jamaat and Federation leadership began to take on the responsibilities for various projects including centralising funds, controlling the movements of religious scholars, unifying the Madrasah syllabus, providing assistance to the needy, planning for the economic upliftment of less fortunate members, and giving educational aid to those intending to go overseas for religious or secular studies.

The most immediate outcome of all this was that closer ties were created between the members of the constituent Jamaats, which allowed them to become aware of and sympathise with the challenges some of them faced. There was increased interaction between community leadership and the religious scholars from Najaf and apart from spiritual guidance, these interactions also led to priorities being set by the Federation for spending towards religious projects within East Africa.

What had begun as an inspiring plea by Marhum Abdulhusein Sachedina had now become a reality in the form of a Federation that brought about the entrenchment of Shia Ithna-Asheri faith as well as unity of purpose and function. "Entrenchment" and "Unity" thus became the core twin pillars that underpinned all the institutions of Khoja Shia Ithna-Asheries in East Africa and beyond.

Externally, the Federation represented the community at various governmental and non-governmental forums and spoke on behalf of the community. Internally, it provided a mechanism for settling disputes within the community. Any member, whose behaviour is unreasonable comes under moral pressure to mend his ways. If this fails, a resolution is passed at the highest forum of the Federation either condemning the conduct of that member or requesting him to rescind or refrain from his actions. As a last resort, the option of a sanction and removal of the offending member is always available to the central body, but seldom used.

5.3 Khoja Shia Ithna-Asheries and the Changing Political Backdrop

As the region began to gain its independence and seek an identity of its own as a continent, the negative consequences of the colonial policy of racial separation began to emerge rapidly. The separate development that the non-European population suffered had left a hostile perception in the psyche of a majority of the African population. East Africa now faced an unwanted legacy of bitter racial animosities left behind by their colonial masters.

In the 1960s, Indians in East Africa had a successful hold over commerce, which formed an essential part of the economy. Despite a lack of comprehensive information, there are some revealing statistics available.[27] Between 1935 and 1946, Kenyan Indians invested £32,709,000 in private companies, £2,379,000 in commercial property and £223,000 in agricultural estates.[28] By 1936, 6680 Kenya Indians compared with 3451 Kenya Europeans held deposits in a Post Office Savings Bank. In Tanganyika, 349 Indians held a combined total of 316,000 acres of land.

In 1946, they paid an estimated £860,000 in import and excise duties on commodities.[29] In 1951, some 3000 Tanganyika Indians were employing 108,860 workers. By 1960, 8,707 Tanganyika Indians were engaged in commerce, 1,999 in manufacturing, 1,953 in public services, 1,852 in transport, 898 in agriculture, and 809 in construction. In Uganda, Indians acquired 42,512 acres and by 1936, they owned 105 of the 137 registered ginneries. In Zanzibar, 20 of the 22 licensed exporters were Indians/Asians. This gives some indication as to the depth of economic penetration achieved by the Indians/Asians in East Africa at the time.

This scale of economic dominance held by Indians became a source of resentment on the part of the Africans as they felt that the Indians, particularly the retail merchants, were an obstacle to their progress. Furthermore, the various educational and welfare institutions that the Indians had established in the country were for the most part confined to members of their own communities, thus socially insulating themselves from the African population. This was not intentional, but the outcome of the colonial racially divisive policy imposed upon the non-European population. Nevertheless, it created an obvious segregated way of functioning that reinforced the tension that was already present.

With the Mau Mau movement[30] creating political uncertainties in Kenya and Uganda, the central leadership of the Khoja Shia Ithna-Asheries felt that the three East African countries could very likely develop dissimilar political strategies after independence. One of the leading lights of our community, Jaffar M Jaffer and other members including Ebrahim Sheriff Dewji, Dost Moledina, Mohamedali

Sheriff, Satchu Gulamali, and Gulam Haji called a conference of the Tanganyika Jamaats to safeguard the interest of the region. They formed the Tanganyika Territorial Council under the aegis of the Africa Federation. Bashir Rahim was entrusted with the task of drafting a constitution for this organisation and the Executive Council of the East African Federation recognized the value of this institution at a later stage.[31]

Under the Tanganyika Territorial Council, a Boarding House for students was established and maintained in Dar es Salaam. Commercial companies like Jamhuri Sisal Estate and National Invest Company Ltd. for leasing residential and commercial estates were established and shares made available to community members. There was an ambitious matchsticks-making company which later was sold.

In 1964, Tanganyika Parliament passed the "Islamic" Law (New Statement) which empowered the Minister of Legal Affairs to compile and publish an Islamic Law. Consultation paper. Mohammed G Dhirani who was the President of the Tanganyika Territorial Council took the initiative of contacting the government and Maulana Akhter Rizvi was tasked with producing a document by the Government official. He wrote out Islamic law papers relating to marriage, divorce, marriage agreement, wills, inheritance and *waqf*.

These papers (with information) were eventually passed on to Mr. Bashir Rahim, a legal member who scrutinized these papers on behalf of the government. They were published under the authority of Mr. Rashid Kawawa, then Vice President of Tanzania, who was also in charge of the Legal Department. After discussion and revision, the collated document became a by-law enacted under the new official Statement of Islamic Law (No. 56 of 1964) (In) Gazette Extraordinary (Government No. 34 of 27 June 1967).[32]

As local animosity towards the Indian settlers increased, the Khoja Shia Ithna-Asheries watched from the sidelines with trepidation the adverse effect the rising tide of African nationalism could potentially bring upon them. The community needed guidance on the way forward and expected their leadership, both local and central, to provide direction regarding their future settled status. However, without having any substantial political influence, all that the respective leadership could do was urge the community to adapt and prepare for the political changes that were inevitably coming.

Although the changes that came with independence were primarily political, they had a huge impact on the economic, social and educational aspirations of Africans, who were the majority. The Khoja Shia Ithna-Asheries had to accept that the days of exclusive community development were over and make a profound re-adjustment in their mentality and perspective. Their resources would now need to be shared with all the citizens of the country irrespective of faith and ethnicity.

The withdrawal of British colonial rule followed by the establishment of independent African governments from the late 1950s to the early 1960s brought a dramatic change within Khoja Shia Ithna-Asheries milieu which had so far prospered in sheltered enclaves during colonial times. The degree and the level of changed circumstances would demand a total overhaul in their social organisation and economic aspirations. Challenging questions arose: How should Khoja Shia Ithna-Asheries respond to this momentous change? What would the repercussions be on their socio-religious identity?

Of course with the passage of time and the preservation of historical records, we have been able to study how the community chose to respond and how it affected their economic prosperity and viability. The answers to these questions are not the subject of this book and will *insha'Allah* be explored in the second volume.

Concluding Remarks: The Identity of the Khoja Shia Ithna-Asheries of East Africa

Upon their arrival in Zanzibar and the East African coastal towns of Lamu, Mombasa, Bagamoyo and Kilwa, the Khoja Shia Ithna-Asheries found themselves in an environment strikingly different from the one they had left. Their new surroundings[1] presented challenges and opportunities, both internally and externally, for the nascent community that required important modifications in their outlook and how they organised the social structure of their community.

At the Belief Level

At a belief level, the *Satpanthi*-Khoja[2] connection is not evident in the beliefs and practices of the East African Khoja Shia Ithna-Asheries. For example, they did not attach a great amount of reverence to Pir Sadr al-Din, who is widely accepted as a Satpanthi *Dai* (preacher) nor to readings of *ginans*.[3] This connection has not been observed from the records examined so far. However, what is noticeable is the retention of the terms such as *dharm*,[4] *matam*,[5] *alam*,[6] *azadari*,[7] as well as terms that later emerged from within the East African Ithna-Asheries such as Hussein Day,[8] *Julus*,[9] *Khushali Bankro*,[10] *Nai Misit*[11] and *Mehfile Private*.[12] The practices of these terminologies gave the Khoja Shia Ithna-Asheries their own distinction in Zanzibar.

Beliefs and values are two closely linked facets within the Khoja Shia Ithna-Asheri community. In some instances, the relationship between the two is straightforward, as evident when one studies the constitutions of Khoja Shia Ithna-Asheri Jamaats of East Africa and its regional federation. In other instances, particularly when one studies the Khoja Shia Ithna-Asheri global diaspora, it becomes more subtle and demands a complex interpretation.

Overall, however, the fact remains that Khoja Shia Ithna-Asheries of East Africa developed their organisational structures based on the reciprocity of beliefs and values and continue to maintain this principle to date. Why and how these factors became more entrenched within the organisational structures of the community is the subject matter of the second volume of this book.

When considering the conflicts that preceded the Khoja Case of 1866, we noted the inherent ambiguities regarding the primary, dominant beliefs of the Khoja community. There is consensus among scholars that the Khoja beliefs and practices pre-1866 comprised of Hindu ideas integrated with Islamic tenets or vice versa, depending on which framework one chooses for analysis.

What is certain is that the eventual outcome of the 1866 Khoja Case brought about splits within the Khoja community. One of the groups that broke away and evolved its own identity was the Khoja Shia Ithna-Asheri.

The process had been gradual but began to accelerate after 1866. Whilst the parting gave a vivid sense of independence to the Khoja Shia Ithna-Asheries, the process itself placed severe strains on this small community that emerged from the secure umbrella of a larger Khoja community into a tentative future. The early pioneers of the Khoja Shia Ithna-Asheri community had to undergo physical and mental struggles in the face of ostracization for their religious principles. Their willingness to change their foundational beliefs is a testament to their search for truth.

The next struggle, as we have described and analysed to some extent in this work, was to maintain and strengthen this faith. They knew the importance of unity and organisation required for this journey and immediately set about to put structures in place where possible.

By 1960, the Khoja Shia Ithna-Asheries of East Africa had emerged from their mission with a secure sense of their distinctive identity. They had succeeded in organising themselves into elaborate rule-based communities that fulfilled the objectives they had originally set out. An extremely important point to note is that in East Africa, Khoja Shia Ithna-Asheries built their structures around the principles of the Ithna-Asheri faith. I did not find any obvious *Satpanthi*-Khoja connection evident in community practices. Instead, everything revolved around Shia Ithna-Asheri tenets, including the flag they adopted in 1960. The Shia Ithna-Asheri faith mattered to the community above all else. In the ultimate analysis, therefore, the root of their distinct identity is based on the Ithna-Asheri faith that in turn determines their functioning values.

At the Structural Level

At a broad glance, we do see various aspects of the Khoja's organisational practices that match those within the Khoja communities in Kachchh, Kathiawad and Mumbai. For example, they adopted an autonomously-functioning *jamaat*[13] ethos with a regular congregation gathering in the *Imambada*[14] (or *Imamwada* or *Imambargah*). The titles *Mukhi*[15] and *Kamadia*[16] that originated from the Khoja community are still accepted functioning roles in many Khoja Shia Ithna-Asheri Jamaats[17] in East Africa.

Historically, the Khoja community in India met a number of times annually to discuss matters important to the community, to appoint leaders, set yearly contributions for various communal expenses, and arbitrate or decide on various issues including cases relating to marriage and divorce. These modes of functioning also exist in many Khoja Shia Ithna-Asheri Jamaats in East Africa albeit in a more formal setting.

At this level, the predominant drive amongst the Khoja Shia Ithna-Asheries of East Africa was towards self-sufficiency and preservation of their faith. It was this that motivated them to keep evolving their organisational structures to adapt to the times; a tactic which would enable the community to achieve prosperity whilst preserving its faith.

The *jamaat* is the oldest, most powerful, autonomous institution that can be found within the hierarchy of the East African community. Khoja Shia Ithna-Asheries closely guarded this autonomy and by 1960, each *jamaat* in East Africa had its own constitution. In this way, they continued to maintain, under this constitutional accountability, the organisational practices that existed within the Khoja community before the arrival of Aga Khan I in India in 1844. This method of working suited them as it provided for regular meetings and appointments of leaders at Jamaat and Federation levels. It also included a voluntary mechanism to resolve disputes and actively seek contributions for communal work.

As the economic, cultural and political arena began to change in the East Africa of the late 1950s, the drive to organise and grow became urgent. To overcome the new challenges they faced, the community needed to review their mode of functioning. This was achieved by shifting their focus on institutionalisation and centralisation. However, the *jamaats* only ceded their autonomy to a regional federation after consultation with other *jamaats* led to the conclusion that a central functioning body was necessary.

Even as they adapted and changed their structural framework, they were keen to preserve their Ithna-Asheri faith identity on a deeper principle level, as well as retain their Khoja identity on an observable plane. This aimed to sustain the harmony between their "religious" and "social" identity. The acculturation and the subsequent shift in interaction patterns between the Ithna-Asheri beliefs and the cultural life of the community form an essential part of their core behaviour.

By the 1960s, the Khoja Shia Ithna-Asheries were able to develop a centralised way of working that was a catalyst for their further religious, social and economic growth within East Africa and beyond.

The organisational experiences of East African Khoja Shia Ithna-Asheries and their impact on the global community were succinctly articulated by the Secretary-General of the World Federation of Khoja Shia Ithna-Asheries in his report to the 1997 World Federation conference held in London, UK. He writes:

Let history of ours (sic) record that our community from Africa in particular and Khoja communities throughout the world who originate from there gave the World Federation[18] all - unfailingly. From our community in Africa, the assistance came in the form of guidance, for they had more than 30 years of institutional history at the time of the birth of the World Federation. More importantly, the absolute support given to the World Federation was in the form of funding. From these funds, the World Federation supported many projects, such as providing shelter for the poor of our community, building schools for the children of our community, Islamic centres for the community to carry out its socio-religious activities, publication of religious books for Tabligh in the community and supporting Zainabiya Child Sponsorship Scheme.

When the community in the West required imambadas, masjids and madrasahs to be established, the community in Africa donated generously and beyond expectation. It is no exaggeration to state that nearly 25% of the cost for such centres in the West has been borne by the Khoja Shia Ithna-Asheries of Africa. This is the extent of generosity from this part of our community that today we have more than 25 mosques, imambadas and socio-religious centres for Khoja Shia Ithna-Asheries in the West.[19]

At the Communal Identity level

By 1880[20], the construction of the identity of Khoja Shia Ithna-Asheries had begun. It was shaped in the first instance by the adversities they had to face when they separated from the main Khoja community on religious grounds and later on, largely fashioned by the experiences they underwent in East Africa. According to Woodward[21] and Pilkington[22] the construction of identities based on oppositions[23] when applied to Khoja Shia Ithna-Asheries is simplistic.

This way of constructing identity - based on antagonism - misses out on the underlying complexity that underpins the evolution of the Khoja Shia Ithna-Asheri community. In the case of the Khoja Shia Ithna-Asheries, oppositional dynamics were not as important as their fundamental search for truth. This search and the dynamism surrounding it continues to play an important role even today. For many pioneers, parting from the larger Khoja community where they had built strong socio-religious ties and transiting to a new, smaller and not yet identifiable group of people was an anxious time of uncertainty. As Mercer puts it succinctly, this anxiety takes over deeply '...when something assumed to be fixed, coherent and stable is displaced by the experience of doubt and uncertainty....'[24]

Nevertheless, the community remained firm in their newly chosen beliefs, wrestled with doubts and chose for itself the name "Khoja Shia Ithna-Asheri" as it resonated with the principles that mattered to them deeply. For an identity of an ethnic group like Khoja Shia Ithna-Asheri to exist, it is not necessary for all within the community to agree on how or what defines them. It is sufficient to establish the terms of identity over which they can debate and negotiate.[25]

Writing the history of the Khoja Shia Ithna-Asheri community in the East African context is also a search for theories on how the community evolved its identity. Scholars have surmised the various ways in which identities are constructed and I share some of my thoughts on this below.

Randall Pouwels[26] talks about the High Islam of the Qur'an and the Ulama (learned teachers) versus Popular Islam which is practised by ordinary people. For Pouwels, the arrival of Sayed Said and his court in Zanzibar in the 1840s is a key factor in the formation of the communal identity. He examines at length the changes brought about by the introduction of new types of Ulama, the administrative types who brought literacy and a higher form of Islam as well as the charismatic types who gave rise to Sufi brotherhoods that shaped the identity of communities in Zanzibar.

In the case of Khoja Shia Ithna-Asheries, their communal rise and evolution was not Ulama-led but based on a search for the right faith spearheaded largely by scholars and leaders from amongst themselves. It was these men who led the separation and survival, as a faith-based community, from the main Khoja community. Many also believe that the identity of the Muslim community is constructed solely by the ideals of Islamic faith and practice. The problem here is not so much of having to explain events without reference to Islam but of weaving many sub-cultures within it that are different to each other.

Some like anthropologist Jean-Loup Amselle's notion of syncretism and negotiation offer a continuity approach that would emphasize every culture dissolves into a series of conflictual or peaceful practices used by its actors to continually renegotiate their identity.[27] In the case of Khoja Shia Ithna-Asheries, this is a process which began perhaps with Pir Sadrudin almost 700 years ago and continues as the community globalises and crosses cultural boundaries, especially for the Khoja Shia Ithna-Asheries in the West.

Talal Asad[28] explains that in the performance of a ritual like the *Maulidi ya Kiswahili*[29], we can read both agency and domination. According to him, this is a first step toward creating richness and complexity from small bits and pieces of the relics we call evidence. Applying Foucault's[30] notion that power can be both generative and destructive and is embedded in and created by both discourse and practice into the construction of identity, one can begin to investigate ways in which power was negotiated and produced at "multiple sites".

In the case of the Khoja Shia Ithna-Asheries of Zanzibar - and one can argue this for all within East Africa - the "Swahili" ethos was a comfortable space to practice their faith and in time "Swahili language and culture" was also subsumed within the East African Khoja Shia Ithna-Asheries as a distinct part of their identity compared to Khoja Shia Ithna-Asheries from the sub-continent. This provides, perhaps an understanding of why people in East Africa defined what it meant to be a Muslim and to be Swahili in a complimentary way.

All these works point to a continual process of evolving, forming and re-forming relationships between individuals as well as groups in a society. When we study the social relationships of settled Khoja Shia Ithna-Asheri communities of East Africa, we can see these inter-relationships playing out within a society that was guided by the Shia Ithna-Asheri ethos in its constituent parts and everyday life. We can also uncover the dynamic nature of religious tenets engaged with social reality (colonial and Indian influences) and the tensions that these engagements sometimes create. We observe the community developing its own unique social-religious identity as a product of trading relations that encompassed the Indian Ocean, extending from India to the Middle East and Africa.

The Swahili culture that had been influenced over centuries by African and Arab cultural and linguistic forms as well as Islam, now shaped the Khoja Shia Ithna-Asheri community. The Khoja community's experience of syncretising Islam/Hindu heritage could have provided a template to use and easily adapt to the nature of Swahili society within a predominantly Islamic value matrix. A blend of the Khoja (Islam/Hindu) and Swahili (Islam/Bantu) cultures created a comfortable "space" for appropriate interaction with/adaptation to/diffusion from the host Swahili community that then contributed to the construction of an identity the Khoja Shia Ithna-Asheries of East Africa could comfortably live with.

Being part of the Indian diaspora in East Africa also had its nuanced complexity. In this regard, the Zanzibar Khoja Case of 1956[31] was instructive. The case centred on, among other issues, the non-Khoja identity of one of the defendants, who was a member of the Khoja Shia Ithna-Asheri community of Zanzibar. As a result, he could not hold the trusteeship of a *Waqf*[32] as the constitution clearly stated that the trustee must be a Khoja Shia Ithna-Asheri. This was an internal dispute within the Kuwwatul Islam Jamaat of Zanzibar. I do not want to dwell on the internal dispute but instead explore one of the main issues the court had to decide i.e. whether a person could claim to be a Khoja when he or she was not born Khoja or whether the term embraced only those who were Khoja by birth, meaning both parents or at least their father was a Khoja.

In arriving at the meaning of the term "Khoja", the court had to address two irreconcilable views that had emerged during the hearing of the case. The court found that the historical origin of the Khoja was not in dispute; all parties agreed that the name "Khoja" originally applied to a community of Indians who first converted to a Shia branch of faith and belonged to the Ismailia sect.[33] The logic that flowed from this common understanding was that in Zanzibar, a "Khoja by birth" was descended from the original Khoja community some 500 - 700 years ago. The point of dispute, however, was whether one could call oneself a "Khoja by adoption" on the ground that he or she had joined the Khoja Shia Ithna-Asheri community from an early age, was embraced by them and, in turn, embraced the culture of the community.

In order to resolve this particular conundrum, the court explored whether "Khoja" was a description of a caste in an Indian sense, involving membership through heredity, or merely that of a community, which on certain conditions one may join without having been born into it. Here, the judge accepted that, in a strict sense, "Khoja" referred to those born into the community from a member who descended from the original Khoja community. However, from this position, the judge pragmatically gave credibility also to the claim of being a Khoja by adoption. He took his authority from the decision delivered on 17 April 1955 at the Central Council of the Federation of Khoja Shia Ithna-Asheri Jamaats that a person ought to be a true Khoja based on his record of interaction and involvement within the community.

The 1956 decision was peculiar to the circumstances present and unlikely to be repeated given that Kuwwat Jamaat's constitution was amended since then to only admit members of "Khoja" origin. Nevertheless, it created an option for the Khoja Shia Ithna-Asheri community to define the term "Khoja" on its own terms and grant membership to non-Khojas based on their embracing the tenets of faith and cultural norms of the community.

The approach of the Central Body of the Federation of Khoja Shia Ithna-Asheri Jamaats in dealing with identity is instructive. It was moving away from the strict hereditary notions of "Khoja" to a pragmatically evolved position set by the community itself. Professor Iqbal who explored late 19th century identity formation and caste boundaries among the Khoja of colonial Zanzibar candidly writes:

> ...the central concern regarding children born to a non-Khōjā parent was what status, particularly regarding rights of inheritance, the multiracial children born of these relationships had within the Khoja community. The case of *Nasur Jesa v. Hurbayee*[34] suggests that the attitude toward these children was inconsistent; sometimes they were embraced, and at other times they were shunned by the Khoja community. Nasur Jesa

was recognized as Khoja because his father willed it. Nasur Jesa was known by the prominent Khoja leaders in Zanzibar, despite living in Kilwa Kivinje, because he had attended caste functions, had been instructed in the rudiments of Gujarati, and was included in his father's last will and testament. He became Khoja through his father's insistence and public recognition, though with the adjective *chotara* attached to his person. For a *chotara* child to be Khoja means to be raised in full view of and with the community.[35]

The Nasur Jesa case of 1878 and the Zanzibar Khoja case of 1956 brought out the complexity of identity issues, which was expressed well by Gijsbert Oonk who wrote:

> It is acknowledged that Indian migrants abroad tend to reproduce their own religions, family patterns, and cultures as much as possible. At the same time, however, they adjust to local circumstances. Caste and language issues have to be negotiated in new environments. This is not a natural process, but one in which great efforts need to be made-sometimes in an effort to maintain one's own culture, but also with regard to the host society....[36]

In dealing with who a Khoja is, the globalised Khoja Shia Ithna-Asheri may want to take on board what the court in 1956 decided. This issue of the "Khoja" part of its identity, comfortably accepted within the East Africa ethos, remains an anomaly for the younger generation - particularly those born and settled in the West.

This is because the social environment that the Khoja Shia Ithna-Asheries encountered upon settling in Europe, Canada, and United States was religiously plural and multi–cultural. They found themselves in a world completely different from the one they left in East Africa, so whilst they organised themselves into Jamaats - a form of organised functioning they were used to - they quickly realised that they could not remain aloof from other Muslim communities. They needed to build relationships with other Shia Ithna-Asheries and open up to other cultures and ideologies.

It is natural that the community would want to retain its Khoja Shia Ithna-Asheri identity in the West but increasingly, they came under pressure to open up membership to those who were not Khoja. Inevitably, how a Khoja is defined in the 21ˢᵗ century within a globalising community generates interesting points of view.

From the late 1970s, when the Khoja Shia Ithna-Asheries first began migrating to the West, to this day, the word "Khoja" generates passionate debates around its inclusion as a mark of identity. At its core, the main point of contention for the Khoja Shia Ithna-Asheri diaspora is the same one the 1956 court in Zanzibar had to deal with. In addition, the Khoja Shia Ithna-Asheries settled in the West also wrestle with reconciling their Khoja identity and the need to evolve into a cohesive Shia community.

On the issue of diaspora, Gijsbert Oonk also remarks that

> [the] Indian diaspora, whilst embracing all those whose roots originate from India, has complexity within the words 'Indian' and the word 'Diaspora' that needs to be unveiled and research made available.[37]

Diaspora has alternative definitions, different approaches, and new suggestions that are constantly emerging in academic journals. Steven Vertovec[38] proposes three meanings of the term diaspora: A. as a social form; B. as a type of consciousness; C. as a mode of cultural production. In the case of Khoja Shia Ithna-Asheries, given its unique diaspora narrative, the nearest meaning that can perhaps match this narrative is a "type of consciousness", but one that did not tie them to the homeland of Kachchh and Kathiawad.

I say this because by the late 1950s, there was no "diaspora longing" for Kachchh or Kathiawad in the hearts of the Khoja Shia Ithna-Asheries. In my research, I did not find - anecdotally or otherwise – record of such sentiments that the "heart" was somewhere other than where the "body" was. They did not suffer a split of belongingness between two or more distinct and distant geographical sites. By 1960, Khoja Shia Ithna-Asheries did not differentiate between "residence" and "homeland", where people keep their connections alive through nostalgia, stories, tangible networks, religious and cultural practices, and so on. In fact, they saw East Africa as their home and Kachchh and Kathiawad as mere places of origin. Hence, the language of diaspora that overemphasises connections with an acknowledged homeland and highlights what differentiates the diaspora people, did not apply to Khoja Shia Ithna-Asheries in the 1960s. In East Africa, they were comfortably at "home".

The construction of the Khoja Shia Ithna-Asheri identity relies on multiple factors: their experiences upon arrival in East Africa, the separation from the greater Khoja community and the cohesive manner in which they blended their faith and the Swahili culture.

Their identity can also be said to have evolved from its Indian geographical and cultural roots, the religious change from Hinduism to Ismailism to the Shia Ithna-Asheri faith as well as the influence of colonialism and nationalism from their new land. In this respect, they are no different from any other Indians who had migrated and settled in East Africa. However, there are some unique defining values that allow Khoja Shia Ithna-Asheries to emerge as a distinct community.

'Khoja Shia Ithna-Asheri' - A Definition

The earlier pioneers[39] were in search of a deep-rooted religious identity based on the love for Prophet Muhammad (pbuh), his family, and the Twelve Imams (pbut). This was the raison d'être for the pioneers to part from the main Khoja community. The love and respect they had for these figures and the values they held became central to their sense of self. At the same time, they retained certain cultural values such as respect for elders, an attachment to food and a healthy value for home life.

Every member of the community was connected through their shared experiences so that they were all considered part of one large extended family. Identity construction for Khoja Shia Ithna-Asheries was about more than just an individual's background, values, interests, relationships or a way of life; it also took into account his or her social and communal dimensions. Both individual and communal identities developed from religion, culture, societal participation, and personal relationships. These distinctions have evolved from earlier pioneers to now 2nd, 3rd, 4th and 5th generations via family units, that act as a secure vehicle of transmission. With every new experience, the ideas of selfness were redefined and reshaped.

For Khoja Shia Ithna-Asheries, the family unit is foundational.[40] In order to safeguard it, the early Khoja Shia Ithna-Asheries built strong relationships between themselves. As we have already observed, when two families settled in one area, they would meet at each other's houses to keep the tradition of mourning, praising and understanding the Ahlulbayt (pbut) alive.

As the number of families increased, *imambadas* were built as soon as the small community could manage. A *mimbar*[41], would be placed in one corner for religious lectures that were aimed at drawing the people into the *imambada*. For Khoja Shia Ithna-Asheries without centralised religious leadership, the *mimbar* provided a platform for scholars to offer guidance at religious gatherings. These gatherings offered opportunities for social connectivity and networking that made it possible for unique bonds to be established between community members.[42]

The *madrasah*, as an institution, became the backbone of religious education for youngsters of Khoja Shia Ithna-Asheries.[43] These were initially set up within homes and then transitioned to *imambadas* until separate *madrasah* buildings could be built. Children were taught religious fundamentals and as they grew older, given the basic knowledge for religious understanding and practice. It seems that wherever there has been a Khoja Shia Ithna-Asheri *imambada* in East Africa, a *madrasah* has been established beside it.

These developments strongly suggest that the first generation of Khoja Shia Ithna-Asheries in East Africa wanted to make sure that the values and practices of the Ahlulbayt (pbut) were passed on to their children. The cohesiveness within the Khoja Shia Ithna-Asheries was based on respect, love, and a religious upbringing. They understood at a very early stage of their evolution that the moral fabric that they wanted to weave throughout the community was wholly dependent on there being spiritual and healthy family units.

The early pioneers also understood and appreciated their vulnerabilities in the new land. They remembered first-hand the difficult dhow journeys they endured together, how they served each other's needs and were able to form durable bonds with each other through these support systems. They aimed at - and succeeded in - creating a sense of belonging within a network of social relationships built around their newly found faith. This connectedness gave profound meaning, self-worth and identity to their existence.

By 1960, Khoja Shia Ithna-Asheri had organised their identity according to several deliberate and distinct characteristics.

Firstly, they abandoned the Khojki script for Gujarati, breaking that connection with their traditional past. When the Khoja Shia Ithna-Asheries moved from the Khojki script to the Gujarati script, as Iqbal Akhtar puts it that

> ...they created the first systematic transliteration system to represent the Arabic script in Gujarati, as it was heavily laden with Persian and Arabic terminology.[44]

This transition was a calculated orientation towards their Muslim identity, whilst still keeping a vernacular script. They also preferred to take their Islamic authority from Najaf and later on from Qum, as their relationship with the *Marja e taqlid* (religious reference) became an important source of communal advice from the 1960s onwards.

Secondly, they had a communal history of exclusion from the Khoja community, but at the same time retained the caste name "Khoja". Official documents in the archive section of the Africa Federation provide no rationale for this. One plausible explanation could be that the word reminded them of their struggle in search of a new faith that eventually led to excluding themselves from their main community. At the same time, they wanted to distinguish their move towards a positive and better understanding of their beliefs and added "Shia Ithna-Asheri" to their chosen title.

Thirdly, the Khoja Shia Ithna-Asheries became aware of their multi-locality in India, Pakistan, Tanzania, Uganda, Kenya, Mauritius,

Reunion, Madagascar, and Aden. The notion of sharing the same roots made them aware of their connection with each other through their shared identity. Their struggle in search of faith had on one hand led to their exclusion from the Khoja community and on the other, to bridging gaps with other communities in East Africa and beyond.

Fourthly, the Khoja Shia Ithna-Asheries of East Africa being local and connected beyond geographical boundaries created a further 'consciousness' of being able to identify with the locality within the country e.g. Khoja Shia Ithna-Asheri Jamaat of Zanzibar, Dar es Salaam, Mombasa, Kampala, Arusha and Moshi. Here we observe their ability to fashion multiple identities under the over-arching umbrella identity of 'Khoja Shia Ithna-Asheri'. This gave them an identity within specific religious beliefs i.e. 'Khoja Shia Ithna-Asheri' and not only a 'Khoja' identity.

Taylor expresses ideas on identity around which a useful definition of the Khoja Shia Ithna-Asheries of East Africa can be constructed. He states that

> one's 'identity' is defined by the commitments and identifications which provide the frame or horizon within which [one] can try to determine from case to case what is good, or valuable, or what ought to be done, or what [one can] endorse or oppose.[45]

The above definition of identity can be seen within the history of the Khoja Shia Ithna-Asheri community of East Africa. It has taken on what is good or valuable to its development and as a rule-based community collectively decided on what needs endorsing or opposing.

Based on all this, I have defined the Khoja Shia Ithna-Asheri identity as follows:

> *'Primarily, it is shaped by being part of the main Khoja community that, seemingly, originated from mainly Lohanas of Gujarat. These early Lohanas were converted to a mixture of beliefs by Persian Pirs who bestowed upon them the honorific title "Khwaja" (Khoja in Gujarati). This identity was then moulded by the hardships they faced when they changed their beliefs to Shia Ithna-Asheri and separated*

from the main Khoja and then further fashioned by their experiences as a diaspora community.

'Identity construction for Khoja Shia Ithna-Asheries, therefore, involves more than just an individual's cultural background, uniqueness, dignity, values, interests, relationships or personal way of life; it also includes his or her social or communal dimension.

'Both individual and communal aspects of identity originated and developed from religion, culture, societal participation, and personal relationships formed with each other. The evolving identity of Khoja Shia Ithna-Asheries has passed on from earlier pioneers to successive generations through the family units which acted as a secure vehicle of transmission.'

For a small community, it is indeed remarkable that the Khoja Shia Ithna-Asheries were able to build their own identity and keep it alive for almost 170 years in the face of massive cultural, religious, economical and political challenges globally.

As we navigate the 21st century and the rise of the global village, the question arises whether the Khoja Shia Ithna-Asheries of and from East Africa will be able to retain their current identity or whether they will go on to reconstruct or deconstruct. I hope to explore this in my next book, *Khoja Shia Ithna-Asheries from East Africa: The Quest for a New Socio-religious Identity (1960 – 2020)*.

NOTES

INTRODUCTION

1. Akhtar, Iqbal. "Ismāʿīl, Gulāmalī (1864–1943)." *Islam, Judaism, and Zoroastrianism*, Florida International University, 2018, pp. 334-8., https://doi.org/10.1007/978-94-024-1267-3_1939. Accessed 1 June 2022.
2. See: "History of the Formation of the Africa Federation." *Africa Federation*, 18 Jan. 2021, https://africafederation.org/2021/01/18/history-of-the-formation-of-the-africa-federation/. Accessed 14 June 2022.
3. Jaffer, Asgharali M. M. "An Outline of the History of Khoja Shia Ithna-Asheri in East Africa." Conference of World Ahlulbayt League, 5 August 1983, pp. 16-17. Conference Paper.
4. For a fuller explanation of the distinction between history and historiography, see: Lorenz, C. "History: Theories and Methods." *International Encyclopedia of the Social & Behavioral Sciences,* edited by Wright, James D., 2nd ed., Elsevier, 2015, vol. 11, pp. 131–137. https://doi.org/10.1016/b978-0-08-097086-8.62142-6.
5. Ibid.,132.
6. See: Hall, Brian C. *Quantum Theory for Mathematicians.* Springer, 2016.
7. Khaldūn Ibn. *The Muqaddimah: An Introduction to History.* Translated by Franz Rosenthal, Princeton University Press, 2015, p. 47.
8. Ibid., 46.
9. McCarney, Joseph. *Routledge Philosophy Guidebook to Hegel on History.* Routledge, 2000, p. 86.
10. See: Al-Sadr, Muhammad Baqir. *Al-Tafsir al-Mawdui wa al-Falsafutu al-Ijtma'iyyah fi al-Madrasti al-Qur'aniyyah*. Beirut, Dar al-ʿAlamiyyah, 1989.
11. Al-Sadr, Muhammad Baqir. "What is Topical Exegesis." *Trends of History in the Qur'an*, translated by Mustajab Ahmad Ansari, Islamic Seminary Publications, https://www.al-islam.org/trends-history-Qur'an-sayyid-muhammad-baqir-al-sadr/what-topical-exegesis-2#need-expansion-juristic-studies. Accessed 29 April 2022.
12. *The Qur'an*. Translation by Ali Q. Qarai. Surah Baqarah, 2:257.
13. Al-Sadr. "Norms of history mentioned in the Qur'an." *Trends of History in the Qur'an,* https://www.al-islam.org/trends-history-Qur'an-sayyid-muhammad-baqir-al-sadr/norms-history-mentioned-Qur'an. Accessed 29 April 2022.

14. *The Qur'an*. Translated by Ali Q. Qara'i. Surah Rum, 12:109. http://al-Qur'an.info/#12. Accessed 22 May 2022. See also 'Ali ibn Abi Talib's words to one of his sons in a letter of his: "I advise you to fear Allah, O my child, abide by His commands, fill your heart with remembrance of Him and cling to hope from Him. No connection is more reliable than the connection between you and Allah provided you take hold of it. Enliven your heart with preaching, kill it by denial, energise it with firm belief, enlighten it with wisdom, humiliate it by recalling death, make it believe in mortality, make it see the misfortunate of this world, make it fear the authority of the time and the severity of some changes during the nights and the days, place before it the events of past people, recall to it what befell those who were before you and walk among their cities and ruins, then see what they did and from what they have gone away and where they have gone and stayed. You will find that they departed from (their) friends and remain in loneliness. Shortly, you too will be like one of them. Therefore, plan for your place of stay and do not sell your next life with this world": Al-Radi, Abu al-Hasan Muhammad bin al-Husayn bin Musa. *Nahj al-Balagha – Imam Ali bin Abi Talib's Sermons, Letters, and Sayings – Arabic and English*. Translated by Syed Ali Raza, Volume 2, Letter 3, Qum, Ansariyan Publications, 2007. https://www.al-islam.org/nahjul-balagha-part-2-letters-and-sayings/letter-31-advice-one-his-sons-after-returning-battle. Accessed 22 May 2022.
15. Al-Tabrisi, Ali al-Fadl b. Al-Hasan b. al-Fadl. "Surat al-Yusuf, 12:109", *Majma' al-Bayan*. https://www.hodaalQur'an.com/rbook.php?id=1787&mn=1. Accessed 21 May 2022.
16. Tabatabai, Muhammad Husayn. "Surat al-Yusuf, 12:109", *Tafsir al-Mizan*. https://www.hodaalQur'an.com/rbook.php?id=4184&mn=1. Accessed 21 May 2022.
17. Al-Kashani, Muhammad b. Murtada b. Mahmud. "Surat al-Yusuf, 12:109", *Tafsir al-Safi*. https://www.hodaalQur'an.com/rbook.php?id=7006&mn=1. Accessed 21 May 2022.
18. See: Lorenz. "History: Theories and Methods." p. 132. See also the distinction between *khabr al-wahid* (the solitary report) and *mutawatir* (multiple, successive report) in *'ilm al-hadith* (the science of narration). The former requires significant investigation as "multiple successive transmission has not been attained, whether it has one reporter in its chain or more than one" (p. 104) whereas the latter is "one that has been narrated by such a great number of reporters that it would be impossible for them all to have agreed to fabricate it" (p. 94): Al-Fadli, 'Abd al-Hadi. *Introduction to Hadith (including Dirayat al-Hadith by al-Shahid al-Thani)*. Translated by Nazmina Virjee, ICAS Press, 2002.
19. For a detailed work in English of Muslim historiography, see: Rosenthal, Franz. *A History of Muslim Historiography*. Brill, 1968.
20. Lorenz. "History: Theories and Methods." p.132.
21. Ibid., 133.
22. Ibid., 135.
23. For further explanation on syllogisms and logic in general, see: Al-Muzaffar,

Muhammad Rida. *Al-Mantiq*. Beirut, Dar al-Ta'aruf wa Al-Matbu'at, 2006 and Hurley, Patrick J. and Watson, Lori. *A Concise Introduction to Logic.* Cengage Learning, 2016.
24. *The Qur'an*. Translation by 'Ali Quli Qara'i. Surah Rum, 30:22, http://al-Qur'an.info/#30. Acessed 22 May 2022.
25. Ibid, 49:13.
26. Tabrisi. *Majma' al-Bayan*. 49:13: https://www.hodaalQur'an.com/rbook.php?id=1897&mn=1. Accessed 22nd May 2022.
27. Ibid.
28. See: Muir, Sir William. *The Life of Mohammad From Original Sources.* J. Grant, 1923, p. 59.
29. See: Said, Edward. *Orientalism*. Vintage, 1979.
30. Lorenz, C., 'History: Theories and Methods', p. 133.
31. See for example *Trade Directory and History of the Community* published by The Federation of K.S.I. Jamaats of Africa in Arusha, 30 December 1960.
32. Writing a 'people's history' appears to be an increasing trend in history books. See for example: Purkis, Diane. *The English Civil War – A People's History.* Harper Perennial, 2007 which uses letters, memoirs, ballads and plays to bring to life the Roundheads and Cavaliers, the foot soldiers, war widows and witchfinders of one of the most significant turning points in British history, culminating in Oliver Cromwell's triumph and the execution of Charles I.
33. The courage to migrate to a new land, safeguard and/or reinterpret their faith and not lose hope are arguably the defining characteristics of hijrah (migration) in the Qur'an as per what Prophet Muhammad (pbuh) himself experienced when he migrated from Makkah to Madinah. See 2:218, 4:97-101, 8:71-75, 16:41 and 110, 29:26 amongst several other verses of the Qur'an.

PART 1: OUR COLLECTIVE PAST

1. *Satpanth*, a significantly different creed, grew inside the Khoja community expressing itself within a local Indian religious culture. (The evidence of Khojki script is found in manuscripts with *Satpanthi* poetry and hymns, commonly known as *ginans*. As Khojas transited from a Hindu merchant caste to a broader Muslim community, the development of Khojki played a role in their identity. The Nizari Ismailis Khojas claimed that the script, as well the teaching of the ginans by the Pirs, was used to convert the Lohanas from Hinduism to Shia Ismailism.) See Bruce, Juan. "Typographic development of the Khojki script and printing affairs at the turn of the 19th century in Bombay", *Khoja Studies Conference*, Paris, CNRS-CEIAS, 2016. https://www.academia.edu/30529028.Accessed 29 May 2022.
2. Parpia, Amir A. "The Evolution of Khoja identity in South Asia: A literature review." *Interdisziplinäre Zeitschrift für Südasienforschung*, vol. 2, 2017, p. 153. https://doi.org/10.11588/izsa.2017.2.1529.
3. Nanji, Azim. *The Nizārī Ismā'īlī Tradition in the Indo-Pakistan Subcontinent.* Caravan Books, 1978.

4. Descendants of the Raghuvanshi dynasty were divided into Gujarati Lohanas, Sindhi Lohanas and Kuchchhi Lohanas.
5. A caste found in Punjab, Rajasthan, Sindh and Gujarat and divided into different sub-castes such as Jakhar, Kuchchhi, Veha, Halai, Kanthi, Pavrai, Navgam, Pachisgaam and Thattai. From Kachchh are the Kachchhi Bhatias; from Jamnagar the Halai Bhatias; from Sindh the Sindhi Bhatias and from Punjab the Punjabi Bhatias.
6. Parpia. "The Evolution of Khoja identity." 1.
7. Nanji. *The Nizārī Ismāʻīlī Tradition.* 72-7.
8. Devotional song rooted in the musical and poetic matrix of Indian culture. The term *ginan* carries a double significance; on one hand meaning "religious wisdom" analogous to the Sanskrit word *jnana* (knowledge), and on the other translating as "song" or "recitation".
9. Parpia. "The Evolution of Khoja identity." 152.
10. *Satpanthi* literature or *ginans*, according to Ismaili sources, were composed by nine Ismaili Pirs and twenty-two Sunni *sayyids*. This evidences that Sufi *sayyids* were deeply involved which shows that Khoja inherited a much more complex creed from their ancestors. See "Fictitious Narratives in the Satveni'ji Vel." *Amir Pir Mela in Sindh and its Origin.* www.ismaili.net.
11. Ivanow, Vladimir. "Satpanth." *The Ismaili Society Collectanea*, vol. 1, Brill, 1948, as cited by Parpia, "The Evolution of Khoja identity." p. 152.
12. Daftary, Farhad, editor. *A Modern History of the Ismailis.* I. B. Tauris Publishers, 2011, p. 484.
13. The doctrine of the Imamate in Isma'ilism differs from that of the Twelvers because the Isma'ilis had living Imams for centuries after the last Twelver Imam went into concealment. They followed Isma'il ibn Jafar, elder brother of Musa al-Kadhim (peace be upon him), as the rightful Imam after his father, Ja'far al-Sadiq (pbuh). The Ismailis believe that whether Imam Ismail did or did not die before Imam Ja'far (pbuh), he had passed on the mantle of the imamate to his son Muhammad ibn Isma'il as the next imam. See "Isma'ilism." *Encyclopaedia Iranica*, https://iranicaonline.org/articles/ismailism-xvii-the-imamate-in-ismailism.
14. Madelung, Wilferd. "Shiism: Ismaʻiliyah." *Encyclopedia of Religion*, edited by Mircea Eliade, vol. 13, Macmillan, 1986, p. 257.
15. Nanji. *The Nizārī Ismāʻīlī Tradition.*
16. Khan, Dominique-Sila. *Conversions and Shifting Identities: Ramdev Pir and the Ismailis in Rajasthan.* New Delhi, Manohar Publishers and Distributors, 2003.
17. Purohit, Teena. *The Aga Khan Case.* Harvard University Press, 2012.
18. Shodhan, Amrita. "The Entanglement of the Ginans in the Khoja Governance." *Ginans : texts and contexts*, edited by Tazim R. Kassam and Françoise Mallison, Delhi, Primus Books, 2010, pp. 169-80.
19. Masselos, Jim. "The Khojas of Bombay: The Defining of Formal Membership Criteria during the Nineteenth Century." *Caste and Social Stratification among Muslims in India*, edited by Imtiaz Ahmed, 2nd ed., Columbia, South Asia

Books 1978, pp. 97-116.
20. Asani, Ali. "From Satpanthi to Ismaili Muslim: The Articulation of Ismaili Khoja Identity in South Asia." *A Modern History of the Ismailis: Continuity and Change in a Muslim Community*, edited by Farhad Daftary, I. B. Tauris, 2011, pp. 95-128.
21. The '*Satveni*' ginan compiled by the Imam-Shahis sect around 1520. This sect was attached to the Hindu part of the Satpanth creed. They are known for concealing and denying any connections to Ismailism and accentuating their Hindu beliefs and use of Hindu symbology. The '*Satveni*' ginan originally contained 100 verses, however, according to Ismaili scholars, the manuscript was in a private collection of the Imam-Shahis in Pirana and when it was brought for printing, it contained 150 verses. This may indicate that at some point an interpolation occurred. This is the reason why '*Satveni*' never became a standard text in Ismaili literature and is hardly recited in the Jamaatkhana. See "Fictitious Narratives in the Satveni'ji Vel."
22. Ranjan, Amit. "A History of Syncretism of the Khoja Muslim Community." *The Apollonian*, vol.4:1-2, 2017, pp. 53-65.
23. In pre-modern time, Khojas were simultaneously a Vaishnav panth (a Hindu denomination), a Sufi order, a trader's guild and a caste. See Asani in Daftary. *A Modern History of the Ismailis*. p. 97.
24. Parpia. "The Evolution of Khoja identity."
25. In the 1866 Khoja Case, some time was spent debating whether the Khojas were a caste or tribe as part of the attempt by the British to classify them. Tribe seems to have been most often associated with Muslim groups while caste was applied primarily to Hindu groups. See Mawani, Rizwan. *Tradition As Rupture: Caste, Community And The Colonial Courts - Forging Religious Identity in The 1866 Khoja Case*. 2017. Berkeley, MA dissertation.
26. Mawani. *Tradition As Rupture*.
27. Arnold, Sir Joseph. "Judgment delivered Nov. 12, 1866 on the Khoja Case (Aga Khan Case)." *Bombay Gazette Steam Press*, 1866.
28. The newspaper reporter wrote around the 1866 Khoja Case that 'Statistics as to the Mahomedan population of Bombay were next produced by Mr. Howard, the lawyer for Aga Khan I and his party, showing that up to 1809, the Khojahs were not recognized here as Mahomedans', Ibid.
29. McMurdo, James. "An Account of the Province of Cutch, and the Countries Lying Between Guzerat and the River Indus: With Cursory Remarks on the Inhabitants, Their History, Manners, and State of Society." *Transactions of the Literary Society of Bombay*, vol. 2, 1820, pp. 205-55.
30. "Heterodox Mahomedans." *Asiatic Journal and Monthly Register for British India and Its Dependencies XII*, no. 69, July-December, 1821, p. 257. See also Mawani. *Tradition As Rupture*.
31. Perry, Erskine. *Cases Illustrative of Oriental Life and the Application of English Law to India, decided in H.M. Supreme Court at Bombay.* London, S. Sweet, 1853, pp. 110-29. He also noted on Khojas that 'their language is Cutchi; their religion Mahomedan; their dress, appearance and manners, for

the most part Hindu…they call themselves Shias to a Shia, and Sunniys to a Sunniy….'

32. Habib Ebrahim was part of the Barbhai group that had testified that theirs was a separate religion as cited by Shodhan and Asani.
33. Aga Khan I
34. Parpia, "The Evolution of Khoja identity."
35. The sixth Holy Imam of Shia Ithna-Asheries.
36. *Ibratul Afza* is a Persian language autobiography of Aga Khan I. It was translated into Gujarati in 1865 A.D. by Bawa Karim Dadaji and printed by the Oriental Press in Bombay. See Dewji, Muhammedjaffer Sheriff. *Imame Zaman Hazrat Mahdi (A.S.).* Translated by Murtaza A. Lakha, Dar es Salaam, Literary Section Ithna-Asheri Union, 1982.
37. Ismail I (17 July 1487-23 May 1524), also known as Shah Ismail I, was the founder of the Safavid dynasty ruling from 1501-1524 as Shah of Iran (Persia).
38. *Aga Khan I.* Sambat, India, Litho Press,1918.)
39. Shah, Aga Jahangir. *Risala*. Translated into Gujarati Adelji Dhanji Kaba, Amreli, Kathiawad, 1912. Reprint by 'Rokaria' (Jaffer Ali Writer) as part of *Satpanth,* Bombay, Alamdar Book Depot, 1962, pp. 50-68.
40. Form of salutation on the Prophet Muhammad and his family members and descendants (pbut).
41. Of Shia Ithna-Asheri sect of Islam.
42. Mulla Asghar Memorial Library & Resource Centre (MARC), Toronto, Canada.
43. The Khojas of Kachchh and Kathiawad mostly preserved their history through oral narrations. I have relied upon such oral testimonies, collective memory, and interviews in my research.
44. Some of the questions that arise based on the oral testimonies in the famous Khoja Case of 1866 include: Why did Judge Arnold define the Khoja community the way he did? Why did the Khojas choose to identify themselves with certain beliefs over others? Why did various factions that parted from the main community after 1866 choose to organise as they did?
45. Hickling, Carrisa. *Disinheriting Daughters: Applying Hindu Laws of Inheritance to the Khoja Muslim Community in Western India.* 1998. University of Manitoba, MA dissertation as cited by Mawani. 'The reason they were brought to the courts at this stage provides an interesting reflection. Was the authority of the Jamaat being questioned in the new urbanized environment? Was the Aga Khan utilizing the influence on his followers to reclaim power from the Jamaat? Was there an increasing feminist consciousness rising in the community? What we do know is that this single act likely set in motion a third node of power in the community in which the courts now enmeshed themselves within the relationship between the Khojas and the Aga Khan.'
46. "The Khoja Case." *The Times of India*, 24 April 1866. ("Letter of Aga Khan to the Khoja Community." c. 1846 and "Statement of Aga Khan in the 1850 Khoja Case.")
47. Wilson, Peter Lamborn. "Ismailis and Nimatullahis." *Studia Islamica*, vol. XLI,

1975, pp. 113-36. The use of words like *Murshid* (guide) and *Murid* (one who seeks guidance) is aligned with Sufi *tariqas* (ways) and the proof of Aga Khan's involvement with Sufi *tariqas* in Persia, especially the Nimatullahis exists in studies. See also Bose, Mihir. *The Aga Khans*. Surrey, World's Work, 1984 and Algar, Hamid. "The Revolt of Aga Khan Mahallati and the Transference of the Ismaili Imamat to India." *Studia Islamica 29*, 1969, pp. 55-82.

48. "Judgment delivered Nov. 12, 1866 on the 'Khoja Case' (Aga Khan Case)." *Bombay Gazette Steam Press*, 12 November 1866. http://heritage.ismaili.net/node/27983.
49. Goswami, Chhaya. *Globalization Before Its Time: The Gujarati Merchants from Kachchh*. India, Penguin, 2016.
50. Nanji. 27, 81-821.
51. Obligatory tithe collected from the members of the Khoja community.
52. Bose, *The Aga Khans*. pp. 77-78.
53. This was not unique to Khojas. India's castes and communities were often under British scrutiny for classification to better govern them. In this sense, there was often a struggle on which boxes that the British colonial state provided to tick. Amongst others who faced this challenge were the Memons. See Perry, *Cases Illustrative of Oriental Life*.
54. See sub-section "1.5. Khoja Case of 1866" this chapter.
55. Bombay High Court. *Haji Bibi v H H Sir Sultan Mahomed Shah.* 2 Ind Cas 874, 1908.
56. Parpia. "The Evolution of Khoja identity." 156.
57. Mawani. *Tradition As Rupture*. The variety of religious sites in use by the Khojas further complicated the way in which the British understood who they were. The *durga*, associated with a deceased *sayyid* of the caste, was usually situated in the Khoja burial ground alongside one of its *masjids* (mosques). The *jamaatkhana* was found at another site and hosted different practices. This co-existence of space, and the rites associated with each, is a fertile area for study.
58. In 1870s Zanzibar, British officials documented the governing structure of the community, especially since they had risen to such prominence and dominated a large portion of the island's trade. 'The Khoja community is governed of a Council of 5 Elders (the *Amuldavi* [the Amaldari?] who on the occurrence of a death vacancy elect the successor. There are two officers chosen yearly by the Council to attend to routine business, these are Muki [*Mukhi*] and Kamaria [*Kamadia*], but their position is altogether subordinate to the Council or Jemad [*Jamaat*]', Kirk, John, 1873 as cited by Mawani. In the Ismaili Nizari tradition, the term is also used for the guardian of each jamaatkhana where the Mukhi acts as the tangible symbol of the Imam's authority.
59. Masselos. "The Khojas of Bombay." 100-03; Asani. "Satpanthi to Ismaili." 97-8.
60. Masselos. "The Khojas of Bombay." 99.
61. Asani. "Satpanthi to Ismaili." 6.
62. Nanjiani, Sachedina. *Khoja Vruttant*. India, 1892, p. 262; Husain, Mulla Qadir. *Memoirs of Mulla Qadir Husain Sahib*. India, Peermohammed Ebrahim Trust,

1972, pp. 14-5.
63. Parpia. "The Evolution of Khoja identity." 156-7.
64. Daftary. *A Modern History of the Ismailis.* 513
65. Masselos. "The Khojas of Bombay." 106-7.
66. Daftary. *A Modern History of Ismailis.* 475.
67. Asani in Daftary. *A Modern History of Ismailis.* 95-128.
68. Masselos. "The Khojas of Bombay." 97-116.
69. Purohit. *Aga Khan Case.* 22-28.
70. Shodhan. "Entanglement of Gināns." 169-180.
71. The papers detailed verbatim speeches and submissions from the lawyers alongside commentary and observations from the courtroom reporters. This allowed for a deeper insight into the intricacies of Khoja community with its religious practices and rituals of the time. (The role and impact of this media exposure needs more research.)
72. Purohit. *Aga Khan Case.* 79.
73. Imamate is a concept in Nizari Ismailism which defines the political, religious and spiritual dimensions of authority/leadership over followers.
74. Asani in Daftary. *A Modern History of Ismailis.* 95-128.
75. When the dissenting Khojas publicly joined the Sunni fold, Agha Khan I circulated a general announcement declaring the Khojas to be 'Shi'ites' (20 October 1861) in which he also expressed his desire to bring the Ismailis to conform to the practices of the Shia Imami Ismaili creed of his holy ancestors regarding marriage ceremonies, ablutions, funeral rites, etc. The decree ended thus: "He who may be willing to obey my orders shall write his name in this book that I may know him." Habib Ebrahim, his following and 20 other families in Mahuva refused to sign it. See Khoja Timeline, http://khojapedia.com/wiki/index.php?title=Khoja_Timeline.
76. Aga Khan I. *Ibratul Afza.* p. 20.
77. There were already conflicting dynamics present within the Khoja community i.e. the presence of and competition between multiple Indic traditions, rivalry between mercantile groups, and emergence of new ideas regarding caste authority. These may have assisted Aga Khan I in his efforts to establish himself.
78. Some of the major opponents of Aga Khan's financial claims were the Jamaat's wealthiest members, including Habib Ebrahim and Datoobhoy Soomar. There were tensions between Aga Khan I and this group and in 1835, a temporary compromise was reached. See Masselos. "The Khojas of Bombay." 103-5.
79. Purohit. *Aga Khan Case.* 22-8; Daftary. *A Modern History of Ismailis.* 33-4.
80. Because of the circumstances described, Asani, and to some extent Masselos and Purohit as well, suggest that the internal strife within the Khoja jamaat was essentially a struggle for power and authority.
81. Perry came to the conclusion after an exhaustive inquiry that if a custom otherwise valid was found to prevail amongst a race of Eastern origin and non-Christian faith, a British Court of Justice would give effect to it, if it did not conflict with any express Act of Legislature; and he held that the attempt of the

daughters to disturb the course of succession which had prevailed among their ancestors for many hundred years had failed and their appeals were dismissed with costs. See Perry. *Cases Illustrative*, O.C. 110 - "Kojahs and Memons' Case."
82. Ibid.
83. Mawani. *Tradition As Rupture*. 32-41.
84. These social codes determined position, status and purpose that categorised individuals; the aim being to achieve the ultimate goal of British Colonial System i.e. control of its subjects.
85. Shodhan. "The Entanglement of the Gināns."; Purohit. *Aga Khan Case*.
86. Mawani. *Tradition As Rupture*.
87. Ibid.
88. Purohit. *Aga Khan Case*. 43.
89. Masselos. "The Khojas of Bombay." 110-2; Purohit. *Aga Khan Case*. 45-9.
90. Shodhan. "The Entanglement of the Gināns." 171.
91. Orientalism is a way of seeing that imagines, emphasizes, exaggerates and distorts the differences of Arab and Asian cultures as compared to that of West. It often views these cultures with a bias, defining them as exotic, backward, uncivilized, and at times dangerous.
92. Parpia. "The Evolution of Khoja identity." 160-1.
93. Ironically, although *Dasa Avatara* was used by the courts to clarify the origins of the community and considered a primary text for the followers of the Aga Khan at the time, it is no longer part of their religious education. This dismissal of Hindu teachings in the Ismaili community began when Aga Khan III started to remodel the community into its modern form.
94. Most studies have based their analysis on two sources. The first is a speech by the defence lawyer for the Aga Khan, Edward Irving Howard, who argued for his spiritual guardianship and authority over the Khojas. See 'The Great Khoja Case', 1866. Howard essentially summarized the local history of the Khojas after their settlement in Bombay as well as the lineage of Aga Khan I. He asserted that the Khojas were in fact Ismailis but that their religion seemed confusing because of the practice of pious dissimulation (*taqiyya*). The second source is the judgement of Sir Joseph Arnold who provided the case's verdict. The judgement weighs in upon various articles and lays out the logic behind his decision. It sets in motion a new destiny for the Khojas in which the Aga Khan's authority reigned supreme. See "Judgment delivered Nov. 12, 1866."
95. Asani. "Satpanthi to Ismaili." 13-14.
96. Purohit. *Aga Khan Case*.
97. A form of a visitation to sites associated with Prophet Mohammed (pbuh). and his family members and descendants (including the Shia Imams).
98. A person accepted as an authority in Islamic law.
99. Those who preach and hold public discourse on religious subjects.
100. Husain, Mulla Qadir. *Memoirs of*.
101. Ibid.
102. Jaffer, Hassan Ali M. *The Endangered Species: An Account of the Journey*

of Faith by the Khoja Shia Ithna-Asheri Community. Ontario, Mulla Asghar Memorial Library & Islamic Resource Centre, 2012.

103. Alarakhia, Haji Karimbhai. Personal account. *Trade Directory and History of the Community.* Arusha, The Federation of K.S.I. Jamaats of Africa, 1960, p.181.
104. Religious scholar.
105. It was Mulla Qadir Husain's wish that the Khoja Shia Ithna-Asheri should have their own mosque. He recited thanksgiving prayers in the mosque and returned to Karbala where he passed away in August 1902 at the age of 60.
106. *A History of the Agakhani Ismailis.* Canada, 1991, https://insideismailism.files.wordpress.com/2014/11/history-of-agakhani-ismailis.pdf.
107. Ibid.
108. Decree issuing direct instructions by Aga Khan III to his community.
109. Aga Khan III (b. 1877) was Aga Khan I's grandson.
110. *Haji Bibi v H. H. Sir Sultan Mohamed Shah.* http://ismaili.net/heritage/node/29459
111. Parpia. "The Evolution of Khoja identity." 162.
112. In 1894, Aga Khan III went for *ziyarats* (visitation) to the holy shrines in Kadhmayn and Samarrah where the 7th, 9th, 10th and 11th Imams of Shia Ithna-Asheries are buried. On his return, he published a book in Gujarati (*Khoja Kaum na Madhhab*) in which he described the five times of *salat* (prayers), the regulations of *sawm* (fasting), and ritual cleanliness, all according to Shia Ithna-Asheri interpretations and not according to Ismaili interpretations (from personal interviews and communal sources.).
113. *Haji Bibi v H. H. Sir Sultan Mohamed Shah.*
114. Ruthven, Malise. "Aga Khan III and the Ismaili Renaissance." *New Trends and Developments in the World of Islam*, edited by Peter B. Clarke, London, Luzac Oriental, 1997, pp. 371-95. See also Asani, "Satpanthi to Ismaili" and Purohit, *Aga Khan Case* who both provide detailed accounts of the changes instituted by the Aga Khan.
115. Asani. "Satpanthi to Ismaili." 110.
116. Ruthven. "Aga Khan III."
117. Ibid., 382-90.
118. Ibid., 385.
119. *Haji Bibi vs H.H. Sir Sultan Mahomed Shah.*
120. Ibid.
121. From June to September 1899, Sir Sultan Mohammed Shah, Aga Khan III visited the Jamaats of Zanzibar. He issued many *farmans* for the wordly and spiritual betterment of Ismailis.
122. Aga Khan III visited Zanzibar in 1905 and stayed for 29 days. He brought with him the owner of Saraswati Press, Mr Vithaldas N Suratia, to write his *farmans*. Mr Suratia later published these *farman* as books. In Book No. 154, he mentions that the first constitution of the Jamaat was prepared and ordained during the days in Zanzibar.
123. Alarakhia. *Trade Directory.* The mentioned *masjid* and *imambada* still stand

in the same position.
124. Ibid.
125. Jaffer. *The Endangered Species*. Aga Khan III had visited Mombasa in 1899 and - frustrated by the growing number of Khojas formally rejecting his authority - issued a *farman* that predicted the demise of the Ithna-Asheri faith within 100 years. He instructed his following to keep well clear of them.
126. Ruthven. "Aga Khan III." 382-90.
127. In the Gujarati book written by Aga Khan III (see note 112), he wrote: 'God is not surrounded by anything; He is not made of anything; neither did He beget anyone nor was He begotten by anyone'. By 1908, the *du'as* recited with his approval in the Jamaatkhanas referred to him as God, although he did not fulfil any of the conditions he had stipulated for Divinity in 1894. (From personal interviews and communal sources.)
128. Ali Shah, the 47th Ismaili Imam, appointed Vazir Esmail's son, Kassam, as the supreme *vazir*. The appointment came with unlimited powers while the latter governed the *jamaats* in the Subcontinent. Kamadia Haji (his grandmother was the great, grand-daughter of *Pir* Vazir Esmail Gangji) accompanied the 48th Imam in the first three visits to Africa in 1899, 1905, and 1914. In 1908, he visited Africa in the capacity of the Aga Khan's special envoy in connection with the historic Haji Bibi Case.
129. Later these gatherings were forbidden altogether.
130. *Ma'sumeen* are fourteen figures in Islam which are deemed by Twelver Shiites to be infallible and include the Holy Prophet (pbuh) and thirteen of his Ahl al-Bayt (people of his household) that is: his daughter Lady Fatima al-Zahra, Imam Ali and their children, Imam al-Hasan and Imam al-Hussain and their descendants (pbut) constituting the twelve Shiite Imams.
131. Ruthven. "Aga Khan III." 385.
132. Alarakhia. *Trade Directory*. 182.

PART 2: MIGRATION TO A NEW LAND

1. Alarakhia. *Trade Directory*. 181. (Interviews with elderly community members corroborate this fact.)
2. *Trade Directory*. 174.
3. *Zanzibar National Archives* HC7/106. See also Akhtar, I. "Negotiating the Racial Boundaries of Khōjā Caste Membership in Late Nineteenth-Century Colonial Zanzibar (1878–1899)." *Journal of Africana Religions*, 2014, vol 2, no. 3, pp. 297-316, doi.org/10.5325/jafrireli.2.3.0297.
4. Gundara, Jagdish S. "Aspects of Indian Culture in Nineteenth Century Zanzibar." *South Asia: Journal of South Asian Studies*, 1980, vol. 3, issue 1, pp. 14-7. doi.org/10.1080/00856408008722996. However, according to Prideaux, W. F. officiating Political Agent and Consul General to C. U. Aitchison, Secretary to Government of India, 8 February 1875, Zanzibar, *Administrative Report for 1873-74*, MSA, PD, vol. 294, 1875, p. 2, there

were 850 males, 650 women, and 725 children.
5. *Trade Directory.* pp. 6-206.
6. Ibid.
7. *Trade Directory.* 174. We can expect this date and narrative to change as more data is gathered. There is also a view by Alhaj Mohammedbhai Khalfan that 1835 is the year of first entry when Versi Advani migrated to Zanzibar from Bhuj, Gujarat with his three brothers: Khalfan, Abdulrasul and Gulamhussein. This has yet to be explored.
8. *Mji Mwema* was expanded by Sultan Majid of Zanzibar who renamed it *Dar es Salaam.*
9. *Mzizima* (Swahili for 'healthy town') was a coastal fishing village.
10. Dar es Salaam from Arabic, meaning "Place of Peace".
11. Panjwani, Sibtain. "In Conversation with Alhaj Murtaza Jivraj." *YouTube*, uploaded by The Awakening Project, 29 Feb 2020, https://www.youtube.com/watch?v=G-0_YUK6OnQ.
12. Brown, Walter T. *A Pre-colonial History of Bagamoyo: Aspects of the Growth of an East African coastal town.* 1970. University of Michigan, Ph.D. dissertation.
13. Swahili/Shirazi plantation owners, who had settled there from Barawa, Somalia.
14. Bantu tribe from Uluguru Mountain region (200 miles inland) who moved to Mzizima for better prospects.
15. A type of unbleached cotton cloth imported from the US. *Merikani* is a Swahili noun derived from the adjective 'American', indicative of the place it originated from.
16. Colourful patterned cotton fabric worn by women throughout the African Great Lakes region.
17. LeRoy, Père. "Archives Générales Spiritains, Chevilly-la-Rue, France." 17 April 1886. Steven Fabian made notes on this source, and these are available at the *Archives Générales Spiritains.*
18. Bagamoyo comes from the Swahili phrase '*bwaga moyo*' meaning 'lay down your heart'. In the mid-19th century, it was a trading port for ivory and the slave trade with traders coming from places as far interior as Mwanza, Tabora, Lake Tanganyika and Usambara on their way to Zanzibar Island.
19. Gray, John M. "Dar es Salaam under the Sultans of Zanzibar." *Tanganyika Notes & Records (TNR)* 33, 1952, pp. 10-7.
20. Sayyid Majid bin Said Al-Busaidi (1834-1870) ruled Zanzibar from 19 October 1856 to 7 October 1870.
21. Glassman, Jonathan. *Feasts and Riot: Revelry, Rebellion, and Popular Consciousness on the Swahili Coast 1856-1888.* Portsmouth, Heinemann, 1995, p. 183.
22. Gray, "Dar es Salaam under the Sultans."
23. Johnston, Harry, H.F.R.G.S. Her Majesty's Consul, Mozambique. "The Asiatic Colonisation of East Africa." *Journal of The Society of Arts*, February 1889, p. 160.

24. Casson, W. T. "Architectural notes on Dar es Salaam." *TNR* 71, 1970, pp. 183-4.
25. Johnston, "The Asiatic Colonisation."
26. The other Khoja Shia Ithna-Asheri was Bhai Versi Advani. See *Africa Federation Archives*.
27. *Africa Federation Archives Section*. 29 December 2017.
28. Dar es salaam Jamaat Community Archive. 1969.
29. Goswami, Chayya. *The Call of the Sea – Kachchi traders in Muscat and Zanzibar, c. 1800-1880.* New Delhi, Orient Blackswan, 2011.
30. Shah, Bipin. "The Famines of India and the formation of Indian Diaspora." https://www.academia.edu/8753763.
31. *Trade Directory*. p. 174.
32. Jaffer. *The Endangered Species*. p. 65. See also Daftary, Farhad. *The Ismailis: An Illustrated History.* United Kingdom, Azimuth Editions, 2008, pp. 480-1.
33. The Slavery Abolition Act 1833 (3 & 4 Will. IV c. 73) abolished slavery throughout the British Empire and made the purchase or ownership of slaves illegal within the British Empire with the exception of Ceylon and Saint Helena which were in possession of the East India Company.
34. The Indian indenture system was a system of servitude through which 2 million Indians were transported to labour in the European colonies as a substitute for slave labour. This resulted in the development of a large Indian Diaspora in the Caribbean, Natal, Reunion, Mauritius, Sri Lanka, Malaysia, Mayanmar and Fiji.
35. The term 'coolie' is said to be derived from an aboriginal tribe in the Gujarat region of India. Others believe it comes from the Tamil word '*Kuli*' meaning 'payment for occasional menial work'.
36. Mungai, Christine. "15 facts about the Indian diaspora in Africa." *World Economic Forum*, 2015, https://www.weforum.org/agenda/2015/06/15-facts-about-the-indian-diaspora-in-africa/. Accessed 31 May 2022.
37. *Trade Directory*.
38. Swahili is a native language of East African cost which belongs to the Bantu branch of the Niger-Congo family.
39. Goswami, Chhaya. "India and Africa Unique Historical Bonds and Present Prospects, with Special Reference to Kutchis in Zanzibar." Working paper, issue 5, University of Mumbai, 2008.
40. Al-Tirmizi, S. "Indian Sources for African History, Volume I", *UNESCO*, 1988, p. 525.
41. "The Kenya Protectorate." *Weekly News*, 19 KNA, CA/10/126, 16 September 1960. See also Freeman-Grenville, G.S.P. *The East African Coast: Select Documents from the First to the Earlier Nineteenth Century.* Oxford, Clarendon Press, 1966, p. 10.
42. Middleton, John. *The World of the Swahili; An African Mercantile Civilization.* Yale University Press, 1992, p. 28.
43. Goswami. "India and Africa."
44. Kirk, William. "The N.E. Monsoon and Some Aspects of African History." *The*

Journal of African History, vol.3, no.2, University of London, 1961, pp. 263-7.
45. Chaudhuri, K. *Trade and civilisation in the Indian Ocean: An Economic History from the Rise of Islam to 1750*. Cambridge University Press, 1985.
46. Pearson, Michael. "A Bibliography." *The Journal of Indian Ocean World Studies*, 3(1):82, 2019, doi:10.26443/jiows.v3i1.56.
47. Sheriff, Abdul. *Slaves, Spices and Ivory in Zanzibar.* Oxford, James Curry Ltd, 1987. See also, Sheriff. *The Indian Ocean – Oceanic Connections and the Creation of New Societies*, edited by Abdul Sheriff and Enseng Ho, London, Hurst & Co., 2014, p. 19.
48. The Indian Ocean is surrounded by some of the most populous nations and most advanced civilizations of the world, allowing for a tremendous opportunity to exploit its resources for the advancement of the people living around it.
49. Palat, Ravi A. "Maritime Trade, Political Relations, and Residential Diplomacy in the World of the Indian Ocean." *The Indian Ocean: Oceanic Connections and the Creation of New Societies,* London, Hurst Publishers, 2014, pp. 45-68.
50. Larsen, Kjersti, editor. "Knowledge, Renewal and Religion - Repositioning and changing ideological and material circumstances among the Swahili on the East African Coast." Uppsala, *Nordiska Afrikainstitutet*, 2009.
51. Deckard, Sharae. *Paradise Discourse, Imperialism, and Globalization- Exploiting Eden.* Routledge, 2010, p. 110.
52. Gilbert, Erik. "Coastal East Africa and the Western Indian Ocean: Long-Distance Trade, Empire, Migration, and Regional Unity, 1750–1970." *The History Teacher*, vol. 36, no. 1, 2002, pp. 7-34.
53. Glassman. "Feasts and Riot."
54. Larsen, Kjersti. "Spirit Possession as Historical Narrative: The Production of Identity and Locality in Zanzibar Town." in N. Lovell, editor. *Locality and Belonging*, Routledge, 1998, pp. 125-46.
55. Kachchh was one of the places where the Arabs built their *vahans* (dhows). Kachchhi sailors and traders usually went wherever the Arabs went and it is most likely that by the 15th century, Kachchhi Khojas merchants were amongst these early visitors, trading as they also did along the entire Indian Ocean Littoral areas.
56. Simpson, Edward. *Muslim Society and the Western Indian Ocean: The Seafarers of Kachchh*. Routledge, 2006, pp. 44-5.
57. Alpers, E.A. "Gujarat and the trade of East Africa,1500–1800." *International Journal of African Historical Studies*, vol. 9, no.1, 1976, pp. 22-44.
58. Sheriff. *Slaves, Spices and Ivory*. p. 21. Also, in 1825, Captain Owen visited Muscat and he found that the town was 'inhabited by every caste of Indian merchants'.' See Owen, W. "Narrative of voyages to explore the shores of Africa, Arabia and Madagascar, vol 1." London, 1833, pp. 336-40.
59. Goswami. *The Call of the Sea*. 79-80.
60. Simpson. *Muslim Society*.
61. Ibid.
62. Smee, T. and Lt. Hardy. "Observation during a voyage of Research on the

East Coast of Africa from Cape Guardafui south to the Island of Zanzibar in the H. C's cruiser Ternate." The Secretary, editor. *Transactions of the Bombay Geographical Society from September 1841 to May 1844*, Vol. # VI, Bombay, the Times Press, p. 45.

63. Goswami. "India and Africa." Although Smee refers to Indian traders, by most accounts they are most likely to be Khoja from Kachchh and Kathiawad.
64. Dhows are ubiquitous to the Indian Ocean. These are large sailing ships, which are still present on the Indian, Persian Gulf and African coasts
65. The first historical source was based on archaeological evidence found at Unguja Ukuu in Zanzibar dated 798 A.D. A second source comes from Al-Masudi (d. 945 A.D.) who mentions that the East African coast in the 10th century had a mixed population of Muslims and Zenj pagans. Al-Idrisi (d.1066 A.D.) mentions that Zanzibar people were mostly Muslims. Shirazis from Iran came to Kilwa which became the leading coastal town in the 14th century. Shirazi influence on the East African coast dated back to 1217. See Hiskett, M. *The Course of Islam in Africa*, Edinburgh University Press, 1994, p. 154.
66. Mehta, Makrand. "Gujarati Business Communities in East African: Major Historical Trends." *Economic and Political Weekly*, vol. 36, no.20, May 2001, p. 1742.
67. Lodhi, Abdulaziz Y. "Indians and Indic languages in Eastern Africa: The Status of South Asian Languages in Eastern Africa." *Dept. of Linguistics & Philology*, Uppsala University, Sweden.
68. Chaudhuri. *Trade and Civilization.* And by the same author, *Asia before Europe: Economy and civilization of the Indian ocean from the rise of Islam to 1750*, Cambridge, 1990; Alpers. *East Africa and the Indian Ocean.*; Sheriff. *Dhow Cultures of the Indian ocean.* London, 2010.
69. Salvadori, Cynthia. *We came in Dhows*. Nairobi, Paperchase Kenya Ltd.,1996.
70. The word *bhadala* meant a hardworking businessman and sea rider in the Kachchhi language, According to their traditions; they were originally settled in the town of Keti Bandar in Sindh. They were invited to settle in Kachchh by the Mughal Emperor Shahjahan. Their original settlement was the village of Mota Salaya in Mandvi. Many Bhadalas moved to Mombasa, Lamu and Dar es Salam in East Africa. They were pioneers in the Asian settlement of East Africa. The community now speaks Kachchhi, while those in Saurashtra also speak Gujarati.
71. Indian city, second-largest urban agglomeration in the State of Kerala. See Mehta. "Gujarati Business Communities." p.1742.
72. Sheriff. *Slaves, Spices and Ivory.* 84.
73. Ibid., 203.
74. The Busaidi Sultanate of Zanzibar (ca. 1850 – 1888).
75. Pouwels, R. "The Battle of Shela: the climax of an era and a point of departure in the modern history of the Kenya Coast." *Cahiers d'Études Africaines* 31 (123), 1991, pp. 363–89.
76. Zanzibar had their own ruler, called the *Mwinyi Mkuu* or Great Lord. The kings and queens who held this title enjoyed an uneasy truce with the invaders, being

allowed to keep their status as spiritual leaders of the Zanzibari people provided they did not interfere in government.
77. Goswami. "India and Africa."
78. Sheriff. *Slaves, Spices & Ivory*. Also see Cooper, F. *Plantation Slavery on the East Coast of Africa.* Yale University Press, 1977.
79. Coupland, R. *East Africa and Its Invaders.* The Clarendon Press, 1938. See also Stigand, Chauncy Hugh. T*he land of Zinj: Being an account of British East Africa, its ancient history and present inhabitants.* London, Constable & Company Ltd., 1913.
80. Goswami. "India and Africa."
81. Sheriff, Abdul. *The Rise of a Commercial Empire: An Aspect of the Economic History of Zanzibar, 1770-1873.* 1971. University of London, pp. 348-9. Ph.D. dissertation.
82. Ibid.
83. Al-Tirmizi. "Indian Sources for African History."
84. Frere, Sir Bartle. "Memorandum regarding Banyans." *British Parliamentary Papers.* It appears that Gujaratis were a highly mobile trading community that adapted well to new areas. This made the state of Gujarat both linguistically and religiously heterogeneous.
85. For instance, the economic recession that struck England during the period 1806-10 forced Britain to search for raw materials along the East African coast.
86. Also known as Said bin Sultan (1790–1856), he was a resourceful and energetic Omani sultan who moved the capital from Arabia to Zanzibar in order to initiate clove production.
87. Coastal culture is the culture of the Swahili people inhabiting Tanzania, Kenya, Uganda and Mozambique as well as the adjacent islands of Zanzibar and Comoros and some parts of the Congo and Malawi. They speak Swahili as their native language.
88. Deckard. *Paradise Discourse.*
89. Ibid.
90. *Trade Directory.* p. 181.
91. Here, the most likely period being described is 1830-1880.
92. Captain Hammerton who was the British Consul in Zanzibar from 1841-1857.
93. Sheriff. *Slaves, Spices and Ivory.* p. 211.
94. The Anglo-French Declaration signed on 10 March 1862. This provided: United Kingdom of Great Britain and France to take into consideration the importance of maintaining the independence of Muscat and Zanzibar as cited in Sheriff, 1998, p. 217.
95. Middleton, John. "The Immigrant Communities: The Arabs of the East African Coast." *History of East Africa*, edited by D.A. Low and Smith, vol.3, Clarendon, 1976, p. 499.
96. Jackson, Mabel V. *European Powers and South-East Africa*, Longmans, Green and Company, 1942, p. 171.
97. Lofchie, Michael. *Zanzibar: background to revolution.* Princeton University Press, 1965, p. 56.

98. Morris, H.F. and Read, J. S. *Indirect Rule and the Search for Justice: Essays in East African Legal History*. Clarendon Press, 1972, p. 43.
99. Heligoland (also known as Helgoland) is the coastal area on the Danish German border which was granted to Germany in exchange for Zanzibar.
100. British colonial officials working in African territories had a collective vision of controlling the whole of the African continent. The policy was earlier envisioned by Cecil Rhodes with his ambitious project of connecting the Cape with Cairo by establishing a Trans-African railway. Leonel Decle of the UK-based Daily Telegraph defined the project by stating that 'The British African Empire means freedom and civilisation, the amelioration of the people, the fostering of trade, the industrial development of vast countries for the British enterprise, British capital and British administrative ability'. See "British Success in Africa." *Official Gazette of Zanzibar and East Africa,* vol. 474, 27 February 1901.
101. Whether the decision of Judge Arnold in 1866 Khoja Case to declare Aga Khan 1 as the head of Khoja Community has anything to do with presence of a large Khoja Community in Zanzibar with considerable economic power could be the subject of an interesting analysis.
102. Gregory, Robert. *India and East Africa: A History of Race Relations within the British Empire 1890-1939.* London, 1971, p. 96
103. Warah, Rasna. *Triple Heritage: A Journey to Self-discovery.* Nairobi, 1998, p. 22.
104. The fertile white lands were eventually allocated to the Europeans. The colonizer also tried to monopolize the sale of German assets in German East Africa. Nevertheless, here the Indians managed to get access to the auctions and were allowed to bid. Eventually, the Asians would buy several sisal estates. See Oonk, G. *The Karimjee Jivanjee family: Merchant Princes of East Africa, 1800-2000.* Amsterdam, 2009.
105. One of the first leaders of the South Asian community in East Africa was Alibhai Jeevanjee (1856-1936). He was born in 1856 in Karachi (now in Pakistan) in a traditional Bohra home where education centred almost entirely on religion. Around the age of 20, Jeevanjee left Karachi, looking for a world of new trade opportunities. Among other things, he was the first non-white to be appointed to represent the interests of the Indians in the Legislative Council, which was established in 1905. See the biography written by his grand-daughter: Patel, Zarina. *Challenge to colonialism - The struggle of Allibhai Jeevanjee for equal rights in Kenya.* Nairobi, 1997. Jevanjee with Manila Ambalal Desai represented the Indian community in a delegation to London for an audience with the Duke of Devonshire. The meeting resulted in the Devonshire White Paper, which whilst failing to meet Indian demands, also rejected the European settlers' demands for dominion status in favour of African Paramountcy. In 1924, Desai spent six weeks in prison for participating in a campaign to boycott participation in a poll tax. The following year, he was nominated to the Legislative Council.
106. Ibid.

107. Refer to Part 1: the Khoja Case of 1866.
108. Ibid. See also Purohit.
109. Mnazi Moja ground was a 27-acre land in Zanzibar used by the Khoja community as a burial ground.
110. 'I would urge that the Aga Khan and his followers are a useful asset from an Imperial point of view, and it would help us here if we could show to him that his support is appreciated not only in India, but throughout the Empire.' British Library, *India Office Records (IOR)/L/PS/10/588/2*, Viceroy of India to Foreign Office, 08-02-1912
111. Pelgrim, Maarten. *The Mnazi Moja Dispute: Exploring the relationship between the Khojas, the Aga Khan and the British on the island of Zanzibar during the period 1899-1912*. 2017. Leiden University, pp. 18-30. MA Dissertation.
112. Ibid.
113. IOR/L/PJ/6/525 File 2280, Foreign Office, 03-10-1899.
114. Kaba, Adelji Dhanji. *Kilwa na Sawal Jawab*. Amarsinhji Printing Press, 1918, pp. 9-27.
115. Ibid.
116. "History of Mombasa KSIJ Cemetery (Qabrastan)." *Africa Federation Archives*, 7 August 2020.
117. Ibid.
118. OR/L/PJ/6/525 File 2280, Foreign Office, 03-10-1899. See also IOR/L/PS/10/588/2: File 748/1916 Pt 2 *The Aga Khan; the Khoja community.*
119. 47fn6 IOR/L/PJ/6/525 File 2280, Cave to Foreign Office, 03-10-1899.
120. Sheriff. *Slaves, Spices and Ivory.* 53, 65.
121. Muslims honour the *Prophet Muhamm*ad and his family with the salutation, 'peace be upon him' ('alayhi al-salaam) or in the case of a female, 'peace be upon her' ('*alayha al-salaam*).
122. 'Khadijah was a merchant woman of dignity and wealth. She used to hire men to carry merchandise outside the country on a profit-sharing basis. Now when she heard about the Prophet's truthfulness, trustworthiness and honourable character, she sent for him and proposed that he should take her goods to Syria and trade with them, while she would pay him more than she paid others. He was to take a lad of her called Maysara.' Guillaume, A. *The Life of Muhammad - A Translation of Ishaq's Sirat Rasul Allah*. Oxford University Press, 1998, p. 82.
123. 'Khadijah was a determined, intelligent woman possessing the properties with which God willed to honour her. So when Maysara told her these things she sent to the apostle of God and-so the story goes-said: "O son of my uncle I like you because of our relationship and your high reputation among your people, your trustworthiness and good character and truthfulness." Then she proposed marriage. Now Khadijah at that time was the best born in Quraysh, of the greatest dignity and too, the richest. All her people were eager to get possession of her wealth if it were possible' and 'Khadijah believed in him and accepted as true what he brought from God and helped him his work. She was

the first to believe in God and His apostle and in the truth of his message. By her God lightened the burden of His Prophet. He never met with contradiction and charges of falsehood, which saddened him, but God comforted him by her when he went home. She strengthened him, lightened his burden, proclaimed his truth and belittled men's opposition. May God Almighty have mercy upon her!' Ibid., p. 111.

124. Smith, Jane I. "Women in Islam: Equity, Equality, and the Search for the Natural Order." *Journal of the American Academy of Religion*, volume XLVII, issue 4, December 1979, pp. 517-537, https://doi.org/10.1093/jaarel/XLVII.4.517. Accessed 1 June 2022 and Tausch, Arno and Hesmati, Almas. "Islamism and Gender Relations in the Muslim World as Reflected in Recent World Values Survey Data." *IZA Network*, Discussion Paper No. 9672, January 2016. http://ftp.iza.org/dp9672.pdf. Accessed 18 June 2022.
125. *Trade Directory*. See also Jaffer, Mulla Asgharali. "An Outline of the History of Khoja.*"*
126. *Trade Directory*. 4 -13.
127. "History of Lamu KSI Community - Pirbhai Visram (Part 1)." *Africa Federation Archives*, 12 February 2016
128. *Trade Directory*.
129. Goswami. "India and Africa."
130. *Trade Directory*. Also, Khoja oral tradition confirms that one Musa Kanji and his brother Sajan Kanji, originally from Surat and working through Zanzibar, had already set up their business on the mainland before 1820. The first South Asian known to have settled upcountry was Musa "Mzuri", a Khoja from Surat. In 1825, he and his brother Sajan, set out on an expedition from Zanzibar and were probably the first non-Africans to reach Unyamwezi territory in western Tanzania, where they traded cloth and beads for ivory, turning a handsome profit. On their return, Sajan died. Musa, however, continued conducting caravans for another 30 years, reaching as far inland as Buganda in Uganda and Maragwe. (Karagwe). According to some evidence it is Musa "Mzuri" Kanji who helped Burton and Speke at Tabora. Musa "Mzuri" is also mentioned by Capt. James Grant as having 'an establishment of 300 native men and women round him. His abode had, three years ago, taken two months to build and it was surrounded by a circular wall which enclosed his houses, fruit and vegetable trees, and a stock of cattle'. It was also Musa "Mzuri" Kanji, who told the explorer Speke about the great river flowing north out of Lake Nyanza. All these needs to be corroborated.
131. Stephens, J.E.R. "The Laws of Zanzibar." *Journal of the Society of Comparative Legislation,* vol.13, no. 3, 1913, p. 603.
132. The relationship between the two ruling dynasties was cemented through Arab traders. Ahmad b. Ibrahim taught Islam to Kabaka of Buganda who later became a Muslim. Nimitz Jr., A. *Islam and Politics in East Africa*. University of Minnesota Press, 1980, p.10.
133. It was through these trade routes that trade transactions and intermarriages occurred, and local people were influenced by Islamic culture and then later

converted to Islam. Ibid., p. 8.
134. Rizvi, Seyyid Saeed Akhtar and King, Noel. "Some East African Ithna-Asheri Jamaats (1840-1967)." *Religion in Africa,* vol. 5, fasc. 1, 1973, pp. 12-22.
135. Oral narration.
136. Tukuyu is a small hillside town that lies about 36 miles (58 km) south of the city of Mbeya, at an elevation of around 5,000 ft (1,500 m) in the highland Rungwe District of southern Tanzania, East Africa.

PART 3: THE ARRIVAL OF KHOJAS IN ZANZIBAR

1. IOR, L/P&S/9/49 Abdul Azeez bin Saeed to Burghash bin Saeed (n.d., ca. 1871), Muscat.
2. Prestholdt, Jeremy. "Zanzibar, the Indian Ocean, and Nineteenth-Century Global Interface - Connectivity in Motion." *Palgrave Series in Indian Ocean World Studies*, 2017, pp. 135-157, doi: https://doi.org/10.1007/978-3-319-59725-6_6.
3. Sheriff. *Slaves, Spices and Ivory.*
4. The Zanzibari Swahili was dynamic and diverse and markedly different from other parts of East African coast. Those from Mombasa dismissively referred to Kiunguja (Zanzibar Swahili) as "foolish words" (*maneno ya kijingajinga*). Prestholdt. "Zanzibar, the Indian Ocean."
5. Ibid.
6. Oonk, Gijsbert. *Settled Strangers: Asian Business Elites in East Africa (1800-2000).* Sage, 2013, p. 77.
7. Ibid.
8. Gundara. "Aspects of Indian culture."
9. Goswami, Chayya. *The Call of the Sea-Kachchi traders in Muscat and Zanzibar, c. 1800-1880.* New Delhi, Orient Blackswan, 2011, p. 175.
10. Oonk, Gijsbert. "South Asians in East Africa, 1800–2000. An entrepreneurial minority caught in a 'Catch-22'." Rotterdam, Erasmus University, 2013.
11. Honey, M. "A History of Indian Merchant Capital and Class Formation in Tanganyika, c. 1840-1940," University of Dar es Salaam, 1982, p. 74. See also Sheriff. *Slaves, Spices and Ivory.*
12. Vaughan, J. H. *The Dual Mandate in Zanzibar.* Zanzibar Government Printers, 1935, pp. 11-12.
13. *Bania,* also spelled *Baniya,* (from Sanskrit *vaṇiya,* meaning "trade"). An Indian caste consisting generally of moneylenders or merchants, found chiefly in northern and western India; strictly speaking, however, many mercantile communities are not *Banias,* and, conversely, some *Banias* are not merchants.
14. Christie, James. *Cholera Epidemics in East Africa: An account of the several epidemics in that country from 1821 till 1872.* Macmillan, 1876, pp. 345-6.
15. The Sultanate of Zanzibar was created on 19 October 1856 after the death of Said bin Sultan who had ruled both Oman and Zanzibar since 1804.
16. Sayyid Bargash bin Said Al-Busaid (1837-1888) ruled Zanzibar from 7 October 1870 to 26 March 1888. He is credited with building Stone Town, including

piped water, public baths, a police force, roads, parks, hospitals and large administrative buildings such as the Bait el-Ajaib (House of Wonders). He maintained a measure of true independence from European control and was often able to play one country off the other.

17. Topan, Tharia. *KHOJAwiki.org*. http://khojawiki.org/Tharia_Topan
18. Fazal, Abdulrazak Sheriff. *My Zanzibar Recollections*. 2014, pp. 28-9.
19. Paroo, Sewa Haji. *KHOJAwiki.org*. http://khojawiki.org/Sewa_Haji_Paroo
20. Visram, Allidina. "Uganda Asians." https://ismailimail.files.wordpress.com/2011/06/allidina-visram-pgs.pdf
21. Patron or guardian.
22. Surti, Shariff Jiwa. "Community Services." *Khojapedia*, http://khojapedia.com/wiki/index.php?title=Shariff_Jiwa_Surti
23. Jaffer, Sabera. Personal interview. 2021.
24. *Federation Samachar*, vol 36, no 5, p. 64.
25. Ibid.
26. Ibid.
27. Bhalloo, Zahir. *Khoja Shia Ithna-Asheris in Lamu and Mombasa: 1870-1930*. Zahir Bhalloo, 2008, p. 5.
28. Pilgrimage to Mecca.
29. Jaffer, Sabera. Personal interview. 2021.
30. Ibid.
31. An MBE is one of five classes of appointment to the Order of The British Empire and it stands for Member of The Most Excellent Order of The British Empire. It is given for an outstanding achievement or service to the community.
32. *Trade Directory*. pp. 138-9.
33. *Africa Federation Archives,* 16 August 2019.
34. "Haji Dewji Jamal remembered on his 200th Birth Anniversary." *Africa Federation Archives*. 19 June 2020.
35. *Transregional Trade and Traders: Situating Gujarat in the Indian Ocean from Early Times to 1900*. Edited by Edward A. Alpers and Chhaya Goswami, Oxford Scholarship Online, 2019, doi: 10.1093/oso/9780199490684.001.0001.
36. Sheriff, Abdul. "Migration & Creation of New Societies: A story from the Indian Ocean." *Transregional Trade and Traders: Situating Gujarat in the Indian Ocean from Early Times to 1900*, edited by Edward A. Alpers and Chhaya Goswami, Oxford Scholarship Online, 2019, doi:10.1093/oso/9780199490684.003.0016.
37. Trading in slaves was abolished by the British who were patrolling the seas to curtail the trading in slavery.
38. Traditional name for the part of the East African coast facing Zanzibar.
39. NAZ: AA 2/4: *Letters from H.M. Consul Zanzibar*, 1859-1861.
40. Sheriff, *Slaves, Spices and Ivory*. p. 121.
41. Contract for the purchase of a plot by Dewji bin Jamal from Ahmad bin Ibrahim bin Malallah al-Basri, 10.5.1866, in the family's possession, Arusha. Purchase of House at Malindi by Dewji Jamal from Ghanem b. Muhammad b.

Abbas Al-Shi'i, 17.10.1866, NAZ: AM 1/1 (31 & 51/1867)
42. Sheriff, Abdul. Personal interview.
43. Jaffer. *The Endangered Species.*
44. Ibid.
45. The devotion to Aga Khan was so considerable that in 1888, Rashid accompanied his aunt (Natha's sister) to Mumbai for the *deedar* (visitation) of the Mola Bapa i.e. the Aga Khan Aqa Ali Shah (Aga Khan II) who passed away in Pune, India in 1885.
46. Khatau, Dharamsi. *KHOJAwiki.org.* http://khojawiki.org/Dharamsi_Khatau
47. 'The sociologist Georg Simmel in the late 19th century defines "strangers" as traders and businessmen who come and go and maintain some distance from local society for cultural and economic reasons'. Simmel, Georg. *The Sociology of Georg Simmel.* Simon and Schuster, 1950, pp. 402-8
48. Christie. *Cholera Epidemics.*
49. Ibid., pp. 337, 342
50. Sheriff, Abdul. *The History & Conservation of Zanzibar Stone Town.* London, Dept. of Archives, Museums & Antiquities in association with J. Curry, 1995.
51. From around the 8th century, the Swahili people were part of the Indian Ocean Trading World. Through this, they were exposed to and influenced by Arabic, Persian, Indian, and Chinese cultures. As a result, during the 10th century, the several city-states that flourished along the East African coast and adjacent island were Muslim, cosmopolitan, and politically independent of one another.
52. He was born in 1888. His father Peera Khataw Chagla Dossa migrated to Zanzibar from India around 1870s. Habib bhai Peera passed away on 27th February 1963 after a long illness at the age of 75. Habibbhai's elder son, Jaffer Bhai operated the Kiosk after the death of his late father. *Africa Federation Archives,* 28 June 2019.
53. Sayyid Sir Khalifa ruled Zanzibar and Pemba Islands for 49 years (1911-1960) and was a popular Sultan of Zanzibar.
54. *Jati* is a self- governing group of clans, tribes, communities, and sub-communities, and religions. Under the *Jātati* system, a person is born into a *Jātia* construct with ascribed social roles and endogamy, i.e. marriages take place only within that *Jaāti*. The *Jāti* provides identity, security and status and has historically been open to change based on economic, social and political influences.
55. One example being endogamy practice of marriage.
56. Ibid.
57. The words *Azadari* (lamentation), *Sogvari* (mourning) and *Majalis-e Aza* have been exclusively used in connection with the remembrance ceremonies for the martyrdom of Imam Hussain (pbuh).
58. Oonk. "South Asians in East Africa." 101-4.
59. *Bombay Chronicle.* 19 December 1913, p. 6.
60. Jivanjee, Yusufali Esmailjee. Memorandum on the report of the commission on agriculture, 1923. Poona, 1924.
61. *The Tanganyika Herald.* 12 September 1933, p. 13.

62. *Trade Directory.* pp. 181 - 196.
63. By contrast, Hindu traders and entrepreneurs had the mindset largely of temporary residence. They made frequent trips back home (India). They sent home a relatively large proportion of their profits and anticipated an eventual retirement in the vicinities of their places of birth and Jati community. The same pattern is discernible in the lives of sons or other relatives who succeeded them in the family businesses.
64. *Trade Directory.* 181
65. Fazal. *My Zanzibar Recollections.* This book is based on historical facts, both written as well as oral. He says: 'The Jamaatkhana in Zanzibar was probably renovated and refurbished in 1905, but its existence in the Stone town in Zanzibar must have been earlier as the list of Mukhis and Kamadias suggest that they go as far back as 1838. Incidentally, the first Mukhi of the Jamaatkhana reads Kassambhai Pirani (1838).'
66. Panjwani, Sibtain. "In Conversation with Alhaj Murtaza Jivraj." *YouTube,* uploaded by The Awakening Project, 29 Feb 2020, https://www.youtube.com/watch?v=G-0_YUK6OnQ.
67. *Trade Directory.*
68. *Trade Directory.* Page 181
69. Sheriff. "Migration & Creation of New Societies."
70. The building referred to as old Faize School Building was transformed into a school in 1928. At its inception, it had three tutors: M.M. Jaffer (Mulla Asgher's father), H.M.Rashid and Hassanali Rashid. When it became a night school, Arabic, Farsi and Urdu were taught. Abdulrasul Alidina Saleh became its first principal followed by Gulamhusein Satchu Lalji, Mohamed Jivraj and Mohamedhusein Satchu Lalji. The teaching staff consisted of Agha Mehdi Shustary (grandson of Agha Husain), Mohamedjaffer Nathani (Maalim Miya), Gulamhusein Peera, Najaf Tejani, Ahmed Issa and many more. In 1958, the old Faize School was replaced by a new Faize School building built by Husain Dharamsi Ganji and known to the community as Ithna-Asheri School.
71. Prior to the arrival of the Khojas, the Shia communities in Zanzibar were mainly from Bahrain, Muscat and Iran. They were already well-settled having found work in the Sultan's army or in setting up small retail shops.
72. Major Mohamed Ahmed Khan because of his honesty and devotion to the religion was often called by the Sultan Baragash "*Kalbe Ali Khan*" which meant a *Muhib* or a devotee of Imam Ali (pbuh). The Sultan would welcome Major Mohamed Ahmed Khan as "*Kalbe Ali Khan*" whenever he would call at the court and enjoyed a special closeness from the Sultan. (See the history purporting to the *Matam Baharani* was given by Al-Haj Syed Kazim Syed Abbas, the current custodian of the *Matam Baharani*, to Mr. Bashir H. Peera at his office on 5 September, 1988. *Africa Federation Archives.*
73. Ibid. According to Syed Kazim Syed Abbas, Sultan Syed Khalifa who succeeded Sultan Bargash had also had a special respect for the Shias of Zanzibar. In fact, the Sultan had made an intention that if he was blessed with a baby boy he would supply Persian carpets for in the entire *Matam Baharani.*

Soon after, his late wife Bibi Matuka conceived and gave birth to a baby boy they named Abdulla, who later became the Sultan of Zanzibar.
74. The circular '*Saf Matam*' was is a circular arrangement of carrying out commemoration most likely brought to Zanzibar by Persians and adopted by Bahrainis. Later, the Khoja Sshia Ithna-Asheries. adopted it into their commemorations and it is now part of Muharram traditions within the East African Khoja Shia Ithna-Asheri communities.
75. Fazal. *My Zanzibar Recollections*.
76. Haji Gulamhussein Sachoo Lalji was one such volunteer who served many roles:e headmaster of Faize night school, secretary to the Faize and an assistant honorary treasurer and a founder members of Zanzibar's reading room. He was also active in governmental services and was awarded "a third class brilliant star" by the Sultan of Zanzibar. See *Federation Samachar*. January, 1962.
77. *Trade Directory*. p. 181.
78. Mohamedjaffer Rawji was buried at the Kuwwat mosque and his grave still lies there. Fazal. *My Zanzibar Recollections*.
79. *Trade Directory*. p. 187.
80. The Hijri year or era follows the Islamic lunar calendar, which begins its count from the Islamic New Year in 622 CE. During that year, Prophet Muhammad (pbuh) and his followers migrated from Mecca to Yathrib (now Medina). This event, known as the *Hijra*. In the West, this era is most commonly denoted as AH ('in the year of the *Hijra*') in parallel with the Christian (AD), Common (CE) and Jewish eras (AM) and can similarly be placed before or after the date. Because the Islamic lunar calendar has only 354 or 355 days in its year, it slowly rotates relative to the Gregorian calendar year.
81. An endowment made by a Muslim to a religious, educational, or charitable cause.
82. Fazal. *My Zanzibar Recollections*. pp. 3-4.
83. *Ibadism* or *Ibaḍiyya*, is a school of thought dominant in Oman. It is also found in parts of Algeria, Tunisia, Libya and East Africa.
84. That included saying '*Ashahdun Aliyun Waliyullah*' (I bear witness that 'Ali is guardian/vicegerent of Allah) in the Adhan (Call to prayer) that was recited from the Kuwwatul mosque.
85. He was the *wazir* (minister) in the Sultanate of Zanzibar
86. The Busaidis instituted unprecedented religious freedoms in Zanzibar. As a result, the island became a centre for both Sunni and Ibadi scholarship. See Bang, A. K. *Sufis and Scholars of the Sea: Family Networks in East Africa, 1860–1925*. Routledge Curzon, 2003.
87. Muslim religious judges
88. Policy of categorizing the colonised people led to the creation of a three-tier court system: English, Islamic and customary courts. By manipulating ethnic identities, the British colonial authorities applied the strategy of inclusion and exclusion. On the one hand, 'foreign' persons were excluded from the application of 'Native' regulations, and on the other hand, 'indigenous' persons were subjected to 'Native' laws. This would have implications for the Khoja

Shia-Ithna-Asheri as they began to establish in Zanzibar and elsewhere in East Africa. For example, British judges adopted a liberal policy of giving judgement according to the *madhhabs* of the litigants, as opposed to the local custom practiced by *qadhis* who gave judgement in accordance with their *madhhabs*. In cases where litigants followed different *madhhabs*, British judges applied common law principles of fairness and equity. The colonial judges also adopted a liberal approach of applying the texts of a particular *madhhab* to litigants who followed a different *madhhab*.

89. Fazal. *My Zanzibar Recollections.* p. 31.
90. *Wazir* means 'minister' in several West and South Asian languages and is found in English as 'vizier'.
91. Arabic phrase in call to prayer meaning: 'I bear witness that Imam Ali (pbuh) is the vicegerant of Allah.'
92. Muslim call to prayer.
93. Excerpts of interview with late Agha Mehdi by Fidahusain Hameer, editor, *The Light Magazine*. Africa Federation.
94. Following the *Unguja Yetu* program by Africa Federation, Fazal writes that 'for that matter it is doubtful if initially even the Kuwwat Jamaat had a President designate or Secretary designate though we do give mention to Peera Walli or Ali Nathoo as presidents in that era. This could be presumption considering that they probably headed a team of Trustees and thus the designations '*pramukh*' or '*mantri*' can be ascribed to them. They could have even been '*Mukhi*' as in the Khoja set up this was the foremost authority'.
95. Ibid.
96. *Ashura*: the day of the martyrdom of Imam Hussain (pbuh), grandson of Prophet Mohammed (pbuh).
97. Commemorating the martyrdom of Imam Ali (pbuh), son-in-law and cousin of Prophet Mohammed (pbuh).
98. *Trade Directory.* p.167.
99. Husain Rahim introduced the Ithna-Asheri Voluntary Corps with Ibrahim Husain Shariff as its Chairman, Ali Jivraj its Secretary and Abbas Tejani its Treasurer.
100. Jaffer. *The Endangered Species*.
101. Ibid., p. 181.
102. *Kaba ni Kahani Part 1, Kaba Kutum.* p.15 onwards, https://www.yumpu.com/xx/document/view/58393230/book-53-kiba-ni-kahani-part-1-kaba-kutum.
103. Kaba, Adelji Dhanji. *Khoja Panth Darpan.* Part 6, Kathiawad, The Khoja Printing Press, 1915, p. 53.
104. Fazal. *My Zanzibar Recollections.*
105. Ibid., p. 101
106. Ibid.
107. There is also a version in the community that this Mehfil at Mtendeni was run by Hassanali Peera and frequented by the members of the other sects. Interestingly the Hazrat Abbas' *ladu* (sweets) that we observe annually is an event that dates back to the Ismaili days (*Abbasali ja laddu* – Indian

sweets of Abbas) and to date given lot of sanctity by them. Likewise, the official positions *Mukhi* and *Kamadia* are traditionally Khoja designations to which we adhere even today.
108. Fazal. *My Zanzibar Recollections*. p. 102.
109. *Trade Directory.* p. 197-8.
110. *Trade Directory.* p. 181.
111. Muhammad Walji and Sheriff Dewji were among the four trustees. Excerpts of an interview with late Agha Mehdi. Fidahusain Hameer, editor. *The Light Magazine*. Africa Federation.)
112. Ibid. Sayyid Abdulhussain made the following conditions: (1) There should not be immorality for three days (2) That all people fast for three days (3) That all people should make Istighfar (repent), On the third day he came out in congregation with the Shia community and led the prayers at Mnazimoja ground when rain started to pour which continued for some days.
113. Agha Sayyid Abdulhusein Mar'ashi was succeeded by his son-in-law, Agha Sayyid Husain Habibullah Shushtari Musawi. Sayyid Husain was a pious, humble man. He remained the Residential Alim till his passing away 1945. He was followed by Agha Sayyid Mohamedhusain Nashirul Islam Musawi, Sayyid Jabir Hassan, Tahzibul Hassan and few others. Agha Hussain and Agha Abdulhusein had large families in Zanzibar. They were held in high esteem by the Khoja Shia Ithna-Asheries.
114. Fazal. *My Zanzibar Recollections*. p. 44 - 59
115. Initially, it appears from the communal conversations that the Khoja community was run by trustees or *mutwallis*, and a *mukhi*, whose words were held in very high esteem. As rule-based Jamaats like Kuwwat and Hujjat were formed, the post of president and other office bearers came into being.
116. It is reported within the communal archives that one of the highest donors was Saleh Lakha Kanji who is believed to have spent his entire wealth on financing this Hujjat mosque.
117. These were donated by Ismail Subzali Thawer.
118. This dispensary, also known as Ithna-Asheri Dispensary, is a finely decorated historical building in Stone Town, Zanzibar. The building was commissioned in 1887 by Tharia Topan, a prominent Khoja Ismaili Indian merchant and brought to completion in 1894. In 1900, it was the building, bought by a prominent Khoja Shia Ithna-Asheri Indian merchant, a member of Zanzibar Hujjat Jamaat, Hajji Nasser Noormohamed Kasmani who decided that the ground floor would be used as a dispensary, while the upper floors were partitioned into apartments. The dispensary ran on a charitable basis for all the Khojas and with minimal charges.
119. *Africa Federation Archives*. Section and article by Br. Abdulrazak Sheriff of Dar es Salaam, Tanzania.
120. Ibid.
121. Fazal. *My Zanzibar Recollections*. pp. 44 - 59.
122. 'The Hazrat Abbas *ladu nyaz* held annually at Nai Misid was traditionally the Jamnagar/Jodia/Khambhalia/Khoja-Ismaili event prior to the secessionist

days. It had to coincide with the Hindu month of 'Ashad' and was celebrated with great fervour. The Jamnagris abided by this tradition and in the early days it was always held during 'Ashad'. Later this factor was nullified but the *ladu nyaz* continues till today. Also to this very day some old Khoja Ismailis seek '*Abbas Alija laddu nyaz*' when this feast is held. See Fazal. *Zanzibar's Mysterious Nai Misid*. 8 July 2020

123. *Rahenajaat*. Edition 30 and earlier.
124. Dewji, Mohamed Jaffer Sheriff. *Al-Musawaat*. Mombasa, Arunoday Printing Press, 1923.
125. *Mehfil* is a Hindustani term for a shrine which is of Persian extraction. They can range from a multi-story complex to a small spare room in a family dwelling and share some common features in the Khoja Shia Ithna-Asheri culture. *Mehfils* (shrines) have certain common features. The foremost is that they contain a *zari* which is a model of a particular shrine that exists mainly in Kerbala and Najaf in Iraq and Mashad in Iran. Near the *zari* are the *alams* (or *uhlums*). They are sticks, one to two meters high, with black cloth draped over it which is a symbolic representations of the saints being venerated. On the head of the stick is attached an open right hand with the palm side facing the congregation and representations of major characters from the story of the passion of Hussain or the life of the Prophet (pbut).
126. 'The Institution of *Majlis* (lecture, lamentations and recitations) of Imam Husain (pbuh) created several *Zakirs* (reciters) ordinarily known as the Mullas. In earlier days, these Mullas read from the books published by Marhum Allama Haji Gulamali Haji Esmail. These had proven to be of considerable assistance as well as magazines like al-Burhan from Ludhiana, Punjab, India. There were Mullas from Iran and Iraq as well as some within the community by 1960s. These included: 1. Mulla Abdulrasul Dewji (Zanzibar), 2. Mulla Kassamali Ladha (Mombasa), 3. Mulla Moledina Jaffer (Tanga), 4. Mulla Ahmad A. Lakha Kanji (Zanzibar), 5. Mulla Husein A. Rahim (Zanzibar), 6. Mulla Mohamed Mulla Jaffer (Zanzibar). Other familiar names are: Mulla Nanji Bhanji, Mulla Faateh Ali, Mulla Jaffer Pardhan, Mulla Ali Mohamed Nanji, Mulla Mohamedjaffer Nazerali, Mulla Rashid Nurmohamed, Mulla Gulamhusein A.D. Musa, Mulla Ali Khaku Rajpar, Mulla Hasanali Rashid Kermalf, Mulla H. M. Rashid, Mulla H. M. Nasser, Mulla Gulamlhusein Kanji, Mulla Abdulrasul Hassanali G. Khaki and many others from the community. See Jaffer. "An Outline of the History of Khoja."
127. Akhtar, Iqbal. "A Study of The Proliferation of Mehfils (Shrines) Among The Khoja Shia Ithna-Asheri Community Of Dar Es Salaam." *Department of Religious Studies*, University of Denver, 2008.
128. An example of this is '*kiejemu*' and '*saf matam*' with '*eki*' and '*bishin*' included within it (Persian/Farsi/Bahraini way of lamentation).
129. *Africa Federation Archives*. 30 August 2019.
130. Ibid., 23 April 2018.
131. "Khoja Shia-Ithna-Asheri Jamaat of Dar es Salaam: Mehfile Abbas Section." *Executive Committee of Dar es Salaam Jamaat*. Dar es Salaam Printers, 1962.

132. The name is common in Ithna-Asheri Tanzanian culture, which involves a shortening of the first name. For instance, the name Fatima as in this case can be shortened to Fatu, Fatim, or Fati.
133. *Africa Federation Archives.* 18 January 2019.
134. '*Sauti Ya Unguja*' (Voice of Zanzibar) was launched in 1951.
135. Fazal. *My Zanzibar Recollections.* p. 95. Alhaj Murtaza Bandali presently lives in the UK and still contributes actively.
136. Copies of Msimuliza can be found in the library of the United Society for the Propagation of the Gospel in London, in the SOAS library (i, 1–19, 21–45; 48), and in the Bodleian. (i, 1–48; ii).
137. *The Gazette*, 192, 2 October 1895, p. 6.
138. Sturmur, Martin. *Media History of Tanzania.* Tanzania, Ndanda Mission Press, 1998, pp. 273-303.
139. Ibid., pp. 20, 22, 34. It also started coverage of politics in English in 1918.
140. There were two community print media companies who established the printing press in Zanzibar: Hassanali Fazel Master in Shangani area in the 1940s and Anwar Ahmed Ladha in Sokomuhogo in the early 1950s. The newspapers were "*Samachar*" and "*Zanzibar Times*" respectively. "Mistakes: an opportunity to pass experience." *Africa Federation Archives.* 22 March 2019.
141. Ibid., and *The Samachar. Silver Jubilee N*umber, 1929, p. 10.
142. Ibid., and *The Chequered*, p. 10., The Union Press was at no. 345, Sokokuu, a property owned by Mohsin bin Seif Khanjiri. The Meher Printing Press was at no. 821 Kiponda, a property owned by Esmailji Jivanji & Co.
143. Ibid., and Scotton, Growth, p. 68.
144. Ibid., and "Report of an Inspector in the Zanzibar Police dated 25/11/1911" in *Zanzibar Archives,* AC 1/151. Document 90 in AL 2/38.
145. Ibid., and *Chequered,* 12 and *Blue Book,* 1918, Q4. Scotton, Growth, 36 says the Samachar first appeared in 1901; Hamdani, 8 and Sturmer, 183 give the date as 1902, confusing it with the *Islam Samachar.* The Zanzibar Archives have a copy of the issue vol. 15, no. 260, Saturday 30 March 1918, all in Gujarati. It ceased to appear in 1968. Few copies are available from these early years.
146. Ibid.
147. Ibid.
148. Ibid.
149. Ibid.
150. Ibid.
151. Ibid.
152. Ibid.
153. Means 'Spring in Paradise'.
154. Gulamhusein Mohamed Vali Dharsi and MohamedJaffer Sheriff Dewji were acknowledged for their religious scholarship. Syed Aqa Hasan Taba Sarah conferred the title of '*Hami-e-Islam*' upon Gulamhusein bhai in 1910. Mohamed Jaffer Sheriff Dewji wrote on diverse themes. He covered religious as well as social subjects. He has about twenty books, some of which are acclaimed as his masterpieces. Two books by Mohamed Jaffer Sheriff Dewji:

"*Ruyate Hilal*" and "*Imame Zaman*" were translated into Urdu, a first example of Gujarati work to be rendered into a language which was a principle source of reference by Khoja Shia Ithna-Asheries. See Jaffer. "An Outline of the History of Khoja."

155. Known in the community as '*Alams* with *panjas*'.
156. Ashura is marked by all Muslims, but for Shia Muslims it is a major religious commemoration.
157. Means 40th or *Arbaeen* in Arabic.
158. The Chehlum Juloos is an elaborate programme that starts with sad recitals followed by *majlis*. At around 11.00 pm *julus* starts from *imambada* of Kuwwat *masjid* and makes various stops religious places such as *matam baharani, mehfile abbas, mehfile shahe khurasan*. Then, in the morning, the *julus* procession starts again visiting *mehfile zainab, mehfile bibi fatema* and eventually the procession ends at the local burial ground. Fazal. *My Zanzibar Recollections*.
159. Procession.
160. Fazal. *My Zanzibar Recollections*. p. 94-9.
161. *Salsabil*. January, 1957.
162. Ibid., pp. 92-4.
163. *Africa Federation Archives*. 22 March 2019.
164. In metaphoric *ginan* "Eji Dhan Dhan Aajano", the word *melavado* appears twice meaning 'Meet with affection' and 'Meeting of minds'. *Melavado* is popularly understood as a gathering or meeting.
165. A long coat-like garment traditionally associated with the aristocracy of the Indian subcontinent. It is worn over the *Kurta* and *Churidar, Khara pajama* and *salwar*.
166. On the wedding night the garlanded groom would be escorted to the mosque for *nikaah* (a simple ceremony consists of reading from the Qur'an, and the exchange of vows in front of witnesses for both partners) and then backwards to his house by a large group chanting *asalamualaik* (Peace be upon you). In the very early days the groom was made to wear a *sherwani* and golden satin *pagri* (turban), hold a sword and ride on a horse. The *jamaat* elders would also wear the *pagri*. The ladies would gather at the bride's residence from where at around midnight they accompanied the heavily-clad bride to the groom's house. It would be a slow march through the Zanzibar narrow lanes and the neighborhood would be awakened by loud shouts and cheery singing of '*maso maso manangu usimone maso*' (Swahili marriage song). Fazal. *My Zanzibar Recollections*.
167. Ibid.

PART 4A: SOCIO-ECONOMIC AND SOCIO-RELIGIOUS CHANGE

1. Al-Tirmizi. "Indian Sources for African History."
2. *British and Foreign State Papers*, Vol. LXII. Compiled by The Librarian And Keeper Of The Papers, Foreign Office, UK, 1871-1872.
3. Ibid.

4. Originally from Persia (Iran) who sought refugee in India.
5. Ibid.
6. *Trade Directory.*
7. The East Africa Protectorate (also known as British East Africa) was an area occupying roughly the same terrain as present-day Kenya (approximately 639,209 km^2 (246,800 sq mi)) from the Indian Ocean to the border with Uganda in the west. Although part of the dominions of the Sultanate of Zanzibar, it was controlled by Britain in the late 19th century; it grew out of British commercial interests in the area in the 1880s and remained a protectorate until 1920.
8. Gregory, Robert G. *The Rise And Fall of Philanthropy in East Africa - The Asian Contribution.* New Jersey, Transaction Publishers, 1992.
9. Khalfan, Mohammed. *Dastan.* 2008.
10. Ibid.
11. Ibid.
12. Burton, Eric. "'…what tribe should we call him?' The Indian Diaspora, the State and the Nation in Tanzania ca. 1850." *Vienna Journal of African Studies,* vol 13, issue 25, pp. 1-28
13. Panjwani, Sibtain. "Preserving while Redefining the Khoja Shia Ithna-Asheri Muslim Identity Today: The Importance of the Mimbar, Madrasa, and Family." http://awakeningproject.page.tl/
14. Fabian, Steven. "Locating the local in the Coastal Rebellion of 1888–1890." *Journal of East African Studies,* vol. 7, 2013, pp. 432-49, doi: https://doi.org/10.1080/17531055.2013.770680.
15. There is no direct textual evidence that I have seen linking Khoja Shia Ithna-Asheries to slave trade. This, of course, does not dismiss the possibility of it existing within the Khoja community.
16. The Shirazi are either descendants of Muslim Arab traders who had intermarried with Africans along the central Kenyan coastline and then migrated southwards, or a prestigious rank within East African coastal society.
17. Zaramo is the ethnic group that populated Bagamoyo's immediate hinterland.
18. See Baker, E.C. "Notes on the Shirazi of East Africa." *Tanganyika Notes and Records,* vol.11, pp.1-10. See also Glassman. "Feasts and Riot."
19. Ibid., and see Brown. *A Pre-Colonial History.* Rockel suggests that it may have begun around the 1780s based on oral traditions of the Baganda in Uganda; Rockel, Stephen. *Carriers of Culture: Labor on the Road in Nineteenth-Century East Africa.* Praeger, 2006, pp. 19.
20. Ibid., and for a detailed breakdown of each group, see Brown, *A Pre-Colonial History.*
21. *Africa Federation Archives* and communal sources.
22. Ibid., and see *Bundesarchiv Berlin (BAB),* R1001/397: Trade Statistics for the year 1885/1886. The next highest single grossing mainland port was Kilwa, which earned just under half of Bagamoyo's total.
23. Ibid. These form roughly the northern and southern borders of present-day Tanzania, respectively. The ports included Bagamoyo, Dar es Salaam, Kilwa,

Lindi, Mikindani, Pangani, and Kilwa.
24. *Africa Federation Archives* and communal sources
25. Anthony, David H. "Islam in Dar es Salaam, Tanzania." *Studies in Contemporary Islam 4*, 2002, pp. 21-40.
26. Ibid.
27. Ibid.
28. *Trade Directory.* p. 121.
29. *Africa Federation Archives.* 20 October 2018.
30. *Trade Directory.* p. 119
31. Ibid.
32. Constitution Document. Courtesy of Alhaj Marhum Mohammedbhai Dhirani (Ex Chairman of Africa Federation and Dar es Salaam Jamaat. *Africa Federation Archives,* 12 March 2021 / 27 Rajab 1442 A.H.
33. Ibid.
34. Ibid.
35. Ibid.
36. Ibid.
37. Ibid.
38. "Mistakes: an opportunity to pass experience." *Africa Federation Archives*, 22 March 2019.
39. *Africa Federation Archives*, 2 November 2018.
40. For a general economic history of East Africa in this period see Sheriff. *Slaves, Spices and Ivory.*
41. McDow, Thomas F. and Rolingher, Louise. "Frontier Geography And Boundless History - Islam And Arabs In East Africa - A Fusion Of Identities." *Networks And Encounters*, The MIT Electronic Journal of Middle East Studies, vol. 5, Fall 2005,
42. Ibid.
43. Sheriff. *Slaves, Spices and Ivory*.
44. *Trade Directory.* p. 6.
45. Known as Usumbura in the early to mid 20th century and pronounced in the community as Uzumbura.
46. *Africa Federation Archives*, 19 February 2016.
47. *Trade Directory.* p. 6.
48. *Africa Federation Archives*, 15th November 2019.
49. Three teachers were employed: Ebrahim Master, Daya bhai Patel and P. Z. Shah, who lived in teachers' quarters. The school also had a volleyball ground. In 1959, the Kharumwa team participated in the Regional tournament held in Kahama, Mwanza.
50. Khoja Shia Ithna-Asheries in surrounding villages were: Sarawi - Ramzanali M. Bhimji, Husein B. Suleiman and Nurmohamed Jivraj, Usambiro - Pyarali Moledina, Bukoli - Mohamed H. Somji and Ushetu - Mulla Kassam Murji.
51. *Africa Federation Archives*, 13 May 2016.
52. *Africa Federation Archives*, 19 February 2016.
53. *Trade Directory.* p. 7.

54. Ibid., 111.
55. Information provided by Roshan Fazal.
56. *Africa Federation Archives*, 21 August 2009.
57. Ibid., 123.
58. *Trade Directory.*
59. Ibid., 125-6.
60. In 1913 at Dosa Thaver's people used to walk barefooted on the fire (*khandaq*) in the open compound (*Lawani*) of his house in the name of Imam Hussain (pbuh).
61. Ibid., 73, 75.
62. *The Journal of Uganda Society*, vol. 30, part 1, 1966.
63. Ibid.
64. Ibid.
65. Ibid., 75. See also *Africa Federation Archives*, 24 February 2017.
66. Ibid., 79.
67. Ibid., 81.
68. Ibid., 83.
69. Ibid., 81.
70. Ibid., 87.
71. Ibid., 53.
72. Ibid., 55.
73. Ibid., 57.
74. Ibid., 71.
75. Ibid., 65.
76. Ibid., 69.
77. *Africa Federation Archives*, 11 April 2020.
78. *Trade Directory.* p. 72.
79. Ibid., 43.
80. Ibid.
81. Ibid., 49.
82. Omukama of Bunyoro is the title given to rulers of the East African kingdom of Bunyoro, Kitara, The kingdom lasted as an independent state from the 16th to the 19th century. This kingdom is closely related to the Omukara of Toro Kingdom.
83. *Trade Directory.* p. 49.
84. The Kumam (also known as Ikumama, Ikokolemu and Akokolemu referred to by the Iteso) are a Ugandan ethnic group living mainly in the western areas of Teso sub-region and the south-east of Lango sub-region in Kaberamaido district in Eastern Uganda
85. "City Population, Kaberamaido." https://www.citypopulation.de/en/uganda/eastern/admin/kaberamaido/SC1077__kaberamaido/ Accessed 11 March 2022.
86. *Africa Federation Archives*, 18 December 2015.
87. Ibid., 42
88. *Africa Federation Archives*, 2 March 2018. Conversation with Jafferali Merali, grandson of Dewji Kanji. See also, Salvadori, Cynthia. "Muharram in Lamu

from an interview with Jafferali Merali." *We Came in Dhows*, pp. 30-1.
89. *Africa Federation Archives*, 2 March 2018. Interview with Hassan A. M. Jaffer. The family mentioned in the letter probably also included two of Nazerali Dewji's younger brothers, Nasser Dewji and Jaffer Dewji, who were sent to manage the branch of Dewji Jamal & Co. on the island.
90. *Trade Directory*.
91. Ibid.,17.
92. *Trade Directory*. p. 23.
93. Or 1880
94. The same "*shaheed*" Killu Khatau, the student of Mulla Qader Husayn who was martyred in Bombay.
95. Khatau, Dharamsi. "A Pioneer and Merchant Prince." Personal interview with Akberali A. Khatau, grandson of Dharamsi Khatau.
96. There is an interesting incident narrated by Akberali Khatau (told to him by his father) that shows their influence at all levels of commerce including European businesses. One day, Walji Bhanji was delayed in paying for goods bought from the German firm Messrs. Hansing & Co. He was sent a notice threatening court action. When the news reached Jivraj Khatau, he became very angry and told the firm German representative: "Walji Bhanji is my brother." Later that day the notice was torn up by the German in Jivraj s office. The Germans knew if they didn't take the notice back, all business dealings between Dharamsi Khatau & Co. and Messrs. Hansing & Co. would stop.
97. *Trade Directory*. p. 19.
98. Ibid., 20.
99. Ibid., 20.
100. A small bunaglow from Maryam bint Mohamed bin Mbarak Karooso was purchased.
101. *Trade Directory*. p. 20.
102. There is no material evidence available to understand how similar the discords in Zanzibar, Lamu and Mombasa were and there is a need to explore the discord if the materials are available.
103. There is also a view that Kuwwat Masjid and Imambada were built in 1904 on land donated by the family of Hashambhai Gulamhussain.
104. *Trade Directory*. p. 25.
105. Ibid., 21.
106. Ibid., 27.
107. Ibid., 29.
108. Ibid., 28,190.
109. Ibid., 28.
110. He was a son of Dewji Jamaal.
111. Mulla Mohamedjaffer Sherriff Dewji left behind two notable children: a daughter who was the mother of Marhum Mulla Asgharali M. M. Jaffer and a son, Haji Ali Mohamedjaffer Sheriff who served Bilal Muslim Mission of Kenya with utmost dedication.
112. "Allamah Syed Saeed Akhter Rizvi." *Africa Federation Samachar*, vol. 31,

issue 3, April 1999.
113. A well known scholar who was one of the founders of Bilal Muslim Mission in Tanzania. He headed this mission and carried out exemplary work in introducing Islam according to the family of Prophet Mohammed (pbut).
114. *Africa Federation Archives*, 29 June 2018.
115. Ibid.
116. *The Light Magazine*, vol.33, no.2, April 1999.
117. *Trade Directory.* p. 31.
118. Ethnic group that inhabits northern, central, southern Kenya and northern Tanzania. They are among the best known local populations internationally due to their residence near the many game parks in East Africa and their distinctive customs and dress.
119. *Trade Directory.* p. 19.
120. From interviews with Mulla Anverali Valimohamed Walji who passed away in 2019 in the UK.
121. Ibid., 32, 33, 34.
122. Ibid., 33, 34.
123. Ibid., 34.
124. Mumtazali Kassam settled with his family in South London, United Kingdom in 1984 and contributed his time for community work in London.
125. *Africa Federation Archives*, 3 August 2018.
126. Ibid.
127. Mangat, J.A. *History of Asians in East Africa c. 1886–1945.* New York, Oxford University Press,1969.
128. Ibid, 475.
129. Ibid, 477.
130. *Trade Directory.* p. 15.
131. Ibid., p. 102.
132. Biginagwa, Thomas John. *Historical archaeology of the 19th century Caravan Trade in North-eastern Tanzania: A zooarchaeological perspective.* 2012. University of York. Ph.D. thesis. http://etheses.whiterose.ac.uk/2326/1/Dr_Bigi_THESIS.pdf, p.108.
133. *Trade Directory.* pp. 15 and 133.
134. Korogwe is a town in Tanzania nearby Usambara mountain range.
135. *Africa Federation Archives,* 10 June 2016.
136. *Trade Directory.*
137. Ibid.
138. Red Water Disease (Babesiosis) is caused by a single-celled parasite which infects red blood cells, eventually causing them to burst.
139. Ibid.
140. *Trade Directory.* p. 162.
141. Ibid., 167.
142. *Trade Directory; Africa Federation Archives,* 8 July 2016.
143. Ibid.,168.
144. *Africa Federation Archives; Trade Directory.*

145. Ibid., 131.
146. Ibid., 96.
147. Ibid., 102.
148. Shermohamed liked recounting his stories to his grandchildren. One such story was that while going from Arusha to Babati with a truck full of goods, their vehicle broke down at around 9 p.m. There was nothing they could do until somebody passed by the next morning; Shermohammed told the driver and his helper to sit inside the cabin and decided to stretch out on his prayer mat on the ground next to the truck. He fell fast asleep and woke up at around 2 a.m., He immediately sensed he was not alone and because of his experience in the jungle, knew to slow down his breathing completely in the presence of a wild animal. When he took stock of his surroundings, he spotted a lion not more than 15 feet from him. After what seemed to be an eternity as he recited chapters from the Qur'an and prayed to God, the lion slowly away. Shermohamed waited at least another half hour before he got up slowly, opened the passenger side door, and squeezed back into the cabin. Neither the helper nor the driver had seen anything until daylight found the whole lion family resting under a tree about a quarter mile from the truck.
149. Mangat. *History of Asians.*
150. *Africa Federation Archives,* 18 March 2016.
151. *Trade Directory.* p.103-4.
152. *Africa Federation Archives,* 18th March 2016.
153. *Trade Directory.* p.104..
154. Ibid.
155. Ibid., 141.
156. *Trade Directory.* p.149.
157. Ibid., 145.
158. Ibid., 147, 149.
159. *Trade Directory.* p. 161.
160. Ibid, 129.
161. *Kilwa na Sawaal Jawaab* (Questions and Answers in Kilwa), *Aftab e Hidayat* (Light of Guidance). Composed and Published by, Adelji Dhanji Kaba, Amerali- Kathiawar, 1918, pp. 2 and 3.
162. Ibid., 2.
163. Al-Qadiri, Mwallimu Mzee bin Ali bin Kidigo, *Shairi la Makunganya [The War against Hassan bin Omari].* 2002, p. 287.
164. *Trade Directory.* pp. 87-9.
165. *Africa Federation Archives,* 3 June 2016.
166. *Africa Federation Archives,* 30 June 2017.

4B. A SINGULAR RULE-BASED COMMUNITY

1. Gregory, Robert. *The Rise And Fall of Philanthropy in East Africa – The Asian Contribution.* Transaction Publishers, 1992, p. 35.
2. Walji-Moloo, P., Palriwala R. and Risseeuw. *Women's position and fertility:*

The case of the Asians in Kenya. 1996. See also Palriwala and Risseeuw. *Shifting Circles of Support: Contextualising Kinship and Gender in South-Asia and Sub-Saharan Africa.* New Delhi, p. 226.
3. Pelgrim. *The Mnazi Moja Dispute.*
4. Gregory, Robert. *An Economic and Social History, 1890 – 1980,* Boulder, CO: Westview Press, 1993, p. 25-36.
5. Brahmins, Kshatriyas and Vaishya and Shudras.
6. Lodhi, Abdulaziz Y. "Muslims in Eastern Africa - Their Past and Present." *Nordic Journal of African Studies* 3(1): 88-98, Uppsala University, Sweden, 1994.
7. Ibid. under "Islamic Denominations and Muslims in Eastern Africa."
8. Souvenir of ten years of social, cultural, religious and educational services of The East African Muslim Welfare Society, published in December 1954.
9. *Trade Directory.*
10. *Trade Directory.*
11. Giving a high value to charity is among the fundamental principles for Muslims.
12. Gregory. "The Rise And Fall of Philanthropy."
13. Means perpetual charity.
14. Jaffer, Hassan Ali M. *Mombasa Jamaat Chronicle.* vol.3. no.1, 18 April 2003.
15. Ibid.
16. Ibid.
17. Ibid.
18. In Islam, *Barakah* or *Baraka* (Arabic: بركة) is a blessing power, a kind of continuity of spiritual presence and revelation that begins with God and flows through those closest to God. *Baraka* can be found within physical objects, places, and people, as chosen by God.
19. "We Exist to Serve." Report for the Term 1994-1997. Presented at the *7th Ordinary Conference Of The World Federation of Khoja Shia Ithna-Asheri Muslim Community.*
20. Wilson, E.G., editor, "Who's Who in East Africa, 1965-66." Nairobi, marco, 1966, Tanzania section, p. 35.
21. *Trade Directory.*
22. However, some did retain their ties with their relations back in Kuchh and Kathiawad, especially true of the first generation immigrants who arrived in East Africa. For example, Abdulla Fazal from Bukoba earned 25 shs per month when he arrived in 1910. Of that, he sent 10 shs to his mother in Kuchh. There are many examples of such obtained during conversation with elders of the community but the mindset among the Khoja Shia Ithna-Asheries was to permanenmtly settle in East Africa and call it their home.
23. Assuming married couple with average of three children.

5. Structural Institutionalization

1. Alloo, Abbas. Alhaj Peera, Ukera G. and Alhaj Nasser, Mohib Ali. "A

Historical Chronicle, The first Ever Khoja Shia Ithna-Asheri Conference held in Mundra, Kachchh, India in 1933." *Africa Federation Archives,* 12 May 2017.
2. Ibid.
3. Ibid.
4. *Munadee* means 'Herald'.
5. *Trade Directory.* p. 166.
6. Jaffer, "An Outline of the History of Khoja." pp. 16,17.
7. *Munadee,* 1932.
8. AFED was formed in 1946.
9. Means revolution.
10. *Africa Federation Archives,* 22 March 2019.
11. 'In 1946 a constitutional conference of the East African Federation of the Khoja Shia Ithna-Asheri Jamaats was convened in Dar-es-Salaam.The youth of Kumar Mandal felt convinced that the Federation is a panacea for to solve the challanges in the community. They felt so convinved and pinned their hopes on it that they collected twenty-five shillings from their spending allowances and contributed the princely amount to the Foundation Fund.' *Africa Federation Archives,* 22 March 2019.
12. *Africa Federation Archives,* 12 April 2019. See also Appendix A. Chairman Abdulhussein Noormohamed's address at the Federation's 2nd Conference held in Mombasa, 1949.
13. Ibid.
14. See Appendix 2.
15. Ibid.
16. *Africa Federation Archives,* 7 February 2009.
17. Ibid.
18. Panjwani, Sibtain. "In Conversation with Alhaj Anverbhai Merali and Mama Keki Merali." *YouTube,* uploaded by The Awakening Project, 23 Jan 2020, https://youtu.be/3-aGeenC_1U.
19. "A Tentative Outline History of Council of European Jamaats (COEJ) - A Generic Working Document." *Secretariat, CoEJ,* https://www.world-federation.org/sites/default/files/KHF%20Itinerary.pdf. Presented at *Khoja Heritage Festival.* 6 April 2019, Watford, United Kingdom.
20. 1971, the expulsion of Asians from Uganda created an urgent need to accommodate large influx of community members with different social and religious demands and needs. In the same year, the East African Ithna-Asheri Union resolved to form a Jamaat. In 1972, a constitutional conference was held and KSI Jamaat of London came into existence.
21. From "Our Leaders - Our History - Our Pride." *Africa Federation Archives,* 12 April 2019
22. One who calls Muslims to prayer.
23. See Appendix C. A Tribute to Maulana Rizvi on his demise.
23. Jaffer. "An Outline of the History of Khoja." 1983, 24-27.
24. Ibid. Also see Appendix D. Extracts from tributes in memory of Ebrahimbhai.
25. *Trade Directory.*

26. From the official colonial records of Kenya, Uganda, Tanganyika, Zanzibar.
27. Taxation enquiry 1947. pp. 10-11.
28. Ibid.
29. The Mau Mau movement of Kenya was a nationalist armed peasant revolt against the British colonial state, its policies, and its local supporters. The overwhelming majority of the Mau Mau fighters and of their supporters, who formed the "passive wing," came from the Kikuyu ethnic group in Central Province.
30. *Africa Federation Archives,* 22 March 2019.
31. http://www.islamkutuphanesi.com/swahilibooks/ebooks/online/maktaba/fiqh/comUtetezi/02.html.

Concluding Remarks

1. 'Arrival of Khojas in the 19th century coincided with two main trends influencing the Zanzibar society. They were 1. Arab and Persian Islamic influences and 2. Growing colonial influence which opened up infra structure into the interior of East Africa and the establishment of order and security. Burton, "'…what tribe should we call him?'"
2. *Satpanthi*-Khoja connection is evident in various aspects of the Khoja beliefs and practices. See Asani, 2011.
3. Ibid., Ginan (derived from a Sanskrit word meaning 'gnosis') e.g. *Jannatpuri* is attributed to Syed Imam Shah and *Dasa Avatara* (historically a key aspect of the Khoja belief and practices) is attributed to Ṣadr al-Din.
4. Obligations with respect to caste, social custom and sacred law.
5. Acts of lamentation for the martyrs of Karbala.
6. Sacred or a symbol for Shia Muslims associated with Imam Hussain's family and especially his brother Hazrat Abbas (pbuh), the flag bearer of Banu Hashim (tribe of Imam Hussain (pbuh)).
7. Mourning practices of the anniversary of the Martyrdom of Imam Hussain (pbuh) in 680 A.D.
8. Special day to remember contributions to human progress of Imam Hussain (pbuh).
9. Procession in memory of Imam Hussain (pbuh).
10. Zanzibari term to describe special celebration of the birthday of Prophet Mohammed (pbuh).
11. Kachchhi word to describe new mosque.
12. Private gathering.
13. Rule-based community with aims and objectives.
14. *Imambada* is a congregation hall used for religious events.
15. Head of the Khoja community is *mukhi* or headman in a *jamaatkhana* (Khoja communal spaces).
16. *Mukhi* is assisted by *kamadiya* (assistant to *Mukhi*).
17. *Jamaat* here means 'a rule-based community'.
18. A forum, formed in 1976, that brings all the federations and their institutions under it.

19. "We Exist to Serve." Report. 1994 -1997.
20. When Khoja Shia Ithna-Asheries organised and opened their own mosque and *imambada* in Zanzibar.
21. Woodward, Kathryn. *Identity and Difference*. London, Sage, 1997.
22. Pilkington, Andrew, *Racial Disadvantage and Ethnic Diversity in Britain*. New York, Palgrave Macmillan, 2003.
23. Such as what happened within the larger Khoja community, primarily 'us' (as Khoja Shia Ithna-Asheri) and 'them' (as Aga khanis or Khoja Ismaili).
24. Mercer, K. "Welcome to the Jungle: Identity and Diversity in Postmodern Politics." *Identity: Community, Culture and Difference,* edited by Jonathan Rutherford, London, Lawrence & Wishart, 1990, p. 43.
25. Amselle, Jean-Loup. *Mestizo Logics: Anthropology of Identity in Africa and Elsewhere.* Translated by Claudia Royal, Stanford University Press, 1998, p. 41.
26. Pouwels, Randall L. *Horn and crescent: cultural change and traditional Islam on the East African coast, 800-1900*, vol. 53, Cambridge University Press, 2002 and also *The East African Coast, C. 780 to 1900 C.E.,* in *The History of Islam in Africa*, edited by N. Levtzion and R.L. Pouwels, Athens, Ohio University Press, 2000, p. 265.
27. Amselle. *Mestizo Logics.* See Mark, Peter. *Portuguese Style and Luso-African Identity: Precolonial Senegambia, Sixteenth-Nineteenth Centuries*. Indiana University Press, 2002.
28. Asad, Talal. *Genealogies of Religion: Discipline and Reasons of Power in Christianity and Islam*. Johns Hopkins University Press, 1993, p. 210.
29. Kiswahili celebrations.
30. Foucault, Michel. *Truth and Power, in Power/Knowledge: Selected Interviews and Other Writings.* Edited by Colin Gordon, Pantheon Books, 1980, pp. 82-3.
31. *High Court of Zanzibar*, Civil case No 18 - 1956.
32. A charitable endowment under Islamic law that involves donating a building, plot of land or other assets for Muslim religious or charitable purposes with no intention of reclaiming the assets.
33. The judge refers to the 1866 Khoja case and the judgment of Arnold J. (refer to the section under 1866 Khoja Case.
34. Civil case, *Nasur Jesa V. Hirbayee, widow of Jesa Damani*, tried in 1878 in the court of the consul general in Zanzibar (no. 382), A copy of the proceedings can be found in the Zanzibar National Archives, HC7/106.
35. Akhtar, Iqbal. "Negotiating the Racial Boundaries of Khōjā Caste Membership in Late Nineteenth-Century Colonial Zanzibar (1878–1899)." *Journal of Africana Religions* 2.3, 2014.
36. Oonk, G. *Global Indian diasporas: Exploring trajectories of migration and theory*. Amsterdam University Press, 2007, pp. 12 -14.
37. Ibid.
38. Vertovec, Steven. *The Hindu diaspora Comparative patterns*. London and New York, Routledge, 2000.
39. *Trade Directory.*

40. *The Awakening Project*, https://awakeningproject.page.tl/About.htm.
41. Steps used as a platform by a preacher in a mosque or *imambada.*
42. *The Awakening Project.*
43. Ibid.
44. Akhtar, Iqbal. *The Oriental African: The Evolution of Postcolonial Islamic Identities among the Globalized Khōjā of Dar es Salaam.* 2013. University of Edinburgh, p. 90, Ph.D. dissertation.
45. Taylor, Charles. *The Sources of the Self: The Making of the Modern Identity.* Harvard University Press, 1989, p. 27.

BIBLIOGRAPHY

Africa Federation Archives. AFED.
Aga Khan 1, A Sindhi Book, India, Litho Press, 1918.
Ahmad, Aziz. *Studies in Islamic culture in the Indian environment*. Oxford University Press, 1967.
Akhtar, Iqbal. "Ismāʻīl, Gulāmalī (1864–1943)." *Islam, Judaism, and Zoroastrianism*, Florida International University, 2018, pp. 334–8., https://doi.org/10.1007/978-94-024-1267-3_1939.
---. *The Khōjā of Tanzania: Discontinuities of a postcolonial religious identity*, Brill, 2016.
---. "Negotiating the Racial Boundaries of Khōjā Caste Membership in Late Nineteenth-Century Colonial Zanzibar (1878–1899)." *Journal of Africana Religions* 2.3, 2014.
---. *The Oriental African: The Evolution of Postcolonial Islamic Identities among the Globalized Khōjā of Dar es Salaam*. 2013. University of Edinburgh, p. 90, Ph.D. dissertation.
---. "Religious citizenship: the case of the globalised Khōjā." *Journal of the Indian Ocean Region* 10.2, 2014, pp. 219-36, doi:10.1080/19480881.2014.956392.
---. "A Study of The Proliferation of Mehfils (Shrines) Among The Khoja Shia Ithna-Asheri Community Of Dar Es Salaam." *Department of Religious Studies*, University of Denver, 2008.
Algar, Hamid. "The Revolt of Aga Khan Mahallati and the Transference of the Ismaili Imamat to India." *Studia Islamica 29*, 1969, pp. 55-82.
Alpers, E.A. "Gujarat and the trade of East Africa,1500–1800." *International Journal of African Historical Studies*, 9.1, 1976, pp. 22-44.
Amselle, Jean-Loup. *Mestizo Logics: Anthropology of Identity in Africa and Elsewhere*. Translated by Claudia Royal, Stanford University Press, 1998, p. 41
Anthony, David H. "Islam in Dar es Salaam, Tanzania." *Studies in Contemporary Islam 4*, 2002, pp. 21-40.
Arnold, Sir Joseph. "Judgment delivered Nov. 12, 1866 on the Khoja Case (Aga Khan Case)." *Bombay Gazette Steam Press*, 1866.
Asad, Talal. *Genealogies of Religion: Discipline and Reasons of Power in Christianity and Islam*. Johns Hopkins University Press, 1993, p. 210.
Asani, Ali. *Ecstasy and Enlightenment: The Ismaili Devotional Literature of South Asia*. Vol. 6, I.B. Tauris, 2002.
---. "From Satpanthi to Ismaili Muslim: The Articulation of Ismaili Khoja Identity in South Asia." *A Modern History of the Ismailis: Continuity and Change in a Muslim Community*, edited by Farhad Daftary, I.B. Tauris, 2011, pp. 95-128.
Baker, E.C. "Notes on the Shirazi of East Africa." *Tanganyika Notes and Records*, vol.11, pp.1-10.

Bang, A. K. *Sufis and Scholars of the Sea: Family Networks in East Africa, 1860–1925.* Routledge Curzon, 2003.

Bhalloo, Zahir. *Khoja Shia Ithna-Asheris in Lamu and Mombasa: 1870-1930.* Zahir Bhalloo, 2008, p. 5.

Biginagwa, Thomas John. *Historical archaeology of the 19th century Caravan Trade in North-eastern Tanzania: A zooarchaeological perspective.* 2012.

British and Foreign State Papers, Vol. LXII. Compiled by The Librarian And Keeper Of The Papers, Foreign Office, UK, 1871-1872.

"British Success in Africa." *Official Gazette of Zanzibar and East Africa*, vol. 474, 27 February 1901, 3.

Brown, Walter T. *A Pre-colonial History of Bagamoyo: Aspects of the Growth of an East African coastal town.* 1970. University of Michigan, Ph.D. dissertation.

Bruce, Juan. "Typographic development of the Khojki script and printing affairs at the turn of the 19th century in Bombay", *Khoja Studies Conference*, Paris, CNRS-CEIAS, 2016. https://www.academia.edu/30529028.

Bombay Chronicle. 19 December 1913, p. 6.

Bose, Mihir. *The Aga Khans.* Surrey, World's Work, 1984.

Bundesarchiv Berlin (BAB), R1001/397: Trade Statistics for the year 1885/1886.

Burton, Eric. "'…what tribe should we call him?' The Indian Diaspora, the State and the Nation in Tanzania ca. 1850." *Vienna Journal of African Studies*, vol 13, issue 25, pp. 1-28.

Casson, W. T. "Architectural notes on Dar es Salaam." TNR 71, 1970, pp. 183-4.

Christie, James. *Cholera Epidemics in East Africa: An account of the several epidemics in that country from 1821 till 1872.* Macmillan, 1876, pp. 345-6

Clarence-Smith, Gervase. "Indian and Arab entrepreneurs in Eastern Africa (1800-1914)." *Publications de la Société française d'histoire des outre-mers* 2.1 (2001): 335-349.

Cooper, F. *Plantation Slavery on the East Coast of Africa.* Yale University Press, 1977.

Coupland, R. *East Africa and Its Invaders.* The Clarendon Press, 1938.

Chaudhuri, K. *Asia before Europe: Economy and civilization of the Indian ocean from the rise of Islam to 1750.* Cambridge, 1990.

---. *Trade and Civilisation in the Indian Ocean: An Economic History from the Rise of Islam to 1750.* Cambridge University Press, 1985.

Daftary, Farhad, editor. *The Ismailis: An Illustrated History.* United Kingdom, Azimuth Editions, 2008, pp. 480-1.

---. *The Isma'ilis: Their History and Doctrines.* Cambridge University Press, 1992.

---. *A Modern History of the Ismailis.* I. B. Tauris Publishers, 2011, p. 484.

Deckard, Sharae. *Paradise Discourse, Imperialism, and Globalization- Exploiting Eden.* Routledge, 2010, p. 110.

Devji, Faisal. "The Idea of Ismailism." *Critical Muslim*, edited by Ziauddin Sardar & Robin Yassin-Kassab 10, 2014, 51-62.

Dewji, Mohamed Jaffer Sheriff. *Imame Zaman Hazrat Mahdi (A.S.).* Translated by Murtaza A. Lakha, Dar es Salaam, Literary Section Ithna-Asheri Union, 1982.

---. *Al-Musawaat.* Mombasa, Arunoday Printing Press, 1923.

Fabian, Steven. "Locating the local in the Coastal Rebellion of 1888–1890." *Journal of East African Studies*, vol. 7, 2013, pp. 432-49, doi: https://doi.org/10.1080/17531055.2013.770680.

Fazal, Abdulrazak Sheriff. *My Zanzibar Recollections*. 2014.

"Fictitious Narratives in the Satveni'ji Vel." *Amir Pir Mela in Sindh and its Origin*. www.ismaili.net.

Foucault, Michel. *Truth and Power, in Power/Knowledge: Selected Interviews and Other Writings*. Edited by Colin Gordon, Pantheon Books, 1980, pp. 82-3.

Freeman-Grenville, G.S.P. *The East African Coast: Select Documents from the First to the Earlier Nineteenth Century*. Oxford, Clarendon Press, 1966, p. 10.

Frere, Sir Bartle. "Memorandum regarding Banyans." *British Parliamentary Papers. The Gazette*, 192, 2 October 1895, p. 6.

Gilbert, Erik. "Coastal East Africa and the Western Indian Ocean: Long-Distance Trade, Empire, Migration, and Regional Unity, 1750–1970." *The History Teacher* 36.1, 2002, pp. 7-34.

Glassman, Jonathan. *Feasts and Riot: Revelry, Rebellion, and Popular Consciousness on the Swahili Coast 1856-1888*. Portsmouth, Heinemann, 1995, p. 183.

Goodman, Zoe. *Tales of the everyday city: geography and chronology in post-colonial Mombasa*. 2018. SOAS University of London, Ph.D. dissertation. https://pdfs.semanticscholar.org/defb/8b9b26705fd18b11afc9f18bb18cde48f290.pdf

Goswami, Chhaya. *Globalization Before Its Time: The Gujarati Merchants from Kachchh*. India, Penguin, 2016.

---. *The Call of the Sea – Kachchi traders in Muscat and Zanzibar, c. 1800-1880*. New Delhi, Orient Blackswan, 2011.

---. "India and Africa Unique Historical Bonds and Present Prospects, with Special Reference to Kutchis in Zanzibar." Working paper 5, University of Mumbai, 2008.

Gray, John M. "Dar es Salaam under the Sultans of Zanzibar." *Tanganyika Notes and Records* 33, 1952, pp. 1-21.

Gregory, Robert. *An Economic and Social History, 1890 – 1980,* Boulder, CO: Westview Press, 1993, p. 25-36.

---. *"The Rise and Fall of Philanthropy in East Africa – The Asian Contribution,"* 1992.

---. *India and East Africa: A History of Race Relations within the British Empire 1890-1939*. London, 1971, p. 96.

Guillaume, A. *The Life of Muhammad - A Translation of Ishaq's Sirat Rasul Allah*. Oxford University Press, 1998, p. 82.

Gundara, Jagdish S. "Aspects of Indian Culture in Nineteenth Century Zanzibar." *South Asia: Journal of South Asian Studies*, 3.1, 1980, pp. 14-7. doi.org/10.1080/00856408008722996.

Hall, Brian C. *Quantum Theory for Mathematicians*. Springer, 2016.

Haji Bibi V. H.H. Sir Sultan Mohamed Shah Aga Khan. Legal case. http://ismaili.net/heritage/node/29459.

"Heterodox Mahomedans." *Asiatic Journal and Monthly Register for British India and Its Dependencies XII*, no. 69, July-December, 1821, p. 257.

Hickling, Carrisa. *Disinheriting Daughters: Applying Hindu Laws of Inheritance to the Khoja Muslim Community in Western India*. 1998. University of Manitoba, MA dissertation.

Hiskett, M. *The Course of Islam in Africa*, Edinburgh University Press, 1994, p. 154.

A History of the Agakhani Ismailis. Canada, 1991, https://insideismailism.files.wordpress.com/2014/11/history-of-agakhani-ismailis.pdf.

"History of the Formation of the Africa Federation." *Africa Federation*, 18 Jan. 2021, https://africafederation.org/2021/01/18/history-of-the-formation-of-the-africa-federation/.

Honey, M. "A History of Indian Merchant Capital and Class Formation in Tanganyika, c. 1840-1940." 1982. University of Dar es Salaam, Ph.D. Dissertation.

Hurley, Patrick J. and Watson, Lori. *A Concise Introduction to Logic*. Cengage Learning, 2016.

Husain, Mulla Qadir. *Memoirs of Mulla Qadir Husain Sahib*. India, Peermohammed Ebrahim Trust, 1972, pp. 14-5. In Gujarati: *Hidayat Prakash*. Bombay, 2nd ed.,1960. First edition, Bombay, 1888 is available for viewing in the British Library.

India Office Records (IOR)/L/PS/10/588/2, Viceroy of India to Foreign Office, 08-02-1912. British Library.

Ivanow, Vladimir. "Satpanth." *The Ismaili Society Collectanea*, vol. 1, Brill, 1948.

"Isma'ilism." *Encyclopaedia Iranica*, https://iranicaonline.org/articles/ismailism-xvii-the-imamate-in-ismailism.

Jaffer, Asgharali M. M. "An Outline of the History of Khoja Shia Ithna-Asheri in East Africa." Conference of World Ahlulbayt League, 5 August 1983, pp. 16-17. Conference Paper.

Jaffer, Hassan Ali M. *The Endangered Species: An Account of the Journey of Faith by the Khoja Shia Ithna-Asheri Community*. Ontario, Mulla Asghar Memorial Library & Islamic Resource Centre, 2012.

---. *Mombasa Jamaat Chronicle* 3.1, 18 April 2003.

Jackson, Mabel V. *European Powers and South-East Africa*. Longmans, Green & Company, 1942.

Jivanjee, Yusufali Esmailjee. Memorandum on the report of the commission on agriculture, 1923. Poona, 1924

Johnston, Harry H. "Asiatic Colonisation of East Africa." *Journal of the Royal Society of Arts* 37, 1889, pp. 161-172.

"Judgment delivered Nov. 12, 1866 on the 'Khoja Case' (Aga Khan Case)." *Bombay Gazette Steam Press*, 12 November 1866. http://heritage.ismaili.net/node/27983.

Kaba, Adelji Dhanji. *Kaba ni Kahani Part 1, Kaba Kutum*. https://www.yumpu.com/xx/document/view/58393230/book-53-kiba-ni-kahani-part-1-kaba-kutum

---. *Khoja Panth Darpan*. Part 6, Kathiawad, The Khoja Printing Press, 1915, p. 53.

---. *Kilwa na sawal jawab*. 1918.

---. Trans. *Risala* of *Aga Jahangir Shah*. 1912.

Karimdadji, Nazarali, translator. *Aga Khan I's 'Ibrat Afza' (An Autobiography)*, Bombay, Oriental Press.

Kashani Al-, Muhammad bin Murtada bin Mahmud. *Tafsir al-Safi*. https://www.hodaalQur'an.com/rbook.php?id=7006&mn=1

Kassam, Tazim. *Songs of Wisdom and Circles of Dance: an Anthology of Hymns by the Satpanth Ismāʿīlī Saint, Pīr Shams.* 1992. McGill University. Ph.D. thesis.

Khalfan, Mohammed. *Dastan.* 2008.

Khaldūn Ibn. *The Muqaddimah: An Introduction to History*. Translated by Franz Rosenthal, Princeton University Press, 2015, p. 47.

Khan, Dominique-Sila. *Conversions and Shifting Identities: Ramdev Pir and the Ismailis in Rajasthan*. New Delhi, Manohar Publishers and Distributors, 2003.

---. *Crossing the Threshold: Understanding Religious Identities in South Asia.* I.B. Tauris, 2004.

"The Khoja Case." *The Times of India*, 24 April 1866.

Khojapedia. https://khojapedia.com.

KHOJAwiki.org. khojawiki.org.

Kirk, William. "The N.E. Monsoon and Some Aspects of African History." *The Journal of African History* 3.2, University of London, 1961, pp. 263-7.

Larsen, Kjersti, editor. "Knowledge, Renewal and Religion - Repositioning and changing ideological and material circumstances among the Swahili on the East African Coast." Uppsala, *Nordiska Afrikainstitutet*, 2009.

---. "Spirit Possession as Historical Narrative: The Production of Identity and Locality in Zanzibar Town." in N. Lovell, editor. *Locality and Belonging*, Routledge, 1998, pp. 125-46.

LeRoy, Père. "Archives Générales Spiritains, Chevilly-la-Rue, France." 17 April 1886.

Lodhi, Abdulaziz Y. "Indians and Indic languages in Eastern Africa: The Status of South Asian Languages in Eastern Africa." *Dept. of Linguistics & Philology*, Uppsala University, Sweden.

---. "Muslims in Eastern Africa - Their Past and Present." *Nordic Journal of African Studies* 3.1, pp. 88-98, Uppsala University, Sweden, 1994.

Lofchie, Michael. *Zanzibar: background to revolution.* Princeton University Press, 1965, p. 56.

Lorenz, C. "History: Theories and Methods." *International Encyclopedia of the Social & Behavioral Sciences,* edited by Wright, James D., 2nd ed., Elsevier, 2015, vol. 11, pp. 131–137. https://doi.org/10.1016/b978-0-08-097086-8.62142-6.

Madelung, Wilferd. "Shiism: Isma`iliyah." *Encyclopedia of Religion*, edited by Mircea Eliade, vol. 13, Macmillan, 1986, p. 257.

Mangat, J.A. *History of Asians in East Africa c. 1886–1945.* New York, Oxford University Press, 1969.

Mark, Peter. *Portuguese Style and Luso-African Identity: Precolonial Senegambia, Sixteenth-Nineteenth Centuries*. Indiana University Press, 2002.

Masselos, Jim. "The Khojas of Bombay: The Defining of Formal Membership Criteria during the Nineteenth Century." *Caste and Social Stratification among*

Muslims in India, edited by Imtiaz Ahmed, 2nd ed., Columbia, South Asia Books, 1978, pp. 97-116.

Mawani, Rizwan. *Tradition As Rupture: Caste, Community And The Colonial Courts - Forging Religious Identity in The 1866 Khoja Case*. 2017. Berkeley, MA dissertation.

McCarney, Joseph. *Routledge Philosophy Guidebook to Hegel on History*. Routledge, 2000, p. 86.

McDow, Thomas F. and Rolingher, Louise. "Frontier Geography And Boundless History - Islam And Arabs In East Africa - A Fusion Of Identities." *Networks And Encounters*, The MIT Electronic Journal of Middle East Studies, vol. 5, Fall 2005,

McMurdo, James. "An Account of the Province of Cutch, and the Countries Lying Between Guzerat and the River Indus: With Cursory Remarks on the Inhabitants, Their History, Manners, and State of Society." *Transactions of the Literary Society of Bombay*, vol. 2, 1820, pp. 205-55.

Mehta, Makrand. "Gujarati Business Communities in East African: Major Historical Trends." *Economic and Political Weekly* 36.20, May 2001.

Mercer, K. "Welcome to the Jungle: Identity and Diversity in Postmodern Politics." *Identity: Community, Culture and Difference,* edited by Jonathan Rutherford, London, Lawrence & Wishart, 1990, p. 43.

Middleton, John. "The Immigrant Communities: The Arabs of the East African Coast." *History of East Africa*, edited by D.A. Low and Smith, vol.3, Clarendon, 1976, p. 499.

---. *The World of the Swahili; An African Mercantile Civilization.*Yale University Press, 1992, p. 28.

Morris, H.F. and Read, J. S. *Indirect Rule and the Search for Justice: Essays in East African Legal History*. Clarendon Press, 1972, p. 43.

Muir, Sir William. *The Life of Mohammad From Original Sources*. J. Grant, 1923, p. 59.

Mungai, Christine. "15 facts about the Indian diaspora in Africa." *World Economic Forum*, 2015, https://www.weforum.org/agenda/2015/06/15-facts-about-the-indian-diaspora-in-africa/.

Muzaffar Al-, Muhammad Rida. *Al-Mantiq*. Beirut, Dar al-Ta'aruf wa Al-Matbu'at, 2006.

Nanji, Azim. *The Nizārī Ismā'ili Tradition in the Indo-Pakistan Subcontinent*. Caravan Books, 1978.

Nanjiani, Sachedina. *Khoja Vruttant*. India, 1892, p. 262.

Nasur Jesa V. Hirbayee, widow of Jesa Damani. Zanzibar National Archives, HC7/106. 1878.

Nimitz Jr., A. *Islam and Politics in East Africa*. University of Minnesota Press, 1980, p.10.

Oonk, Gijsbert. *Global Indian diasporas: Exploring trajectories of migration and theory*. Amsterdam University Press, 2007, pp. 12 -14.

---. *The Karimjee Jivanjee family: Merchant Princes of East Africa, 1800-2000.* Amsterdam, 2009.

---. *Settled Strangers: Asian Business Elites in East Africa (1800-2000)*. Sage, 2013, p. 77.
---. "South Asians in East Africa, 1800–2000. An entrepreneurial minority caught in a 'Catch-22'." Rotterdam, Erasmus University, 2013.
Palat, Ravi A. "Maritime Trade, Political Relations, and Residential Diplomacy in the World of the Indian Ocean." *The Indian Ocean: Oceanic Connections and the Creation of New Societies,* London, Hurst Publishers, 2014, pp. 45-68.
Panjwani, Sibtain. *The Awakening Project.*
Patel, Zarina. *Challenge to colonialism - The struggle of Allibhai Jeevanjee for equal rights in Kenya.* Nairobi, 1997.
Pearson, Michael. "A Bibliography." *The Journal of Indian Ocean World Studies,* 3(1), p. 82, 2019, doi:10.26443/jiows.v3i1.56.
Pelgrim, Maarten. *The Mnazi Moja Dispute: Exploring the relationship between the Khojas, the Aga Khan and the British on the island of Zanzibar during the period 1899-1912.* 2017. Leiden University, pp. 18-30. MA Dissertation.
Perry, Erskine. *Cases Illustrative of Oriental Life and the Application of English Law to India, decided in H.M. Supreme Court at Bombay.* London, S. Sweet, 1853, pp. 110-29.
Pilkington, Andrew, *Racial Disadvantage and Ethnic Diversity in Britain.* New York, Palgrave Macmillan, 2003.
Pouwels, Randall L. "The Battle of Shela: the climax of an era and a point of departure in the modern history of the Kenya Coast." *Cahiers d'Études Africaines* 31 (123), 1991, pp. 363–89.
---. *The East African Coast, C. 780 to 1900 C.E.,* in *The History of Islam in Africa,* edited by N. Levtzion and R.L. Pouwels, Athens, Ohio University Press, 2000, p. 265.
---. *Horn and crescent: cultural change and traditional Islam on the East African coast, 800-1900,* vol. 53, Cambridge University Press, 2002.
Prideaux, W. F. *Administrative Report for 1873-74.* MSA, PD, vol. 294, 1875, p. 2.
Purkis, Diane. *The English Civil War – A People's History.* Harper Perennial, 2007.
Purohit, Teena. *The Aga Khan Case.* Harvard University Press, 2012.
Qadiri Al-, Mwallimu Mzee bin Ali bin Kidigo, *Shairi la Makunganya [The War against Hassan bin Omari].* 2002, p. 287.
Ranjan, Amit. "A History of Syncretism of the Khoja Muslim Community." *The Apollonian,* vol.4:1-2, 2017, pp. 53-65.
Rizvi, Seyyid Saeed Akhtar and King, Noel Q. "Some East African Ithna-Asheri Jamaats (1840-1967)." *Religion in Africa,* vol. 5, fasc. 1, 1973, pp. 12-22.
Rockel, Stephen. *Carriers of Culture: Labor on the Road in Nineteenth-Century East Africa.* Praeger, 2006, pp. 19.
Rosenthal, Franz. *A History of Muslim Historiography.* Brill, 1968.
Ruthven, Malise. "Aga Khan III and the Ismaili Renaissance." *New Trends and Developments in the World of Islam,* edited by Peter B. Clarke, London, Luzac Oriental, 1997, pp. 371-95.
Sadr Al-, Muhammad Baqir. *Al-Tafsir al-Mawdui wa al-Falsafutu al-Ijtma'iyyah fi al-Madrasti al-Qur'aniyyah.* Beirut, Dar al-'Alamiyyah, 1989.

---. *Trends of History in the Qur'an*, translated by Mustajab Ahmad Ansari, Islamic Seminary Publications, https://www.al-islam.org/trends-history-Qur'an-sayyid-muhammad-baqir-al-sadr/what-topical-exegesis-2#need-expansion-juristic-studies.

Said, Edward. *Orientalism*. Vintage, 1979.

Simpson, Edward. *Muslim Society and the Western Indian Ocean: The Seafarers of Kachchh*. Routledge, 2006, pp. 44-5.

Shah, Bipin. "The Famines of India and the formation of Indian Diaspora." https://www.academia.edu/8753763.

Shah, Hasan Ali (Aga Khan I). *Ibratul Afza*. Autobiography. Bombay, Oriental Press, 1865.

---. *Aga Khan I*. Sambat, India, Litho Press, 1918.

Sheriff, Abdul. *Dhow Cultures of the Indian ocean*. London, 2010.

---. *The History & Conservation of Zanzibar Stone Town*. London, Dept. of Archives, Museums & Antiquities in association with J. Curry, 1995.

---. *The Indian Ocean – Oceanic Connections and the Creation of New Societies*, edited by Abdul Sheriff and Enseng Ho, London, Hurst & Co., 2014, p. 19.

---. "Migration & Creation of New Societies: A story from the Indian Ocean." *Transregional Trade and Traders: Situating Gujarat in the Indian Ocean from Early Times to 1900*, edited by Edward A. Alpers and Chhaya Goswami, Oxford Scholarship Online, 2019, doi:10.1093/oso/9780199490684.003.0016.

---. *The Rise of a Commercial Empire: An Aspect of the Economic History of Zanzibar, 1770-1873*. 1971. University of London, pp. 348-9. Ph.D. dissertation.

---. *Slaves, Spices and Ivory in Zanzibar*. Oxford, James Curry Ltd, 1987.

Shodhan, Amrita. "The Entanglement of the Gināns in the Khoja Governance." *Gināns : texts and contexts*, edited by Tazim R. Kassam and Françoise Mallison, Delhi, Primus Books, 2010, pp. 169-80.

---. "Legal Formulation of the Question of Community: Defining the Khoja Collective." *Indian Social Science Review* 1.1, 1999, pp. 137-51.

---. *A Question of Community: Religious Groups and Colonial Law*. Kolkata, Samya, 2001.

Smee, T. and Lt. Hardy. "Observation during a voyage of Research on the East Coast of Africa from Cape Guardafui south to the Island of Zanzibar in the H. C's cruiser Ternate." The Secretary, editor. *Transactions of the Bombay Geographical Society from September 1841 to May 1844*, Vol. # VI, Bombay, the Times Press, p. 45.

Smith, Jane I. "Women in Islam: Equity, Equality, and the Search for the Natural Order." *Journal of the American Academy of Religion*, volume XLVII, issue 4, December 1979, pp. 517-537, https://doi.org/10.1093/jaarel/XLVII.4.517.

Steinberg, Jonah. *Isma'ili modern: globalization and identity in a Muslim community*. Univ of North Carolina Press, 2011.

Stephens, J.E.R. "The Laws of Zanzibar." *Journal of the Society of Comparative Legislation*, vol.13, no. 3, 1913, p. 603.

Stigand, Chauncy Hugh. T*he land of Zinj: Being an account of British East Africa,* *its ancient history and present inhabitants.* London, Constable & Company Ltd., 1913.

Sturmur, Martin. *Media History of Tanzania.* Tanzania, Ndanda Mission Press, 1998, pp. 273-303.

"A Tentative Outline History of Council of European Jamaats (COEJ) - A Generic Working Document." *Secretariat, CoEJ,* https://www.world-federation.org/sites/default/files/KHF%20Itinerary.pdf.

Tabatabai, Muhammad Husayn. *Tafsir al-Mizan.* https://www.hodaalQur'an.com/rbook.php?id=4184&mn=1.

Tabrisi Al-, Ali al-Fadl b. Al-Hasan b. al-Fadl. *Majma' al-Bayan.* https://www.hodaalQur'an.com/rbook.php?id=1787&mn=1.

The Tanganyika Herald. 12 September 1933, p. 13.

Tausch, Arno and Hesmati, Almas. "Islamism and Gender Relations in the Muslim World as Reflected in Recent World Values Survey Data." *IZA Network*, Discussion Paper No. 9672, January 2016. http://ftp.iza.org/dp9672.pdf.

Taylor, Charles. *The Sources of the Self: The Making of the Modern Identity.* Harvard University Press, 1989, p. 27.

Trade Directory and History of the Community. Federation of K.S.I. Jamaats of Africa, Arusha, 30 December 1960.

Transregional Trade and Traders: Situating Gujarat in the Indian Ocean from Early Times to 1900. Edited by Edward A. Alpers and Chhaya Goswami, Oxford Scholarship Online, 2019, doi: 10.1093/oso/9780199490684.001.0001.

Tirmizi Al-, S. "Indian Sources for African History, Volume I", *UNESCO*, 1988, p. 525.

Virani, Shafique N. *The Ismailis in the Middle Ages: a History of Survival, a Search for Salvation.* Oxford University Press, 2007.

Vaughan, J. H. *The Dual Mandate in Zanzibar.* Zanzibar Government Printers, 1935, pp. 11-12.

Vertovec, Steven. *The Hindu diaspora Comparative patterns.* London and New York, Routledge, 2000.

Walji-Moloo, P., Palriwala R. and Risseeuw. *Women's position and fertility: The case of the Asians in Kenya.* 1996. See also Palriwala and Risseeuw. *Shifting Circles of Support: Contextualising Kinship and Gender in South-Asia and Sub-Saharan Africa.* New Delhi, p. 226.

Warah, Rasna. *Triple Heritage: A Journey to Self-discovery.* Nairobi, 1998, p. 22.

"We Exist to Serve." Report for the Term 1994-1997. Presented at the *7th Ordinary Conference Of The World Federation of Khoja Shia Ithna-Asheri Muslim Community.*

Wilson, E.G., editor, "Who's Who in East Africa, 1965-66." Nairobi, marco, 1966, Tanzania section, p. 35.

Wilson, Peter Lamborn. "Ismailis and Nimatullahis." *Studia Islamica*, vol. XLI, 1975, pp. 113-36.

Woodward, Kathryn. *Identity and Difference.* London: Sage, 1997.

Zanzibar National Archives HC7/106.

INTERVIEWS & TALKS

(In Chronological Order)

"In Conversation with Alhaj Hassanalibhai Merchant." *YouTube*, uploaded by The Awakening Project, 13 Feb 2019, https://youtu.be/pS9rDDWZq5Y.

"In Conversation with Alhaj Mohammed Raza Virjee." *YouTube*, uploaded by The Awakening Project, 14 Feb 2019, https://youtu.be/sbbtiyNGHxM.

"In Conversation with Alhaj Aunalibhai Salehmohammed." *YouTube*, uploaded by The Awakening Project, 2 Mar 2019, https://youtu.be/sFsaBy475UM.

"In Conversation with Alhaj Muhsin Dharamsi." *YouTube*, uploaded by The Awakening Project, 2 Mar 2019, https://youtu.be/fGZzowkx7IU.

"In Conversation with Professor Abdul Sheriff." *YouTube*, uploaded by The Awakening Project, 3 March 2019, https://youtu.be/tlgH8KaApFM.

"In Conversation with Alhaj Mohamedbhai Dhirani." *YouTube*, uploaded by The Awakening Project, 24 April 2019, https://youtu.be/ru7NYabqDQI.

"In Conversation with Alhaj Riyazbhai Masani." *YouTube*, uploaded by The Awakening Project, 2 Jun 2019, https://youtu.be/7Mj6hDi8w3A.

"In Conversation with Nazneenbai Verteji." *YouTube*, uploaded by The Awakening Project, 4 Jul 2019, https://youtu.be/x-y8K4bREwA.

"In Conversation with Haji Saheb." *YouTube*, uploaded by The Awakening Project, 9 Jan 2020, https://youtu.be/MdDJD_AU8og.

"In Conversation with Alhaj Anverbhai Merali and Mama Keki Merali." *YouTube*, uploaded by The Awakening Project, 23 Jan 2020, https://youtu.be/3-aGeenC_1U.

"In Conversation with Professor Karim Manji-Part 1." *YouTube*, uploaded by The Awakening Project, 6 Feb 2020, https://youtu.be/k_912llhlAM.

"In Conversation with Professor Karim Manji-Part 2." *YouTube*, uploaded by The Awakening Project, 13 Feb 2020, https://youtu.be/wy45chx0qpk.

"In Conversation with Murtazabhai Jivraj." *YouTube*, uploaded by The Awakening Project, 29 Feb 2020, https://youtu.be/G-0_YUK6OnQ.

"In Conversation with Alhaj Asgarali Bharwani." *YouTube*, uploaded by The Awakening Project, 21 April 2020, https://www.youtube.com/watch?v=J_318jISGco.

"In Conversation with Alhaj Mohamed Abdulla Khalfan." *YouTube*, uploaded by The Awakening Project, 12 Sept 2020, https://youtu.be/J9VO55ng_Tk.

"In Conversation with Sabira Jaffer." *YouTube*, uploaded by The Awakening Project, 18 Mar 2021, https://youtu.be/4ultxowaKq8.

"In Conversation with Anverbhai Rajpar." *YouTube*, uploaded by The Awakening Project, 24 Mar 2021, https://youtu.be/Uq5h9TIBUvI.

"In Conversation with Arzu Merali." *YouTube*, uploaded by The Awakening Project, 5 April 2021, https://youtu.be/E5Fe3ziAnbs.

"In Conversation with Iqbal Asaria." *YouTube*, uploaded by The Awakening Project, 10 April 2021, https://youtu.be/W65GfgPrmw8.

"In Conversation with Sajjadbhai Rashid." *YouTube*, uploaded by The Awakening Project, 23 Jul 2021, https://youtu.be/9Wv0HzW1oIY.

Other videos (chronological)

"'Mari Bhasha'-'My Language', Marhum Kassimali Nazerali Panju." *YouTube*, uploaded by The Awakening Project, 23 Sept 2015, https://youtu.be/EtWv6kpLRxc.

"KHOJA SHIA ITHNA-ASHERI IDENTITY (SPEECH IN GUJARATI)." *YouTube*, uploaded by The Awakening Project, 23 Sept 2015, https://youtu.be/LHZX_fw-gjg.

"A short talk on Khoja Shia Ithna-Asheries of East Africa (1839-1960) PART 1." *YouTube*, uploaded by The Awakening Project 9 Apr 2018, https://youtu.be/M_wyol_h4Uk.

"A short talk on Khoja Shia Ithna-Asheries of East Africa (1839-1960) PART 2." *YouTube*, uploaded by The Awakening Project 9 Apr 2018, https://youtu.be/OglgtEGhtME.

"Abul Ghuraba" (Father of the Needy) - Haji Gulamabbas Kassamali Bahadurali Mawji - Son's Reflection." *YouTube*, uploaded by The Awakening Project, 3 Jun 2019, https://www.youtube.com/watch?v=9vLq6F7-m5A.

"The Khoja Shia Ithna-Asheri Community Diaspora: An Exploratory Overview." *YouTube*, uploaded by The Awakening Project, 23 Oct 2019, https://youtu.be/4ttvhK8_oRY.

"Khoja Shia Ithna-Asheries - 'Our journey - Who we are and Where we are'." *YouTube*, uploaded by The Awakening Project, 23 Oct 2019, https://youtu.be/PihYSd-lfoY.

"Khoja Shia Ithna-Asheries of East Africa: Quest for New Socio-religious Identity 1." *YouTube*, uploaded by The Awakening Project, 23 Oct 2019, https://youtu.be/cXvZELagHcQ.

"Q and A - Khoja Shia Ithna-Asheries of East Africa: Quest for New Socio-religious Identity 2." *YouTube*, uploaded by The Awakening Project, 23 Oct 2019, https://youtu.be/iWjSngmJXpA.

"Understanding Our Present Through Our Past - Quest for KSI Socio-religious Identity - Part 1." *YouTube*, uploaded by The Awakening Project, 31 Mar 2021, https://youtu.be/OmnRerY4QYk.

Q & A. Understanding Our Present Through Our Past - Quest for KSI Socio-religious Identity - Part 2." *YouTube*, uploaded by The Awakening Project, 31 Mar 2021, https://youtu.be/-DRvsn8IrSM.

APPENDICES

Appendix A.

FEDERATION'S 2ND CONFERENCE (MOMBASA) - 1949

Chairman Abdulhussein Noormohamed's Address

After about three and half years, we are meeting for our Second Conference. I appreciate the Mombasa Jamaat's effort of hosting this conference with a warm welcome. The first time we met in Dar es Salaam in 1945, we established the provisional council to unite different Jamaats under one roof.

In 1946, we had met again in Dar es Salaam to set the constitution and I could see the support, encouragement and enthusiasm from the community then. In that conference we established the Federation and the Council's central body, we laid a foundation for brotherhood among our Community members, we created one community in East Africa and continued the society's business and religious activities. I am here to inform you about the developments as well as the problems faced within this period. This will help us in our future plans. The Central Council had introduced the following:

- The Census - Community population.
- Birth and Marriage Certificates.
- Higher education grant and scholarship (studying abroad).
- Scholars for Tabligh.
- Grant to acquire religious courses.

We have not been able to follow up on other main programs especially the "levy" and despite all our efforts in past three years, we have not been able to establish a boarding house in Uganda like the one in Tanganyika.

According to our census records, we are able to give you the figures for the Jamaat and their strengths under the Federation. However according to my understanding this report has to be updated every year so the Council can have an account of the increased population. When we first tried introducing the birth and marriage certificates, we faced a tough discussion against it. Since then, the community has realized its importance especially after the introduction of the new 1947 immigration bill. In the future these documents will be necessary and it is my sincere request to the community to register all their children and acquire marriage certificates. For higher education from 1946 to date, we have given a total of seven scholarships and the students have been pursuing good courses. At the end of 1952, two students will Insha'Allah, complete their MBBS degrees and when they return to Zanzibar to practice, the community will realise the importance of this project.

As for the Tabligh project, Maulana Zaminhussein Saheb's travel report has been received by every Jamaat and by the grace of Almighty it has been a success. Arusha's Aalim, Maulana Sayyid Razahussein has submitted his report as well, but due to the load of work it is not yet completed.

Furthermore we are allocating a grant for Arusha's religious scholar's salary. We have given a grant to a student from Kilwa teaching in Arusha's Government's school and another from Arusha studying in Mwanza. A request from some Jamaats has been submitted to do the same for their resident scholars, which will be discussed by the new Council's committee.

Despite of several reminders through circulars the Council has not yet received any request for higher education in religious courses, if there would be any, the Council would have definitely presented it. I don't find it very important to present all the communication of the Central Council's Secretariat, but if anyone is interested to know more about the contents, the letters are available on file.

Comment on original transcript:
We can observe that higher education was given the same importance in the past by our leaders as it is today. It is really amazing to see the far-sightedness and the vision of our forefathers. May Allah (SWT) grant them *maghferat* and rest their souls in the proximity of our fourteen infallibles – *Masumeen* (pbut).

Source: Extracted from "*Rehbar*" October 1949
Translated: F. Ali.
Edited: F. Jaffer.

APPENDIX B.

FEDERATION'S 3ᴿᴰ CONFERENCE (ZANZIBAR) - 1952

Alhaj Abdulhussein Noormohamed's Address

Your Excellency, Prince Abdulla, The Chairman, Brother Delegates, and Gentlemen:

It is a great honour and privilege for me to preside over the 3rd Conference of the Federation of my Community particularly on the soil of this peaceful and lovely island of Zanzibar, where I was born, bred, and educated. I express the grateful thanks of my Community and myself to Your Excellency for kindly accepting to open the conference this afternoon.

If I may recollect it as a happy coincidence, Sir, it was in 1950 that Your Excellency, as Acting Governor of Kenya, opened an Economic Conference in Mombasa - a session of the Federation of the Indian Chambers of Commerce and Industry of Eastern Africa, which was also presided over by me. Today it is a social Conference of the Ithna-Asheri Section of the Khoja Community of East Africa, which belongs to the main Shia Sect of Islam, and Your Excellency, as British Resident of the Dominions of His Highness the Sultan, in performing the opening is doing us a great honour, and I can assure you, Sir, that your presence this afternoon will encourage the deliberation of our organization with a spirit of enthusiasm.

With the increasing number of population of my community spread over in all the parts of East Africa, which now totals over 14,000, it was in 1946 that at a Conference of my community held in Dar es Salaam that the Federation of the Khoja Shia Ithna-Asheri Jamats of Africa was created with an Executive body known as the Central Council. The constitution of our organisation embodies religious principles based on democratic lines, and its aim and objects include social, education, and cultural activities for the welfare and well-being of the whole Community.

In the last six years, we have been successful in the co-ordination of some of our activities under the central organisation, and hope, Sir, to do more useful work for the general uplift of our society.

Our history goes back to about two hundred years when the pioneer members of the Khoja Community first migrated to Zanzibar for trade and commerce from the Cutch and Kathiawar states of Western India, and gradually with the increasing number of people some of them with foresight and with a spirit of initiative and enterprise opened businesses on the mainland and penetrated even in the remote corners of Kenya, Uganda, Tanganyika, Congo Belgium and Somaliland.

Today we are happy to be called and known as permanent East African Citizens having little left in India, except trade relations and family ties and similarly, trade, cultural and religious ties with Pakistan, which we wish to maintain. As law-abiding and peaceful British subjects of this part of the Commonwealth, which we have adopted as our permanent homeland, I would re-iterate, Sir, on behalf of my community and myself, our unswerving loyalty and humble devotion to the person and throne of Her Gracious Majesty the Queen.

As you may be aware, Sir, the enterprising members of my community have played their useful part in the economic expansion and development of East Africa, and have contributed a fair share to the progress and prosperity of the Community and the Country as a whole. Prominent Ithna-Asheri industrialists, agriculturists, and well-known business firms will be found in all the parts of East Africa.

They own sisal and coffee plantations, coffee estates, and coffee curing works, timber concessions, cotton ginning industries, rice, oil and soap milling, and several other secondary and small industries including aluminium factories, etc., throughout East Africa. Some of them hold large agricultural *shambas*, particularly in Uganda, Tanganyika and Zanzibar. Some of them are among the largest Exporting and Importing firms.

With trade and commerce as the backbone of their main occupation, the members of my community have no doubt shared in the general prosperity of the Country. In the Educational field, through our organisation, we have so far sent, with the aid of scholarships, a number of students for higher education, and I am glad to say that two students from Zanzibar will return back in Zanzibar next year as qualified M.B.B.S. doctors. With the increased interest evinced by the parents, we have done a great deal in improving the educational standard of our children.

A number of our boys are also in the Muslim Institute, in Mombasa, in technical lines. Now, I take the opportunity to express our deep sense of appreciation to Sir Phillip Mitchell, whose sympathy and invaluable services to the Muslim Community include the establishment of the Muslim Institute of Mombasa, for which the whole Muslim Community of East Africa, including my community will ever remain grateful. I hope, Sir, that it is the intention of my community to contribute to this important Muslim Educational Institution in the near future.

In public life, Sir, there are a number of public-spirited gentlemen among the members of my community, who find time to serve the people. There could be no better example than to mention Hon. Mr. Fazel Nasser, M.L.C. and, Hon Mr. H.K. Jaffer C.B.E. M.L,C., who are both senior unofficial members of the Legislative Council in Zanzibar and Uganda respectively. In Zanzibar Government Administration, the Ithnasheris have always held senior posts, and it is a pleasure to see Mr. Husein A. Rahim appointed to the dignified post of First Class Magistrate in Zanzibar. I take this opportunity to congratulate Mr. Rahim on his promotion.

Everywhere in East Africa, the members of my community have always maintained a friendly relation with the other sections of the multi-racial community, and I believe, Sir, that with such a spirit of friendliness, cooperation and tolerance, all the sections should get together and do everything possible for the good of East Africa and its people as one community. Zanzibar is a shining example where harmonious relations always exist between the different sections of the community under the protection of the glorious rule of His Highness the Sultan, whose love and paternal care for his subjects are well known. I pray Almighty to spare his Highness for a long time with health and happiness to rule over his beloved subjects.

Before I sit down, Sir, I take this opportunity to thank the Chairman and Members of our Reception Committee for doing an excellent arrangement for the Conference and to my brother Delegates, who have spared time to come to Zanzibar to attend the Conference from all parts of East Africa, and to you Gentlemen, for your presence this afternoon. I would now request you, Sir, to open the Conference with your blessings.

APPENDIX C.

A GLOBAL TRAGEDY
ALLAMAH SAYYID SAEED AKHTAR RIZVI PASSES AWAY

The sudden and sad demise of Allamah Sayyid Saeed Akhtar Rizvi in Dar-es-Salaam on Thursday 20th June 2002 (8th Rabi-ul-Aakhar 1423) came as a shock to the community and Muslims at large around the world. Marhum Maulana Rizvi was more like an institution rather than an individual considering his intense involvement in propagating the Shia faith around the world. He was a scholar, a preacher and a writer. He acquired deep knowledge of religion as well as of secular subjects and his books have been used by children learning Islam, adults wanting to know further about our religion and by new converts and outsiders for whom Marhum spent many hours enlightening them on the true concepts of the Shia faith.

As a prolific writer he has over 140 titles to his credit some of these have been translated into twenty-two languages. His books and correspondence have been instrumental in spreading the true Islam from Philippines to Guyana and around the world. His books on the Elements of Islamic Studies, harmful effects of music, the ill effects of pork and many others are a household name because they provide simple and crucial explanations on many issues pertaining to Islam. He also wrote numerous articles while excerpts from his "Your Questions Answered" editions have been regularly carried in the Federation Samachar.

His writing erudition also extends to the English translation of the profound *Tafsir Al Mizan* of Ayaullah Tabatabai. A *faqih* and a *muhadddith* in his own right, he was also expert in *tafseer* and scholastic theology, a *rijali* and historian, a poet and a linguistic that all made him one of the greatest Muballighs the Shia World has ever known.

A multi-talented communicator, he spoke and wrote in Urdu, English, Arabic, Persian and Kiswahili while also knowing Hindi and Gujarati. As a historian, his last mammoth work, on the History of the Shia Communities, is in the process of being published. In his tribute, the World Federation President, Hasnainbhai Walji points out that Allama Rizvi authored the very first monograph he ever read on the history of the Khoja Shia Ithnaasheries. This was authored in conjunction with Professor Noel King of Makerere University about a quarter of a century ago. The World Federation Secretary General, Sibtain Panjwani in his condolence message says, "I am reflecting on those momentous and far-sighted decisions made by the Supreme Council of the Africa Federation in 1964 to create the Bilal Muslim Mission with the support of Allama Syed Saeed Akhtar Rizvi and others who remained committed to this substantial task during their life time." He adds, "History will record the work of the Bilal Muslim Mission as a legacy from our community to the indigenous people of Africa."

Born in Ushri, Bihar, India on 5th January 1927 (1st Rajab, 1345) Maulana was first appointed as a resident Aalim in Lindi after coming to

Tanzania in 1959. Realizing that he could only propagate the true faith by understanding and speaking the local language he was quick to learn Kiswahili and improved his English as a result of which he could write the many books that he authored. As a man with vision he was thus involved in the establishment of the Bilal Muslim Mission in Africa.

In 1962 he prepared a scheme for tabligh and sent it to Haji Ebrahim H. Sheriff in Arusha. He then amended and improved the first plan and when Allama was transferred to Arusha in 1963 a pilot scheme was put into effect. Before the triennial Conference of the Africa Federation in Tanga in 1964, Allamah Rizvi's recommendations were circulated as a Secretariat paper and this got a boost following a resolution of Hussein Nasser Walji (approved in the general meeting of Dar es Salaam Jamaat) that called upon the Federation to become involved in *tabligh* activities among African people. In his booklet, 'Outline of Shia Ithnaashari History in East Africa', Marhum Mulla Asgharali M.M. Jaffer states, "...the 1964 memorandum was received with mixed feelings but it got a boost from a resolution sent by Dar es Salaam Jamaat to do something in this (*tabligh*) connection."

An appreciative majority ultimately adopted this scheme as a policy and this is how a new field of activity appropriately called the Bilal Muslim Mission came into being. In his same book, Marhum Mulla Asghar mentions, "The incessant and untiring efforts and contributions by Maulana Syed Saeed Akhtar Rizvi in this direction have been decisive and of great importance. His knowledge of Kiswahili and English enabled him to offer his service without any undue hesitation. He was appointed Chief Missionary of the Bilal Muslim Mission – an appellation signifying the new role of an Aalim among the Khoja Shia Ithna-Asheris. For the first time in its history, the community lent its credence to this new appointment and realized that the function of an Aalim could be much more beneficial, varied and discursive."

From Arusha, Marhum Allamah Rizvi was transferred to Dar es Salaam Jamaat. The expansion of the Mission's activities in Dar es Salaam necessitated the formation of an autonomous body and in July 1967 Allamah Rizvi went to Mombasa and had a meeting with the office-bearers of the Supreme Council in which it was decided to establish two institutions, the Bilal Muslim Mission of Tanzania and the Bilal Muslim Mission of Kenya. The former was registered on 16th April 1968 and the latter in 1971 with Marhum Maulana Rizvi being one of the founder members and the Chief Missionary.

He was also the Tableegh Advisor of the Late Chairman of the Africa Federation, Late Mohamedali Meghji and to Marhum Mulla Asghar M.M. Jaffer, Alhaj Mohamed Dhirani and Alhaj Habibbhai Mulji. Thereafter, with his enthusiastic missionary activities into the interior regions of East Africa his name became synonymous with the word "*tabligh*" among the indigenous people of East Africa. In his endeavour to spread Islam, Marhum introduced correspondence courses in Islamic studies in English and Kiswahili besides several other courses for Shia students through the Bilal Muslim Mission. These courses are not only pursued in Africa but throughout the world.

He also traveled widely in Africa, Europe, Canada and the USA where he recited thought-provoking majlises and lectured university students and various other audiences. While his audiences at some gatherings were intellectuals he always reached out to new converts and those wishing to know more about religion.

Source: Federation Samachar, Vol 33 No 3, September 2002.

APPENDIX D.

EXTRACTS
from letters and articles in the Federation Samachar of May, 1964
in memory of Haji Ebrahim Shariff Dewji (1923-1964)

Alhaj Mohamed A. Khalfan

Alhaj Khalfan wrote his glowing tribute in Gujarati. In his long tribute he recalled an extra-ordinary commitment demonstrated by Marhoom Ebrahimbhai as personally experienced by him.

'After assuming the first term Chairmanship of the Africa Federation, one of the projects embarked upon by Ebrahimbhai was carrying out a census of the population of all the Jamaats which had already joined with the Africa Federation. He gave great importance to completion of the census and set a time frame for it. As Dar es Salaam had the largest Jamaat and the city was spread out into suburbs, the whereabouts of some very few families could not be established and visited. Ebrahimbhai volunteered to come down to Dar es Salaam from Arusha and assist me in tracing these families because he wanted the work completed sooner. I was the Hon. Secretary General of the Jamaat then. In the case of one family which I had traced in a suburb of the city, we were informed that the head of the family would be late in returning home that evening. Mobile phones were unknown then.

At the request of Ebrahimbhai, we both waited in the car and later when the brother arrived, and as some time was already lost, Ebrahimbhai spread out the census form across the bonnet of the car and filled the form under a municipal street light. He thanked the brother profusely for his co-operation.'

Abbas S. Alloo, Dar es Salaam

The impression of personality of Alhaj Ebrahim Hussein Shariff remains vivid upon the minds of his friends and the sense of his loss is in no way dimmed among the community. All feel poorer that he has gone from us. In these days of greater social and economical problems gathering upon the community, we are conscious of a lack of outstanding leaders with whose help to overcome them. He was a man in whom there existed not only an immense capacity for service but also a touch of genius that made everything he touched successful. He always left a favourable impression over those with whom he came in contact. They felt themselves in presence of an active being; they felt that his latent reserves of force and willpower were beyond measurement.

His influence upon the community has been remarkable and it will continue to be felt for still many more years to come. By the end of his first term, he had already put the Federation on solid footing and made it financially independent. The second term was marked by the developments on the economical side in the formation of the limited liability companies, for the welfare of the community in my view. The companies are: The Ithna-asheri Investments Ltd., The Jamhuri Sisal Estates Ltd. and The First Tanganyika Safety Matches Mfg. Co. Ltd.

These companies have no direct affiliation with the Federation except that Alhaj Ebrahim was the spearhead of the companies as well as the Head of the Federation. All the companies have thrived well under him. He possessed and practiced the art of always appearing interested in any subject that was raised or in any person with whom he was talking. He allowed the talk to flow as his companion wished, appreciating in the most complimentary manner anything that was said in good will. All who met him come away with a feeling that they had been at their very best, and they found someone who, whether he agreed or differed, understood their point of view. Very often they remembered the things they had said to him, which he had welcomed or seemed to agree with, better than he had said to them.

He loved general conversation and knew exactly how to rule it, so none was left out. He has gone, and gone when sorely needed. His records remain. He seemed to have a double dose of human nature. He burned all his candles at both ends. His physique and constitution seemed to be capable of supporting indefinitely every form of mental and physical exertion. When they broke, the end was swift. Alhaj Ebrahim Shariff banked his treasures in the hearts of his friends and they will cherish his memory till their time to come. His message to the community is "*Ek Bano, Nek Bano*".

Hussein A. Rahim, Zanzibar

Throughout East Africa and throughout the Ithna-asheri world, the community mourns the passing of a great leader, a unique personality, a champion of the rights of orphans and widows and a fighter to eradicate ignorance, poverty and suffering within the community. Alhaj Ebrahim Hussein Shariff was a man of warmth and passion, of vitality and conviction, of independent and forthright opinions, and of towering personality. All these qualities were magnificently displayed during his term of office as the President of the Federation of Khoja Shia Ithna-asheri Jamaats of Africa.

He assumed office as President at a time when the fortunes of the Federation were at their lowest ebb. By his qualities of unflinching moral courage, deep sincerity and complete selflessness, he raised the Federation to a pinnacle of power and influence and, vigour, goodwill and bounty. He imbued and inspired the spirit of love, sympathy and sacrifices amongst the members of the community and attained a position of influence amongst the rich and the poor alike unequalled by anyone else in the community in East Africa. Perhaps he was the first

East African Ithna-asheri to have had the honour of presiding over a session of the Imamia Mission Conference in Pakistan where he was also held in high esteem.

In carrying out the duties of his great office as the President of the Federation, there was nothing mean and petty about Alhaj Ebrahim. He was upright, he was downright, he was forthright. As a highly religious and devoted Muslim, he led the community onto the path of progress and advancement within the bound of the Holy Sheria.

In private life, he was true, sincere and lovable friend of great natural charm and gentleness whose memory every one of us will long cherish. Before the tears shed for Alhaj Ebrahim had ceased to trickle, the community had the second misfortune of losing also his devoted lieutenant in the person of Haji Mohamed Taki Remtulla Pirbhai, the Honorary Treasurer of the Federation. As a son of a distinguished philanthropist, Haji Mohamed Taki had dedicated himself to the service of the community and died a martyr in harness.

We, the Ithna-asheris of East Africa, are the poorer by the deaths of these two leaders. May they both be accorded the companionship of Ahlulbayt (AS) whom they so dearly loved.

Hajee Dawood Nasser, Karachi, Pakistan

Our heart bleeds on this great loss at a young and premature age at a time when we needed him the most, when especially complicated and serious problems are facing the country. Alas, Haji Ebrahimbhai is no more with us. There may hardly be any man in the country whose heart has not been wounded. I go further than the community - Africans, Hindus, Muslims and Europeans have also been moved greatly by the permanent departure of this young but gallant hero.

I visited Arusha at his home where I stayed for 2 days only, during most of which time he explained to me the commercial, religious, social and economic problems of the community and his efforts towards improving them and his marvellous plans for the future. I was wonderstruck at his extreme keenness to work for the betterment of the Community at the cost of his own business and health and alas! the latter took the toll. I cannot describe what marvelous deeds he would have achieved if he was alive for only a few years more. His life was studded with exemplary, unsurpassable achievements for the betterment of the community. May he live forever in our hearts, Ameen.

Seyed Saeed Akhtar Rizvi, Arusha

Ebrahimbhai left us on 9th January, 1964. Takibhai followed him within one month. Sorrow, grief and shock are inadequate words to express the profound feeling which has penetrated the very heart of the Shia world. Well-wishers of the community they were from the start; leaders they became in 1958. They had zeal; they had courage. Sincere and selfless servants of Allah (SWT) who found a way to please Him through the services of His chosen religion. Ebrahimbhai took the leadership of the Federation; and accomplished seemingly impossible tasks during the short period of five years.

First he was lucky enough to get a team of office-bearers, superbly efficient, deeply sincere, and highly prestigious. They invested not only their time and money but their zeal and prestige also. And they got the dividend in the shape of a highly organized community, stretching from Somalia in the North upto Mauritius in the South, and from

Zanzibar in the East upto Congo in the West. What was formerly, 'The Federation of the East African Jamaats' is now 'The Federation of the African Jamaats'. They found Shias in Africa like scattered beads; they transformed them in a TASBIH, using the Federation as the unifying cord. This was their foremost achievement. Ebrahimbhai and Takibhai have died; but they made the Federation so strong, it will live for ever.

Bashirali Habib Peera, Zanzibar

The economic position of East Africa and in particular of the working class people of our community including retail traders had always been a big concern to Hajji Ebrahimbhai. He tried to find ways and means to solve this acute problem facing the community and at last resulted in the launching by him of a number of projects, among them being the First East Africa Match Factory, the Ithna-Asheri Investment Ltd. and the Jamhuri Sisal Estate Ltd. There is no shadow of doubt, the speed with which he was working would have enabled him to embark upon other major projects if only time and health permitted him to do so.

One of the major contributions, which the late Haji Ebrahimbhai made towards the development of the community was the raising of the Foundation Fund to the extent of eight hundred thousand shillings. He managed to collect this huge amount by visiting all the constituent Jamaats in East Africa. His interest in the expansion of education, and in particular higher education, resulted in the formation of the Education Board. The community is rightly proud to see that today there are nearly 80 students from the various Jamaats in East Africa taking up degree courses in different fields of education.

The thirteen Jamaats of the Malagasy and Mauritius, which were functioning as individual Jamaats, welded together into a Federation because of a visit to these places by a delegation from the Africa Federation headed by the late Haji Ebrahimbhai. Thus, our brethren there were brought into closer contact with East Africa than ever before. Not only did he strengthen the ties of brotherly relations among these thirteen Jamaats but he even went so far as to help them in raising funds for them in order to establish their own Territorial Council building, Imamwadas and rest houses. His untimely death has marked the end of the career of a devoted leader and a great personality who had the welfare of his community at heart.

Abdulla Fazal, Bukoba

The recent demise of Mr. Ebrahim Sheriff has come to the community as the greatest and the least expected set-back. Destiny knew no better time to take Ebrahimbhai away from us than in the state of his brilliant youth at the helm of the Community and selflessly dedicated to our service in order to better our lot and that of our progeny.

Ebrahimbhai took over the leadership of the Federation at a time when the diversity of opinion regarding the functions of the Federation had grown so wide as to render any further progress almost impossible. The constitution pleased only few. The resultant impasse gave rise to more and more presumptuous voices within the Federation, marshalling on their sides small groups of dissidents advocating the dismantling of the Federation. The financial position of the Federation had weakened considerably as the confidence in the institution had reduced funds to meager proportions; but the needs and the necessities of the Community kept growing. Only leadership with grim determination could pull the community out of this rut and activate it again.

This leadership the Community found in Ebrahimbhai. My mind shall hold fresh forever my memories of him. In all associations with him, both as a personal friend and co-worker in the Federation, I was struck by the sincerity of his purpose. His writings and his speeches to us clearly revealed this. This sincerity in him was clearly reflected when in the face of terrific pressure sometimes brought to bear on him to change his mind, he was seen determined not to compromise with his convictions, which he believed to be the true dictates of his conscience.

This does not imply Mr. Ebrahimbhai was quite infallible; I recall the time when he first took office on a condition that he be promised a target sum in order to re-align the whole Federation. Promises made to him then turned out in effect so real and far-reaching that when I once had an occasion to remind him of the condition he had set, he admitted to me his fallacy with a smile and said, "Abdulbhai, I had then underestimated the philanthropic capacity of my community; it is very wide indeed." This reply pleased me tremendously and further strengthened my confidence in Ebrahimbhai as a leader.

On assuming the leadership of the community, Ebrahimbhai first set to the task of reviving that confidence that he had sipped off so rapidly for sometime. This he did by going out on tours to meet every Jamaat under the Federation. His message to the Community was to be united and to put forward to the Supreme Council suggestions for a new constitution. This was achieved and soon a new spirit, a sense of belonging to a larger group than their own, was inculcated in every Jamaat. Funds rose as Ebrahimbhai's personal contacts with individual Jamaats increased. Dawdlers and talkers had a surprised awakening and soon, awed by Ebrahimbhai's personality and convinced by his policy, they shook off their lethargy and got into stride with the rest of the workers.

What amazed one was the way in which Ebrahimbhai himself, without the least feeling of tiredness, annoyance or frustration dealt with queries from both young and old personally, and to their entire satisfaction. Any hour for attending to such was convenient to him. This in itself is a great achievement for a leader and an inspiration for the masses to follow him united in thought and action. Ebrahimbhai's seriousness of thought, action and personality were evident from the reading on his face and in his words, and this was more so when he was observed engaged in deliberation over matters pertaining to religion, I mean the problems of keeping the religious torch of Shia-ism burning both in the young and old of the community, no matter how big or small the size of the community or how far or near resident.

Today the community is proud of its organized religious services. A short time ago, prior to the sad death of Ebrahimbhai, opinion was expressed from some quarters that the Federation should inaugurate industries to help uplift the community economically and to create employment opportunities for the unemployed in the community. This is easier said than done. Not that Ebrahimbhai did not consider this aspect very seriously. I was associated with him in this thought all the time. It was then felt by Ebrahimbhai that before taking the rash step of plunging the community into this vortex, with the possibility of frustrating its future, the whole problem be first studied carefully and tried outside the Federation by a few individuals with business acumen. This experience could then be of greater help.

I remember the seriousness with which Ebrahimbhai studied, for example, the Sisal Industry for a couple of months. The knowledge he acquired of the industry baffled the oldest and the best of experts in this industry when we sat down to discuss it with them. And couldn't we ascribe the heart attack that Ebrahimbhai sustained to the fatigue that he felt but never complained in his study of the match-box industry and the industries besides this that Late Ebrahimbhai kept concentrating on day and night.

May the Almighty grant us the will to carry on from where he has left. To the young men and women of the community, the brilliant and youthful state of Ebrahimbhai, dedicated selflessly and to the best of its ability to communal service, is an ever-shining example of how they, the youths, could pull their minds and energies together to form a strong nucleus for social work.

And in this context, I am reminded of the sad and tragic death of Mr. Mohamed Takki Rhemtulla, our treasurer, a young silent worker with an exacting job well done to the satisfaction of the entire Federation. Mr. Takki's charming personality cheerful nature and strict self-discipline both at his job and in his personal life were indeed a great inspiration to Late Ebrahimbhai right from beginning. We need more and more of such self-discipline and strong sense of duty. May the Almighty grant peace to the departed soul. And so I end this rather protracted tribute to the leader whose desire for good, social reform, love of religion, resentment of preferential treatment and prejudicial opinions and whose constant action have elevated the Community to a noble status.

Ebrahimbhai leaves behind a proud record of an exacting job well done through the maturity of his wisdom. May the Almighty grant peace to the departed soul and may He grant strength to the bereaved families of both Ebrahimbhai and Mohamed Takki to bear their loss. Amen.

J. A. Green, Town Clerk, Arusha

The death of Ebrahim Hussein Shariff has meant not only a great loss to his family and community, but to Tanganyika and in particular to the Northern Region. It was a great privilege for me to have known and worked with him for a period of nine years, and I was proud to be able to call him a friend. He was indeed, a friend to everyone he met, an honourable man of business, an extremely keen and conscientious social worker, and one, who spent an incredible part of his time in public service. He was particularly interested in the town of Arusha, where he had been engaged in establishing his family business, and where he did a great deal for the Seed Bean Industry.

He also gave a great deal of his time to the Arusha Town Council, and it was on this body, where he served as Councillor, as Chairman of a number of Committees, and as Chairman of the Council that I had the privilege of working with him and getting to know him so well.

I think it can be truly said of Ebrahim Hussein Shariff that his life was an example and an inspiration to others.

Pakistan High Commission Mr S. A. Afzal seen with Late Ebrahim bhai in Arusha

Appendix E.

Maps of East Africa drawn and labelled in Gujrati script.

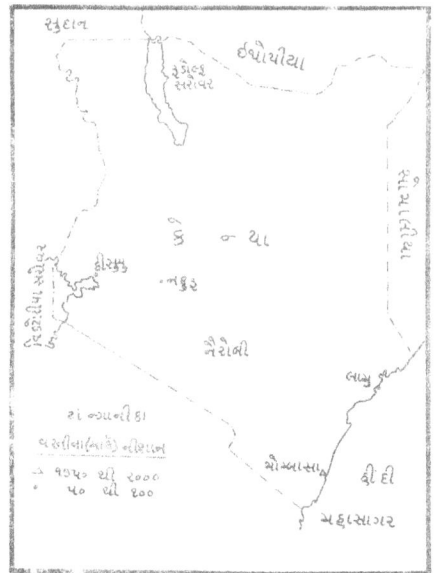

Kenya

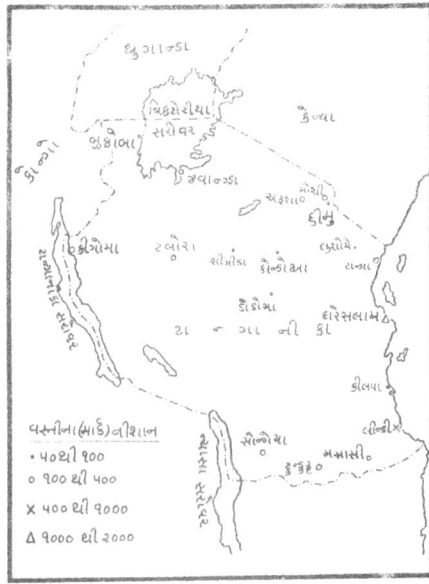

Tanganyika

These maps reflect the demographics of 1960s that the pioneer Khoja communities lived in.

UGANDA

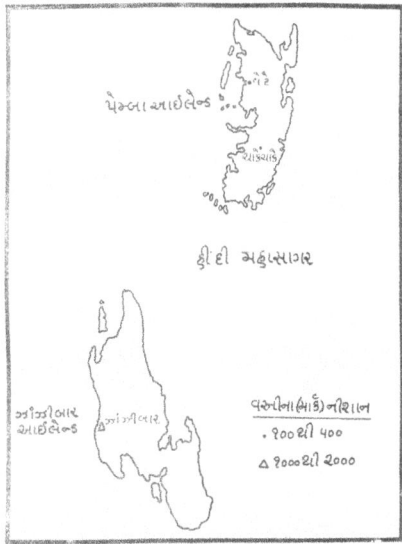

ZANZIBAR AND PEMBA ISLANDS

About the Authors

Dr Sibtain Panjwani is the Director of the Awakening Project KSIMC, a non-profit community project that raises awareness on the role of three major institutions of the Khoja Shia Ithna-Asheri community – the *mimbar* (pulpit), *madrasah* (school) and family.

Having qualified as a dentist from the University of Manchester, he obtained an MA in Medical Law & Ethics from King's College London and a Ph.D. in Law from the University of Essex. He went on to work closely with Mulla Asgharali M M Jaffer as the Secretary-General of the World Federation of KSIMC during 1997-2003.

Dr Sibtain Panjwani continues to be active in Muslim community affairs and Western academia as a lecturer in Khoja heritage, Gujarati exegesis of the Qur'an and Islamic bioethics.

Dr Imranali Panjwani is a Senior Lecturer in Law at Anglia Ruskin University and Head of Diverse Legal Consulting, UK where he writes country expert reports for asylum seekers. He completed his Islamic seminary studies at Al-Mahdi Institute, Birmingham, UK, and post-doctoral research at Jami'at al-Mustafa, Mashhad.

He pursued law at the University of Sheffield, the University of Law, and Western Sydney University and completed his Ph.D. at King's College London.

www.ingramcontent.com/pod-product-compliance
Lightning Source LLC
Chambersburg PA
CBHW041134110526
44590CB00027B/4007